The following guides by Dawn Apgar are available from Springer Publishing to assist social workers with studying for and passing the ASWB® examinations necessary for licensure.

Bachelors

The Social Work ASWB® Bachelors Exam Guide: A Comprehensive Guide for Success

Test focuses on knowledge acquired while obtaining a Baccalaureate degree in Social Work (BSW). A small number of jurisdictions license social workers at an Associate level and require the ASWB Associate examination. The Associate examination is identical to the ASWB Bachelors examination, but the Associate examination requires a lower score in order to pass.

Masters

The Social Work ASWB® Masters Exam Guide: A Comprehensive Guide for Success

Test focuses on knowledge acquired while obtaining a Master's degree in Social Work (MSW). There is no postgraduate supervision needed.

Clinical

The Social Work ASWB® Clinical Exam Guide: A Comprehensive Guide for Success

Test focuses on knowledge acquired while obtaining a Master's degree in Social Work (MSW). It is usually taken by those with postgraduate supervised direct practice experience.

Advanced Generalist

The Social Work ASWB® Advanced Generalist Exam Guide: A Comprehensive Guide for Success

Test focuses on knowledge acquired while obtaining a Master's degree in Social Work (MSW). It is usually taken by those with postgraduate supervised nonclinical experience.

Dawn Apgar, PhD, LSW, ACSW, has helped thousands of social workers across the country pass the ASWB® examinations associated with all levels of licensure. In recent years, she has consulted in numerous states to assist with establishing licensure test preparation programs, including training the instructors.

Dr. Apgar has done research on licensure funded by the American Foundation for Research and Consumer Education in Social Work Regulation and is currently chairperson of her state's social work licensing board. She is a past President of the New Jersey Chapter of NASW and has been on its National Board of Directors. In 2014, the Chapter presented her with a Lifetime Achievement Award. Dr. Apgar has taught in both undergraduate and graduate social work programs and has extensive direct practice, policy, and management experience in the social work field.

Social Work ASWB® Advanced Generalist Exam Guide

A Comprehensive Study Guide for Success

Dawn Apgar, PhD, LSW, ACSW

SPRINGER PUBLISHING COMPANY
NEW YORK

Springer Publishing Company, LLC
11 West 42nd Street
New York, NY 10036
www.springerpub.com

Acquisitions Editor: Stephanie Drew
Composition: diacriTech

ISBN: 978-0-8261-3352-6
e-book ISBN: 978-0-8261-3353-3

16 17 18 19 20 / 5 4 3 2 1

Publisher's Acknowledgements
Springer Publishing Company recognizes that the ASWB® is a registered service mark of the Association of Social Work Boards and has applied this service mark to the first mention of the association in each of the chapters in the book and on its cover. The Association of Social Work Boards neither sponsors or endorses this product.

The author and the publisher of this Work have made every effort to use sources believed to be reliable to provide information that is accurate and compatible with the standards generally accepted at the time of publication. The author and publisher shall not be liable for any special, consequential, or exemplary damages resulting, in whole or in part, from the readers' use of, or reliance on, the information contained in this book. The publisher has no responsibility for the persistence or accuracy of URLs for external or third-party Internet websites referred to in this publication and does not guarantee that any content on such websites is, or will remain, accurate or appropriate.

Library of Congress Cataloging-in-Publication Data
Names: Apgar, Dawn, author. | Association of Social Work Boards.
Title: Social work ASWB advanced generalist exam guide : a comprehensive
   study guide for success / Dawn Apgar.
Description: New York, NY : Springer Publishing Company, [2016] | Includes
   bibliographical references and index.
Identifiers: LCCN 2015051157 | ISBN 9780826133526
Subjects: LCSH: Social workers—Certification—United States. | Social
   service—United States—Examinations—Study guides. | Social
   service—United States—Examinations, questions, etc.
Classification: LCC HV40.52 .A7347 2016 | DDC 361.3076—dc23 LC record available at
http://lccn.loc.gov/2015051157

Special discounts on bulk quantities of our books are available to corporations, professional associations, pharmaceutical companies, health care organizations, and other qualifying groups. If you are interested in a custom book, including chapters from more than one of our titles, we can provide that service as well.

For details, please contact:
Special Sales Department, Springer Publishing Company, LLC
11 West 42nd Street, 15th Floor, New York, NY 10036-8002
Phone: 877-687-7476 or 212-431-4370; Fax: 212-941-7842
E-mail: sales@springerpub.com

Printed in the United States of America by McNaughton & Gunn.

Contents

Preface

Congratulations on getting to this point in your social work career. The decision to become licensed is significant, and passing the licensing examination demonstrates that you have the basic knowledge necessary to safely practice. Social workers are employed in all kinds of settings including hospitals, correctional facilities, mental health and addictions agencies, government offices, and private practices. It is essential that those served have some assurance that these practitioners are competent to provide the services that they are charged with delivering.

Regulation through certification and licensure helps to assure that social workers will interact in an ethical and safe manner, and there is oversight to address actions that are not consistent with this standard.

Passing the licensing exam is only one step in becoming certified or licensed, but it is usually the most difficult challenge faced after graduating with your degree.

This guide aims to assist helping you through this process in several important ways. It will:

1. Increase your knowledge of the Association of Social Work Boards ASWB® examination, including testing conditions and scoring

2. Provide valuable test-taking strategies that will assist in developing a good study plan and in analyzing question wording in order to select the correct answer

3. Summarize content areas that may be included on the examination as per the Knowledge, Skills, and Abilities (KSA) statements published by ASWB, which are used by test developers to formulate actual questions

4. Supply sample questions that can be used to simulate an actual examination experience

Although there are other test preparation materials produced, this guide provides all these essential elements in a single, manageable, easy-to-use guide.

Individuals who are studying for the social work licensing examination have a primary concern and request. They are worried that they do not know important information about the tests that will prove to be a barrier to passing, and they want a "place" to go that will have all the necessary materials in a single location. They want to focus their efforts on studying for the exam—not hunting around for what needs to be studied!

This guide was created based on this important information, and it has been gathered from thousands of social workers just like you. Although it is not produced by or affiliated with ASWB in any way, and does not guarantee a passing score on the examinations, the test-taking techniques have been developed and used successfully by others who were faced with the same challenge that you are—others who are now certified and licensed social workers! They found this information so helpful in passing because the skills that it takes to be a good social worker in practice can be very different than the skills that it takes to pass the examination.

Best wishes as you study for the examination. And remember that there is never only one way to achieve a goal, so use this guide in a way that works for you as you prepare. In choosing this guide as your roadmap, you have taken an important first step on the journey of passing the examination for certification and licensure.

Acknowledgments

Although I have taught this material for nearly 20 years and have helped tens of thousands of social workers pass the examinations, writing this guide proved to be a challenging undertaking. Many people assisted in getting the guide written and produced in an aggressive time frame. In some instances, they provided direct support in ensuring that the guide was comprehensive and easy to use, whereas others gave me strength throughout the process.

I want to thank:

- The National Association of Social Workers (NASW), who granted permission for me to reprint a section of the Code of Ethics, which was essential material for Unit V, Professional Values and Ethics: National Association of Social Workers. (1999). *Code of ethics of the National Association of Social Workers*. Washington, DC: NASW Press.

- Trainers with whom I have worked to help countless social workers prepare for the examinations

- Social workers in my examination preparation classes who were the best educators about what works and what doesn't in preparing for and passing the examinations

- Stephanie Drew, my editor at Springer Publishing Company, who was enthusiastic about creating this guide as there were virtually no resources for social workers studying for the Advanced Generalist ASWB® test

- Bill, Ryan, and Alex, who are my support system and always inspire me to be a better person

Social Work ASWB® Advanced Generalist Exam Guide

Introduction

About the Examination

Generally, when social workers are getting ready to take the ASWB® tests, they are anxious not only about knowing the content, but also about the examinations themselves. They have many questions about the number of questions that will be asked and the number of correct answers required to pass. Becoming familiar with the examination basics will assist in making you more comfortable with the examination conditions and structure, thereby reducing your anxiety about the unknown.

10 THINGS THAT YOU SHOULD KNOW ABOUT THE ASWB EXAMINATIONS

1. All of the ASWB examinations have the same format, meaning that each has the same number of questions that each test-taker is given the same amount of time to complete. There are **170 multiple-choice questions** and you will have **4 hours** from the time that you start answering the questions. You can take a brief restroom break or stand to stretch, but the clock does not stop and these activities will be included in your 4-hour limit, so you want to be judicious with your time.

2. Although you will be answering a total of 170 questions, **20 of these questions are non-scored items** that are being piloted for possible inclusion as scored questions on future ASWB examinations. Thus, only 150 questions will determine whether you pass or not. However, you will never know which 20 are pilot items because they are mixed in with scored items, so you will need to try to select the right answers on all 170 questions.

3. You **do not want to leave any questions blank**; answer all 170 questions in the 4 hours.

4. The examination is **computerized**, but requires no specialized computer knowledge. There is a brief computer tutorial that will assist you when you first sit down and look at the screen, and spending time getting to feel comfortable with the device at that time is a good idea, since it will not count toward your 4-hour time limit.

5. You will be taking your examination at a **testing center with others who are being tested in different disciplines** and may be taking shorter or longer examinations, so do not be concerned if they finish before or after you.

6. Testing center activities are **closely monitored**, and you will need to leave all of your belongings, including your watch, in a provided locker. You can ask for earplugs, scrap paper, or a pencil, but will not be able to bring anything into the room with you. The room may be hot or cold, so you should dress in comfortable layers. All testing accommodations related to documented disabilities must be approved by your state licensing board and arranged in advance with ASWB. *Some* states allow for extra time or foreign language dictionaries as accommodations for those who do not have English as a first language.

7. You will leave the testing center with an unofficial copy of your examination results. It will tell you how many questions you were asked and how many you got correct in each of the four areas or domains. You will never know which specific answers were correct and incorrect. You will also not find out the correct answers for those that you answered incorrectly. **The exam is pass/fail**, and a passing score can be used for certification or licensure in any state.

8. Although the KSAs are in four content areas and you may structure your studying to learn all the related material in a given domain before moving on to the next, **the questions on the examination are in random order** and skip across topics. There is not a separate section of questions labeled Human Development, Diversity, and Behavior in the Environment, or so on. You may have a human behavior question followed by one on ethics, so you really need to clear your head between questions and avoid trying to relate them to one another in any way. Each question stands alone as a way to assess knowledge related to a distinct KSA.

9. Social workers always want to know how many questions of the 150 scored items they will need to answer correctly to pass the exam. Although this sounds like an easy question, it is not! Not all questions on the ASWB examinations are the same level of difficulty as determined by the pilot process, so individuals who are asked to

answer harder questions that have been randomly selected from the test bank will need to answer fewer questions correctly than those who were lucky enough to have easier questions randomly assigned. This method ensures that the examination is fair for all those who are taking it, regardless of which questions were chosen. **The number of questions that you have to get correct *generally* varies from 93 to 106 of the 150 scored items.** You will find out how many needed to be answered correctly only after you are finished with your examination and it is immediately scored electronically. When you examine your unofficial test results, which are provided in a printout prior to leaving the testing center, you will be able to gauge the difficulty of your examination. If you needed to get closer to 93 correct, you had a harder combination of questions, and if you needed to get 106 or above correct, you had an easier combination.

10. **If you do not pass the examination, you will not have the same questions repeated on any of your examinations in the future.** Other questions in the four areas will be selected from the test bank. As the four domains are so broad, you may find that the topics of the questions may be quite different than those on a previous examination. To be adequately prepared, it is best to go back and study all the KSAs listed for a content area and not just those that may have caused you problems. If you do not pass, you will have to wait 90 days before taking the examination again.

If you have questions about the examination or scoring, such as the process for sending your passing exam score to another state in which you want to be licensed, visit the ASWB website at www.aswb.org for additional information and necessary forms. The *ASWB Examination Candidate Handbook*, which is free and located on this website, provides additional information about registering for the examination that may be useful.

Test-Taking Strategies

Social workers studying for the ASWB® examinations always want to know techniques that will assist them in studying wisely and answering questions correctly. Remember that there are no replacements for good old-fashioned work, and test-taking strategies are not enough on their own to eliminate all of the incorrect answers. Usually, applying test-taking strategies can help you dismiss two of four possible multiple-choice responses and it is your knowledge of the content area that will be needed to select the correct answer from the two that are remaining. Thus, you will need to make sure that you are well versed in the examination content in order to pass the examination.

However, there are two types of strategies that may assist. The first concerns things to remember when developing your study plan. These are important pieces of information that may help when you are trying to decide what to learn and how to learn it. The second includes those strategies that can assist you when actually answering the questions. These "tips" are important to remember after you have learned all the needed content and are tasked with applying it in the proper way to select the correct answer.

As both of these strategy types are keys to success on the examinations, they are outlined here.

10 ESSENTIAL STRATEGIES FOR STUDY SUCCESS

Tip 1

This is an examination to assess knowledge of social work content, so you will need to make sure that you can describe an overview of the key concepts and terms related to each of the KSAs. You will know if you are ready to take the examinations when you are able to briefly explain these areas to someone who does not have any prior knowledge of them. The difference between passing and not passing the examinations almost always is a result of gaps in knowledge, not application of test-taking strategies, so you need to make sure that the bulk of your studying is aimed at filling in knowledge gaps or refreshing information already learned.

Tip 2

You will never be "ready" to take the ASWB examination. Not unlike other standardized examinations, such as the Scholastic Aptitude Test (SAT) or Graduate Record Examination (GRE), you cannot judge readiness as knowing everything about the content areas. The ASWB® examinations are not designed for test takers to "know it all" in order to pass. Often, picking a test date is the hardest task; as with the SAT or GRE, a deadline for admission to college or graduate school forces individuals to select a date even when they do not feel ready. For the ASWB examination, you will need to select a date in the next few weeks or months, perhaps dictated by job opportunities or promotions predicated on being licensed. You will walk into the examination without feeling totally ready, but this is typical of others who have passed.

Tip 3

You need to limit your study materials to this guide or other key resources that summarize material. This is *not* the time to go back and read your textbooks! There are so many topics that you are asked to know about under each KSA that you cannot and are not expected to know everything related to the topic. This guide is geared to provide important information on these areas "under one roof." It will be hard enough to read through all this material. You should only use outside materials if something in this guide is unclear or you feel that you need more than the information included, perhaps because you never learned this area in the first place. In these instances, you can use free resources on the Internet or any other documents that have no more than a paragraph summarizing key points. Remember, you do not need to read a book on Freud to understand his work and its importance in explaining human development.

Tip 4

Although individuals like to study from sample questions, this is *not* advisable. There are many reasons why using this technique will hurt you on the examinations, but here are just a few:

1. Although it makes individuals feel better when they get an answer correct on a sample test, getting an answer correct is not a valid indicator of really knowing the content in the KSA for which the question was developed. Studying from the KSAs and the topics within them will ensure that you are able to answer any question, not just the one that is in a sample test.

2. Your answers to sample questions inappropriately influence your decisions on the actual examinations when asked about similar topics. For example, you may see an answer that is similar to one that was correct or incorrect in a practice test and you will be more apt or less apt to select it based upon this prior experience. However, the question in the "real" examination will not be exactly the same as the one on the practice test, and you must evaluate all four answers independently without any undue bias that may be caused by your practice question experience.

3. The sample questions that you study are not going to be on your examination and probably are not even written by those who developed items for your test. Thus, the idea that many social workers have of wanting to "get into the head" of the individuals writing the exam or understand their logic is not valid—though it might make them good clinicians in real life!

Tip 5

If you have access to sample questions, such as those in the last section of this guide, you should use them to create a "mock" examination. Most people have trouble resisting the urge to look at the answer key to see if they were correct immediately after selecting a response. However, a far better way to use these questions is to pretend that they are an actual examination.

1. *After* you are done studying the content and think you are ready to take the ASWB examination, select a 4-hour period where you can create a quiet environment without interruptions.

2. Answer the questions as you would on the actual examination—using the strategies and having to pick *one* answer—even if you are not completely sure that it is correct.

3. If you do not take unnecessary breaks, you will see that you can easily get through 170 questions in the 4 hours allotted. This experience should relieve some of your anxiety about the timed nature of the examination.

4. See which answers that you got correct and incorrect. The "mock" examination is not to be used to determine whether you are ready to take the actual test—even if getting 93 to 106 puts you in the range of having the knowledge to pass the actual examination. Instead, it gives you some idea of the length of the examination and how long you will need to focus, while giving you the confidence that you can get most of the answers correct within the time period allotted.

Tip 6

It probably has been a long time since you had to sit for a 4-hour examination—if ever! Our lives are hectic, and we rarely get a chance to really focus on a single task or have the luxury of thinking about a single topic in a way that allows us to really understand it. Thus, many people find it helpful to study in 4-hour blocks of time rather than for a few minutes here and there. This may be difficult, but it will be beneficial because it will get you prepared to not lose your concentration or focus during such a long period. Remember, runners do not start with marathons, they need to build their strength and endurance over time before they can tackle 26.2 miles. Your preparation is similar: You do not want the first time that you have to sit and engage in critical thinking to be your actual examination.

Tip 7

There is always a time lag between the generation of new social work content and when it appears on the ASWB examinations. It takes time to write and pretest questions on new material. For example, when the Health Insurance Portability and Accountability Act (HIPAA) of 1996 was passed, there were several years before questions related to this law were asked. Although the *DSM-5* was published in 2013, ASWB announced that it would not be included on examinations until July 2015. This lag is good and bad. The good news is that you do not have to know the "latest and greatest" in all content areas. It is hard to keep completely up to date in a profession that is changing so rapidly. Now for the bad news! For many, especially if they are working in a particular specialty area, some of the content or answers may appear to be dated. This is often the case in the area of psychopharmacology, because new medications are being approved and used rapidly. Remember the time lapse in your studying, and do not rely on breaking news or even practices in your own agency as information sources.

Tip 8

As you think about what is important to learn or remember when you are reviewing this guide, you should recognize that social workers who have attended social work programs at different schools, as well as courses within a program taught by various instructors, have passed the examinations. Thus, although there is always information to add to a KSA related to experience or depth of knowledge, there are "core" elements included in any overview or lecture on the topic, regardless of school or professor. These elements are the ones that have to be learned and remembered because they are the basis of the knowledge being tested. In addition, there are also "core" or essential areas that contain information that is seen as critical to competent practice. Can you imagine a social worker leaving an undergraduate or graduate program without reviewing the signs of child abuse and neglect and his or her duty as a mandatory reporter? Of course not! This is a "core" topic that often is the basis of examination questions. The list of these areas is not fixed, but includes confidentiality, assessment of danger to self and others, cultural competence, and so on. You should ask yourself when studying, "Is this something that every social worker needs to know, regardless of setting or specialization?" If so, it may be essential to include it in your review of a topic because it is likely to be included on the examination.

Tip 9

When studying, it is not necessary to memorize the content because you will not have to recall a term or definition from memory. The ASWB examinations are not tests geared to test your memory. Instead, they require you to be able to pick the one of several answers that most directly relates to the topic or is the best based on your knowledge of the content area. Thus, it is much more important that you understand each of the KSAs and are not focused on memorizing fancy terms or facts. If you stumble when asked a question about something that you are saying about a KSA, or cannot go off script when discussing these areas, you may be just memorizing the material instead of really understanding it.

Tip 10

Often, social workers are focused on using the clinical and other jargon that they learned in their MSW programs; however, they may be unable to explain what these concepts mean in plain and understandable terms. For example, when asked what should happen when meeting with a client for the first time, social workers often use phrases such as "You need to build rapport," "It is essential that you start where a client is," or "Social workers should show empathy as to what a client is going through." Though all true, these statements give little insight into any real actions that a social worker should take in this first meeting. What should a social worker do to "build rapport"? How would a client know if a social worker was being "empathetic"? What would a social worker be doing or saying? Having to explain the KSAs to someone who knows little about social work practice and will ask you *lots* of questions about the content area can be a far better strategy than studying with a social work colleague who will not challenge you when you use jargon or technical terms without having to explain the basics.

20 TIPS YOU NEED TO USE TO ANSWER QUESTIONS CORRECTLY

Tip 1

This is an examination of your knowledge of social work content. Often, what we learn in the classroom and how we might act in practice based upon practice wisdom and clinical judgments are different. **When selecting an answer, you should base it upon the content that you studied from this guide and what you learned in the classroom.** Each question is written to make sure that you know requisite information about the KSAs. Thus, ask yourself—"What did I study in the guide that relates to this question?" or "Which KSA is being tested and what do I know about this content area?" If you are inappropriately asking, "What would I do in this case vignette?" or "How should I handle this situation?" you will be drawing upon your practice experience rather than the existing knowledge in a domain that is the basis for selecting the correct answer.

Remember, there is only one correct answer for each question. Since everyone has different practice experience, basing your answers on what you see or do in the field may lead you to a different response than someone else taking the examination. However, the textbook or existing body of knowledge on the KSAs is universal, regardless of setting or practice experience. Basing your responses on the information that is taught in the classroom and in social work textbooks, as outlined in this guide, will ensure that you get to the same correct response as others.

Tip 2

You may have a negative opinion about the need to take a standardized 4-hour examination after having successfully graduated from your social work program and even gotten the requisite clinical experience. However, it is a requirement for licensure and seen as a way of determining whether social workers possess the knowledge needed to practice safely. Just as the SAT and GRE are viewed as ways of determining the ability to perform in college or graduate school, the ASWB examinations are seen as indicators of proper social work preparation to successfully practice at various levels. You probably know individuals who have done well on the SAT and GRE and did not do well in postsecondary education and vice versa.

The use of standardized tests in social work and other life areas "is what it is" and **it will hurt your performance if you "fight" the use of such examinations**—in other words, *do not* approach the test with negative attitudes and resentment about having to take it.

It is important to approach the examination with a positive attitude and realize that your performance on this examination will not define your social work career. Passing it should not be viewed as an end in itself, but rather a step in the licensure process—just as the SAT is a step in the college acceptance process. Being resentful about the use of standardized testing as an indicator of competence or future performance will only get in your way.

Tip 3

Although there may be some questions that require you to simply "recall" content in a content area, many of them will be focused on you "applying" information to a particular situation or scenario. These questions come in the form of case vignettes and are often the ones in which social workers make mistakes. In practice, social workers often alter their actions based on many contextual variables. However, remember that the questions on the examination are about the application of social work knowledge within the KSAs, and this knowledge does not change regardless of the setting in the vignette. **You should not get "lost" in the scenario**. For example, the core components of a discharge plan are the same if it is prepared for a client leaving the hospital, a drug treatment facility, or an inpatient psychiatric treatment setting. The content within the components (i.e., history/assessment, treatment provided, follow-up needed) may be different, but each discharge plan has to contain information in these critical areas.

Thus, you need to stay focused on the content being tested and remember that it is not necessary to have worked in all the settings mentioned in the vignettes (schools, hospitals, drug treatment centers, nursing homes, etc.) to pass the examination; the KSAs or core social work content being tested is universal, regardless of venue.

Tip 4

The ASWB examination that you are taking is used for licensure in virtually every state. The correct answer to a question is the same for all social workers taking the examination. However, the systems of care and laws in each state differ; thus, responses to situations may be varied in real-life, everyday work. This is not the case on the examination, as **there is only one correct answer to each question**. Thus, if you are thinking about "rules" or laws that apply in your state, or resources that may be available, you are likely to get yourself in trouble on the examination because these vary between states and cannot influence your answer selection.

A simple way to avoid unconsciously using state-specific information when answering questions is to think of a state that you envision is very different than your own and ask yourself, "What answer would a social worker living in [insert name of state here] pick as the correct answer?" If your response is, "I don't know because I am not sure how things are done there," you are mistakenly drawing upon practice systems and rules that may differ between states and should *not* be considered. However, if your response is, "It would be the same as mine," you have considered the core social work content that applies to practice in all states.

Tip 5

Standardized examinations are often difficult and test-takers often find themselves struggling to identify the correct answer from several listed. In these instances, social workers can make a common mistake such as selecting the answer that has catchy social work phrases, such as "from a client's perspective" or "focus on a client's strengths and skills." Although these are important social work concepts, you need to make sure that these answers fit the scenario or question asked. **The "best" answer is not always the correct answer.** If you are judging answers solely based on the inclusion of important social work terms—independent of what the question is really asking—you will often be drawn to the "best" answers (judged to be so solely based on the inclusion of important social work terms or concepts), but they may not be correct. Remember, you always want to ask yourself, "What is the right answer to this question on the examination?"

Tip 6

If you are asked to select between four listed terms, diagnoses, or theories, and you do not know with certainty what all the terms listed mean or the criteria for all of the named diagnoses, you should only choose between those that you know. When they are uncertain about the answer to a question, social workers often mistakenly think that it must be the term, diagnosis, or theory listed that they do not know and will gravitate toward selecting this answer. It seems to make logical sense in their minds—"I am uncertain of the answer to the question and I am uncertain as to what this answer means, so they must go together." Although common, this logic is problematic.

Instead, you should concentrate on choosing between the answers that you know. **Only in instances in which you are able to eliminate with 100% certainty the three choices that you know—which is almost never the case—should you choose the "mystery" term, diagnosis, or theory.**

Tip 7

You will have plenty of time to answer the questions. Although the examination is timed, most people finish with a half-hour or more left in the 4 hours. However, you may be nervous about the time and feel rushed due to your anxiety. Use your time wisely, reading carefully and applying the tips described. You should answer the questions in the order in which they are listed. Skipping around will waste time. The most time that you will spend on a question is determining what the question is asking, so not answering a question after you have done this analysis serves no purpose because you will not have an epiphany or any more information that will be helpful to you later in the examination than you do at that moment. You need to select an answer and move on. You also will need to commit to an answer after having read the question no more than two to three times and applying the strategies. Individuals who run out of time are "stuck" because they are waiting for the feeling of certainty in their answers that does not come in these types of standardized examinations.

Tip 8

Look for qualifying words in examination questions. These words are often capitalized, but not always. Examples of qualifying words are "best," "next," "least," "most," "first," and "not." Whenever you see a qualifying word, it is the key to selecting the correct answer from the others and is directly related to the answer. Thus, when you read each of the response choices or answers, you should put the qualifying word in front of it to ensure that you are focusing on what, in this question, is important. You will repeat the qualifying word before reading each answer. By repeating the word before each response choice, you are making sure that you are focusing on what is important when selecting between the answers.

Tip 9

The examinations require you to have basic knowledge about many theories, practice models, and perspectives related to social work practice. A theory is a set of interrelated concepts that are organized in a way that explain aspects of everyday life. A practice model is a way in which a theory is operationalized. And a perspective is a point of view that is usually broader and at a higher level of abstraction (i.e., strengths perspective). Having a basic understanding of various theories, practice models, and perspectives, as well as the terms that are rooted in them, is necessary. Sometimes there are recall questions about theories, practice models, or perspectives, but knowledge in these areas is often tested through questions related to case vignettes. For example, the last sentence before the response choices or answers may state, "*Using a systems approach,* a social worker can expect this recent medical diagnosis to...." Examining the response choices or answers through the "lens" of systems theory is essential to selecting the correct answer. Systems theory states that individuals are in continual interaction with their environment and that parts within a system are interrelated. Thus, when one subsystem is affected, they are all affected. In this example, you would need to have this knowledge in order to select the correct answer, and you would be looking for the response choice that reflects the medical diagnosis affecting others in the family or other aspects of a client's life beyond health.

You do not have to be an expert in all theories, practice models, or perspectives. Instead, your knowledge base needs to be "an inch deep, but a mile wide." You do not need to know the material in great depth, but you do need to have basic knowledge about a lot of paradigms.

Remember to always make sure that you are determining whether a question asks you to use a particular theory, practice model, or perspective when selecting the correct answer. If so, it is not about what might be best to address the problem; instead, identify which answer most closely relates to the paradigm identified.

When studying the theories, practice models, and perspectives, make sure to also focus on their related terms. Sometimes questions do not specify paradigms, but use related terms that you would only know if you studied them.

Tip 10

Perhaps the biggest mistake that social workers make when taking the examinations is adding material to the questions. This is done unconsciously when social workers mistakenly think of a client or situation in their own lives that is similar to what is described in a question. Unfortunately, when this occurs, information related to this real-life client or situation is added to the information that you are considering when selecting the correct response choice or answer, even when it is not actually included in the question. For example, if a man is described as psychotic, you may inappropriately think that he is a danger to himself or others because you recently worked with someone who was psychotic and was exhibiting harm to self or others. However, being psychotic does not necessarily mean that you are posing any danger. This added information may cause you to choose the incorrect information.

In order to determine whether you are adding material to a question, ask yourself what a non–social worker might answer. If the non–social worker's answer would be different from your answer, you may be adding material based on practice experience, not what is stated in the question. Remember, the question has all the information needed to select the correct answer. **You should stay with the material in the question and not add information based upon practice experience.**

Tip 11

Look for quotation marks throughout the question or clues in the last sentence before the response choices, because both are often the keys to selecting the correct answers. For example, a case vignette may describe a client who walks into the first therapy session and states, "I don't have to tell you anything and I don't want to be here," followed by a question for a social worker's best actions. Although this question does not explicitly state that it is asking how to best address resistance, it is implied by the client's verbal statement as described in the quoted statement. These words are there for a reason and are usually important clues to the KSA being tested or the critical information needed to select between correct and incorrect answers.

In addition, a case vignette may ask you to use a particular practice modality or theoretical approach to select the correct response choice. The "lens" that you should use is often mentioned in the last sentence before the answers are listed. For example, a case vignette that ends with *"using a task-centered treatment approach*, a social worker should. . ."* requires you to look at the response choices to see which relates to an intervention that is brief, highly structured, and focused on quick results in which a client can take a very active role. The correct answer would be very different if a social worker, responding to the same case vignette, was asked to use a "psychodynamic model."

Tip 12

Many of the response choices to questions on the examination often begin with verbs. **If you are debating between multiple answers, the verb choices can often provide some clues**. For example, some answers describe a social worker doing something for a client that he or she should be doing or for which he or she should be taking responsibility. These response choices often begin with the word "provide" when the question asks what a social worker should do in a particular situation.

In addition, some verbs may denote less of an empowerment approach, which may help rule them out. "Explore" and "engage" are active verbs that usually indicate that a social worker is relying on a client to come up with the answer or be responsible for the treatment process. "Ignore" or "wait" may indicate that a social worker is not taking critical information into account or acting when needed.

Although examining the verb used in the response choices is only one piece of information that should be used when selecting the correct response choice, and may not be as critical in some instances as other selection criteria, it is a vital tool to consider when two response choices appear equally viable.

Tip 13

Often, questions on the examinations require social workers to identify what they would do "first" or "next" or to pick out the issue or problem that is "most" important in a case scenario. In practice, such decisions are often somewhat subjective and driven by practice wisdom that takes into account many clinical and contextual factors. However, for the examination, all social workers must select the same correct answer. **A useful framework** for prioritizing client needs and addressing them sequentially is Maslow's hierarchy of needs.

Although it is unlikely that Maslow's hierarchy of needs would ever be explicitly asked about on the examination, it is a tool that will be used repeatedly in questions that want the social worker to prioritize problems or order actions based on client need.

A social worker should always address health and safety issues before moving on to issues that relate to self-esteem and relationships. Thus, when the question includes the qualifying word "first," the answers should be considered in light of the health and safety needs of a client. Social workers should also provide concrete services to meet basic needs, such as housing, employment, and transportation, before moving up the hierarchy. Maslow's framework indicates that without health, safety, and basic needs being met first, a client cannot meet his or her higher level needs.

Tip 14

Another critical tool available to select the correct answer is the problem-solving process (i.e., engagement, assessment, planning, intervention, evaluation, and termination). Understanding the goal of each phase and the tasks to be completed therein is critical because many questions on the examination focus on making sure that things are happening in the correct order. For example, if the question is about the first session or meeting with a client, the activities of a social worker should be focused on engagement. Engagement includes finding out why a client is there and why he or she is seeking services now, explaining the role of a social worker and what to expect in treatment, listening to a client as he or she explains his or her situation, and explaining the limits of confidentiality. Including a reference to a specific session in the question is a clue for a social worker in determining what stage of the problem-solving process a social worker and client are in and what activities are appropriate for this stage.

When a question asks what actions a social worker should take when interacting with a client, attention should be paid to what part of the problem-solving process a social worker and client are theoretically engaged in. A social worker's response may be quite different if it is the beginning of the process versus the end. Although questions will rarely explicitly state the phase, it can be identified by what has occurred, such as "when gathering information on the problem" to indicate assessment or "when developing the contract" to indicate planning. Also, it may be useful to classify response choices into these stages in order to select what comes "first" or "next."

Tip 15

If the age of a client or others is included in a case vignette, it is usually relevant to selecting the correct response choice. For example, having an imaginary friend at age 4 is very different than having one at age 34. Imaginary friends in childhood are an extension of pretend play and part of Piaget's preoperational stage. However, having one in later life might be an indicator of psychosis resulting from a hallucination or delusion. Thus, in the former instance, a social worker would view this behavior as typical, which would require no special intervention, whereas in the latter, a social worker may need to do a mental status examination or refer for a psychiatric evaluation.

When studying, a social worker does not need to memorize the exact age at which an individual leaves one stage of development or reaches a milestone. However, when mentioned in a question, the age can be a useful hint as to where a client is in the life course and what may be expected.

Tip 16

Often, questions on the examinations aim to assess whether a social worker is appropriately placing a client as the priority and respecting his or her right to self-determination. Questions may focus on conflicts between meeting a client's needs versus adhering to practices or policies created by an agency. When there is a barrier to meeting a client's needs, a social worker should always take responsibility for trying to remove the barrier.

Answers indicating that a social worker should provide advice to a client because he or she has better solutions to a client's problems are never correct.

In practice, a social worker may often encounter practices or policies that limit a client's alternatives or rights to self-determination, and fighting to change these "rules" may seem unrealistic and futile. However, whether or not a social worker will be successful does not change the mandate to challenge them. Do not dismiss an answer just because it seems difficult to achieve.

A client is the expert on his or her situation and should be regarded as such. The supervisor in case vignettes is there to ensure that a client receives the most effective and efficient services possible—not to make things easier for a social worker or enforce agency mandates.

Always look at the answers through the lens of what is best for a client. The self-determination of a client is only limited in situations that would cause harm to a client or others. The correct response choice is always the one that puts a client first.

Tip 17

It is essential that the question is thoroughly understood before looking at the answers. The most difficult part of selecting the correct answer is understanding the knowledge area or concept that is being tested. In order to ensure that proper attention is given to understanding the question, a multistep process should be undertaken.

1. Read the question exactly as it is written, paying attention to qualifying words and those in quotes. Do not look at the response choices yet!

2. Ask "What is this question about?" to determine which of the KSAs is being tested.

3. Think about the important concepts related to the KSA; they will be essential in selecting the correct answers from the incorrect ones.

4. Examine the question again to confirm that your assumption about which KSA is being tested is correct and to determine how the important concepts related to the KSA are relevant to the question.

5. Now look at the response choices for the first time! Read each carefully.

6. Eliminate any that do not appear to be correct. If more than one response choice appears to be viable, go back and read the question again—looking only at the remaining viable responses. It is difficult to eliminate three of four possible answers immediately, so this process may involve multiple iterations. Each time a response choice is eliminated, read the question and the answers that are left. Going back to the question each time you are unable to dismiss all but one response choice will assist in selecting the correct answer for that particular question.

Tip 18

It is critical not to be influenced to select a response choice simply because it has social work "buzz words" such as "rapport," "empathy," "support system," "joining with a client," "strengths perspective," "from a client's perspective," and so on. Often, social workers have a hard time eliminating response choices that contain terms that are important to effective service delivery. These are key concepts that are the cornerstone of competent social work services. However, a word or catch phrase does not make a response choice correct. An answer may not be correct because the other parts of it are inadequate, false, or simply do not address what the question is asking. When you see these social work "buzz words" in a response choice, it is essential to read the rest of the answer critically. You might want to ask yourself whether the answer would still be as appealing if a synonym was used in place of the "buzz word." The entire answer has to stand on its merits as correct, even when the actual term that is making it so appealing is omitted.

Tip 19

Often, social workers view the examinations as a vehicle by which to demonstrate their clinical knowledge and skills. They view all client behaviors through a psychotherapeutic lens and are inappropriately quick to attribute actions to symptomology of disorders or dysfunction. Social workers also are more apt on the ASWB examinations to wrongly view clinical attributes as the focus of treatment or intervention.

For example, if a client has just experienced unsuccessful infertility treatments, she may be likely to feel depressed, frustrated, and hopeless. These are typical reactions to her inability to get pregnant as a result of this medical intervention. The presence of these feelings does not mean that they must be the focus of social work treatment or clinically analyzed and diagnosed. Perhaps the client simply needs support for pursuing alternative methods for becoming a mother, such as through adoption or surrogacy.

You should not be quick to diagnose a client with a disorder on the examinations unless ALL the required clinical criteria are present. You should also not make all client feelings or behaviors clinical issues to be addressed as part of an intervention or treatment.

The ASWB examinations, including the Clinical Examination, are taken by social workers employed in all types of settings and roles. Clinical work does not always imply the need for psychotherapy. Unless the setting or type of intervention to be employed is explicitly stated in a case vignette, you should use a more generalist approach to selecting the correct answer.

Tip 20

Most questions do not ask a social worker to "solve the problem" or even take action that will directly lead to resolving the issue or situation. For example, a question may ask what a social worker should do FIRST when having an issue with his or her supervisor or not getting a verbal response from a colleague. Although speaking directly to a supervisor or putting the request to a colleague in writing may likely not result in an acceptable outcome, such as getting a client a service, they are required steps in ensuring adherence to chain of command or appropriate documentation procedures. It is also important to remember that it is possible to speak to your supervisor first, even if it won't achieve the desired outcome, and then go to an agency directly immediately after—perhaps even the same day—in order to follow the proper chain of command.

Social workers like to get results, and this desire can cause them to choose answers that will make a difference even when questions are not asking for resolution.

There are not long waiting lists, scarce resources, or delays in referrals in examination case vignettes unless they are explicitly stated. In actual practice, social workers encounter these realities daily and often base their decisions and actions to ensure results despite these constraints. These factors should not influence selecting a response choice unless they are explicitly stated in the question.

Assessing Examination Difficulties

If you are having difficulty answering practice questions or even passing the examinations, it is useful to try to diagnose what is causing your problem. You should re-examine the tips outlined in this guide to see what strategies may be helpful in preparing for the examinations and/or answering questions. You also might want to relook at the self-assessment to determine which content areas require more studying.

Although strategies are important, failing the examinations is almost always a result of gaps in knowledge of social work content.

The ASWB examinations are very reliable. Thus, if you study using the same strategy or methods, you are likely to get the same results.

Just like in social work practice, a thorough assessment is critical to ensuring a strategy or intervention is created to address the targeted problem(s). A social worker should spend time analyzing what is causing the difficulties before taking an examination again. For example, difficulties with anxiety will not be addressed by "hitting the books." In addition, knowledge gaps cannot be filled by simply reviewing the test-taking strategies.

Although social workers who have failed the examinations may be anxious to start studying so that they can take the tests again in 90 days, it is worth spending time *critically* reflecting on the strategies used to study and answer questions so that corrections can be made before trying again.

Dealing With Test Anxiety

Perhaps one of the biggest issues that social workers have to address when preparing for and actually taking the examinations is anxiety. Although not designed to be an exhaustive resource on how to address test anxiety, this guide would be incomplete if it did not provide some guidance to social workers to assist with anxiety during this stressful time in their professional development.

It is important to acknowledge that anxiety can be useful during this process because it helps you prioritize studying and preparing above other demands placed upon you in everyday life. There are no magic ways to instill the necessary knowledge in your brain besides good old-fashioned studying. Anxiety can be a motivator to keep going over the material even when there are more interesting things you could be doing!

Remember, everyone who is studying for the examinations is feeling the same way. This stress is typical, and you are not alone in feeling anxious.

However, it is essential to manage this anxiety, and there are several strategies that can help.

1. *Make a Study Plan and Work the Plan*
   A great way to instill confidence is being able to walk into the testing center having prepared the way that you set out to do. A study plan will help you break the material into smaller manageable segments and avoid last minute cramming.

2. *Don't Forget the Basics*
   You need to make sure that you don't neglect your biological, emotional, and social needs leading up to and on the day of the examination. Get plenty of rest, build in relaxation time to your study plan, and eat well to give you energy during this exhausting process.

3. *Familiarize Yourself With the Test Environment*
Before the day of the examination, drive to the testing center so you know how to get there. Arrive early so you are not rushed. Take your time reviewing the tutorial on the computer before you start the examination.

4. *Use Relaxation Techniques*
Breathe and give yourself permission to relax during the examination. You may need to shut your eyes and stretch your neck or stand up several times during the 4-hour exam to help you to refocus.

5. *Put the Examination Into Perspective*
Rarely do people get the score that they want the first time taking any standardized test. Taking the SATs or GREs more than once is the rule rather than the exception. Social workers often attach too much meaning to whether or not they pass the examination the first or second time. They walk into the testing center feeling their entire career rests on the results. This is not true. There are many outstanding social workers who have had to take the test multiple times. Remember that you will be able to retake the examination if you do not pass—this is not your only chance. Not passing is not in any way reflective of your ability to practice social work. You *will* eventually pass, whether it is this time or another, so don't let the test define you. Avoid thinking in "all or nothing" terms.

6. *Expect Setbacks*
The road to licensure is not different than other journeys in life and not usually without unexpected delays or even disappointments. It is important to see these as typical parts of the process and not ends in themselves. Try to figure out why these setbacks in studying or passing are occurring and how you can use this information as feedback for making improvements. You did not get a social work degree without some disappointments and challenges. Studying for and passing the examination will also not be easy, but you will be successful if you keep focused and learn from challenges encountered.

7. *Reward Yourself*
You don't have to wait until you pass in order to celebrate. Build some enjoyment into the test-taking experience by creating little incentives or rewards along the way. Go out to dinner after having studied for 4 hours on a Saturday afternoon. Get up early and study before work so you can enjoy a movie when you get home. Improving your attitude about the test-taking experience can actually help you study more and improve your performance on the examination.

8. *Acknowledge and Address the Anxiety*
Ignoring the anxiety that accompanies this process will not help. It is impossible to completely eliminate it through any of the

techniques mentioned. However, you do need to assess whether it is manageable and can be addressed by some of these suggestions or if it is interfering so significantly with the learning process that you are "blanking out" or having problems in other areas of your life because of its presence. If this is the case, you may need more intensive anxiety reduction interventions. Repeatedly studying the content over and over will not reduce your anxiety. Although most people can develop their own strategies for anxiety management, others need outside help. Usually, individuals who need the assistance of others are those who have experienced debilitating anxiety in other areas of life prior to taking the examinations. No matter what the severity—anxiety management is a critical part of every study plan!

Examination Content

Although it is impossible to identify the information that will be tested in your examination, ASWB® provides a listing of all content areas that are used as the basis for all question construction. These areas are identified by social workers in the field via a practice analysis conducted by ASWB. Through this process, a listing of topics that describe the Knowledge, Skills, and Abilities (KSAs) that are important to the job of a social worker are used to make sure that questions focus on the areas of critical importance to social workers.

Although there is a separate set of KSAs for each of the four ASWB examinations (Bachelors, Masters, Advanced Generalist, and Clinical), there is tremendous overlap across these tests. Sometimes a KSA is not listed in the same content area or is described slightly differently (for example, "theories of human development" versus "developmental theories"). However, upon review, you will see a tremendous overlap across the examinations.

This is good news, because doing well on one ASWB examination often means that you will do well on another. It is always easier to refresh your memory about a topic area than to learn it for the first time!

You do not have to be an expert in each of the KSAs, but you will need to recall critical content, as well as key concepts and terms that may be related to the area. Many people question whether they know enough or are ready to take the examination. With regard to content, it is challenging because individuals often define readiness by being an expert or highly skilled in each area.

For the examinations, you can use the following as a guide to assessing your readiness in having the requisite knowledge.

1. Would you be able to summarize the most relevant points related to the content area in a 5-minute "lecture" on the topic?

2. Do you understand the relevancy to social work practice and how social workers use this information to make decisions when interacting with clients?

3. Do you know how this content area relates to the assessment and treatment of clients? Does it in any way impact problems or issues that they may be experiencing?

In order to get the right answers, your exam questions may require you to broadly apply the overall key theme related to a theory or area (e.g., the understanding that what happens to a client early in life can influence later functioning) or specific terms associated with the area, even if the construct is not mentioned (e.g., picking a response that best represents "family homeostasis"). In order to help you to determine the areas in which you need to concentrate in your preparation for the examination, you should review KSAs, listed in the Self- Assessment in this guide. They are the basis for individual test questions.

If you feel that you have the requisite knowledge, you may only need to quickly review by reading through the content outlined in the subsequent pages of this guide. If you have gaps in content, you should mark the sections in this guide that relate to the topic and go over them in detail so you can get to the point that you have enough knowledge to recall the key concepts and terms. If you have never heard of the concept or recall little about its relevance to social work practice, do not worry—everyone has gaps in knowledge, but this just means that you will have to spend some extra time learning about the topic.

There are different learning styles and you will need to determine which one best fits you because researchers have shown that individuals perform better on examinations if they use study techniques that are consistent with their styles of learning.

The following are some suggested techniques for each learning style that can help fill in content gaps that may exist.

VISUAL LEARNERS

Visual learners learn best through what they see. Although lectures can be boring for visual learners, they benefit from the use of diagrams, PowerPoint slides, and charts.

- Use colored highlighters in this guide to draw attention to key terms.
- Develop outlines or take notes on the concepts in the guide.
- Write talking points for each of the KSAs on separate white index cards.
- Create a coding schema of symbols and write them in this guide next to material and terms that require further study.
- Study in an environment that is away from visual distractions such as television, people moving around, or clutter.

AUDITORY LEARNERS

Auditory learners learn best through what they hear. They may have difficulty remembering material that they read in this guide, but can easily recall it if it is read to them.

- Tape record yourself summarizing the material as you are studying it—listen to your notes as a way to reinforce what you read.
- Have a study partner explain the relevant concepts and terms related to the KSAs.
- Read the text from this guide aloud if you are having trouble remembering it.
- Find free podcasts or YouTube videos on the Internet on the content areas that are short and easy to understand to assist with learning.
- Talk to yourself about the content as you study—emphasizing what is important to remember related to each KSA.

KINESTHETIC OR HANDS-ON LEARNERS

Kinesthetic learners learn through tactile approaches aimed at experiencing or doing. They need activities and physical activities as a foundation for instruction.

- Make flashcards on material because writing it down will assist with remembering the content.
- Use as many different senses as possible when studying—read material when you are on your treadmill, use highlighters, talk aloud about content, and/or listen to a study partner.
- Develop mnemonic devices to aid in information retention (for example—EAPIET or *EAt PIE* Today is a great way to remember the social work problem-solving process (Engaging, Assessing, Planning, Intervening, Evaluating, and Terminating).
- Write notes and important terms in your guide margins.
- Ask a study partner to quiz you on material—turn it into a game and see how many KSAs you can discuss or how long you can talk about a content area before running out of material.

One important thing to remember is that success on the examination does not require a lot of memorization of material, but rather the ability to recall terms when you see them and to draw upon your knowledge of multiple concepts to select the correct course of action in hypothetical vignettes or scenarios. Thus, spend your time really understanding the KSAs and not just being able to recite definitions.

Self-Assessment

In order to help you determine the areas in which you need to concentrate in your preparation for the examination, please review the following Knowledge, Skills, and Abilities (KSAs) that describe the discrete knowledge components that may be tested as part of the examination and are the basis for individual test questions.

If you are not able to recall basic content and/or key terms, indicate the need to study this area thoroughly by circling "1." If you have some basic information about the content and/or key terms, indicate the need to fill in knowledge gaps by circling "2." If you are able to summarize the key concepts and terms, as well as answer questions about its applicability to social work practice and impacts on client functioning, you may be well prepared and can circle "3." Adequate preparation should not be indicated until you can synthesize material from multiple content areas and can discuss all aspects of the KSAs easily and fluidly.

Association of Social Work Boards'
Content Outline for *Advanced Generalist* Examination

3	2	1
Well Prepared	Somewhat Prepared	Not Prepared

I.   Human Development, Diversity, and Behavior in the
     Environment (18%)

*Models of Human Growth and Development Throughout the Life
     Span*

	3	2	1
Theories of human growth and development through the life span	3	2	1
The psychosocial model	3	2	1

(continued)

Ego psychology	3	2	1
Feminist theory	3	2	1
Psychodynamic theory	3	2	1
Personality theory	3	2	1
Family systems theory	3	2	1
Psychoanalytic theory	3	2	1
Systems theory	3	2	1
Addiction theories	3	2	1
Conflict theory	3	2	1
Indicators of normal physical growth and development through the life span	3	2	1
The impact of physical, mental, and cognitive disabilities on human development through the life span	3	2	1
The normal life crises			
Emotional development	3	2	1
Normal sexual development	3	2	1
Gerontology	3	2	1
The concept of attachment and bonding	3	2	1
Basic human needs	3	2	1
The adult learning process	3	2	1
Human genetics	3	2	1

Models of Functioning of Various Systems

The effects of family dynamics on individuals	3	2	1
Family life cycle	3	2	1
Abnormal and normal functioning in traditional and nontraditional families	3	2	1
Models of organizational development	3	2	1
Models of group development	3	2	1
Models of community development	3	2	1
Models of couples development	3	2	1

Effects of the Environment on Systems' Behavior

Normal and abnormal behavior	3	2	1
The socialization process	3	2	1
The interplay of biological, psychological, and social factors	3	2	1
Social development	3	2	1
The impact of environment on individuals	3	2	1
The indicators of psychosocial stress	3	2	1
The impact of economic status	3	2	1

The effects of social role on self-image	3	2	1
The impact of poverty on individuals, families, organizations, and communities	3	2	1
The effects of social role on relationships	3	2	1
The effects of addictive behavior on relationships	3	2	1
The effects of defense mechanisms on relationships	3	2	1
The dynamics of work relationships	3	2	1
The dynamics of domestic and other violence in relationships	3	2	1
Theories of crisis intervention	3	2	1

Diversity, Discrimination, and Stereotypes

The influence of culture, race, religion/spirituality, and/or ethnicity on behaviors and attitudes	3	2	1
The influence of sexual orientation, gender, and/or gender identification on behaviors and attitudes	3	2	1
The influence of age and/or disability on behaviors and attitudes	3	2	1
The effects of discrimination based on culture, race, religion/spirituality and/or ethnicity	3	2	1
The effects of discrimination based on sexual orientation, gender, and/or gender identification	3	2	1
The effects of discrimination based on age and/or disability	3	2	1
The relationship between self-image and cultural heritage	3	2	1
The different and similar characteristics of cultural, racial, religious and/or ethnic groups	3	2	1
The different and similar characteristics related to sexual orientation, gender, and/or gender identification	3	2	1
The different and similar characteristics of age groups and types of disability	3	2	1
Stereotypes	3	2	1
The impact of diversity in styles of communicating	3	2	1

II. Micro Assessment and Planning (22%)

Use of Assessment Instruments and Methods

Psychological and educational tests and measurements	3	2	1
The use of assessment/diagnosis instruments in practice	3	2	1

(continued)

The components and function of the mental status examination	3	2	1
The process used in problem formulation	3	2	1
The methods of involving the client and/or systems in identifying the problem	3	2	1
The principles and techniques of interviewing	3	2	1
The methods used to assess the client's communication skills	3	2	1
The methods used to assess motivation and resistance	3	2	1
The methods used to assess needed level of care	3	2	1

Use of Social History

The components of a biopsychosocial history	3	2	1
The types of information available from employment, medical psychological, and school records	3	2	1
The methods used to collect and evaluate collateral information	3	2	1
The methods used to obtain information relevant to a given situation	3	2	1
The components of a sexual history	3	2	1
The components of a marital history	3	2	1
The components of a family history	3	2	1
Basic medical terminology	3	2	1
The exploration of spiritual/religious beliefs and practices	3	2	1

Impact of Life Stressors on Systems

The effects of life stressors on families	3	2	1
The effects of stressors on behavior	3	2	1
The impact of physical and mental illness on family dynamics	3	2	1
The dynamics of loss, separation, and grief	3	2	1
The impact of aging parents on adult children	3	2	1
The factors of child development	3	2	1
The psychological responses to illness and disability	3	2	1
The effects of addiction on individuals, families, organizations, and communities	3	2	1
The impact of economic change on individuals, families, organizations, and communities	3	2	1
The effects of physical, sexual, and psychological abuse on individuals, families, organizations, and communities	3	2	1
The impact of life cycle changes on systems	3	2	1

The effects of life crises on individuals	3	2	1
The effects of life crises on the family	3	2	1
The impact on clients of out-of-home displacement (e.g. hospitalization, jail, foster care, natural disaster)	3	2	1
The impact of defense mechanisms on behavior	3	2	1

Intervention Planning

Criteria used in selecting intervention/treatment modalities	3	2	1
The components of and methods used to develop an intervention/treatment or service plan	3	2	1
The effect of the client's developmental level on the creation of an intervention/treatment plan	3	2	1
Permanency planning	3	2	1
Methods used to develop measurable objectives to assess client change	3	2	1
The client's role in the intervention process	3	2	1
The methods used to develop behavioral objectives	3	2	1
The methods used to formulate a time frame for interventions	3	2	1
The methods used to identify learning needs for clients	3	2	1

Assessment of Strengths and Challenges

The methods used to assess clients' strengths and challenges	3	2	1
The factors used in determining the client's ability to use intervention/treatment	3	2	1
The methods used in assessing ego strength	3	2	1
The indicators of motivation and resistance	3	2	1

Identification of Common Indicators of Risks and Disorders

The effects of body image on self-image	3	2	1
The indicators of somatization	3	2	1
The indicators of malingering	3	2	1
Use of the current *Diagnostic and Statistical Manual of Mental Disorders* of the American Psychiatric Association	3	2	1
Psychopathology	3	2	1
The symptoms of mental and emotional illness	3	2	1
The symptoms of neurologic and organic processes	3	2	1
The symptoms of substance abuse and other addictions	3	2	1

(continued)

The indicators of sexual dysfunction	3	2	1
The dynamics and indicators of neglect and physical, psychological, and sexual abuse	3	2	1
The characteristics of perpetrators of abuse and neglect	3	2	1
The indicators of client danger to self and others	3	2	1
The methods used to assess the client's communication skills	3	2	1
The use of observation to assess client interactions	3	2	1
The ways in which the client's behavior with a social worker is representative of his or her relationship patterns	3	2	1
Common psychotropic and nonpsychotropic prescriptions and over-the-counter medications and their side effects	3	2	1

III. Micro Practice and Social Work Relationships (18%)

Application of Theories, Methods, and Processes to Micro Systems

The problem-solving model	3	2	1
The crisis intervention/treatment approach	3	2	1
Task-centered practice	3	2	1
Behavioral approaches	3	2	1
The selection on theoretical approaches to meet client need	3	2	1
Psychotherapies	3	2	1
Short-term interventions/treatment	3	2	1
Client advocacy	3	2	1
The methods used in working with the unmotivated or involuntary client	3	2	1
Case management	3	2	1
The use of permanency planning as an intervention/treatment method	3	2	1
The phases of intervention/treatment	3	2	1
The indicators of client readiness for termination	3	2	1
The methods of conflict resolution	3	2	1
Small group theories	3	2	1
Other intervention/treatment strategies	3	2	1

Micro Intervention Techniques

The use of partializing, supporting, focusing, clarifying, confronting, interpreting, and reflecting	3	2	1
The techniques used to motivate clients	3	2	1
The techniques used to develop contracts with clients	3	2	1

The techniques used to clarify the responsibilities of the client	3	2	1
The use of goal-setting	3	2	1
The techniques used to teach skills to clients	3	2	1
The differential use of intervention/treatment techniques	3	2	1
Client self-monitoring techniques	3	2	1
The use of timing in intervention/treatment	3	2	1
The technique of role-play	3	2	1
Role-modeling techniques	3	2	1
The techniques used for follow-up	3	2	1
Stress management techniques	3	2	1
Limit setting	3	2	1
The process used to refer clients for services	3	2	1
The approaches to family therapy	3	2	1
Use of clients' strengths	3	2	1
Couples intervention/treatment approaches	3	2	1
Group dynamics	3	2	1
The approaches to social group work	3	2	1
The approaches to group psychotherapy	3	2	1
The differential use of group process	3	2	1
The techniques for developing and maintaining group cohesion	3	2	1
The process of co-therapy	3	2	1
The concept of congruence in communication	3	2	1
The methods used in summarizing communication	3	2	1
Verbal and nonverbal communication techniques	3	2	1
Techniques that elicit the underlying meaning of communication	3	2	1
The methods used to obtain and provide feedback	3	2	1

Dynamics of the Social Worker–Client Relationship

The process of engagement in social work practice	3	2	1
The social worker's role in the change process	3	2	1
The concept of empathy	3	2	1
The concept of a helping relationship	3	2	1
The use of acceptance	3	2	1
The methods used to clarify the role of the social worker	3	2	1
The principles of relationship building	3	2	1
Professional objectivity in the social worker–client relationship	3	2	1
The concept of transference and countertransference	3	2	1

(continued)

The components of the social worker–client relationship   3   2   1

The use of the social worker–client relationship as an
     intervention/treatment tool   3   2   1

The effects of the client's developmental level on the social
     worker-client relationship   3   2   1

The influence of the social worker's own values on the
     social worker–client relationship   3   2   1

The dynamics of power and transparency in the helping
     relationship   3   2   1

The dynamics of diversity in the helping relationship   3   2   1

The dynamics of domestic and other violence in the helping
     relationship   3   2   1

Application of Evidence-Based Practices

The techniques used to evaluate a client's progress   3   2   1

Techniques used to measure the effectiveness of the social
     work intervention   3   2   1

Utilization of research results in practice   3   2   1

Applying evidence-based practices to current programs   3   2   1

IV.   Macro Practice (18%)

Research Methods and Design

The methods of data collection   3   2   1

The difference between quantitative and qualitative data   3   2   1

Data analysis procedures   3   2   1

The methods used to evaluate research instruments   3   2   1

The methods used to assess reliability and validity in
     social work research   3   2   1

Social work research designs   3   2   1

Appropriate uses of statistical data   3   2   1

Research ethics (e.g., institutional review boards, use of
     human subjects, informed consent)   3   2   1

Program Evaluation and Outcomes

The methods used to evaluate agency programs   3   2   1

Assessment/diagnosis instruments used to evaluate social
     work practice   3   2   1

The effects of program evaluation findings on services   3   2   1

Accreditation and program reviews   3   2   1

Determination of appropriate evaluation tools   3   2   1

Record-Keeping and Reporting

Written communication skills	3	2	1
Case recording and record-keeping	3	2	1
The use of appropriate documentation and correspondence in service delivery	3	2	1
The management of agency/practice records	3	2	1

Program Development and Service Delivery Systems

The types of service delivery programs/systems	3	2	1
The methods used to clarify the benefits and limitations of resources	3	2	1
The methods used to interpret and communicate policies and procedures	3	2	1
The development of programs and services to meet community needs	3	2	1
The methods used to establish service networks or community resources	3	2	1
The effects of agency policies, regulation, and function on service delivery	3	2	1
The methods of conducting a needs assessment	3	2	1
Establishing program objectives and outcomes	3	2	1

Interdisciplinary Collaboration

Elements of a case presentation	3	2	1
Range or expertise of professions other than social work	3	2	1
The use of collaterals to obtain relevant information	3	2	1
The approaches used in consultation	3	2	1
The use of networking	3	2	1
The process for interdisciplinary collaboration	3	2	1
The methods used to coordinate services between service providers or agencies	3	2	1
The multidisciplinary team approach	3	2	1
The use of informal and formal power structures	3	2	1
The use of advocacy among agencies and disciplines	3	2	1

Policy Analysis and Advocacy

Interpreting legislation to clients	3	2	1
The impact of social welfare legislation on social work practice	3	2	1
Social policy processes and analysis	3	2	1

(continued)

Legislative advocacy	3	2	1
The methods of advocacy for policy and/or procedural change	3	2	1
The methods of advocacy for resources to meet client needs	3	2	1
The methods of advocacy for policies and services sensitive to ethnic and cultural differences	3	2	1
The methods of advocacy for policies to eliminate discriminatory practices	3	2	1
The policy implications of research findings	3	2	1

Theories and Methods of Social Change

Primary, secondary, and tertiary prevention strategies	3	2	1
The concept of citizen participation	3	2	1
Community organization and development methods	3	2	1
Community resources	3	2	1
Community outreach and advocacy	3	2	1
Social planning methods	3	2	1
The impact of social institutions on society	3	2	1
The theories of social change	3	2	1

Administration and Management

The impact of agency policy and procedures on social work practice	3	2	1
Leadership and management techniques	3	2	1
Time management approaches	3	2	1
Formal and informal organizational structure	3	2	1
The elements of caseload management	3	2	1
The use of delegation as a technique	3	2	1
The methods used to plan and assign work for staff	3	2	1
The concept of authority and responsibility	3	2	1
The models for interpreting agency policies and procedures to staff	3	2	1
The components of a collegial and positive work environment	3	2	1
Fiscal management techniques	3	2	1
The budgetary process	3	2	1
Governance structures	3	2	1
The methods used for strategic planning	3	2	1
Employee recruitment, training, retention, performance appraisal, evaluation, and discipline	3	2	1

Supervision and Consultation

The stages of professional development	3	2	1
The educational components, techniques, and methods of supervision	3	2	1
The models of group supervision	3	2	1
The models of peer supervision and consultation	3	2	1
The methods used to identify learning needs and develop learning objectives for supervisees	3	2	1
Transference and countertransference within supervisory relationships	3	2	1
The social worker's responsibility to seek and receive appropriate supervision	3	2	1
Student/supervisee characteristics and suitability for the profession	3	2	1
The use of case recording/documentation for practice evaluation or supervision	3	2	1

Risk Management

Systems of internal controls that minimize risk for clients, workers, and the agency	3	2	1
The methods to create, implement, and evaluate policies and procedures that minimize risk for clients, workers, and the agency	3	2	1
The social worker's responsibility to respond to client and/or community concerns	3	2	1
The policy implications of risk management	3	2	1
Methods to manage critical incidents, including debriefing for clients and staff	3	2	1

V. Professional Values and Ethics (24%)

Values, Boundaries, and Ethics

The effects of differences in values influenced by culture, political beliefs, race, ethnicity, gender, age, disability, sexual orientation, gender identity, and religion/ spirituality	3	2	1
Intrinsic worth and value of the individual	3	2	1
Professional boundary issues	3	2	1
Dual relationships	3	2	1
Identification and resolution of ethical dilemmas	3	2	1

(continued)

Ethical and legal issues   3 2 1
Medical issues   3 2 1
Ethical issues in supervision and management   3 2 1

Confidentiality

Legal and ethical issues regarding confidentiality, including
    electronic information   3 2 1
The use of client records   3 2 1
Ethical and legal issues regarding mandatory reporting
    of abuse   3 2 1
The process of obtaining informed consent   3 2 1

Self-Determination

The circumstances under which clients have the right to
    refuse services   3 2 1
Individual, group, organization, and community
    self-determination   3 2 1
The limits to self-determination   3 2 1
Clients' rights and grievance procedures   3 2 1

Professional Responsibilities for Ethical Practice

The social worker's ethical responsibility as a professional   3 2 1
The social worker's ethical responsibility to broader society 3 2 1
The social worker's ethical responsibility to the social work
    profession   3 2 1
The social worker's ethical responsibility in practice
    settings   3 2 1
The social worker's ethical responsibility to colleagues   3 2 1

Human Development, Diversity, and Behavior in the Environment (18%)

Models of Human Growth and Development Through the Life Span

1

THEORIES OF HUMAN GROWTH AND DEVELOPMENT THROUGH THE LIFE SPAN

Social work theories are general explanations that are supported by evidence obtained through the scientific method. A theory may explain human behavior by describing how humans interact or how humans react to certain stimuli. Because human behavior is so complex, numerous theories are utilized to guide practice. You need to understand them and use them as conceptual tools.

Often, the name of the theory will not be used in a question, but understanding it is essential to selecting the correct answer.

Study the theories *broadly* to understand their general theme or focus, and *deeply* enough to know the meaning of terms originating from them that may be mentioned in exam questions.

THE PSYCHOSOCIAL MODEL

According to Erikson, there are eight distinct stages, with two possible outcomes. Successful completion of each stage results in a healthy personality and successful interactions with others. Failure to successfully complete a stage can result in a reduced ability to complete further stages and, therefore, a more unhealthy personality and sense of self. These stages, however, can be resolved successfully at a later time.

Trust Versus Mistrust. From birth to 1 year of age, children begin to learn the ability to trust others based upon the consistency of their caregiver(s). If trust develops successfully, the child gains confidence and security in the world around him or her and is able to feel secure even when threatened. Unsuccessful completion of this stage can result in an inability to trust, and therefore a sense of fear about the inconsistent world. It may result in anxiety, heightened insecurities, and feelings of mistrust in the world around them.

Autonomy Versus Shame and Doubt. Between the ages of 1 and 3, children begin to assert their independence by walking away from their mother, picking which toy to play with, and making choices about what they like to wear, to eat, and so on. If children in this stage are encouraged and supported in their increased independence, they become more confident and secure in their own ability to survive in the world. If children are criticized, overly controlled, or not given the opportunity to assert themselves, they begin to feel inadequate in their ability to survive, and may then become overly dependent upon others while lacking self-esteem and feeling a sense of shame or doubt in their own abilities.

Initiative Versus Guilt. Around age 3 and continuing to age 6, children assert themselves more frequently. They begin to plan activities, make up games, and initiate activities with others. If given this opportunity, children develop a sense of initiative, and feel secure in their ability to lead others and make decisions. Conversely, if this tendency is squelched, either through criticism or control, children develop a sense of guilt. They may feel like nuisances to others and will therefore remain followers, lacking self-initiative.

Industry Versus Inferiority. From age 6 to puberty, children begin to develop a sense of pride in their accomplishments. They initiate projects, see them through to completion, and feel good about what they have achieved. If children are encouraged and reinforced for their initiative, they begin to feel industrious and feel confident in their ability to achieve goals. If this initiative is not encouraged but instead restricted, children begin to feel inferior, doubting their abilities and failing to reach their potential.

Identity Versus Role Confusion. During adolescence, the transition from childhood to adulthood is most important. Children are becoming more independent, and begin to look at the future in terms of career, relationships, families, housing, and so on. During this period, they explore possibilities and begin to form their own identities based upon the outcome of their explorations. This sense of who they are can be hindered, which results in a sense of confusion ("I don't know what I want to be when I grow up") about themselves and their role in the world.

Intimacy Versus Isolation. In young adulthood, individuals begin to share themselves more intimately with others and explore relationships leading toward longer term commitments with others outside the family. Successful completion can lead to comfortable relationships and a sense of commitment, safety, and care within a relationship. Avoiding intimacy and fearing commitment and relationships can lead to isolation, loneliness, and sometimes depression.

Generativity Versus Stagnation. During middle adulthood, individuals establish careers, settle down within relationships, begin families, and develop a sense of being a part of the bigger picture. They give back to society through raising children, being productive at work, and becoming involved in community activities and organizations. By failing to achieve these objectives, individuals become stagnant and feel unproductive.

Ego Integrity Versus Despair. As individuals grow older and become senior citizens, they tend to slow down and explore life as retired people. It is during this time that they contemplate accomplishments and are able to develop a sense of integrity if they are satisfied with the progression of their lives. If they see their lives as being unproductive and failing to accomplish life goals, they become dissatisfied with life and develop despair, often leading to depression and hopelessness.

EGO PSYCHOLOGY

Ego psychology focuses on the *rational, conscious processes of the ego*. Ego psychology is based on an assessment of a client as presented in the *present (here and now)*. Treatment focuses on the ego functioning of a client, because healthy behavior is under the control of the ego. It addresses:

- How the person behaves in relation to the situation he or she finds himself or herself in
- Reality testing: a client's perception of situation
- Coping abilities: ego strengths
- Capacity for relating to others

The *goal* is to maintain and enhance ego's control and management of stress and its effects.

FEMINIST THEORY

Feminist theory analyzes the status of women and men in society with the purpose of using that knowledge to better women's lives. Feminist theorists question the differences between women and men, including how race, class, ethnicity, sexuality, nationality, and age intersect with gender.

Themes that are studied include discrimination, objectification (especially sexual objectification), oppression, stereotyping, and so on. Feminist theory is used in the fields of social work, sociology, economics, education, and others.

Feminism is a political, cultural, or economic movement aimed at establishing equal rights and legal protection for women.

PSYCHODYNAMIC THEORY

Psychodynamic approaches aim to help clients review emotions, thoughts, early life experiences, and beliefs in order to gain insight into their lives and their present-day problems. Recognizing recurring patterns helps clients see the ways in which they avoid distress and/or develop defense mechanisms as methods of coping so that they can take steps to change these patterns.

In order to keep painful feelings, memories, and experiences in the unconscious, clients tend to develop defense mechanisms, such as denial, repression, rationalization, and others. Social workers using psychodynamic approaches encourage clients to speak freely about their emotions, desires, and fears in order to reveal vulnerable feelings that have been pushed out of conscious awareness. According to psychodynamic theory, behavior is influenced by unconscious thought; vulnerable or painful feelings are resolved by the use of defense mechanisms.

The therapeutic relationship is central to psychodynamic approaches as it takes an intimate look at interpersonal relationships so that clients can see relationship patterns. It also empowers clients, through insight and self-awareness, to transform dysfunctional dynamics.

PERSONALITY THEORY

Personality theories attempt to explain both personality characteristics and the way these characteristics develop and impact behavior/functioning. Theories that have this aim can be categorized as biological, behavioral, psychodynamic, humanist, or trait focused.

Biological

Biological theories suggest that genetics are responsible for personality. Research on heritability suggests that there is a link between genetics and personality traits.

Behavioral

Behavioral theories suggest that personality is a result of interaction between the individual and the environment. Behavioral theorists study observable and measurable behaviors, rejecting theories that take internal thoughts and feelings into account.

Psychodynamic

Psychodynamic theories emphasize the influence of the unconscious mind and childhood experiences on personality.

Humanist

Humanist theories emphasize the importance of free will and individual experience in the development of personality. Humanist theorists emphasized the concept of self-actualization, which is an innate need for personal growth that motivates behavior.

Trait

Trait theories posit that the personality is made up of a number of broad traits. A trait is basically a relatively stable characteristic that causes an individual to behave in certain ways.

FAMILY SYSTEMS THEORY

Family theory provides a theoretical and therapeutic base for dealing with family-related situations; it is also useful in understanding and managing individual problems by determining the extent to which such problems are related to family issues. A family systems approach argues that in order to understand a family system, a social worker must look at the family as a whole, rather than focusing on its members.

People do not exist in a vacuum. They live, play, go to school, and work with other people. Most anthropologists agree that, next to their peculiar tendency to think and use tools, one of the distinguishing characteristics of human beings is that they are social creatures. The social group that seems to be most universal and pervasive in the way it shapes human behavior is the family. For social workers, the growing awareness of the crucial impact of families on clients has led to the development of family systems theory.

Family systems theory searches for the causes of behavior, not in the individual alone, but in the interactions among the members of a group. The basic rationale is that all parts of the family are interrelated. Further, the family has properties of its own that can be known only by looking at the relationships and interactions among all members.

The family systems approach is based on several basic assumptions:

- Each family is more than a sum of its members.
- Each family is unique, due to the infinite variations in personal characteristics and cultural and ideological styles.
- A healthy family has flexibility, consistent structure, and effective exchange of information.
- The family is an interactional system whose component parts have constantly shifting boundaries and varying degrees of resistance to change.
- Families must fulfill a variety of functions for each member, both collectively and individually, if each member is to grow and develop.
- Families strive for a sense of balance or **homeostasis**.
- Negative feedback loops are those patterns of interaction that maintain stability or constancy while minimizing change. Negative feedback loops help to maintain homeostasis. Positive feedback loops, in contrast, are patterns of interaction that facilitate change or movement toward either growth or dissolution.
- Families are seen as being goal oriented. The concept of **equifinality** refers to the ability of the family system to accomplish the same goals through different routes.
- The concept of hierarchies describes how families organize themselves into various smaller units or **subsystems** that are comprised by the larger family system. When the members or tasks associated with each subsystem become blurred with those of other subsystems, families have been viewed as having difficulties. For example, when a child becomes involved in marital issues, difficulties often emerge that require intervention.
- **Boundaries** occur at every level of the system and between subsystems. Boundaries influence the movement of people and the flow of information into and out of the system. Some families have very open boundaries where members and others are allowed to freely come and go without much restriction; in other families, there are tight restrictions on where family members can go and who may be brought into the family system. Boundaries also regulate the flow of information in a family. In more closed families, the rules strictly regulate what information may be discussed and with whom.

In contrast, information may flow more freely in families that have more permeable boundaries.

■ The concept of **interdependence** is critical in the study of family systems. Individual family members and the subsystems comprised by the family system are mutually influenced by and are mutually dependent upon one another. What happens to one family member, or what one family member does, influences other family members.

Genograms are diagrams of family relationships beyond a family tree allowing a social worker and client to visualize hereditary patterns and psychological factors. They include annotations about the medical history and major personality traits of each family member. Genograms help uncover intergenerational patterns of behavior, marriage choices, family alliances and conflicts, the existence of family secrets, and other information that will shed light on a family's present situation.

PSYCHOANALYTIC THEORY

Originally developed by Sigmund Freud, psychoanalytic theory posits that a client is seen as the product of his past and treatment involves dealing with the repressed material in the unconscious. According to psychoanalytic theory, personalities arise because of attempts to resolve conflicts between unconscious sexual and aggressive impulses and societal demands to restrain these impulses.

Freud believed that behavior and personality derives from the constant and unique interaction of conflicting psychological forces that operate at **three different levels of awareness**: the preconscious, the conscious, and the unconscious.

The **preconscious** contains all the information outside of a client's attention, but readily available if needed—thoughts and feelings can be brought into the consciousness easily.

The **conscious** contains all the information that a client is paying attention to at any given time.

The **unconscious** contains thoughts, feelings, desires, and memories of which clients have no awareness, but that influence every aspect of their day-to-day lives.

Freud proposed that personalities have three components: the id, the ego, and the superego.

■ **Id:** a reservoir of instinctual energy that contains biological urges such as impulses toward survival, sex, and aggression. The id is unconscious and operates according to the **pleasure principle**, which is the drive to achieve pleasure and avoid pain.

■ **Ego:** the component that manages the conflict between the id and the constraints of the real world. Some parts of the ego are unconscious and others are preconscious or conscious. The ego operates according to the reality principle, the awareness that gratification of impulses has to be delayed in order to accommodate the demands of the real world. The ego's role is to prevent the id from gratifying its impulses in socially inappropriate ways.

Ego-Syntonic/Ego-Dystonic:

■ Syntonic = behaviors "insync" with the ego (no guilt)

■ Dystonic = behavior "dis-n-sync" with the ego (guilt)

The ego's job is to determine the best course of action based on information from the id, reality, and the superego. When the ego is comfortable with its conclusions and behaviors, a client is said to be ego-syntonic. However, if a client is bothered by some of his or her behaviors, he or she would be ego-dystonic (ego alien).

Inability of the ego to reconcile the demands of the id, the super-ego, and reality produces conflict which leads to a state of psychic distress known as anxiety.

■ **Superego:** the moral component of personality. It contains all the moral standards learned from parents and society. The superego forces the ego to conform not only to reality but also to its ideals of morality. Hence, the superego causes clients to feel guilty when they go against society's rules.

SYSTEMS THEORY

A system is a whole comprising component parts that work together. Applied to social work, systems theory views human behavior through larger contexts, such as members of families, communities, and broader society.

Important to this theory is the concept that when one thing changes within a system, the whole system is affected.

Systems tend toward equilibrium and can have closed or open boundaries.

Applications to Social Work

1. Social workers need to understand interactions between the micro, mezzo, and macro levels.

2. Problems at one part of a system may be manifested at another.

3. Ecomaps and genograms can help to understand system dynamics.

4. Understanding "person-in-environment" is essential to identifying barriers or opportunities for change.

5. Problems and change are viewed within larger contexts.

Some System Theory Terms

closed system	uses up its energy and dies
differentiation	becoming specialized in structure and function
entropy	closed, disorganized, stagnant; using up available energy
equifinality	arriving at the same end from different beginnings
homeostasis	steady state
input	obtaining resources from the environment that are necessary to attain the goals of the system
negative entropy	exchange of energy and resources between systems that promote growth and transformation
open system	a system with cross-boundary exchange
output	a product of the system that exports to the environment
subsystem	a major component of a system made up of two or more interdependent components that interact in order to attain their own purpose(s) and the purpose(s) of the system in which they are embedded
suprasystem	an entity that is served by a number of component systems organized in interacting relationships
throughput	energy that is integrated into the system so it can be used by the system to accomplish its goals

ADDICTION THEORIES

There are many *risk factors* for alcohol and other drug abuse, including, but not limited to:

1. *Family:* Parents, siblings, and/or spouse use substances; family dysfunction (i.e., inconsistent discipline, poor parenting skills, lack of positive family rituals and routine); family trauma (i.e., death, divorce)

2. *Social:* Peers use drugs and alcohol; social or cultural norms condone use of substances; expectations about positive effects of drugs and alcohol; drugs and alcohol are available and accessible

3. *Psychiatric:* Depression, anxiety, low self-esteem, low tolerance for stress; other mental health disorders; feelings of desperation; loss of control over one's life

4. *Behavioral:* Use of other substances; aggressive behavior in childhood; impulsivity and risk taking; rebelliousness; school-based academic or behavioral problems; poor interpersonal relationships

Different models are believed to explain the causes of substance abuse.

1. *Biopsychosocial model:* There are a wide variety of reasons why people start and continue using substances. This model provides the most comprehensive explanation for the complex nature of substance abuse disorders. It incorporates hereditary predisposition, emotional and psychological problems, social influences, and environmental problems.

2. *Medical model:* Addiction is considered a chronic, progressive, relapsing, and potentially fatal medical disease.

   ■ *Genetic causes:* Inherited vulnerability to addiction, particularly alcoholism
   ■ *Brain reward mechanisms:* Substances act on parts of the brain that reinforce continued use by producing pleasurable feelings
   ■ *Altered brain chemistry:* Habitual use of substances alters brain chemistry and continued use of substances is required to avoid feeling discomfort from a brain imbalance

3. *Self-medication model:* Substances relieve symptoms of a psychiatric disorder and continued use is reinforced by relief of symptoms.

4. *Family and environmental model:* Explanation for substance abuse can be found in family and environmental factors such as behaviors shaped by family and peers, personality factors, physical and sexual abuse, disorganized communities, and school factors.

5. *Social model:* Drug use is learned and reinforced from others who serve as role models. A potential substance abuser shares the same values and activities as those who use substances. There are no controls that prevent use of substances. Social, economic, and political factors, such as racism, poverty, sexism, and so on, contribute to the cause.

Whatever the root causes, a client's substance abuse problem must be addressed before other psychotherapeutic issues. A social worker should also rule out symptoms being related to a substance abuse problem before attributing them to a psychiatric issue.

CONFLICT THEORY

Conflict theory, derived from the works of Karl Marx, posits that society is fragmented into groups that compete for social and economic resources. Social order is maintained by consensus among those with the greatest political, economic, and social resources.

According to conflict theory, inequality exists because those in control of a disproportionate share of society's resources actively defend their advantages. The masses are bound by coercion by those in power. This perspective emphasizes social control, not consensus and conformity. Groups and individuals advance their own interests, struggling over control of societal resources.

There is great attention paid to class, race, and gender in this perspective since they relate to the most pertinent and enduring struggles in society.

Conflict theorists challenge the status quo, encourage social change, and believe rich and powerful people force social order on the poor and the weak. Conflict theorists note that unequal groups usually have conflicting values and agendas, causing them to compete against one another. This constant competition between groups forms the basis for the ever-changing nature of society.

THE INDICATORS OF NORMAL PHYSICAL GROWTH AND DEVELOPMENT THROUGH THE LIFE SPAN

Human growth, development, and learning become progressively complex over time and are influenced through a variety of experiences and interactions. Growth, development, and learning proceed in predictable patterns reflecting increasingly complex levels of organization across the life course. Each developmental stage has distinctive characteristics; however, each builds from the experiences of earlier stages. The domains of development are integrated within the child, so when one area is affected, other areas are also affected. Development proceeds at varying rates from child to child, as well as across developmental domains for individual children, reflecting the unique nature of each. Because growth and development are generally predictable, social workers should know the milestones of healthy development and the signs of potential delay or disability.

Child Behavior and Development

Child development refers to the physical, mental, and socioemotional changes that occur between birth and the end of adolescence, as a child progresses from dependency to increasing autonomy. It is a continuous process with a predictable sequence, yet having a unique course. Individuals do not progress at the same rate, and each stage is affected by the preceding types of development. Because these developmental changes may be strongly influenced by genetic factors and events during prenatal life, genetics and prenatal development are usually included as part of the study of child development.

Infants and Toddlers (Age 0–3)

Healthy Growth and Development

- *Physical*—grows at a rapid rate, especially brain size
- *Mental*—learns through senses, exploring, playing; communicates by crying, babbling, then "baby talk," simple sentences
- *Social-emotional*—seeks to build trust in others; dependent; beginning to develop a sense of self

Key Health Care Issues

- *Communication*—provide security, physical closeness; promote healthy parent–child bonds
- *Health*—keep immunizations/checkups on schedule; provide proper nutrition, sleep, skin care, oral health, routine screenings
- *Safety*—ensure a safe environment for exploring, playing, sleeping

Examples of age-specific care for infants and toddlers:

- Involve child and parent(s) in care during feeding, diapering, and bathing
- Provide safe toys and opportunities for play
- Encourage child to communicate—smile, talk softly to him or her
- Help parent(s) learn about proper child care

Young Children (Age 4–6)

Healthy Growth and Development

- *Physical*—grows at a slower rate; improving motor skills; dresses self; toilet trained
- *Mental*—begins to use symbols; improving memory; vivid imagination, fears; likes stories
- *Social-Emotional*—identifies with parent(s); becomes more independent; sensitive to others' feelings

Key Health Care Issues

- *Communication*—give praise, rewards, clear rules
- *Health*—keep immunizations/checkups on schedule; promote healthy habits (good nutrition, personal hygiene, etc.)
- *Safety*—promote safety habits (use bike helmets, safety belts, etc.)

Examples of age-specific care for young children:

- Involve parent(s) and child in care—let child make some food choices
- Use toys and games to teach child and reduce fear
- Encourage child to ask questions, play with others, and talk about feelings
- Help parent(s) teach child safety rules

Older Children (Age 7–12)

Healthy Growth and Development

- *Physical*—grows slowly until a "spurt" at puberty
- *Mental*—understands cause and effect; can read, write, do math; active, eager learner
- *Social-Emotional*—develops greater sense of self; focuses on school activities; negotiates for greater independence

Key Health Care Issues

- *Communication*—help child to feel competent, useful
- *Health*—keep immunizations/checkups on schedule; give information on alcohol, tobacco, other drugs, sexuality
- *Safety*—promote safety habits (playground safety, resolving conflicts peacefully, etc.)

Examples of age-specific care for older children:

- Allow child to make some care decisions (in which arm do you want vaccination?)
- Build self-esteem—ask child to help you do a task, recognize his or her achievements, and so on
- Guide child in making healthy, safe, lifestyle choices
- Help parent(s) talk with child about peer pressure, sexuality, alcohol, tobacco, and other drugs

Adolescent Behavior and Development

The development of children ages 13 to 18 years old is a critical time as children develop the ability to understand abstract ideas, such as higher math concepts; develop moral philosophies, including rights and privileges; and move toward a more mature sense of themselves and their purpose. This development continues between the ages of 18 and 21 as adolescents reach the physical, mental, and emotional milestones that signal their transition into adulthood.

Healthy Growth and Development

- *Physical*—grows in spurts; matures physically; able to reproduce
- *Mental*—becomes an abstract thinker (goes beyond simple solutions, can consider many options, etc.); chooses own values
- *Social-Emotional*—develops own identity; builds close relationships; tries to balance peer group with family interests; concerned about appearances, challenges authority

Key Health Care Issues

- *Communication*—provide acceptance, privacy; build teamwork, respect
- *Health*—encourage regular checkups; promote sexual responsibility; advise against substance abuse; update immunizations
- *Safety*—discourage risk-taking (promote safe driving, violence prevention, etc.)

Examples of age-specific care for adolescents:

- Treat more as an adult than child—avoid authoritarian approaches
- Show respect—be considerate of how treatment may affect relationships
- Guide teen in making positive lifestyle choices (i.e., correct misinformation from teen's peers)
- Encourage open communication between parent(s), teen, and peers

Young Adult Behavior and Development

The development of adults ages 21 to 39 years old focuses on family, career, and community involvement.

Healthy Growth and Development

- *Physical*—reaches physical and sexual maturity, nutritional needs are for maintenance, not growth
- *Mental*—acquires new skills, information; uses these to solve problems
- *Social-Emotional*—seeks closeness with others; sets career goals; chooses lifestyle, community; starts own family

Key Health Care Issues

- *Communication*—be supportive and honest; respect personal values
- *Health*—encourage regular checkups; promote healthy lifestyle (proper nutrition, exercise, weight, etc.); inform about health risks (heart disease, cancer, etc.); update immunizations
- *Safety*—provide information on hazards at home, work

Examples of age-specific care for young adults:

- Support the person in making health care decisions
- Encourage healthy and safe habits at work and home
- Recognize commitments to family, career, community (time, money, etc.)

Middle Adult Behavior and Development

The development of adults ages 40 to 64 years old focuses on recognizing abilities and contributions while planning for older adulthood.

Healthy Growth and Development

- *Physical*—begins to age; experiences menopause (women); may develop chronic health problems
- *Mental*—uses life experiences to learn, create, solve problems
- *Social-Emotional*—hopes to contribute to future generations; stays productive, avoids feeling "stuck" in life; balances dreams with reality; plans retirement; may care for children and parents

Key Health Care Issues

- *Communication*—keep a hopeful attitude; focus on strengths, not limitations

- *Health*—encourage regular checkups and preventive exams; address age-related changes; monitor health risks; update immunizations
- *Safety*—address age-related changes (effects on sense, reflexes, etc.)

Examples of age-specific care for middle adults:

- Address worries about future—encourage talking about feelings, plans, and so on
- Recognize the person's physical, mental, and social abilities/ contributions
- Help with plans for a healthy active retirement

Older Adult Behavior and Development

The development of adults ages 65 to 79 focuses on social activities, physical health maintenance, and promoting independence.

Healthy Growth and Development

- *Physical*—ages gradually; natural decline in some physical abilities, senses
- *Mental*—continues to be an active learner, thinker; memory skills may start to decline
- *Social-Emotional*—takes on new roles (grandparent, widow or widower, etc.); balances independence, dependence; reviews life

Key Health Care Issues

- *Communication*—give respect; prevent isolation; encourage acceptance of aging
- *Health*—monitor health closely; promote physical, mental, social activity; guard against depression, apathy, update immunizations
- *Safety*—promote home safety; especially preventing falls

Examples of age-specific care for adults ages 65 to 79 years:

- Encourage the person to talk about feelings of loss, grief, and achievements
- Provide information, materials, and so on, to make medication use and home safe
- Provide support for coping with any impairments (avoid making assumptions about loss of abilities)
- Encourage social activity with peers, as a volunteer, and so on

The development of adults ages 80 and older focuses on health issues, encouraging independence, and planning for care needs.

Healthy Growth and Development

- Physical—continues to decline in physical abilities; at increasing risk for chronic illness, major health problems
- Mental—continues to learn; memory skills and/or speed of learning may decline; confusion often signals illness or medication problem
- Social-Emotional—accepts end of life and personal losses; lives as independently as possible

Key Health Care Issues

- Communication—encourage the person to express feelings, thoughts, avoid despair; use humor, stay positive
- Health—monitor health closely, promote self-care; ensure proper nutrition, activity level, rest; reduce stress; update immunizations
- Safety—prevent injury and ensure safe living environment

Examples of age-specific care for adults ages 80 and older:

- Encourage independence—provide physical, mental, social activities
- Support end-of life decisions—provide information, resources, and so on
- Assist the person in self-care—promote medication safety; provide safety grips, ramps, and so forth

THE IMPACT OF PHYSICAL, MENTAL, AND COGNITIVE IMPAIRMENT DISABILITIES ON HUMAN DEVELOPMENT THROUGH THE LIFE SPAN

The impacts of disabilities on human development are extremely varied depending upon the manifestations of the disability and when it occurs during the life course. Some disabilities are short-term, whereas others are lifelong. Critical to mitigating the negative impacts is the development of coping skills that strengthen a client's ability to deal with his or her limitations. Support (formal and informal) is also critical.

There may also be positive effects of disabilities because familial bonds may be stronger or individuals may develop skills to compensate for other tasks that cannot be performed.

Disability is a normal phenomenon in the sense that it exists in all societies. Although medical explanations remain primary in defining disability, the history of disability took an important turn in the latter half of the 20th century that has significantly influenced responses to it. Disability rights scholars and activists rejected the medical explanation for disability, since such explanations of permanent deficit did not advance social justice, equality of opportunity, and rights as citizens. Rather, these leaders proposed the intolerance and rigidity of social institutions, rather than medical conditions, as the explanation for disability. Words such as *inclusion*, *participation*, and *nondiscrimination* were introduced into the disability literature and reflected the notions that people who did not fit within the majority were disabled by stigma, prejudice, marginalization, segregation, and exclusion. This notion of disability requires the modification of societal structures to include all, rather than "fixing" individuals with varying abilities.

THE NORMAL LIFE CRISES

Crisis is an essential component in the understanding of human growth and development. It has important implications for quality of life and subjective well-being. Crisis situations are viewed as unusual, mostly negative events that tend to disrupt the normal life of a person.

A crisis is an upset to a steady state. When a stressful event becomes a crisis, the individual or family is vulnerable and feels mounting anxiety, tension, and disequilibrium. A *precipitating event of a crisis does not have to be a major event*. It may be the "last straw" in a series of events that exceed a client's ability to cope.

An individual or family, at this point, may be emotionally overtaxed, hopeless, and *incapable of effective functioning or making good choices and decisions. The person or family is at a "critical turning point" of coping effectively or not effectively.*

The way in which life crises are addressed—whether surviving trauma, parental divorce, or a personal loss—has a very significant role to play in determining quality of life. When crises are understood, dealt with, and overcome, clients emerge as healthier and happier.

EMOTIONAL DEVELOPMENT

Emotional milestones are often harder to pinpoint than signs of physical development. This area emphasizes many skills that increase self-awareness and self-regulation. Social skills and emotional development are reflected in the ability to pay attention, make transitions from one activity to another, and cooperate with others.

During childhood, there is a lot happening during playtime. Children are lifting, dropping, looking, pouring, bouncing, hiding, building, knocking down, and more. Children are busy learning when they are playing. Play is the true work of childhood.

During play, children are also learning that they are liked and fun to be around. These experiences give them the self-confidence they need to build loving and supportive relationships all their lives.

NORMAL SEXUAL DEVELOPMENT

Many people cannot imagine that everyone—babies, children, teens, adults, and older adults—are sexual beings. Some inappropriately believe that sexual activity is reserved for early and middle adulthood. Teens often feel that adults are too old for sexual intercourse. Sexuality, though, is much more than sexual intercourse. Humans are sexual beings throughout life.

Sexuality in infants and toddlers—Children are sexual even before birth. Males can have erections while still in the uterus, and some boys are born with an erection. Infants touch and rub their genitals because it provides pleasure. Little boys and girls can experience orgasm from masturbation, although boys will not ejaculate until puberty. By about age 2, children know their own gender. They are aware of differences in the genitals of males and females and in how males and females urinate.

Sexuality in children (age 3–7)—Preschool children are interested in everything about their world, including sexuality. They may practice urinating in different positions. They are highly affectionate and enjoy hugging other children and adults. They begin to be more social and may imitate adult social and sexual behaviors, such as holding hands and kissing. Many young children play "doctor" during this stage, looking at other children's genitals and showing theirs. This is normal curiosity. By age 5 or 6, most children become more modest and private about dressing and bathing.

Children of this age are aware of marriage and understand living together, based on their family experience. They may role play about being married or having a partner while they "play house." Most young children talk about marrying and/or living with a person they love when they get older. Most sex play at this age happens because of curiosity.

Sexuality in preadolescent youth (age 8–12)—Puberty, the time when the body matures, begins between the ages of 9 and 12 for most children. Girls begin to grow breast buds and pubic hair as early as 9 or 10. Boys' development of the penis and testicles usually begins between 10 and 11. Children become more self-conscious about their bodies at this age and often feel uncomfortable undressing in front of others, even a same-sex parent.

Masturbation increases during these years. Preadolescent boys and girls do not usually have much sexual experience, but they often have many questions. They usually have heard about sexual intercourse, homosexuality, rape, and incest, and they want to know more about all these things. The idea of actually having sexual intercourse, however, is unpleasant to most preadolescent boys and girls.

Same-gender sexual behavior can occur at this age. Boys and girls tend to play with friends of the same gender and are likely to explore sexuality with them. *Same-gender sexual behavior is unrelated to a child's sexual orientation.*

Some group dating occurs at this age. Preadolescents may attend parties that have guests of both genders, and they may dance and play kissing games. By age 12 or 13, some young adolescents may pair off and begin dating and/or "making out." Young women are usually older when they begin voluntary sexual intercourse. However, many very young teens do practice sexual behaviors other than vaginal intercourse, such as petting to orgasm and oral sex.

Sexuality in adolescent youth (age 13–19)—Once youth have reached puberty and beyond, they experience increased interest in romantic and sexual relationships and in genital sex behaviors. As youth mature, they experience strong emotional attachments to romantic partners and find it natural to express their feelings within sexual relationships. There is no way to predict how a particular teenager will act sexually. Overall, most adolescents explore relationships with one another, fall in and out of love, and participate in sexual intercourse before the age of 20.

Adult sexuality—Adult sexual behaviors are extremely varied and, in most cases, remain part of an adult's life until death. At around age 50, women experience menopause, which affects their sexuality in that their ovaries no longer release eggs and their bodies no longer produce estrogen. They may experience several physical changes. Vaginal walls become thinner and vaginal intercourse may be painful because there is less vaginal lubrication and the entrance to the vagina becomes smaller. Many women use estrogen replacement therapy to relieve physical and emotional side effects of menopause. Use of vaginal lubricants can also make vaginal intercourse easier. Most women are able to have pleasurable sexual intercourse and to experience orgasm for their entire lives.

Adult men also experience some changes in their sexuality, but not at such a predictable time as with menopause in women. Men's testicles slow testosterone production after age 25 or so. Erections may occur more slowly once testosterone production slows. Men also become less able to have another erection after an orgasm and may take up to 24 hours to achieve and sustain another erection. The amount of semen released during ejaculation also decreases, but men are capable of fathering a baby even when they are in their 80s and 90s. Some older men develop an enlarged or cancerous prostate gland. If the doctors deem it necessary to remove the prostate gland, a man's ability to have an erection or an orgasm is normally unaffected.

Although adult men and women go through some sexual changes as they age, they do not lose their desire or their ability for sexual expression. Even among the very old, the need for touch and intimacy remains, although the desire and ability to have sexual intercourse may lessen.

GERONTOLOGY

Aging is scientifically defined as the accumulation of diverse deleterious changes occurring in cells and tissues with advancing age that are responsible for an increased risk of disease and death. Life expectancy is defined as the average total number of years that a human expects to live. The lengthening of life expectancy is mainly due to the elimination of most infectious diseases occurring in youth, better hygiene, and the adoption of antibiotics and vaccines.

The notion that aging requires treatment is based on the false belief that becoming old is undesirable. Aging has at times received a negative connotation and become synonymous with deterioration, approaching pathology, and death. Society should learn to value old age to the same extent as it presently values youth.

There are physical changes that naturally occur. In older adulthood, age-related changes in stamina, strength, or sensory perception may be noticed and will vary based on personal health choices, medical history, and genetics.

Social workers understand that old age is a time of continued growth and that older adults contribute significantly to their families, communities, and society. At the same time, clients face multiple biopsychosocial–spiritual–cultural challenges as they age: changes in health and physical abilities; difficulty in accessing comprehensive, affordable, and high-quality health and behavioral health care; decreased economic security; increased vulnerability to abuse and exploitation; and loss of meaningful social roles and opportunities to remain engaged in society. Social workers are well positioned and trained to support and advocate for older adults and their caregivers.

THE CONCEPT OF ATTACHMENT AND BONDING

Attachment theory originated with the seminal work of John Bowlby. Bowlby defined attachment as a lasting psychological connectedness between human beings that can be understood within an *evolutionary* context in which a caregiver provides safety and security for a child. Bowlby suggests that children come into the world biologically preprogramed to form attachments with others because this will help them to survive. They initially form only one primary attachment (monotropy), and this attachment figure acts as a secure base for exploring the world. Disrupting this attachment process can have severe consequences because the critical period for developing attachment is within the first 5 years of life.

There is another major theory of attachment that suggests attachment is a set of *learned behaviors*. The basis for the learning of attachments is the provision of food. A child will initially form an attachment to whoever feeds him or her. This child learns to associate the feeder (usually the mother) with the comfort of being fed and, through the process of classical conditioning, comes to find contact with the mother comforting. The child also finds that certain behaviors (i.e., crying, smiling) bring desirable responses from others and, through the process of operant conditioning, learns to repeat these behaviors in order to get the things they want.

In both of these theoretical approaches, parents have important impacts on their children's attachment system. Insecure attachment systems have been linked to psychiatric disorders and can result in clients reacting in a hostile and rejecting manner as children or adults.

These theories are, however, criticized because there are cultural influences that may impact on attachment and the ways in which children interact with caregivers. Much of Bowlby and others' work has not fully considered these differences.

John Bowlby also discussed typical stages of attachment, which included stranger and separation anxieties.

Stranger anxiety, manifested by crying when an unfamiliar person tries to hold or closely approaches a child, usually begins between 5 and 9 months, intensifies at about a year, and usually stops by approximately age 2.

Separation anxiety typically begins at about 6 to 8 months, peaks in intensity between 14 and 18 months, and generally resolves by 24 to 36 months or so. It is characterized by being upset and anxious when a caregiver is out of sight or leaves the room.

The onset and intensity of stranger and separation anxieties vary with each child, but these are typical developmental processes related to attachment and bonding, as opposed to Separation Anxiety Disorder, which occurs later in childhood, is characterized by excessive worrying about being away from a caregiver, and is not age typical.

BASIC HUMAN NEEDS

Maslow's hierarchy of needs implies that clients are motivated to meet certain needs. When one need is fulfilled, a client seeks to fulfill the next one, and so on. This hierarchy is often depicted as a pyramid. This five stage model can be divided into basic (or deficiency) needs (i.e., physiological, safety, social, and esteem) and growth needs (self-actualization).

1. Deficiency needs—also known as D-Needs
2. Growth needs—also known as "being needs" or B-Needs

Deficiency Needs

- Physiological
- Safety
- Social
- Esteem

Maslow called these needs "deficiency needs" because he felt that these needs arise due to deprivation. The satisfaction of these needs helps to "avoid" unpleasant feelings or consequence.

Growth Needs

- Self-actualization

These needs fall on the highest level of Maslow's pyramid. They come from a place of growth rather than from a place of "lacking."

A client must satisfy lower-level basic needs before moving on to meet higher level growth needs. After meeting lower levels of needs, a client can reach the highest level of self-actualization, but few people do so.

Every client is capable and has the desire to move up the hierarchy toward a level of self-actualization. Unfortunately, progress is often disrupted by failure to meet lower level needs. Life experiences, including divorce and loss of job, may cause a client to fluctuate between levels of the hierarchy.

Physiological needs: These needs maintain the physical organism. These are biological needs such as food, water, oxygen, and constant body temperature. If a person is deprived of these needs, he or she will die.

Safety needs: There is a need to feel safe from harm, danger, or threat of destruction. Clients need regularity and some predictability.

Social needs: Friendship, intimacy, affection, and love are needed—from one's work group, family, friends, or romantic relationships.

Esteem needs: People need a stable, firmly based level of self-respect and respect from others.

Self-actualization needs: There is a need to be oneself, to act consistently with whom one is. *Self-actualization is an ongoing process.* It involves developing potential, becoming, and being what one is capable of being. It makes possible true objectivity—dealing with the world as it is, rather than as one needs it to be. You are free to really do what you want to do. There are moments when everything is right (peak experience); a glimmer of what it is like to be complete. One is in a position to find one's true calling (i.e., being an artist, writer, musician). Only 1% of the population consistently operates at this level.

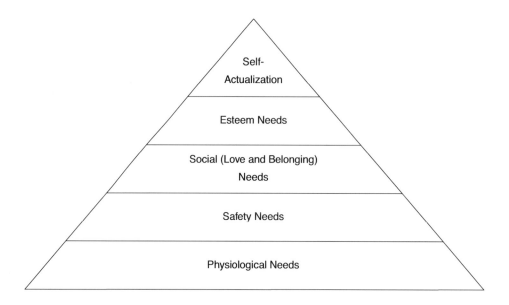

On the examination, Maslow's hierarchy of needs is often not explicitly asked about, but it can be applied when asked about the order of prioritizing problems or issues with a client. A client with an acute medical problem should focus on getting a medical evaluation first; a victim of domestic violence should prioritize medical and safety issues; and a refugee must initially meet basic survival needs (shelter, food, income, clothing, etc.) before working on fulfilling higher level needs.

THE ADULT LEARNING PROCESS

Learning theory is a conceptual framework describing how information is absorbed, processed, and retained during learning. Cognitive, emotional, and environmental influences, as well as prior experience, all play a part in how understanding, or a worldview, is acquired or changed, as well as how knowledge and skills are retained.

There are many learning theories, which can be conceptualized as fitting into four distinct orientations.

   1. Behavioral (Pavlov, Skinner)—learning is viewed through change in behavior and the stimuli in the external environment are the locus of learning. Social workers aim to change the external environment in order to bring about desired change.

2. Cognitive (Piaget)—learning is viewed through internal mental processes (including insight, information processing, memory, and perception) and the locus of learning is internal cognitive structures. Social workers aim to develop opportunities to foster capacity and skills to learn better.

3. Humanistic (Maslow)—learning is viewed as a client's activities aimed to fulfill his or her full potential and the locus of learning is to meet cognitive and other needs. Social workers aim to develop the whole person.

4. Social/situational (Bandura)—learning is obtained through clients' interactions with and observations of their environment in social contexts. Social workers establish opportunities where conversation and participation can occur.

HUMAN GENETICS

Social workers in all settings must educate themselves about the process of genetic inheritance and understand the primary reasons that clients seek genetic testing and counseling. Minimally, a social worker must understand the types of genetic conditions, including single gene disorders, chromosome anomalies, and multifactorial disorders, and the effect of harmful environmental toxins on development. Furthermore, an understanding of the patterns of inheritance between generations (autosomal dominant, autosomal recessive, and X-linked recessive) is essential in working with families.

It is important that social workers be educated about the specific application of skills to genetic cases. Social workers are already trained to view people from a biopsychosocial–spiritual–cultural perspective. In order to identify the patterns of disease in a family, a social worker may need to develop a genogram as part of the assessment.

Because a client's genetic test produces information about the whole family, the biology of a genetic condition must be thoroughly understood and explained to a client and his or her family in order to make informed decisions about whether or not to be tested. Sensitivity to the principle of self-determination is essential in the process of informing clients and family members.

Social workers must take care to ensure that clients are fully informed about all aspects of genetic testing. Social workers should provide counseling before and after the decision to have a genetic test and after the test itself.

Models of Functioning of Various Systems

2

THE EFFECTS OF FAMILY DYNAMICS ON INDIVIDUALS

Family dynamics significantly impact on a client's biological, psychological, and social functioning in both positive and negative ways. Having a close-knit and supportive family provides emotional support, economic well-being, and increases overall health. However, the opposite is also true. When family life is characterized by stress and conflict, well-being can be poor.

Social support is one of the main ways that family positively impacts well-being. Social relationships, such as those found in close families, have decreased the likelihood of negative outcomes, such as chronic disease, disability, mental illness, and/or death.

Though good familial relations and social support serve as protective factors and improve overall well-being and health, not all familial relations positively impact these areas. Problematic and nonsupportive familial interactions have a negative impact. For example, growing up in an unsupported, neglectful, and/or violent home is associated with poor physical health and development.

FAMILY LIFE CYCLE

The emotional and intellectual stages from childhood to retirement as a member of a family are called the family life cycle. In each stage, clients face challenges in family life that allow the building or gaining of new skills.

Not everyone passes through these stages smoothly. Situations such as severe illness, financial problems, or the death of a loved one can have an impact. If skills are not learned in one stage, they can be learned in later stages.

Stage 1: **Family of origin experiences**
  Main tasks
- Maintaining relationships with parents, siblings, and peers
- Completing education
- Developing the foundations of a family life

Stage 2: **Leaving home**
  Main tasks
- Differentiation of self from family of origin and parents and developing adult-to-adult relationships with parents
- Developing intimate peer relationships
- Beginning work, developing work identity, and financial independence

Stage 3: **Premarriage stage**
  Main tasks
- Selecting partners
- Developing a relationship
- Deciding to establish own home with someone

Stage 4: **Childless couple stage**
  Main tasks
- Developing a way to live together both practically and emotionally
- Adjusting relationships with families of origin and peers to include partner

Stage 5: **Family with young children**
  Main tasks
- Realigning family system to make space for children
- Adopting and developing parenting roles
- Realigning relationships with families of origin to include parenting and grandparenting roles
- Facilitating children to develop peer relationships

Stage 6: **Family with adolescents**
  Main tasks
- Adjusting parent–child relationships to allow adolescents more autonomy
- Adjusting family relationships to focus on midlife relationship and career issues
- Taking on responsibility of caring for families of origin

Stage 7: **Launching children**

Main tasks

- Resolving midlife issues
- Negotiating adult-to-adult relationships with children
- Adjusting to living as a couple again
- Adjusting to including in-laws and grandchildren within the family circle
- Dealing with disabilities and death in the family of origin

Stage 8: **Later family life**

Main tasks

- Coping with physiological decline in self and others
- Adjusting to children taking a more central role in family maintenance
- Valuing the wisdom and experience of the elderly
- Dealing with loss of spouse and peers
- Preparation for death, life review, and reminiscence

Mastering the skills and milestones of each stage allows successful movement from one stage of development to the next. If not mastered, clients are more likely to have difficulty with relationships and future transitions. Family life cycle theory suggests that successful transitioning may also help to prevent disease and emotional or stress-related disorders.

The stress of daily living, coping with a chronic medical condition, or other life crises can disrupt the family life cycle. Ongoing stress or a crisis can delay the transition to the next phase of the life cycle.

ABNORMAL AND NORMAL FUNCTIONING IN TRADITIONAL AND NONTRADITIONAL FAMILIES

The concept of family has certainly changed in American society over the last few decades. Statistics continue to show that fewer Americans are getting married, and those who do so are having fewer children or none at all. More marriages are ending in divorce. More people are living alone, cohabiting with someone, or marrying more than once and creating "blended" families.

Historically, a "traditional" family consisted of a husband, a wife, and their biological children. Today, however, society displays greater diversity and most American households are "nontraditional" under this definition.

Despite the recognition of same-gender marriage, children in these households are often worried about being viewed differently and recognize that many are uncomfortable with or have questions about their conception or daily life with two same-gender parents.

In addition, although at one time there was a stigma associated with single parenthood, it is now considered more acceptable. One-parent families can result from the death of a significant other, divorce, or an adult's decision to have a child alone. Poverty is more prevalent in single-parent homes.

Cohabitation is the sharing of a household by an unmarried couple. Cohabitating couples and their children function similarly to those with married parents. However, though widely accepted in American society today, cohabitation does not receive the same formal recognition or legal benefits as marriage and is viewed as sinful or immoral by some.

Many children are also growing up with adults other than their parents. For example, they may live with their grandparents or other family members. Children may also live with foster or adoptive parents.

Monogamous families, with only two partners, is the norm, but there are some who live in polygamous families. Polygamy includes a man "married" to more than one wife at a time or a woman "married" to more than one husband at a time. Often, polygamy is tied to religious beliefs. As polygamy is illegal in many societies, those who choose to live a polygamist lifestyle are typically legally married to one spouse and cohabitating with the other spouses.

MODELS OF ORGANIZATIONAL DEVELOPMENT

There are many ways to measure the functioning and effectiveness of organizations. For example, the functioning can be analyzed related to productivity, turnover, stability, cohesion, and so on. Usually, functioning is assessed as it relates to organizational structures, processes, and outcomes.

Structural indicators influence the capacity of the organization for effective performance. Assessments aimed at organizational structure evaluate organizational features, such as training, equipment, office space, and so on, or worker characteristics including degrees attained and licenses held. Structural characteristics form the basis for accreditation reviews and licensing. When an organization is not operating efficiently or effectively, a review of the available structural resources is often completed to determine the extent to which they may be responsible for the problems.

Evaluations of organizational processes assess effort rather than effect. Formative evaluations look at how the work gets done in organizations and the satisfaction of those doing the work, rather than the ultimate outcome or performance. Given that the majority of social work services are delivered in organizations with complex structures, it is essential to determine the extent to which processes inhibit or promote quality outcomes.

Outcome assessments determine the extent to which tangible, defined differences have been made. Though essential, these assessments can be difficult to make because extraneous factors must be controlled in order to determine whether changes are truly attributable to organizational goods or services.

The complexity of organizational assessments varies widely. They can be as simple as asking stakeholders for feedback on how the organization is operating or can involve intensive, structured work plans, information collection and analyses, and reporting. Typically, this complexity is driven by financial and time constraints and the degree to which there is concern about the organization's performance and effectiveness.

MODELS OF GROUP DEVELOPMENT

Humans are small group beings. Group work is a method of social work that helps individuals to enhance their social functioning through purposeful group experiences, as well as to cope more effectively with their personal, group, or community problems. In group work, **individuals help each other** in order to influence and change personal, group, organizational, and community problems.

A social worker focuses on helping each member change his or her environment or behavior through interpersonal experience. Members help each other change or learn social roles in the particular positions held or desired in the social environment.

The stages of group development are:

1. Preaffiliation—development of trust (known as forming)

2. Power and control—struggles for individual autonomy and group identification (known as storming)

3. Intimacy—utilizing self in service of the group (known as norming)

4. Differentiation—acceptance of each other as distinct individuals (known as performing)

5. Separation/termination—independence (known as adjourning)

MODELS OF COMMUNITY DEVELOPMENT

There is no one way to define community development. Over the years, community development has been defined as an occupation, a movement, an approach, and a set of values. It has been labeled the responsibility of social workers because it is seen as the most practical framework for creating lasting change for clients.

Community development has been used to the benefit of communities of place, of interest, and of identity. But despite these differences, there are certain principles, characteristics, and values that underpin nearly every definition of community development—neighborhood work aimed at improving the quality of community life through the participation of a broad spectrum of people at the local level.

Community development is a long-term commitment. It is not a quick fix to address a community's problems, nor is it a time-limited process. It aims to address imbalances in power and bring about change founded on social justice, equality, and inclusion. Its key purpose is to build communities based on justice, equality, and mutual respect.

Community development is ultimately about getting community members working together in collective action to tackle problems that many individuals may be experiencing or to help in achieving a shared dream that many individuals will benefit from.

MODELS OF COUPLES DEVELOPMENT

Models of couples development attempt to describe how two people bond to form an intimate relationship. This process has similarities to that described by Margaret Mahler who chronicles the experiences of a parent and child who ultimately learn to balance and support the separate needs of each other. Using this model, there are five developmental stages:

1. **Symbiosis:** The first stage of couplehood is the attachment phase, when partners are "madly in love," passionate, nurturing, and selflessly attentive to each other's needs. During this time of high emotional and physical stimulation, the couple strives to find common ground and effortlessly attempts to please each other. Differences are easily minimized and accommodating to the desires of the other is a pleasure. Partners place few demands on each other, especially demands that might create annoyance or displeasure. The intense merging that takes place during this stage of the relationship (at cognitive, emotional, physical, and behavioral levels) is essential for creating the bond that eventually will lead to the mutual decision to form a couple. The enduring attachment created early in the relationship is the foundation that allows the individuals to proceed from symbiosis to differentiation, the next stage of a couples' development.

2. **Differentiation:** Differentiation is the re-emergence of the self in relation to the partner. It is the active, ongoing process of (a) defining the self, (b) activating (expressing) the self, and (c) managing the anxiety of risking intimacy, separation, or loss resulting from self-expression. In this stage, the individuals in the couple begin to notice differences and experience annoyance with things that were previously unnoticed or minimized. What once was acceptable (cute, silly, not important) is now irritating.

Time spent away from the partner is appreciated. Different feelings, desires, and opinions begin to emerge. Break-ups are common at this point. If the connection between the two individuals was based predominantly on the illusion of symbiosis, the relationship may abruptly end. For those who are able to manage the stresses of this stage, differentiation opens the way for undertaking the work of the next stage; that is, balancing the desire for self-discovery with the desire for intimacy.

3. **Practicing:** The practicing stage is the time of self-rediscovery. This is a time when autonomy and individuality become primary and a partner rediscovers him or herself as an individual. Developing the self becomes more important than developing the relationship. Practicing is characterized by the redirection of a person's attention, time, and activities away from the partner and toward the self. The practicing partner begins to focus on personal needs in a self-centered manner. While the symbiotic partner may experience the redirection of attention as loss, the practicing partner views this time as necessary for survival.

4. **Rapprochement:** Rapprochement is the stage when openness and vulnerability begin to re-emerge. Because the partners have succeeded in developing a sufficiently well-defined sense of self in the prior (practicing) stage, identity and separateness are no longer threatened by the desire for companionship and intimacy. The partners feel comfortable with their own individuality and no longer fear being engulfed in the earlier symbiosis that threatened separate identities. In this stage, the partners are able to show weakness and to seek comfort and support from one another. Yet this is a time when there is still some back and forth between intimacy and independence. The individual is able to regain the internal sense of balance that enables openness, vulnerability, and the desire for intimacy while not sacrificing the necessary countervailing state of separateness.

5. **Mutual interdependence:** Constancy is the hallmark of this later stage in a couple's development. Just like the child who is able to internalize and maintain the image of the mother and use it to soothe itself in stressful moments, the couple in this stage is able to do something similar. Each partner is able to value and respect the separateness of the other. Likewise, each partner is also able to experience the wholeness and intimacy that comes from the ability to trust and from the knowledge that one is loved. In this stage, the image of the ideal or perfect partner is reconciled with the image of the real partner. The foundation of the relationship is no longer personal need, but the appreciation and love of the other and the support and respect for mutual growth.

Homosexual couples also go through these developmental stages, but have unique challenges that impact relationship formation. For example, heterosexual couples have a much wider variety of public role models for their partnerships than their homosexual peers. In addition, there may be heightened concerns by partners about acceptance of their mates or even the very existence of their intimate relationships by their respective families.

Effects of the Environment on Systems' Behavior

3

NORMAL AND ABNORMAL BEHAVIOR

Many factors influence people and their behaviors. The first influence is *individual characteristics* or differences that are unique to each client, such as knowledge, attitudes, beliefs, general personality style, and disposition. There are also *interpersonal factors* that impact how clients behave and feel. These may include social support, social cohesion, work relationships, friendships, and/or religious belonging. A third influence comes from *institutional factors*. These are the rules, regulations, and informal structures in the organizations where clients live and work. Institutional rules may include prohibition of certain behaviors (i.e., smoking), dress expectations, and/or rules about social interaction. A fourth influence is *community factors*, which come from the social environment in which clients live, including social resources/networks and community norms. The last influence is *public policy*, which may mandate regulations and laws such as wearing seat belts, not using drugs, and/or limits on physical aggression. These hierarchical factors are the basis of the ecological perspective or model.

In social work, there are many theoretical perspectives that help to explain the human behavior of clients, including, but not limited to, systems, conflict, rational choice, social constructionist, psychodynamic, developmental, social behavioral, and humanistic perspectives.

Systems

Systems are made up of interrelated parts; each part impacts all other parts, as well as the system as a whole. The dynamic interactions within, between, and among systems produce both stability and change.

Conflict

Clients try to advance their own interests over the interests of others as they compete for scarce resources. Power is unequally divided and some social groups dominate others. Members of nondominant groups become alienated from society. Social change is driven by conflict.

Rational Choice

Clients are rational and goal-directed, and human interaction involves exchange of social resources, such as love, approval, information, money, and physical labor. Clients have self-interest and try to maximize rewards and minimize costs. Power comes from unequal resources in exchanges.

Social Constructionist

Social reality is created when clients, in social interaction, develop a common understanding of their world. Clients are influenced by social processes that are grounded in customs as well as cultural and historical contexts.

Psychodynamic

Unconscious, as well as conscious, mental activity serves as the motivating force in human behavior. Early childhood experiences are central and clients may become overwhelmed by internal or external demands. Defense mechanisms are used to avoid becoming overwhelmed.

Developmental

Human development occurs in defined, age-related stages that build upon one another and are distinct. Human development is a complex interaction of biological, psychological, and social factors.

Social Behavioral

Human behavior is learned when clients interact with the environment through association, reinforcement, and imitation. All human problems can be formulated as undesirable behavior and can be changed through techniques such as classical and operant conditioning.

Humanistic Perspective

Each client is unique and is responsible for the choices he or she makes. Clients have the capacity to change themselves because human behavior is driven by a desire for growth, personal meaning, and competence. Behaving in ways that are not consistent with the true self causes clients anxiety.

THE SOCIALIZATION PROCESS

Socialization is the process by which children and adults learn from others, beginning in the early days of life. During socialization, language and social roles are learned. Most people continue their social learning all through life (unless some mental or physical disability slows or stops the learning process). Sometimes social learning is fun while, at other times, it is painful. The general process of acquiring culture is referred to as socialization.

Socialization is important in the process of personality formation. Although much of human personality is the result of genes, the socialization process can mold it in particular directions by encouraging specific beliefs and attitudes, as well as selectively providing experiences.

Natural socialization occurs when infants and youngsters explore, play, and discover the social world around them. Planned socialization occurs when other people take actions designed to teach or train others—from infancy on.

Positive socialization is the type of social learning that is based on pleasurable and exciting experiences. It involves social learning processes which involve positive motivation and rewards. Negative socialization occurs when punishment, harsh criticisms, or anger are used.

THE INTERPLAY OF BIOLOGICAL, PSYCHOLOGICAL, AND SOCIAL FACTORS

Human development is a lifelong process beginning before birth and extending to death. At each moment in life, every human being is in a state of personal evolution. Physical changes largely drive the process, as our cognitive abilities advance and decline in response to the brain's growth in childhood and reduced functioning in old age. Psychosocial development is also significantly influenced by physical growth, as a changing body and brain, together with the environment, shape a client's identity and relationships with other people.

Thus, development is the product of the elaborate interplay of biological, psychological, and social influences. As children develop physically, gaining greater psychomotor control and increased brain function, they become more sophisticated cognitively—that is, more adept at thinking about and acting upon their environment. These physical and cognitive changes, in turn, allow them to develop psychosocially, forming individual identities and relating effectively and appropriately with other people.

SOCIAL DEVELOPMENT

Human beings are inherently social. Developing competencies in this domain enhances a person's mental health, success in work, and ability to achieve in life tasks.

On a micro level, social development is learning how to behave and interact well with others. Social development relies on emotional development or learning how to manage feelings so they are productive and not counterproductive.

On a macro level, social development is about a commitment that development processes need to benefit people—particularly, but not only, the poor. It also recognizes the way people interact in groups and society, and the norms that facilitate such interaction.

Social development implies a change in social institutions. Progress toward an inclusive society, for example, implies that individuals treat each other fairly in their daily lives, whether in the family, workplace, or public office. Social cohesion is enhanced when peaceful and safe environments within neighborhoods and communities are created. Social accountability exists to the extent that individuals' voices are expressed and heard. Reforms aimed at improving rights and more participatory governance are part of the process by which institutional change is achieved.

THE IMPACT OF ENVIRONMENT ON INDIVIDUALS

The person-in-environment perspective highlights the importance of understanding individual behavior in light of the environmental contexts in which a client lives and acts. The perspective has historical roots in the social work profession.

Environmental factors can have strong positive or negative impacts on development. Social workers have paid much more attention to the influences of the social environment, as opposed to the physical, on client beliefs, attitudes, and behaviors. However, there is a growing shift, and social workers are recognizing the importance of physical and environmental issues such as water shortages, global warming, depletion of environmental resources, and catastrophic weather patterns on human well-being. Social workers are increasingly being called upon to develop and promote sustainable environment practices. Environmental justice is now widely recognized as part of the social work mandate to engage in advocacy aimed at improving adverse conditions.

THE INDICATORS OF PSYCHOSOCIAL STRESS

Psychosocial stress results when there is a perceived threat (real or imagined). Examples of psychosocial stress include threats to social status, social esteem, respect, and/or acceptance within a group; threats to self-worth; or threats that are perceived as uncontrollable.

Psychosocial stress can be caused by upsetting events, such as natural disasters, sudden health problems or death, or breakups/divorce.

Although current upsetting events certainly create stress, events from the past can also still affect clients. Social workers should assess the impacts of events such as childhood abuse, bullying, discrimination, violence, and/or trauma.

Often, psychosocial stress is not caused by single events, but by ongoing problems such as caring for a parent or a child with disabilities.

Stress may manifest itself in many different ways, such as high blood pressure, sweating, rapid heart rate, dizziness, and/or feelings of irritability or sadness.

When psychosocial stress triggers a stress response, the body releases a group of stress hormones which lead to a burst of energy, as well as other changes in the body. The changes brought about by stress hormones can be helpful in the short-term, but can be damaging in the long run.

It is essential that clients learn to manage psychosocial stress so that the stress response is only triggered when necessary and not for prolonged states of chronic stress.

THE IMPACT OF ECONOMIC STATUS

Family income has selective but, in some instances, quite substantial impacts on child and adolescent well-being. Family income appears to be more strongly related to children's ability and achievement than to their emotional outcomes.

Children who live in extreme poverty or who live below the poverty line for multiple years appear, all other things being equal, to suffer the worst outcomes. The timing of poverty also seems to be important for certain outcomes. Children who experience poverty during their preschool and early school years have lower rates of school completion than children and adolescents who experience poverty only in later years. Although more research is needed, findings to date suggest that interventions during early childhood may be most important in reducing poverty's impact on children.

Social workers must also consider the implications on the biopsychosocial–spiritual–cultural aspects of well-being. Medical care may be neglected in order to meet other needs. Coping skills are needed when there are dramatic changes in income, and opportunities to adapt and return to economic stability are critical.

THE EFFECTS OF SOCIAL ROLE ON SELF-IMAGE

Clients are social beings whose behavior is shaped to some extent by their roles, such as student, mother, homemaker, artist, and so on. Social roles not only help others to understand client experiences, but also help clients know what is expected of them in various situations.

Self-image, or how a client views himself or herself, is usually defined by social roles and/or personality traits (internal or affective aspects such as funny, impatient, or athletic).

Typically, younger people describe themselves more in terms of personal traits, whereas older people feel defined to a greater extent by their social roles.

Understanding the degree to which a client's self-image is linked to his or her social roles is important because changes to these roles is likely to impact self-esteem and worth.

THE IMPACT OF POVERTY ON INDIVIDUALS, FAMILIES, ORGANIZATIONS, AND COMMUNITIES

Clients who are poor often do not have resources to meet their basic needs. There are many social problems that contribute to and result from poverty, including, but not limited to, little or no education, poor basic nutrition and hygiene, disability or illness, unemployment, substance abuse, and homelessness.

Wealth is often poorly distributed. A small minority has all the money. This can be a major cause of social tensions and divisions within a society. There are the "haves" and the "have nots." Communities are often homogeneous—with those comprised of poor people being segregated from those living above the poverty line. Communities comprised of the poor have fewer opportunities and resources to assist their members, leading to a greater likelihood that they will not be able to break out of the cycle that originally resulted in their economic insecurity. Thus, those born into poverty often remain there throughout their life course.

THE EFFECTS OF SOCIAL ROLE ON RELATIONSHIPS

In everyday life, clients take on roles within given social contexts. These roles have typical and expected patterns of behavior. Some social roles result from familial relationships with others, such as mother or father, sister or brother, son or daughter, cousin, and so on. Social roles can be chosen, such as wife or husband, but others are not. All clients have many different social roles.

The ability for clients to successfully function in these roles must start with clear understandings of what is expected of them by others. Just because clients are in social roles does not mean that they have the needed skills or possess the behavioral style to be able to function effectively. Disputes often arise as clients are unclear about role expectations (*role ambiguity*), have different role expectations than others in the relationship (*role discomplementarity*), and/or switch roles (*role reversal*). These disputes lead to incompatible or conflicting expectations (*role conflicts*).

THE EFFECTS OF ADDICTIVE BEHAVIOR ON RELATIONSHIPS

Substance use can disrupt family life and destroy relationships. A client's preoccupation with the substance, plus its impacts on mood and performance, can lead to relationship/marital problems. A client may spend more time on getting and using substances than attending to his or her relationships with others. Drug use can also create destructive patterns of codependency. Codependency occurs when a partner/spouse or members of the family, out of love or fear of consequences, inadvertently enables a client to continue using substances by covering up, supplying money, or denying there is a problem.

In addition, substance abuse or dependence can result in accidental injury, disability, legal involvement, and/or loss of income or employment, which negatively impacts on those who are friends or family members of a client. Neglect of friends and family, as well as anger that can lead to verbal assaults or physical violence, are also seen as a result of substance abuse or dependence.

Clients who are using or dependent on substances may also tend to neglect "old" relationships and find those who also engage in similar behaviors.

Clients with other addictions feel strong cravings or a dependency on whatever they are addicted to and feel afraid or powerless to let it go. Clients may feel ashamed or fear the consequences of their addictions being discovered. They will sometimes lie to conceal engagement in the behaviors or the extent of their problems.

Secrecy and deceit cause breakdowns in trust within relationships. Family members of those who are addicted may question their behavior and feel confused, scared, and angry at changes that they witness. Family members are frightened by unpredictable situations encountered due to those who are addicted experiencing ups and downs. One moment they are happy and positive, but then they can quickly become anxious, irritable, or depressed. Individuals may be preoccupied with their addictions and pay less attention to role responsibilities or the feelings and needs of others. They also may lose interest in family activities and appear withdrawn.

Family members of those who are addicted often take on more responsibility at home to compensate for the unreliability or unpredictability that accompanies addiction. Family members may feel they have to take control of everything as a way of compensating for these feelings of instability. Family members often feel strained as they try to successfully juggle extra responsibilities. Communication in these situations breaks down and relationships become strained or broken. Emotional distance in relationships can result in a loss of interest in sex or intimacy.

Family members may be worried that their behavior will exacerbate the situation or cause clients' addictions to worsen. Children in families with addiction also feel the effects because they are aware of arguments and tensions in the home and feel afraid and confused. They are also more likely to develop addictive behaviors as ways of coping.

THE EFFECTS OF DEFENSE MECHANISMS ON RELATIONSHIPS

Defense mechanisms are ways to cope with unpleasant emotions. While Freud and others believed that they are used to combat sexual or aggressive feelings, defense mechanisms apply to a wide range of reactions from anxiety to insecurity. Defense mechanisms are unconscious ways of distancing oneself from awareness of unpleasant thoughts and feelings. Using defense mechanisms may seem to make situations more tolerable, but they often result in issues going unresolved.

The use of defense mechanisms can be found in relationships. They keep clients protected from getting hurt and serve as ways to cope with relationship-related anxiety. Clients may be able to function on a daily basis by denying or ignoring unpleasant realities of life and relationships. Facing them would cause disruption in families and relationships with loved ones. Therefore, denial, a form of inattention and even blindness to certain realities of relationships, can be adaptive. For example, in marriages or committed intimate relationships, it is often necessary to overlook the flaws of partners or even turn them into positive attributes by viewing them differently. However, denial can be extremely dangerous when clients refuse to see serious or life-threatening problems in members of their families or themselves.

THE DYNAMICS OF WORK RELATIONSHIPS

As much time is often spent in the workplace, well-being may be dramatically impacted by relationships that exist at jobs.

Understanding workplace dynamics is essential because they can have a dramatic impact on the efficiency and effectiveness of an organization and the well-being of its employees. An organization is the sum of its employee relationships that respond and react to the situations occurring within it. Thus, everything that employees do has an effect on the environment and culture and visa versa. The impact can be positive or negative or both.

There are many sources of positive and negative interactions and relationships within the workplace. These include, but are not limited to:

- **Actions of individuals**: An individual action by an employee can disrupt the performance and success of others in efficiently and effectively doing their jobs. Behaviors, such as consistently being late to meetings or acting aggressively, can negatively impact the culture within a workplace. Positive or outstanding performance can also inspire others and advance the mission of the agency or company.

- **Interactions between individuals**: Organizational functioning relies on individuals interacting with others. Differences of opinions or work style need to be addressed quickly so they do not lead to dysfunctional relationships that can negatively impact the entire workforce.

Social workers must be astute in identifying, analyzing, and understanding the dynamics of work relationships to assist their clients if needed in addressing issues that are adversely affecting their well-being. In addition, as most social work practice occurs within organizational contexts, social workers' own actions or the behaviors of their coworkers may contribute to or result in barriers to service efficiency or effectiveness. Social workers have a responsibility to monitor these situations carefully and address issues immediately so clients are not negatively impacted.

THE DYNAMICS OF DOMESTIC AND OTHER VIOLENCE IN RELATIONSHIPS

The common thread in all abusive relationships is the abuser's need for power and control over his or her partner. Domestic violence *occurs across all racial, cultural, and socioeconomic groups* and can involve physical, sexual, psychological/emotional, and economic/financial abuse.

Signs of abuse are varied.

- *Suspicious injury* (not consistent with history of injury; unusual locations; various stages of healing; bites; repeated minor injuries; delay in seeking treatment; old scars or new injuries from weapons)
- *Somatic complaints* without a specific diagnosis (such as chronic pain—head, abdomen, pelvis, back, or neck)
- *Behavioral presentation* (crying; minimizing; no emotional expression; anxious or angry; defensive; fearful eye contact)
- *Controlling/coercive behavior of partner* (partner hovers, overly concerned, won't leave client unattended; client defers to partner; fear of speaking in front of partner or disagreeing with him or her)

Cycle of Violence

Phase I: *Tension building*
Phase II: *Battering incident*—shortest period of the cycle, lasts a brief time
Phase III: *"Loving–contrition"* (absence of tension or "honeymoon" phase)—batterer offers profuse apologies; assures attacks will never happen again and declares love and caring

Batterers often learn abusive behavior from their families of origin, peers, and media, as well as from personal experience of being abused as children. Batterers view their victims as "possessions" and treat them like objects. Victims are dehumanized to justify the battering. Batterers are very self-centered and feel entitled to have their needs (physical, emotional, sexual) met "no matter what." Batterers have control over their impulses and give themselves permission to be abusive.

Some of the reasons that clients stay in abusive relationships are:

- Hope that the abuser will change (if the batterer is in a treatment program, the client hopes the behavior will change; leaving represents a loss of the committed relationship)
- Isolation and lack of support systems
- Fears that no one will believe the seriousness of abuse experienced

- Abuser puts up barricades so client won't leave the relationship (escalates threats of violence, threatens to kill, withholds support, threatens to seek custody of children, threatens suicide, etc.)

- Dangers of leaving may pose a greater danger than remaining with the batterer

- Client may not have the economic resources to survive on his or her own

Leaving is a process. Over time, the client comes to the conclusion that the abuser will not change; each time the client tries to leave, he or she gathers more information that is helpful.

Social exchange theory is based on the idea of totaling potential benefits and losses to determine behavior. People make decisions about relationships based on the amount of rewards they receive from them. A client remains in an abusive relationship because the high cost of leaving lowers its attractiveness (outweighs the benefits) as the best alternative. A client will leave when the best alternative promises a better life (rewards outweigh the costs).

THEORIES OF CRISIS INTERVENTION

A "crisis" is an acute disruption of psychological homeostasis in which a client's usual coping mechanisms fail and there is evidence of distress and functional impairment. While there are many theories used to explain and address crises, there are seven critical stages through which clients typically pass on the road to crisis stabilization, resolution, and mastery. These stages are essential, sequential, and sometimes overlapping in the process of crisis intervention:

1. *Plan and conduct a thorough biopsychosocial–spiritual–cultural and lethality/imminent danger assessment*
   A social worker must conduct a biopsychosocial–spiritual–cultural assessment covering a client's environmental supports and stressors, medical needs and medications, current use of drugs and alcohol, and internal and external coping methods and resources. Assessing lethality is first and foremost.

2. *Make psychological contact and rapidly establish the collaborative relationship*
   In a crisis, a social worker must do this quickly, generally as part of assessment.

3. *Identify the major problems, including crisis precipitants*
   A social worker should determine from a client why things have "come to a head." There is usually a "last straw," but a social worker should also find out what other problems a client is concerned about.

It can also be useful to prioritize the problems in terms of which problems a client wants to work on first.

4. *Encourage an exploration of feelings and emotions*
A social worker should validate a client's feelings and emotions and let him or her vent about the crisis. The use of active listening skills, paraphrasing, and probing questions is essential. A social worker should also challenge maladaptive beliefs.

5. *Generate and explore alternatives and new coping strategies*
A social worker and a client must come up with a plan for what will help improve the current situation. Brainstorming possibilities and finding out what has been helpful in the past are critical.

6. *Restore functioning through implementation of an action plan*
This stage represents a shift from a crisis to a resolution. A client and a worker will begin to take the steps negotiated in the previous stage. This is also where a client will begin to make meaning of the crisis event.

7. *Plan follow-up*
Follow-up can take many forms as it can involve phone or in-person visits at specific intervals. A postcrisis evaluation may look at a client's current functioning and assess a client's progress.

Diversity, Discrimination, and Stereotypes

4

THE INFLUENCE OF CULTURE, RACE, RELIGION/SPIRITUALITY, AND/OR ETHNICITY ON BEHAVIORS AND ATTITUDES

The United States has a racially and ethnically diverse population. The Census officially recognizes six ethnic and racial categories: White American; American Indian and Alaska Native; Asian; African American; Native Hawaiian and Other Pacific Islander; and people of two or more races. The U.S. Census Bureau also classifies Americans as "Hispanic or Latino" and "Not Hispanic or Latino," thus identifying Hispanic and Latino Americans as a racially diverse ethnicity that comprises the largest minority group in the nation.

A social worker must remember that there is tremendous intragroup diversity. In fact, the differences between racial and ethnic groups (intergroup) are often less profound than those found within these groups (intragroup). It is important to view a client as the expert and to not stereotype or make assumptions about values, behaviors, or attitudes based on a client's racial or ethnic group.

The following is an overview of some characteristics recognized as being more prevalent within each of the Census categories/classifications:

White American

■ Family: parents with young children; divorce common; personal desires put over family; parents try to be friends with their children; avoid physical punishment

- Communication: language—American Standard English; communication can be long-winded and impersonal
- Spirituality: religion is a private affair, but mainly Protestant and Bible-based
- Values: capitalism (i.e., the future is what you make it); poverty is a moral failing and wealth is held in high esteem; physical beauty is valued with white skin, blond hair, and thin body being the ideal; sports are an important part of life (baseball, American football, basketball); democracy and freedom; individual rights

American Indian/Alaska Native

- Family: complex family organizations that include relatives without blood ties; strong kinship bonds (multigenerational, extended families); group takes preference over individual; husband and wife show a tendency to communicate more with their gender group than with each other; harmony within the group is very important; common sharing of material goods; group decision making
- Communication: indirectness; being still and quiet; comfortable with silence; value listening and nonverbal communication; may avoid making direct eye contact as a show of respect when talking to a higher status person
- Spirituality: fundamental part of life; interconnectedness of all living things; sacredness of all creation; use of traditional and Western healing practices; medicine man, shaman, or spiritual leaders are traditional healers
- Values: holistic; interconnectedness of mind, body, spirit, and heart; time is viewed as a circular flow that is always with us; follow nature's rhythms rather than linear time

Asian

- Family: patriarchal system in which a wife has lower status and is subservient to her father, husband, and oldest son; obligation to parents and respect for elders; hierarchical family structure with strictly prescribed roles and rules of behavior and conduct
- Communication: often indirect in order to avoid direct confrontation and maintain highly valued harmonious relationships; less emotional expressiveness (reserved) and demonstration of affection
- Spirituality: cultures influenced by Confucian and Buddhist philosophies
- Values: shaming and obligation to others are mechanisms for reinforcing cultural norms; adhering to rules of conduct reflects not

only on the individual, but also on the family and extended kinship network, including past and future generations; usually seek help from the family or cultural community

Asian clients may respond to psychotropic drugs differently than clients from other ethnic groups. They typically require lower doses of medications and may experience more severe side effects from the same doses given to other clients. It is sometimes recommended to start Asian clients on less than the normally prescribed dosage. They are also sometimes resistant and view treatment of symptoms via homeopathic methods as more acceptable.

African American

- Family: multigenerational family systems; strong kinship bonds, including extended families and relatives without blood ties; informal adoption of children by extended family members; flexible family roles; women are often viewed as being "all sacrificing" and the "strength of the family"

- Communication: animated; individuals try to get their opinions heard; often includes physical touch; direct; show respect at all times; history of racism and sense of powerlessness impacts interactions

- Spirituality: turn to community and/or religious leaders if assistance is needed; church is seen as a central part of community life

- Values: strong kinship bonds; strong work orientation; strong religious orientation; use informal support network—church or community; distrust of government and social services—feel "big brother" doesn't care; don't like to admit they need help—strong sense of pride

Native Hawaiian and Other Pacific Islander

- Family: Western concept of "immediate family" is completely alien to indigenous Hawaiians; family is not restricted to those related by blood; "we are all related"; ties that bind cannot be broken, even by death; cherish their ancestors, with generation upon generation of lineage committed to memory and beautiful chants composed to herald their ancestors' abilities

- Communication: many native Hawaiian and Pacific Islander subgroups, representing different languages and customs; ability to speak English has a tremendous impact on access to health information, public services; Hawaii is the only state in the United States that has designated a native language, Hawaiian, as one of its two official state languages

- Spirituality: polytheistic, believing in many deities; belief that spirits are found in nonhuman beings and objects such as animals, waves, and the sky

- Values: importance of culture and welfare of all living in a community; focus on ensuring the health of the community as a whole; everyone has a responsibility to use his or her talents to the benefit of the whole; sharing is central

Hispanic/Latino

- Family: extended family system incorporates godparents and informally adopted children; deep sense of commitment and obligation to family; family unity, welfare, and honor are important; emphasis on group rather than individual; male has greater power and authority

- Communication: often speak Spanish (but do not assume that they wish to receive services in native language); display varied emotional expressiveness depending on language being spoken; when speaking Spanish, client may be very expansive/expressive, friendly, playful, but in switching to English, speech may be more businesslike and guarded

ask what they prefer

- Spirituality: most are Roman Catholic; emphasis on spiritual values; strong church and community orientation/interdependence

- Values: wish to improve their life circumstances; belief in the innate worth of all individuals and that people are born into their lot in life; respect for dignity of self and others; respect for elders; respect for authority; very proud of heritage—never forget where they came from

THE INFLUENCE OF SEXUAL ORIENTATION, GENDER, AND/OR GENDER IDENTIFICATION ON BEHAVIORS AND ATTITUDES

Sexual orientation refers to an individual's pattern of physical and emotional arousal toward other persons. Heterosexual individuals are attracted to persons of the opposite sex, homosexual individuals are attracted to persons of the same sex, and bisexual individuals are attracted to persons of both sexes. Homosexual males are often referred to as "gay"; homosexual females are often referred to as "lesbian." *It is important to not use labels.*

In contrast, **gender identity** is the knowledge of oneself as being male or female. Gender identity usually conforms to anatomic sex in both heterosexual and homosexual individuals. However, individuals who identify as transgender feel themselves to be of a gender different from their biological sex; their gender identity does not match their anatomic or chromosomal sex. Transvestite should not be confused with transgender or transsexual ("person who lives as a member of a sex different from his or her birth sex"). Transvestites simply enjoy being able to cross-dress and do not view themselves as a gender different from their biological sex.

People who are transgender may identify as heterosexual, homosexual, bisexual, pansexual (attracted to individuals outside or independent of gender—blind to gender), polysexual (attracted to many genders), or asexual.

It is important to let individuals define their own sexual orientation and gender identity.

THE INFLUENCE OF AGE AND/OR DISABILITY ON BEHAVIORS AND ATTITUDES

Clearly, age has a profound impact on behavior and attitudes. Most developmental theorists trace physical, psychosocial, and other changes across the life course, marking distinctions in these areas by age. Interestingly, although behavior analysts have contributed to research on aging, the focus has largely been on remedying age-related deficits, rather than a concern with aging as a developmental process. Thus, although there is much documented that confirms that behavior changes with advancing years, there is less known about the sources of those changes.

Age can influence health behaviors, social/emotional patterns, mobility, cognitive functioning, economic well-being, independence, and other areas of life.

Disability also places a set of extra demands on the family system. A disability can consume a lot of a family's resources of time, energy, and money, so that other individual and family needs may go unmet.

Day-to-day assistance may lead to exhaustion and fatigue, taxing the physical and emotional energy of family members. There can be emotional strain, including worry, guilt, anxiety, anger, and uncertainty about the cause or prognosis of the disability, about the future, about the needs of other family members, and about whether the individual is getting enough assistance.

There can be a financial burden associated with getting health, education, and social services; buying or renting equipment and devices; making accommodations to the home; transportation; and acquiring medications and/or special food. The person or family may be eligible for payment or reimbursement from an insurance company and/or a publicly funded program such as Medicaid or Supplemental Security Income. However, knowing about services and programs and then working to become eligible is another major challenge faced by families.

Working through eligibility issues and coordinating among different providers is a challenge faced by families for which they may want a social worker to assist.

Many communities still lack programs, facilities, and resources that allow for the full inclusion of persons with disabilities. Families often report that one burden comes from dealing with people in the community whose attitudes and behaviors are judgmental, stigmatizing, and rejecting.

There are differential impacts, depending upon several factors. For example, a disability in which cognitive ability is limited may be difficult because it may limit the person's ability to complete major life tasks or live independently. In addition, the degree to which a physical disability limits activities or functions of daily living, or the ages of individuals or parents when a disability emerges, are important factors that may impact on adjustment.

THE EFFECTS OF DISCRIMINATION BASED ON CULTURE, RACE, RELIGION/SPIRITUALITY, AND/OR ETHNICITY

There are biopsychosocial–spiritual–cultural impacts of discrimination based on culture, race, and/or ethnicity. These impacts can be long-term or short-term, including having:

- Low self-esteem
- Depression
- Fear of rejection
- Stress
- Low self-worth
- Feelings of being withdrawn from society
- Humiliation
- Fear
- Anger

These impacts can result in long-term effects, including:

- Loss of motivation
- Restricted opportunities
- Limited access to services
- Long-term depression
- Increased behavior problems
- Difficulty communicating
- Lack of education and achievement

Those who have been discriminated against based on culture, race, and/ or ethnicity can become isolated from society and feel embarrassed about the shame imposed on them and/or their family. Internalized racism can occur in which negative discriminatory attitudes based on culture, race, and/or ethnicity can result with those in minority groups applying stereotypes toward their own cultural, racial, and/or ethnic groups.

Those who discriminate against others often do so because they have been discriminated against themselves. They may be unhappy or have watched people close to them discriminate against others and/or are copying and responding to their actions.

THE EFFECTS OF DISCRIMINATION BASED ON SEXUAL ORIENTATION, GENDER, AND/OR GENDER IDENTIFICATION

Discrimination against those who are not heterosexual or gender conforming is commonplace. Mistreatment can range from insulting jokes or verbal insults to unequal treatment to physical violence. This bias can be encountered in any setting—home, school, work, or community—and be pervasive throughout the life course.

Those who are not heterosexual or gender conforming often receive negative reactions from family members which can lead to physical and/or verbal abuse. In addition, many are forced to leave their family homes due to rejection and, ultimately, become homeless. These familial reactions can lead to depression, use of illegal drugs, and/or suicide attempts.

Bullying of those who are not heterosexual or gender conforming is common in schools and in the workplace. This harassment can turn violent. Many youth miss school because they feel unsafe. Adults experience workplace discrimination, leading to higher levels of psychological distress and health-related problems. These adults also have less job satisfaction, higher rates of absenteeism, and more frequent contemplation of quitting.

There is also unequal treatment under the law for those who are not heterosexual or gender conforming. The denial of marital rights has been found to be linked to higher levels of overall psychological distress, depression, anxiety, and alcohol abuse. Denial of adoption rights based on sexual orientation and gender expression/identity has a similar impact.

Those who are not heterosexual or gender conforming are also at real risk of hate crimes. Hate crime survivors manifest symptoms of depression, anger, anxiety, and posttraumatic stress.

In order to mitigate these effects, family, friendship, school, and workplace supports are needed to reduce psychological distress. Anti-discrimination and anti-hate crime laws help to protect individuals by preventing and/or punishing such acts. Finally, laws that provide equal rights can improve mental health.

THE EFFECTS OF DISCRIMINATION BASED ON AGE AND/OR DISABILITY

The negative impacts of discrimination can be seen on both the micro and macro levels. Exposure to discrimination is linked to anxiety and depression, as well as other mental health and behavioral problems. In addition, there may be physical effects such as diabetes, obesity, and high blood pressure. These health problems may be caused by not maintaining healthy behaviors (such as physical activity) or engaging in unhealthy ones (such as smoking and alcohol or drug abuse).

On a macro level, discrimination also restricts access to the resources and systems needed for good health, education, employment, social support, and participation in sports, cultural, and civic activities. Discrimination and intolerance can also create a climate of despondence, apprehension, and fear within a community. The social and economic effects of discrimination on one generation may flow on to affect future generations, which can lead to or extend cycles of poverty and disadvantage through those generations.

THE RELATIONSHIP BETWEEN SELF-IMAGE AND CULTURAL HERITAGE

Although experiences will differ, most individuals have experienced racism, oppression, or discrimination in some form and are very sensitive to being treated with disrespect or to being exploited. They will be skeptical and cautious about seeking help out of fear of being mistreated or misunderstood.

Trust is an important element in establishing a therapeutic alliance. Clients want to know if a social worker can be trusted and are competent to help them solve their problems. Clients regard and treat social workers as experts and authority figures.

Matching clients and social workers of the same race and ethnicity may decrease dropout rates and increase utilization of services, but the quality of the therapeutic relationship remains the most important factor in predicting the outcome of treatment.

Clients will ascribe credibility to a social worker using their cultural norms as a reference point (role, age, education, gender, etc.).

Understanding the cultural heritage of a client is important to working with him or her. Conflict between older and younger generations can often occur as younger members assume the values and traditions of a majority culture which can conflict with the more traditional values of the original culture that are held by an older generation.

Power and role reversals that threaten and undermine parental authority and leadership can also occur in families as parents rely on younger members of the family to become cultural interpreters. Role reversals may also occur if a woman becomes the main breadwinner because her husband cannot find employment. In a traditional marital relationship with strict gender roles, men may have difficulty dealing with this role reversal.

Members of ethnic minority groups must adapt to being members of two cultures ("bicultural") and learn to function in relationship to their culture of origin and the majority culture. Factors which influence the degree of "bicultural" socialization include:

1. The degree to which the two cultures are alike (i.e., values, beliefs, norms)—less dissonance between cultural factors makes adjustment easier

2. The degree to which bicultural socialization is supported/valued (help in accessing resources and intervening with other social systems, lend assistance in times of crisis, advocate for client, etc.)

3. The degree to which the majority culture and culture of origin provide positive or negative feedback regarding attempts to adapt to the majority culture

4. Language barriers

5. The degree to which a client appears the same in physical characteristics to those members of the majority culture (i.e., skin color, facial characteristics)

A higher degree of psychological well-being, self-esteem, and marital adjustment is reported in clients with higher levels of bicultural socialization.

Although no culture condones child abuse or neglect, there are cultural variations about what constitutes child abuse and neglect, as well as acceptable discipline measures.

There are greater incidences of domestic violence in cultures where women have lower statuses than men.

Cultural groups have various explanations for an illness, particularly mental illness, and also have different ideas of what will help (often depends on the identified cause of the illness)—some illnesses are culture-bound syndromes.

THE DIFFERENT AND SIMILAR CHARACTERISTICS OF CULTURAL, RACIAL, RELIGIOUS, AND/OR ETHNIC GROUPS

Differences *within* cultural, racial, religious, and/or religious groups are much greater than differences *between* groups. Education, social standing, personality, past experiences, and a myriad of other factors affect human behavior.

However, since there are cultural, racial, religious, and/or ethnic differences, it is good to have an understanding about their impact on customs, values, and behavior. Differences can relate to, but are not limited to food choice and preparation, concept of time, definition of family unit, physical contact, emotional expression, gender roles, and so on.

However, danger can arise when generalizations about these differences are acted upon, especially when they are based on faulty observation. Acting on generalizations, or stereotyping, about eye contact, personal space, physical touch, and interest in participation, for example, can have negative consequences.

Thus, social workers who are interacting with others of different cultures must be receptive to interpersonal feedback, use good observation skills, and effectively question clients about their values, beliefs, attitudes, and behavior to understand how they are influenced by their cultural, racial, religious, and/or ethnic backgrounds. Social workers should not be afraid to ask questions as this information is critical to understanding client well-being and problems.

Although the differences between cultures are real, social workers must also remember that clients have much in common, such as the need for appreciation, love, connection with others, being valued, making a contribution, and so on.

THE DIFFERENT AND SIMILAR CHARACTERISTICS RELATED TO SEXUAL ORIENTATION, GENDER, AND/OR GENDER IDENTIFICATION

Science has produced compelling evidence that sexual orientation is biologically based. Scientists are increasingly asserting that sexual orientation results from fundamental developmental differences that are probably caused by hormonal exposures in the womb and/or genetic factors. Similar theories have emerged about gender identification; that is, it is not a choice, but results from biological differences which are present at birth.

Despite any biological differences that drive sexual orientation and/or gender identity, there are many similarities—especially as they relate to relationships—between all individuals. Human beings, regardless of sexual orientation or gender identification, need and want to love and feel loved, to matter to someone special, to have regular and predictable companionship, to have a reliable sexual outlet, and to build a life together based on mutual respect and understanding, shared goals, and common interests. Culture also puts pressure on individuals to couple and form families.

There are some unique challenges for couples who are homosexual or transgender. Sometimes, social, cultural, legal, and familial supports are lacking due to discrimination and biases. In addition, the usual times when young adults are learning how to form intimate relationships and engage in sexual activity occurs in the mid to late teens and early adulthood—in high school and perhaps college. Because youth who are lesbian, gay, bisexual, and/or transgender are often just beginning to come to terms with their own identity during these times, they may feel confused and pressured as they do not have many visible role models for forming relationships or developing dating skills. However, working through these challenges can result in a flexibility and adaptability that can ultimately make these individuals good partners.

THE DIFFERENT AND SIMILAR CHARACTERISTICS OF AGE GROUPS AND TYPES OF DISABILITY

With increasing age comes increased likelihood of disability. As people live longer and do not encounter fatal diseases, their health issues tend to become chronic instead. The association between increasing age and increasing disability has led to a negative image of aging. Some gerontologists have introduced the term "successful aging" to emphasize the point that not all aging is negative.

There are many types of disabilities that can affect vision, movement, cognition, communication, hearing, and mental health. Disabilities can affect people in different ways, even when one person has the same disability as another. Some disabilities may be hidden or largely unnoticeable. Anyone can have a disability, and a disability can occur at any point in a person's life.

Every person has a purpose, special uniqueness, and value, no matter what hurdles he or she faces. Many living with disabilities are fully active in work, their family life, sports, and/or hobbies. Some people with disabilities are able to work full- or part-time while others are unable to maintain gainful or substantial employment, have trouble with daily living activities, and/or need assistance with their care.

The term *invisible disabilities* refers to symptoms such as debilitating pain, fatigue, dizziness, cognitive dysfunctions, brain injuries, learning differences, mental health disorders, and hearing or vision impairments. Although not always obvious to others, these disabilities may limit daily activities and result in mild challenges to severe limitations.

Unfortunately, people often judge others by what they see, and often conclude a person can or cannot do something by the way he or she looks. This can be equally frustrating for those who may appear unable, but are perfectly capable as it is for those who appear able, but are not. Everyone, whether disabled or not, is different, with varying challenges, needs, abilities, and attributes.

STEREOTYPES

Stereotypes are commonly held public beliefs about certain social groups or individuals. The use of stereotypes represents a "cognitive shortcut," allowing the brain to make a snap judgment based on characteristics such as gender, ethnicity, race, age, and so on. While seemingly useful as a way to process information, problems arise when assumptions are made and applied to individuals based on these characteristics. Actions based on stereotypes or assumptions can deny access of some to societal rewards (jobs, career advancement, and so on) and result in discrimination.

It is essential that social workers start by admitting that they too have biases and need to identify and challenge them. Understanding the root causes of these biases and how they may be impacting on interactions with clients is essential. Social workers should expose themselves to different experiences and cultures because such exposure will help to eradicate the use of stereotypes and mitigate biases. Social workers should also challenge the use of stereotypes by others, advocate for those who have been adversely impacted by them, and educate society about their inherent dangers.

THE IMPACT OF DIVERSITY IN STYLES OF COMMUNICATING

Communication styles may be strongly influenced by culture, race, and/or ethnicity.

Communication is far more than an exchange of words. Facial expressions, hand gestures, posture, eye contact, and even silence are constantly sending messages about attitudes, emotions, status, and relationships.

Nonverbal cues are critical. For example, personal space, or the distance two people keep between themselves in order to feel comfortable, is culturally based. Personal space may be influenced by gender or status. It can also be influenced by the intimacy of a relationship.

Eye contact is also influenced by culture. For some, direct eye contact is very brief, with the gaze then sliding away to the side, especially with superiors or members of the opposite sex. In contrast, others may engage in more direct eye contact.

Speaking volume can be nearly as important as the words themselves. Normal baseline volumes vary among cultures and among individuals in these cultures.

The appropriateness of physical touch is also important to understand. In some cultures, individuals rarely touch each other, limiting themselves to handshakes and occasional pats on the shoulder or arm in business relationships and hugs in closer friendships. In other cultures, physical touch such as hugging is part of many interactions, even those that are casual.

Smiling, facial expressions, time, and silence are other communication factors that vary among those from different cultures, races, or ethnic groups.

In order to be effective with those from diverse cultural, racial, and/or ethnic groups, a social worker must:

1. Recognize direct and indirect communication styles

2. Demonstrate sensitivity to nonverbal cues

3. Generate a wide variety of verbal responses, nonverbal responses, and strategies

4. Use language that is culturally appropriate

5. Identify his or her own professional style and recognize limitations and strengths

6. Identify and reduce barriers that will inhibit engagement with persons who are culturally different

Micro Assessment and Planning (22%)

Use of Assessment Instruments and Methods

PSYCHOLOGICAL AND EDUCATIONAL TESTS AND MEASUREMENT

There are many psychological and educational tests in existence for assessment and diagnostic purposes. The following are a few of the most well-known.

Beck Depression Inventory

The Beck Depression Inventory (BDI) is a 21-item test, presented in multiple choice formats, that assesses the apresence and degree of depression in adolescents and adults.

The Minnesota Multiphasic Personality Inventory

The Minnesota Multiphasic Personality Inventory (MMPI) is an objective verbal inventory designed as a personality test for the assessment of psychopathology consisting of 550 statements, 16 of which are repeated.

Myers–Briggs Type Indicator

The Myers–Briggs Type Indicator (MBTI) is a forced-choice, self-report inventory that attempts to classify individuals along four theoretically independent dimensions. The first dimension is a general attitude toward the world, either extraverted (E) or introverted (I). The second dimension, perception, is divided between sensation (S) and intuition (N). The third dimension is that of processing. Once information is received, it is processed in either a thinking (T) or feeling (F) style. The final dimension is judging (J) versus perceiving (P).

Rorschach Inkblot Test

Client responses to inkblots are used to assess perceptual reactions and other psychological functioning. It is one of the most widely used projective tests.

Stanford–Binet Intelligence Scale

The Stanford–Binet Intelligence Scale is designed for the testing of cognitive abilities. It provides verbal, performance, and full-scale scores for children and adults.

Thematic Apperception Test

The Thematic Apperception Test (TAT) is another widely used projective test. It consists of a series of pictures of ambiguous scenes. Clients are asked to make up stories or fantasies concerning what is happening, has happened, and is going to happen in the scenes, along with a description of their thoughts and feelings. The TAT provides information on a client's perceptions and imagination for use in the understanding of a client's current needs, motives, emotions, and conflicts, both conscious and unconscious. Its use in clinical assessment is generally part of a larger battery of tests and interview data.

Wechsler Intelligence Scale

The Wechsler Intelligence Scale (WISC) is designed as a measure of a child's intellectual and cognitive ability. It has four index scales and a full-scale score.

THE USE OF ASSESSMENT/DIAGNOSIS INSTRUMENTS IN PRACTICE

There are advantages and disadvantages of using existing scales and instruments to evaluate one's own practice. Advantages include that clients may already be using them for service authorizations, eliminating the need to separately collect this information for evaluation purposes. There is also considerable time and financial cost with developing new scales and instruments. Thus, using existing scales can be more efficient and less costly.

In addition, existing scales and instruments may have undergone extensive testing, increasing their reliability and validity.

There are also disadvantages to the use of existing scales and instruments. They may not exactly measure the areas or domains in which client progress could have occurred. Thus, it could appear as if no progress and gains were made when in fact they did occur. A social worker also is limited to only the questions contained in the existing scale or instrument. There may be vital information omitted as it relates to a particular client's problem or situation. It is also crucial to understand whether an existing instrument or scale has been tested cross-culturally in order to determine its appropriateness, reliability, and validity with diverse populations.

THE COMPONENTS AND FUNCTION OF THE MENTAL STATUS EXAMINATION

A mental status examination is a structured way of observing and describing a client's current state of mind, under the domains of appearance, attitude, behavior, mood and affect, speech, thought process, thought content, perception, cognition, insight, and judgment. A mental status examination is a necessary part of any client assessment no matter what the presenting problem. It should be documented in the record either in list form or in narrative form. The following client functions should be included:

1. *Appearance*—facial expression, grooming, dress, gait, and so on

2. *Orientation*—awareness of time and place, events, and so on

3. *Speech pattern*—slurred, pressured, slow, flat tone, calm, and so on

4. *Affect/mood*—mood as evidenced in both behavior and client's statements (sad, jittery, manic, placid, and so on)

5. *Impulsive/potential for harm*—impulse control with special attention to potential suicidality and/or harm to others

6. *Judgment/insight*—ability to predict the consequences of his or her behavior, to make "sensible" decisions, to recognize his or her contribution to his or her problem

7. *Thought processes/reality testing*—thinking style and ability to know reality, including the difference between stimuli which are coming from inside himself or herself and those that are coming from outside himself or herself (statements about delusions, hallucinations, and conclusions about whether or not a client is psychotic would appear here)

8. *Intellectual functioning/memory*—level of intelligence and of recent and remote memory functions

A paragraph about mental status in the record might read as follows:

Client is a 43-year-old woman who looks older than her stated age. She is well groomed and appropriately dressed for a professional interview. She is well oriented. Her speech is slow as if it is painful to talk. She has had occasional thoughts of "ending it all," but has not made any suicidal plans or preparations. She talks about future events with the expectation of being alive. She is aware that she is "depressed" and recognizes that the source of some of the feeling comes from "inside moods," although she often refers to the difficulties of her situation. Her thoughts are organized. She is not psychotic.

THE PROCESS USED IN PROBLEM FORMULATION

In both micro and macro practice, social workers must work with clients to identify the problem(s) to be addressed. Problem identification concerns determining the problem targeted for intervention. Although this seems straightforward, it is often difficult to isolate the issue that, when addressed, will result in a change in the symptomology of a client and/or client system.

Part of problem identification is determining the issue in exact definable terms, when it occurs, and its magnitude. When doing macro practice, a social worker may often need to get consensus from the group regarding whether there is agreement as to the nature of the problem and its occurrence and magnitude.

It is often useful in problem identification to determine that which is *not* the problem. Such a technique will ensure that these elements are not grouped in with those that are targeted and will assist in narrowing down the focus.

The problem should always be considered within the person-in-environment perspective and using a strengths-based approach. It should not blame a client and/or client system for its existence.

THE METHODS OF INVOLVING THE CLIENT AND/OR SYSTEMS IN IDENTIFYING THE PROBLEM

Social workers focus on assisting clients and/or system members to identify problems and areas of strength, as well as increasing problem-solving strategies.

It is essential that, throughout the problem-solving process, social workers view clients and/or system members as experts.

Clients and/or system members should be asked about what they would like to see changed and their definitions of problems should be accepted.

Clients and/or system members should be asked about what will be different when problems are solved. Social workers should listen carefully for, and work hard to respect, the directions in which clients and/or system members want to go (their goals) and the words they use to express these directions.

Clients and/or system members should be asked about the paths that they would like to take to make desired changes. Perceptions should be respected and inner resources (strengths) should be maximized.

THE PRINCIPLES AND TECHNIQUES OF INTERVIEWING

In social work, an interview is always purposeful and involves verbal and nonverbal communication between a social worker and client, during which ideas, attitudes, and feelings are exchanged. The actions of a social worker aim to gather important information and keep a client focused on the achievement of the goal.

A social work interview is designed to serve *the interest of a client*; therefore, the actions of a social worker during the interview must be planned and focused. Questions in a social work interview should be tailored to the specifics of a client, not generic, "one size fits all" inquiries. The focus is on the uniqueness of a client and his or her unique situation.

The purpose of the social work interview can be informational, diagnostic, or therapeutic. The same interview may serve more than one purpose.

Communication during a social work interview is interactive and interrelational. A social worker's questions will result in specific responses by a client that, in turn, lead to other inquiries. The message is formulated by a client, encoded, transmitted, received, processed, and decoded. The importance of words and messages may be implicit (implied) or explicit (evident).

There are a number of techniques that a social worker may use during an interview to assist clients, including partializing, supporting, focusing, clarifying, confronting, interpreting, and reflecting.

THE METHODS USED TO ASSESS THE CLIENT'S COMMUNICATION SKILLS

Social workers must involve clients in every aspect of treatment. In order to do so, social workers must assess clients' communication skills and determine effective methods to gather needed information, as well as to ensure that clients understand data that is presented to them. Thus, the expressive and receptive communication of clients must be considered.

Communication can be verbal and nonverbal, so an assessment of clients' communication skills must involve both. Role-playing is a good way to assess and enhance clients' communication skills. It also allows a social worker to see if there is congruence between nonverbal and verbal communication.

As many clients may have experienced trauma, it is essential that social workers understand how such experiences may impact on clients' communication styles and patterns. Much of communication is also cultural and should be viewed within the context of clients' backgrounds and experiences.

Silence is a form of communication and should be considered by a social worker when used by a client.

Social workers should understand how to communicate with clients who are upset and angry, as well as how some wording choices and tones can be upsetting to clients based on their ethnic backgrounds and/or past experiences, such as victimization.

THE METHODS USED TO ASSESS MOTIVATION AND RESISTANCE

Motivation and resistance exist along a continuum of readiness. When assessing motivation and resistance of a client, it is important to determine what stage of change a client is in. This will provide a social worker with appropriate clinical strategies to use to address these issues. If social workers push clients at a faster pace than they are ready to take, the therapeutic alliance may break down.

A lack of motivation and resistance are often found in *precontemplation and contemplation* before making the decision to change. There can also be motivational challenges during preparation, action, and maintenance, but they are more easily addressed. When resistance occurs in these latter stages of change, a social worker should reassess the problem and appropriateness of the intervention to ensure that there have not been new developments in a client's life that need to be considered. They may be distracting a client from making progress or serving as barriers to making real change.

In *precontemplation*, a client is unaware, unable, and/or unwilling to change. In this stage, there is the greatest resistance and lack of motivation. It can be characterized by arguing, interrupting, denial, ignoring the problem, and/or avoiding talking or thinking about it. A client may not even show up for appointments and may not agree that change is needed.

A social worker can best deal with lack of motivation and resistance in this stage by establishing a rapport, acknowledging resistance or ambivalence, keeping conversation informal, trying to engage a client, and recognizing a client's thoughts, feelings, fears, and concerns.

In *contemplation*, a client is ambivalent or uncertain regarding behavior change; thus, his or her behaviors are unpredictable. In this stage, a client may be willing to look at the pros and cons of behavior change, but is not committed to working toward it.

addressing contemplation

A social worker can best deal with lack of motivation and resistance in this stage by emphasizing a client's free choice and responsibility, as well as discussing the pros and cons of changing. It is also useful to discuss how change will assist a client in achieving his or her goals in life. Fear can be reduced by producing examples of change and clarifying what change is and is not.

THE METHODS USED TO ASSESS NEEDED LEVEL OF CARE

Social workers must assess the client's needed level of care, with the belief that there should be a continuum of intensity depending upon the level of crisis. Clients should enter treatment at a level appropriate to their needs and then step up to more intense treatment or down to less intense treatment as needed. An effective continuum of care features successful transfer of a client between levels of care.

Levels of care for behavioral health services, for example, vary from early intervention services/outpatient services to intensive outpatient/partial hospitalization to residential/inpatient services.

Early intervention or outpatient services are appropriate unless a client is experiencing crisis or at risk for residential/inpatient services, which may then warrant a step up to intensive outpatient or partial hospitalization. The goal is to serve clients in the least restrictive environment, while ensuring health and safety.

Use of Social History

6

THE COMPONENTS OF A BIOPSYCHOSOCIAL HISTORY

The biopsychosocial–spiritual–cultural history is a tool that provides information on the current/presenting issue or issues; a client's past and present physical health, including developmental milestones; a client's emotional functioning; educational or vocational background; cultural issues; spiritual and religious beliefs; environmental issues; and social functioning. Each issue may be reviewed for its relationship and/or impact with the presenting issue.

The *biological section* assesses a client's medical history, developmental history, current medications, substance abuse history, and family history of medical illnesses. Issues related to medical problems should be explored because mental health symptoms can exacerbate them. Referrals should be made to address medical concerns that are not being treated. Clients who are on medications should have care coordinated with the treating provider, and more should be known about the medications because side effects can also mask or exacerbate psychiatric symptoms or illnesses.

The *psychological section* assesses a client's current psychiatric illness or symptoms and their history, past or current psychosocial stressors, and mental status. It includes exploration of how the problem has been treated, past or present psychiatric medications, and the family history of psychiatric and substance-related issues.

The *social section* focuses on client systems and unique client context and may identify strengths and/or resources available for treatment planning. Included are sexual identity issues or concerns, personal history, family of origin history, support system, abuse history, education, legal history, marital/relationship status and concerns, work history, and risks.

The assessment should also include information about a client's spiritual beliefs and cultural traditions.

THE TYPES OF INFORMATION AVAILABLE FROM EMPLOYMENT, MEDICAL, PSYCHOLOGICAL, AND SCHOOL RECORDS

Assessment is ongoing within the problem-solving process. In order to ensure that all relevant information is considered, social workers often rely on information available from clients' existing records in addition to the data that they collect directly.

To access this information, it is critical for social workers to be aware of laws governing its release and get the informed consent of clients prior to any request for access. The consent process must make clients aware of the reasons for such requests, as well as the benefits and risks of social workers obtaining this information. When information is obtained, it becomes part of the client record. Although protected by Health Insurance Portability and Accountability Act (HIPAA), clients' records can become subject to subpoenas and/or court orders. Thus, inclusion of this information in their records can have some additional risks associated with the legal duty to release it if court-ordered to do so.

Despite this risk, using existing employment, medical, psychological, psychiatric, and educational records can be very helpful when completing a biopsychosocial–spiritual–cultural history.

Employment records may help social workers construct clients' work histories and obtain data about income earned from their jobs. These records may be essential if clients need assistance with applying for Unemployment Insurance or other public benefits (Temporary Assistance for Needy Families [TANF], Supplemental Nutrition Assistance Program [SNAP], etc.).

Medical records are essential to ensure that client problems are not due to health issues and to better understand the possible impact of past or current medical problems on client functioning.

Psychological and psychiatric records can be helpful as they can contain the results of any psychological testing that has been completed and provide information about whether any mental health diagnoses have been assigned. Whether or not a client has been prescribed psychotropic medications and/or received any subsequent treatment for behavioral health concerns would also be contained in psychiatric records.

When working with children, educational records are often consulted to determine performance in school and whether any problems experienced at home or elsewhere are being manifested in this setting as well. When working with adults, educational records can provide clues as to the age at which problems or difficulties began. Historical educational records are often used to diagnose adults with intellectual or developmental disabilities that were not appropriately identified while in school.

THE METHODS USED TO COLLECT AND EVALUATE COLLATERAL INFORMATION

Collateral information is often used when the credibility and validity of information obtained from a client or others is questionable. For example, child custody cases are inherently characterized by biased data within an adversarial process. Thus, it is often necessary to evaluate the integrity of the information gathered through use of collateral information.

However, social workers should always assess the credibility of collateral informants and understand that data from more neutral parties has higher integrity. In addition, informants who have greater access to key information may produce more valid data.

When an account by a collateral informant agrees with information gathered from a client, it enhances the trustworthiness of the data collected.

Using multiple information sources (or triangulation) is an excellent method for social workers to have accurate accounts upon which to make assessments or base interventions.

THE METHODS USED TO OBTAIN INFORMATION RELEVANT TO A GIVEN SITUATION

Social workers focus on assisting clients to identify problems and areas of strength and improving their problem-solving strategies.

It is essential that throughout the problem-solving process, social workers view clients as experts in their own lives.

Clients should be asked about what they would like to see changed in their lives, and clients' definitions of problems should be accepted.

Clients should be asked to explain what will be different in their lives when their problems are solved. Social workers should listen carefully for, and work hard to respect, the directions in which clients want to go with their lives (their goals) and the words they use to express these directions.

Clients should be asked about the paths that they would like to take to make desired changes. Clients' perceptions should be respected and clients' inner resources (strengths) should be maximized as part of treatment.

THE COMPONENTS OF A SEXUAL HISTORY

Some clients may not be comfortable talking about their sexual history, sex partners, or sexual practices. It is critical that social workers try to put clients at ease and let them know that taking a sexual history may be an important part of the assessment process. A history is usually obtained through a face-to-face interview but can also be gotten from a pencil-and-paper document.

Questions included in a sexual history may vary depending upon client issues. However, they usually involve collecting information about partners (number, gender, risk factors, length of relationships), practices (risk behaviors, oral/vaginal/anal intercourse, satisfaction with practices, desire/arousal/orgasm), protection from and past history of STDs (condom use), and prevention of pregnancy (if desired)/reproductive history.

If clients are experiencing dissatisfaction or dysfunction, social workers will need to understand the reasons for dissatisfaction and/or dysfunction. Medical explanations must be ruled out before psychological factors are considered as causes. A systems perspective should be used to understand issues in this area. For example, a medical/biological condition that decreases satisfaction or causes dysfunction may heavily impact on psychological and social functioning. In addition, a psychological or social issue can lead to a lack of desire, inability to become aroused, or failure to attain orgasm.

Alcohol and/or drug use should also be considered related to concerns about desire, arousal, or orgasm because they can cause decreased interest or abilities in these areas.

THE COMPONENTS OF A MARITAL HISTORY

While clients are often asked about their current marital statuses, more in-depth information about their marital relationships over time should be gathered. It will provide social workers with the number of marriages and their duration as well as how each functioned—what worked and what did not. A marital history also sheds light on any external influences and whether they contributed to problems or enhanced the relationship(s).

A marital history should include a chronology from dating to engagement and eventually marriage, as well as whether clients are still married, divorced, or widowed. It should detail marital issues between spouses and relationship troubles with other family members, including how they impacted on the unions. Topics of disagreements should be noted, including how conflicts were resolved and decisions were made. Financial responsibilities and health issues of each spouse should be outlined as they relate to life events and/or marital issues.

This history should also gather information on pregnancies and births as well as the parenting responsibilities of each party.

THE COMPONENTS OF A FAMILY HISTORY

Understanding a client's family history is an important part of the assessment process. A client is part of a larger family system. Thus, gaining a better understanding of the experiences of other family members may prove useful in understanding influences imposed on a client throughout his or her life course.

One tool used by social workers to depict a client as part of a larger family system is a **genogram**. A genogram is a graphic representation of a family tree that displays the interaction of generations within a family. It goes beyond a traditional family tree by allowing the user to analyze family, emotional, and social relationships within a group. It is used to identify repetitive patterns of behavior and to recognize hereditary tendencies. A social worker can also ask about these relationships, behaviors, and tendencies without using a genogram.

There are no set questions that must be included in a family history; often, they relate to the problem or issue experienced by a client at the time. However, they may include identifying family members':

- Ethnic backgrounds (including immigration) and traditions
- Biological ties (adoption, blended family structures, foster children)
- Occupations and educational levels
- Unusual life events or achievements
- Psychological and social histories, as well as current well-being
- Past and present substance use behaviors
- Relationships with other family members
- Roles within the immediate and larger family unit
- Losses such as those from death, divorce, or physical separation
- Current and past significant problems, including those due to medical, financial, and other issues
- Values related to economic status, educational attainment, and employment
- Coping skills or defense mechanisms

Finding out which adults and/or children get the most attention or recognition and which get the least may also provide insight.

BASIC MEDICAL TERMINOLOGY

Social workers must recognize the relationship between physical well-being and mental status. Social workers should always rule out medical etiology before making psychiatric diagnoses. A **differential diagnosis** is a systematic diagnostic method used to identify the presence of an entity where multiple alternatives are possible.

Social workers must know the major body systems and medical conditions associated with them that can affect psychological functioning and mood.

1. *Circulatory System*

   The circulatory system is the body's transport system. It is made up of a group of organs that transport blood throughout the body. The heart pumps the blood and the arteries and veins transport it.

2. *Digestive System*

   The digestive system is made up of organs that break down food into protein, vitamins, minerals, carbohydrates, and fats, which the body needs for energy, growth, and repair.

3. *Endocrine System*

   The endocrine system is made up of a group of glands that produce the body's long-distance messengers, or hormones. Hormones are chemicals that control body functions, such as metabolism, growth, and sexual development.

4. *Immune System*

   The immune system is a body's defense system against infections and diseases. Organs, tissues, cells, and cell products work together to respond to dangerous organisms (like viruses or bacteria) and substances that may enter the body from the environment.

5. *Lymphatic System*

   The lymphatic system is also a defense system for the body. It filters out organisms that cause disease, produces white blood cells, and generates disease-fighting antibodies. It also distributes fluids and nutrients in the body and drains excess fluids and protein so that tissues do not swell.

6. *Muscular System*

   The muscular system is made up of tissues that work with the skeletal system to control movement of the body. Some muscles—like those in arms and legs—are voluntary, meaning that an individual decides when to move them. Other muscles, like the ones in the stomach, heart, intestines, and other organs, are involuntary. This means that they are controlled automatically by the nervous system and hormones—one often does not realize they are at work.

7. *Nervous System*

   The nervous system is made up of the brain, the spinal cord, and nerves. One of the most important systems in the body, the nervous system is the body's control system. It sends, receives, and processes nerve impulses throughout the body. These nerve impulses tell muscles and organs what to do and how to respond to the environment.

8. *Reproductive System*

The reproductive system allows humans to produce children. Sperm from the male fertilizes the female's egg, or ovum, in the fallopian tube. The fertilized egg travels from the fallopian tube to the uterus, where the fetus develops over a period of nine months.

9. *Respiratory System*

The respiratory system brings air into the body and removes carbon dioxide. It includes the nose, trachea, and lungs.

10. *Skeletal System*

The skeletal system is made up of bones, ligaments, and tendons. It shapes the body and protects organs. The skeletal system works with the muscular system to help the body move.

11. *Urinary System*

The urinary system eliminates waste from the body in the form of urine. The kidneys remove waste from the blood. The waste combines with water to form urine.

THE EXPLORATION OF SPIRITUAL/RELIGIOUS BELIEFS AND PRACTICES

In addition to the biopsychosocial domains of human development, spirituality must also be considered as it relates to well-being. There is often a perceived spiritual basis of many physical and psychological symptoms. Thus, individuals may consult a religious or spiritual adviser instead of or in addition to seeking help from a social worker. In fact, the use of spiritual healers in the non-Western world is so widespread that it is the backbone of many rural health care systems.

Given the central role of spirituality in all cultures, it will certainly have an impact on client functioning in some manner. In a clinical sense, client beliefs about themselves and their worlds are the "spirits" that comprise their personal realities and inform their feelings and actions. Including spirituality when gaining a better understanding of client problems and developing interventions to address them completes the holistic approach required by the ecological perspective of social work.

The Impact of Life Stressors on Systems

7

THE EFFECTS OF LIFE STRESSORS ON FAMILIES

Families experience growing pressures, including those related to managing relationships, finances, and work. Raising a family can be rewarding and demanding even in the best of times with healthy social and economic climates, so traumatic life events and environmental stressors can make things much more challenging.

Many parents report family responsibilities as a significant source of stress. This stress by parents can impact on the well-being of children and affect the health of all family members. It is important to consider the way a parent's stress and corresponding unhealthy behaviors affect the family.

Children model their parents' behaviors, including those related to managing stress. Parents who deal with stress in unhealthy ways, such as overeating or substance use, risk passing those behaviors on to their children. Conversely, parents who cope with stress in healthy ways can not only promote better adjustment and happiness for themselves, but also promote the formation of critically important habits and skills in children.

Stressful events can lead to divorce, depression, illness, substance use, work problems, relationship issues, and so on. These manifestations of stress can have devastating impacts for individual family members as well as the family unit as a whole.

Managing stress can be difficult, but is possible. By taking small, incremental steps to a healthier lifestyle, families can work toward meeting their goals to be psychologically and physically fit. These steps can include becoming aware of maladaptive behaviors used to deal with stress, talking about healthy ways to solve problems including healthy eating and getting enough exercise and sleep, and creating a home space that is safe and relaxing.

THE EFFECTS OF STRESSORS ON BEHAVIOR

Emotional and psychological trauma is the result of extraordinarily stressful events that destroy a sense of security, making a client feel helpless and vulnerable in a dangerous world.

Traumatic experiences often involve a threat to life or safety, but **any situation that leaves a client feeling overwhelmed and alone can be traumatic, even if it does not involve physical harm.** It is not the objective facts that determine whether an event is traumatic, but a subjective emotional experience of the event.

An event will most likely lead to emotional or psychological trauma if:

- It happened unexpectedly
- There was not preparation for it
- There is a feeling of having been powerless to prevent it
- It happens repeatedly
- Someone was intentionally cruel
- It happened in childhood

Emotional and psychological trauma can be caused by one-time events or ongoing, relentless stress.

Not all potentially traumatic events lead to lasting emotional and psychological damage. Some clients rebound quickly from even the most tragic and shocking experiences. Others are devastated by experiences that, on the surface, appear to be less upsetting.

A number of risk factors make clients susceptible to emotional and psychological trauma. Clients are more likely to be traumatized by a stressful experience if they are already under a heavy stress load or have recently suffered a series of losses.

Clients are also more likely to be traumatized by a new situation if they have been traumatized before—especially if the earlier trauma occurred in childhood. Experiencing trauma in childhood can have a severe and long-lasting effect. Children who have been traumatized see the world as a frightening and dangerous place. When childhood trauma is not resolved, this fundamental sense of fear and helplessness carries over into adulthood, setting the stage for further trauma.

Emotional and psychological symptoms of trauma include:

- Shock, denial, or disbelief
- Anger, irritability, mood swings
- Guilt, shame, self-blame
- Feeling sad or hopeless
- Confusion, difficulty concentrating

- ■ Anxiety and fear
- ■ Withdrawing from others
- ■ Feeling disconnected or numb

Physical symptoms of trauma include:

- ■ Insomnia or nightmares
- ■ Being startled easily
- ■ Racing heartbeat
- ■ Aches and pains
- ■ Fatigue
- ■ Difficulty concentrating
- ■ Edginess and agitation
- ■ Muscle tension

THE IMPACT OF PHYSICAL AND MENTAL ILLNESS ON FAMILY DYNAMICS

Physical and mental illness place a set of extra demands on the family system. They can consume a lot of a family's resources of time, energy, and money, so that other individual and family needs go unmet.

Day-to-day assistance, which can be required due to physical and mental illness, may lead to exhaustion and fatigue, taxing the physical and emotional energy of family members. There can be emotional strain, including worry, guilt, anxiety, anger, and uncertainty about the cause or prognosis of the physical and mental illness, about the future, about the needs of other family members, and about whether the individual is getting enough assistance.

There can be a financial burden associated with getting health, education, and social services; buying or renting equipment and devices; making accommodations to the home; transportation; and acquiring medications and/or special food. The person or family may be eligible for payment or reimbursement from an insurance company and/or a publicly funded program, such as Medicaid or Supplemental Security Income. However, knowing about services and programs and then working to become eligible is another major challenge faced by families.

Working through eligibility issues and coordinating among different providers is a challenge faced by families for which they may want a social worker to assist.

Many communities lack programs and resources and families also report burden from dealing with people in the community whose attitudes and behaviors, especially related to mental illness, are judgmental, stigmatizing, and rejecting.

There are differential impacts of physical and mental illness, depending upon several factors. For example, they limit the person's ability to complete major life tasks or live independently. In addition, the ages of individuals or parents when physical and mental illness occur is an important factor that may impact on adjustment.

THE DYNAMICS OF LOSS, SEPARATION, AND GRIEF

Elisabeth Kübler-Ross outlined what has been the traditional five stages of grief. She originally developed this model based on her observations of people suffering from terminal illness. She later expanded her theory to apply to any form of personal loss, such as the death of a loved one, the loss of a job or income, major rejection, the end of a relationship or divorce, drug addiction, incarceration, the onset of a disease or chronic illness, and/or an infertility diagnosis, as well as many tragedies and disasters (and even minor losses).

Denial and isolation: Shock is replaced with the feeling of "this can't be happening to me."

Anger: The emotional confusion that results from this loss may lead to anger and finding someone or something to blame—"why me?"

Bargaining: The next stage may result in trying to negotiate with one's self (or a higher power) to attempt to change what has occurred.

Depression: A period of sadness and loneliness then will occur in which a person reflects on his or her grief and loss.

Acceptance: After time feeling depressed about the loss, a person will eventually be at peace with what happened.

Hope is not a separate stage, but is possible at any stage.

Loss, separation, and grief can occur at any time and each client will be unique in how he or she copes with these issues. Some clients may have responses that are healthy coping mechanisms, while other responses may hinder the grieving process. The acknowledgment of the loss, separation, or grief, as well as time and support, help to assist through the grieving process, allowing an opportunity for a client to appropriately mourn and heal. Emotional, psychological, and physical effects of loss, separation, and grief mirror those for experienced during trauma.

THE IMPACT OF AGING PARENTS ON ADULT CHILDREN

For social workers, there is an increasing need to provide services and supports to adult children as they become caregivers for their parents. In these new roles, adult children may need direct assistance with maintaining adequate nutrition, decent housing, economic stability, and access to appropriate medical care for both their parents and themselves. However, of even greater concern to adult children are a multitude of psychosocial stressors that come with the transitioning of roles and the expectations placed upon them. In these instances, there are often blurred familial roles, boundaries, and expectations.

The responsibility of caring for the aging parent often falls to adult children who are generally accepting of this responsibility. Their reasons for doing so may include fulfilling expectations, religious beliefs, sense of duty, financial rewards, altruism, and/or respect/love.

Adult children may need the assistance of social workers due to feelings of guilt, fatigue, sadness, anxiety, and/or frustration. These feelings are compounded when the assistance of adult children is not appreciated by their aging parents. Often adult children need help getting other family members to share the burden and/or getting their parents' affairs in order.

Seeing parents grow old forces adult children to confront feelings about their own mortality. Feelings can include denial, hostility, resentment, hatred of their parents or themselves, helplessness, fear, anger, and sadness. Clients may have any or all of these emotions at one time and the emotions may vary in range and intensity. In some instances, adult children may feel in a bind and begin to seek reasons for reducing their commitment to their older family members. A social worker can provide help in sorting out these feelings, finding their roots, and reframing them into empowerment, opportunity, and choice.

Clients may want help in areas such as communication (i.e., understanding requests for assistance/resistance of their parents), self-care (i.e., developing coping skills and attending to their own needs), and/or resource identification (i.e., finding services to assist in meeting child/parent needs).

Social workers need to be sensitive to client needs in these situations, since the transforming role of child to adult child of aging parents will most likely leave a client on shaky ground, especially if the role was not expected or anticipated. A social worker may need to act as a consultant, advocate, case manager, catalyst, broker, mediator, facilitator, instructor, mobilizer, and/or clinician in these situations as the family dynamic is complex and the needs are great.

THE FACTORS OF CHILD DEVELOPMENT

Child development occurs naturally as a child grows older and develops physically, biologically, mentally, emotionally, socially, and so on. Child development is extremely important as it represents the "foundation years" which shape and impact the child's future in regard to growth, health, development, happiness, and learning ability.

Child development can be positively or adversely affected by many social, economic, and environmental factors. Because children are so vulnerable, they can be easily affected by things many parents and adults take for granted. While not exhaustive, some of the factors affecting child development are listed below.

■ **Genetic and Environmental Factors**

Child development results from significant interaction between biological/genetic predetermined factors and the environment in which the child is raised. Genes will always play a role with how a child responds to his or her environments. However, a child's behavior cannot be blamed solely on his or her genes, nor can it be blamed solely on the environment he or she is being raised in. Both of these factors affect child development.

Sometimes, a child will need outside help to be able to develop well. There are early intervention programs that can help which are effective and uncostly.

■ **Nutrition**

Early nutrition is essential to health and disease outcomes later in life. However, early nutrition is not the only contributing factor; health is impacted by exercise, genetic and biological factors, medical care, and so on.

■ **Attachment**

Relationships, including early attachment, are extremely important. Parents and children need to attend to forming and maintaining attachments with one another. In addition, being prepared to handle any difficulties or obstacles that might harm these attachments is essential.

Parenting is important. Parents are role models and establish the rules and standards for children to follow.

■ **Culture**

Culture (including family values, practices, and norms) greatly affects children's attitudes, beliefs, and behaviors.

THE PSYCHOLOGICAL RESPONSES TO ILLNESS AND DISABILITY

Change is inevitable during the life course. Depending upon a client's perception and the circumstances involved, these changes may be negative or positive. In either case, changes require adjustment or adaptation and can often be difficult for clients.

Illness and disability produce significant change and are associated with psychological distress as clients may have to cope with modifications in their usual lifestyles, loss of control, pain or discomfort, changes in roles, financial hardship, and/or decreased independence.

When clients perceive that they can control their own destinies or future and that change is manageable, they are less likely to be overwhelmed by the stress of their situations. However, if clients perceive that the illnesses or disabilities are insurmountable or unpredictable, stress associated with these conditions can be overwhelming.

Some psychological responses to illness and disability include threats to:

- Body image and self-concept
- Privacy
- Autonomy and control
- Life goals and future plans
- Relationships with family, friends, and colleagues
- Economic well-being

Responses to these threats can be destructive behaviors such as non-compliance with recommended treatment and/or substance use, anger, depression, and so on. What is essential is working with clients to ensure that they, or family members who have become ill and/or disabled, still have a significant purpose in life and can be contributing members in their homes, workplaces, and society. Interestingly, clients in similar situations do not necessarily experience similar degrees of stress, and the amount of change due to an illness or disability is not necessarily an indicator of the amount of stress experienced by a client. Social work intervention can assist clients with adapting and coping effectively with these changes and mobilizing resources needed to address limitations. Building coping skills can dramatically reduce negative psychological responses and lead to more stable or positive outcomes.

THE EFFECTS OF ADDICTION ON INDIVIDUALS, FAMILIES, ORGANIZATIONS, AND COMMUNICATIONS

There are biopsychosocial–spiritual–cultural impacts of substance abuse or dependence. Those who use drugs experience a wide array of physical effects other than those expected. The excitement or high that results from the use of cocaine is followed by a "crash": a period of anxiety, fatigue, depression, and an acute desire for more cocaine to alleviate these continued feelings. Marijuana and alcohol interfere with motor control and are factors in many automobile accidents. Users of hallucinogenic drugs may experience flashbacks, which are unwanted recurrences of the drug's effects weeks or months after use. Sudden abstinence from certain drugs results in withdrawal symptoms. For example, heroin withdrawal can cause vomiting, muscle cramps, convulsions, and delirium. With the continued use of substances that are physically addictive, tolerance develops; that is, constantly increasing amounts of the drug are needed to duplicate the initial effect.

Substance abuse or dependence also impacts mental health because it causes irrational behavior, violence, and lapses in memory. Chronic use of some substances can cause long-lasting changes in the brain, which may lead to paranoia, depression, aggression, and hallucinations.

In addition, because the purity and dosage of illegal drugs are uncontrolled, drug overdose is a constant risk. Many drug users also engage in criminal activity, such as burglary and prostitution, to raise money to buy drugs.

Family members also can be hugely impacted when one of them becomes addicted to alcohol or drugs. Those who are addicted can be difficult to live with. They may be physically or verbally abusive. Their behavior is often erratic and can cause a great deal of pain and sadness. Some who are addicted can function adaptively, but most will be poor providers. This means that the family will suffer financially. Those addicted to alcohol or drugs also are often unable to provide proper care to their dependents. This neglect can have a traumatic impact on children. Those addicted also may steal from their family members in order to supply their alcohol or drug habits.

The rest of the family will want to help, but they may have no idea about how to assist, causing feelings of helplessness. Eventually family members may decide that their only option is to break off contact with the relative who is addicted, leading to further guilt.

The effects of substance abuse frequently extend beyond the nuclear family. Extended family members may experience feelings of abandonment, anxiety, fear, anger, concern, embarrassment, or guilt; they may also wish to ignore or cut ties with the person abusing substances. Some family members may even feel the need for legal protection from the person. Moreover, the effects on families may continue for generations. Intergenerational effects of substance abuse can have a negative impact on role modeling, trust, and concepts of normative behavior, which can damage the relationships between generations. For example, a child with a parent who abuses substances may grow up to be an overprotective and controlling parent who does not allow his or her children sufficient autonomy.

Neighbors, friends, and coworkers also experience the effects of substance abuse because a person who abuses substances often is unreliable. Friends may be asked to help financially or in other ways. Coworkers may be forced to compensate for decreased productivity or carry a disproportionate share of the workload. As a consequence, they may resent the person abusing substances.

Therefore, the impact of addiction on society is great. Addiction is closely related to criminal activity and is a drain on societal health care resources.

THE IMPACT OF ECONOMIC CHANGES ON INDIVIDUALS, FAMILIES, ORGANIZATIONS, AND COMMUNITIES

Economic changes can dramatically impact client systems. While economic changes can be attributable to many factors, they are often associated with job loss due to business closing, downsizing, disability, and so on. Job loss is devastating given that a client's biggest asset is his or her ability to work and generate income. When losing a job, a client is faced with readjusting household budgets to account for new economic realities and determining the long-term economic impacts.

Clients experience many emotional reactions to economic change. Often, such change occurs suddenly and is accompanied with shock and disbelief. When shock and disbelief fade, clients experience fear and anxiety about paying their bills, maintaining their households, depleting their savings, losing their homes, finding new income sources, telling others about their loss, the impact that their situation will have on their family, and so on.

Economic changes can also undermine self-worth, personal security, and personal control, resulting in sadness and depression. In addition, clients may have to give up activities and/or certain roles, have fewer social contacts, face disruption in daily routines, and find themselves separated from roles and rewards that give meaning or purpose to their lives. These changes may result in both anger and shame. Even when caused by factors outside their control, clients may feel responsible for their changes in circumstances. There may be shame in failing as providers. With socioeconomic status viewed by society as an indicator of social status and respectability, such changes are often associated with feelings of poor self-worth.

Economic changes also impact families, organizations, and communities. Economic changes are associated with shifts in family roles, relationships, and responsibilities that can result in stress. Economic recession can cause citizens to be cautious as they do not know if the overall economy will improve. People may be fearful of spending money or engaging in activities that may have financial implications. Declines can be seen in moving, marriages, car purchases, and so on. Also, enrollment in higher education often edges up during a recession as individuals graduate with their bachelor's degrees and there are no jobs available. Thus, they decide to pursue master's or some other kinds of professional degrees until they become employed. A recession does not necessarily impact on the rich and poor equally. Those who are low-income prior to a recession are likely to be more adversely affected, thus widening the income gap between these groups.

THE EFFECTS OF PHYSICAL, SEXUAL, AND PSYCHOLOGICAL ABUSE ON INDIVIDUALS, FAMILIES, ORGANIZATIONS, AND COMMUNITIES

Abuse and neglect have both immediate and long-term consequences. The impacts are often influenced by various factors including the extent and type of abuse or neglect, whether it was continual or infrequent, the age at which it occurred, the relationship to the perpetrator (if abuse), and how the abuse or neglect was discovered and addressed. Client personality traits, inner strength, and support systems also influence the effects.

For many, the impacts of abuse and neglect will not be immediately evident. Physical injuries, if there are any, are usually temporary. The more damaging and lasting impacts are those that result from, cognitive and physical development and impaired language due to the abuse and neglect. Children who have been abused and neglected are at risk of academic problems and school failure due to difficulty following rules, being respectful, staying in their seats and keeping on-task, temper tantrums, and/or difficult peer relationships.

In addition, social and emotional problems, poor relationships, substance use and dependency, risky or violent behaviors, and delinquency are manifestations of abuse and neglect. The psychological consequences of abuse and neglect include isolation, fear, inability to trust, low self-esteem, anxiety, depression, and hopelessness. These difficulties can lead to relationship problems and the possibility of antisocial behavioral traits.

It is important to note that not all those who have been abused and neglected will experience physical, behavioral, and/or psychological problems—though they are more likely. Thus, a lack of these problems should not be used as evidence that abuse or neglect did not occur.

The social and economic costs of physical, sexual, and psychological abuse are difficult to calculate. Some costs are straightforward and directly related to maltreatment, such as hospital costs for medical treatment of injuries sustained and foster care costs resulting from the removal of children when they cannot safely remain with their families. Other costs, less directly tied to the incidence of abuse, include lower academic achievement, adult criminality, and lifelong mental health problems. Both direct and indirect costs impact our society and economy.

THE IMPACT OF LIFE CYCLE CHANGES ON SYSTEMS

Crisis situations are viewed as unusual, mostly negative life events that tend to disrupt typical functioning. The concept of crisis is an essential component in the understanding of human growth and development.

Erikson's theory of psychosocial development suggests that crises and major life transitions are similar in their components, though they vary in their degree and intensity.

It is difficult to avoid crises, and the ways in which they are handled is significant in determining subsequent quality of life. The same life events can strengthen one system and make another collapse.

Negative life events are not always the causes of crises. Positive events can also trigger them.

1. Life event occurs

2. Life event is seen as threatening

3. Response occurs in a disorganized manner

4. Search for a solution

5. Adoption of new roles, rules, systems, and/or coping strategies

Crises present opportunities for positive change, and social workers should work toward such change. Crises help strengthen problem-solving skills. During a period of intense crisis, when usual methods of coping fail, new strategies of operating are entertained. The goal is to resolve crises constructively and better prepare families for their next challenges. Quick, highly active responses by social workers are essential during crises to mitigate negative effects.

THE EFFECTS OF LIFE CRISES ON INDIVIDUALS

Trauma is the response that a client has to an extremely negative event. Although trauma is a normal reaction to a horrible event, the effects can be so severe that they interfere with a client's ability to live life. Thus, a social worker is needed to treat the stress and dysfunction caused by the traumatic event and to restore a client to his or her previous emotional state.

Trauma often manifests physically, including both physiological and behavioral symptoms. Behavioral manifestations of trauma include, but are not limited to:

- Insomnia or fatigue
- Using harmful substances
- Keeping to oneself
- Overworking
- Lethargy
- Eating problems
- Drug or alcohol use

- Needing to do certain things over and over
- Always having to have things a certain way
- Doing strange or risky things

Clients may have anxiety or panic attacks and be unable to cope in certain circumstances. Social workers must often work with clients to address the underlying emotional impacts of the trauma in order for clients to make behavioral changes.

Emotional reactions are the common effects of trauma. Impacts of trauma on clients' self-image include, but are not limited to:

- Anxiety
- Denial
- Agitation
- Irritability or rage
- Flashbacks or intrusive memories
- Feeling disconnected from the world
- Unrest in certain situations
- Being "shut down"
- Being very passive
- Feeling depressed
- Guilt/shame/self-blame
- Unusual fears
- Impatience
- Having a hard time concentrating
- Wanting to hurt oneself
- Being unable to trust anyone
- Feeling unlikable
- Feeling unsafe

Clients who experience trauma often believe that they cannot trust, the world is not safe, and they are powerless to change their circumstances. Beliefs about themselves, others, and the world diminish their sense of competency. Thus, clients view themselves as powerless or "damaged" and have trouble feeling hopeful.

Clients who have experienced trauma may display intense emotions toward others, such as friends or family members. Clients can also emotionally retreat from these individuals, choosing to isolate themselves. Thus, trauma can be difficult for those who are close to clients as well.

THE EFFECTS OF LIFE CRISES ON THE FAMILY

Couples and families experience both predictable and unanticipated life cycle changes. Some life cycle changes occur with little notice whereas others are fraught with conflict, emotional upheaval, and discomfort or confusion.

Life cycle changes refer to those events that are linked to human development, first as a single individual and then as a member of a couple and head of a family. The birth, raising, and departure of children from the home, retirement, and death require adaptation and reorganization of roles and rules. The life of families evolves through a fairly predictable sequence of stages.

The following are some examples of predictable life cycle changes in couples and families:

- Adjusting to a committed relationship/marriage
- Family planning
- Childrearing
- Children leaving the home ("empty nest syndrome")
- Caring for aging parents
- Disability and/or death of a partner/spouse

However, in the family life cycle, there are also unpredictable life cycle events such as those caused by premature disability/death of a partner/spouse, divorce, health crisis, unemployment, violence, addiction, and so on. These unpredictable changes are usually the source of major stress, throw a family system out of its normal balance, and precipitate long-term change. All unpredictable stresses affect cohesion and adaptability and may modify boundaries.

Family coping capacity is tied to four factors:

1. Number of previous stressors the members faced
2. Degree of role change involved
3. Social support available
4. Institutional support available

A family with a high capacity for adaptation and above-average cohesion is likely to weather stressor events more easily than families who are rigid and fragmented. No two families react to crisis in the same way; however, families usually go through the following stages which follow one another, may overlap, and may be repeated a number of times.

1. Shock, numbness, disbelief, and denial

2. Anger, confusion, blaming, guilt, and bargaining

3. Depression

4. Reorganization, acceptance and recovery

THE IMPACT ON CLIENTS OF OUT-OF-HOME DISPLACEMENT (E.G., HOSPITALIZATION, JAIL, FOSTER CARE, NATURAL DISASTER)

The homes in which clients live are part of their self-definition. They are decorated to reflect likes or dislikes, telling others about their occupants and accommodating interests such as gardening, cooking, and others. Homes are seen as extensions of their residents and distinguish people from each other.

Behavior is also cued by the physical environment. Homes remind inhabitants of experiences which took place in the past, as well as what to do in the future. Homes are familiar and are often viewed as safe havens where clients can behave without being judged.

Thus, involuntary displacement outside the home due to hospitalization, incarceration, needed safety, or long-term care needs can be traumatic for many reasons. First, such movement may be associated with losses such as those due to health issues, financial concerns, or safety problems. These losses alone can cause depression, anxiety, confusion, and/or other emotional reactions, which are compounded from having to move from the communities or homes in which clients live.

In out-of-home placements, clients may have changes in roles, causing them to develop poor self-image. For example, the roles of neighbor, community leader, gardener, and so on, which provided fulfillment and recognition, may be lost and no longer possible. Since there is also status attached to these roles. Their loss can negatively affect self-image.

There also may be a loss of possessions associated with displacement. Precious items that represent a lifetime of memories may have been destroyed, such as by a natural disaster, or sold/given away as there may be no room to keep them in the new settings—especially if they are shared with others.

There also may be a cost associated with involuntary displacement. For example, long-term care can drain client assets and make clients feel guilty about spending money on themselves or fearful about running out of funds for sustained care and housing.

Out-of-home displacement also often accompanies loss of relationships. Relatives and friends who interfaced with clients in their homes may find it inconvenient or impossible to see them in the new settings. Sometimes the lack of private space in which to visit puts up barriers. Visitors may also be intimidated by the sights and sounds of hospitals, jails, or nursing homes.

Clients frequently do not have the same freedom or control that they had when they were at home. In congregate settings, meals, activities, room cleaning, and bathing may be overseen and scheduled for the sake of organization and efficiency, and there are usually numerous rules, policies, and procedures to follow with less individual autonomy and choice.

THE IMPACT OF DEFENSE MECHANISMS ON BEHAVIOR

To manage internal conflicts, people use defense mechanisms. **Defense mechanisms** are behaviors that protect people from anxiety. Defense mechanisms are automatic, involuntary, usually unconscious psychological activities to exclude unacceptable thoughts, urges, threats, and impulses from awareness for fear of disapproval, punishment, or other negative outcomes. Defense mechanisms are sometimes confused with coping strategies, which are voluntary.

The following are some defense mechanisms (the list of defense mechanisms is huge, and there is no theoretical consensus on the exact number).

1. **Acting Out**—emotional conflict is dealt with through actions rather than feelings (i.e., instead of talking about feeling neglected, a person will get into trouble to get attention).

2. **Compensation**—enables one to make up for real or fancied deficiencies (i.e., a person who stutters becomes a very expressive writer; a short man assumes a cocky, overbearing manner).

3. **Conversion**—repressed urge is expressed disguised as a disturbance of body function, usually of the sensory, voluntary nervous system (as pain, deafness, blindness, paralysis, convulsions, tics).

4. **Decompensation**—deterioration of existing defenses.

5. **Denial**—a primitive defense; inability to acknowledge true significance of thoughts, feelings, wishes, behavior, or external reality factors that are consciously intolerable.

6. **Devaluation**—a defense mechanism frequently used by persons with borderline personality organization in which a person attributes exaggerated negative qualities to self or another. It is the split of primitive idealization.

7. **Dissociation**—a process that enables a person to split mental functions in a manner that allows him or her to express forbidden or unconscious impulses without taking responsibility for the action, either because he or she is unable to remember the disowned

behavior, or because it is not experienced as his or her own (i.e., pathologically expressed as fugue states, amnesia, or dissociative neurosis, or normally expressed as daydreaming).

8. **Displacement**—directing an impulse, wish, or feeling toward a person or situation that is not its real object, thus permitting expression in a less threatening situation (i.e., a man angry at his boss kicks his dog).

9. **Idealization**—overestimation of an admired aspect or attribute of another.

10. **Identification**—universal mechanism whereby a person patterns himself or herself after a significant other. Plays a major role in personality development, especially superego development.

11. **Identification With the Aggressor**—mastering anxiety by identifying with a powerful aggressor (such as an abusing parent) to counteract feelings of helplessness and to feel powerful oneself. Usually involves behaving like the aggressor (i.e., abusing others after one has been abused oneself).

12. **Incorporation**—primitive mechanism in which psychic representation of a person (or parts of a person) is/are figuratively ingested.

13. **Inhibition**—loss of motivation to engage in (usually pleasurable) activity avoided because it might stir up conflict over forbidden impulses (i.e., writing, learning, or work blocks or social shyness).

14. **Introjection**—loved or hated external objects are symbolically absorbed within self (converse of projection) (i.e., in severe depression, unconscious unacceptable hatred is turned toward self).

15. **Intellectualization**—where the person avoids uncomfortable emotions by focusing on facts and logic. Emotional aspects are completely ignored as being irrelevant. Jargon is often used as a device of intellectualization. By using complex terminology, the focus is placed on the words rather than the emotions.

16. **Isolation of Affect**—unacceptable impulse, idea, or act is separated from its original memory source, thereby removing the original emotional charge associated with it.

17. **Projection**—primitive defense; attributing one's disowned attitudes, wishes, feelings, and urges to some external object or person.

18. **Projective Identification**—a form of projection utilized by persons with Borderline Personality Disorder—unconsciously perceiving others' behavior as a reflection of one's own identity.

19. **Rationalization**—third line of defense; not unconscious. Giving believable explanation for irrational behavior; motivated by

unacceptable unconscious wishes or by defenses used to cope with such wishes.

20. **Reaction Formation**—person adopts affects, ideas, attitudes, or behaviors that are opposites of those he or she harbors consciously or unconsciously (i.e., excessive moral zeal masking strong, but repressed, asocial impulses or being excessively sweet to mask unconscious anger).

21. **Regression**—partial or symbolic return to more infantile patterns of reacting or thinking. Can be in service to ego (i.e., as dependency during illness).

22. **Repression**—key mechanism; expressed clinically by amnesia or symptomatic forgetting serving to banish unacceptable ideas, fantasies, affects, or impulses from consciousness.

23. **Splitting**—defensive mechanism associated with Borderline Personality Disorder in which a person perceives self and others as "all good" or "all bad." Splitting serves to protect the good objects. *A person cannot integrate the good and bad in people.*

24. **Sublimation**—potentially maladaptive feelings or behaviors are diverted into socially acceptable, adaptive channels (i.e., a person who has angry feelings channels them into athletics).

25. **Substitution**—unattainable or unacceptable goal, emotion, or object is replaced by one more attainable or acceptable.

26. **Symbolization**—a mental representation stands for some other thing, class of things, or attribute. This mechanism underlies dream formation and some other symptoms (such as conversion reactions, obsessions, compulsions) with a link between the latent meaning of the symptom and the symbol; usually unconscious.

27. **Turning Against Self**—defense to deflect hostile aggression or other unacceptable impulses from another to self.

28. **Undoing**—a person uses words or actions to symbolically reverse or negate unacceptable thoughts, feelings, or actions (i.e., a person compulsively washing hands to deal with obsessive thoughts).

Intervention Planning

8

CRITERIA USED IN SELECTING INTERVENTION/TREATMENT MODALITIES

Evidence-based social work practice combines research knowledge, professional/clinical expertise, social work values, and client preferences/circumstances. It is a dynamic and fluid process whereby social workers seek, interpret, use, and evaluate the best available information in an effort to make the best practice decisions.

Decisions are based on the use of many sources, ranging from systematic reviews and meta-analyses to less rigorous research designs.

Social workers often use "evidence-based practice" to refer to programs that have a proven track record. However, it takes a long time for a program or intervention to be "evidence based." Thus, most interventions in social work need more empirically supported research in order to accurately apply the term. "Evidence-informed practice" may be more appropriate.

Some questions guide the selection of intervention modalities:

■ How will the recommended modality assist with the achievement of the treatment goal and will it help get the outcomes desired?

■ How does the recommended treatment modality promote client strengths, capabilities, and interests?

■ What are the risks and benefits associated with the recommended modality?

■ Is there research or evidence to support the use of this modality for this target problem?

- Is this modality appropriate and tested on those with the same or similar cultural background as the client?

- What training and experience does a social worker have with the recommended modality?

- Is the recommended modality evidence-based or consistent with available research? If not, why?

- Was the recommended modality discussed with and selected by a client?

- Will the use of the recommended modality be assessed periodically? When? How?

- Is the recommended treatment modality covered by insurance? What is the cost? How does it compare to the use of other options?

THE COMPONENTS AND METHODS USED TO DEVELOP AN INTERVENTION/TREATMENT OR SERVICE PLAN

The goals of intervention and means used to achieve these goals are incorporated in a contractual agreement between a client and a social worker. The contract (also called an intervention, treatment, or service plan) may be informal or written. The contract specifies problem(s) to be worked on; the goals to reduce the problem(s); client and worker roles in the process; the interventions or techniques to be employed; the means of monitoring progress; stipulations for renegotiating the contract; and the time, place, fee, and frequency of meetings.

The problem-solving process drives the methods used to develop a contract. The steps that precede planning include engagement and assessment, which are both essential to ensuring that a social worker and client have created a therapeutic alliance and collected the information needed to move into planning, the third stage.

In planning, a social worker and client should be:

1. Defining the problem (in a well-defined, clear, and data-driven format)

2. Examining the causes of the problem and how it relates to other positive or negative aspects of a client's life

3. Generating possible solutions that will impact on the problem

4. Identifying the driving and restraining forces related to implementation of each of the possible solutions

5. Rating the driving and restraining forces related to consistency and potency

6. Prioritizing these solutions based on these ratings;

7. Developing SMART objectives—specific, measurable, achievable, relevant, and time-specific—related to the chosen solutions

8. Creating strategies and activities related to the objectives

THE EFFECTS OF THE CLIENT'S DEVELOPMENTAL LEVEL ON THE CREATION OF AN INTERVENTION/ TREATMENT PLAN

A social worker develops an intervention or a treatment plan by consulting the relevant practice research and then flexibly implementing an approach to fit a client's needs and circumstances. The intervention or treatment plan is driven by the data collected as part of assessment. Assessment is informed by current human behavior and development research that provides key information about how clients behave and research about risk and resilience factors that affect human functioning. These theories inform social workers about what skills, techniques, and strategies must be used by social workers, clients, and others for the purpose of improving well-being. These techniques and strategies are outlined in an intervention or a treatment plan.

It should be reviewed during the intervention, at termination, and, if possible, following the termination of services to make adjustments, ensure progress, and determine the sustainability of change after treatment.

PERMANENCY PLANNING

Permanency planning is an approach to child welfare that is based on the belief that children need permanence to thrive. Child protection services should focus on getting children into, and maintaining, permanent homes. Permanency planning received a lot of attention in the 1970s. Legislation in the United States, such as the Adoption Assistance and Child Welfare Act of 1980, promotes permanency planning and creates mandates related to child placements.

In permanency planning, the first goal is to get children back into their original homes. This can be achieved with a thorough investigation into child protection situations to determine if homes are safe and, if needed, exploring ideas for making them safer or more enriching for children.

Supports can include getting caregivers services for meeting needs or providing education, if needed, to ensure adequate and quality care. If children cannot return to their original homes, steps need to be made so that they can get into permanent living situations as quickly as possible with adults with whom they have continuous and reciprocal relationships.

METHODS USED TO DEVELOP MEASURABLE OBJECTIVES TO ASSESS CLIENT CHANGE

When social workers are creating intervention or service plans, it is essential that goals are written in observable and measurable terms. In order to achieve this aim, the following should be included in each goal contained in the intervention or service plan.

- *Criteria*: What behavior must be exhibited, how often, over what period of time, and under what conditions to demonstrate achievement of the goal?
- *Method for evaluation*: How will progress be measured?
- *Schedule for evaluation*: When, how often, and on what dates or intervals of time will progress be measured?

There may also be benchmarks or the intermediate knowledge, skills, and/or behaviors that must be learned/achieved in order for a client to reach his or her ultimate goal.

Objectives break down the goals into discrete components or subparts, which are steps toward the final desired outcome.

THE CLIENT'S ROLE IN THE INTERVENTION PROCESS

The participation of clients in the process of identifying what is important to them now and in the future, and acting upon these priorities, is paramount. Clients' participation in the process will reduce resistance, increase motivation to change, and ensure sustainability of progress made.

In order to involve clients, social workers must continually listen to, learn about, and facilitate opportunities with clients who they are serving. Client involvement should not just occur during intervention planning, but instead during the entire problem-solving process.

In *engagement*, a social worker should be actively involved with a client in determining why treatment was sought; what has precipitated the desire to change now; the parameters of the helping relationship, including defining the roles of a social worker and client; and the expectations for treatment (what will occur and when it will happen). Client involvement is essential in determining what is important to a client now and in the future.

In *assessment*, a client is the source of providing essential information upon which to define the problem and solutions, as well as identifying collateral contacts from which gaps in data can be collected.

In *planning*, a client and social worker must develop a common understanding of a client's preferred lifestyle. Goals are developed from this common understanding in order to provide a direction to help a client move toward this lifestyle. Specific action plans are developed and agreed upon in order to specify who will do what, what and how resources will be needed and used, and timelines for implementation and review.

In *intervention*, a client must be actively involved in mobilizing his or her support network to realize continued progress and sustainable change. A client must bring to the attention of a social worker issues that arise which may threaten goal attainment. Progress, based upon client reports, must be tracked and plans/timelines adjusted accordingly.

In *evaluation*, subjective reports of a client, in conjunction with objective indicators of progress, should be used to determine when goals or objectives have been met and whether new goals or objectives should be set. Client self-monitoring is a good way to involve a client so he or she can see and track progress himself or herself.

In *termination*, a client should reflect on what has been achieved and anticipate what supports are in place if problems arise again. Although this is the last stage of the problem-solving process, it still requires active involvement by both a social worker and client.

THE METHODS USED TO DEVELOP BEHAVIORAL OBJECTIVES

When outlining the goals for treatment, it is important that the broad over-arching aims of treatment are broken down by a social worker and client into smaller, more tangible items that must be achieved in order to reach the overall goal. Behavioral objectives are the smaller, observable, and measurable intermediate steps that lead to broader long-term goals. Behavioral objectives help a social worker and client understand whether the strategies they are using to achieve the goal are resulting in change or whether they need to modify their efforts to improve the likelihood of accomplishing the desired outcome.

There are several important elements of behavioral objectives.

1. Good behavioral objectives are client-oriented and place the emphasis upon what a client will need to do in order for change to occur.

2. Good behavioral objectives are clear and understandable and contain a clearly stated verb that describes a definite action or behavior.

3. Good behavioral objectives are observable and describe an action that results in observable products.

4. Good behavioral objectives contain the behavior targeted for change, conditions under which a behavior will be performed, and the criteria for determining when the acceptable performance of the behavior occurs.

THE METHODS USED TO FORMULATE A TIME FRAME FOR INTERVENTIONS

Evaluating progress is a critical part of the problem-solving process. Examining with a client what has occurred and what still needs to occur involves him or her in treatment decisions.

Evaluation methods can be simple or complex. They can rely on quantitative information that shows data on reductions in target behaviors, health care improvements, or psychiatric symptom increases, and/or qualitative information in which a client and/or social worker subjectively report on progress made in various areas.

When evaluating progress, a social worker and client should gather all needed information and identify factors that helped or hindered progress. Goals outlined in the contract should be modified, if needed, based upon the outcome of the evaluation.

Social workers should assist clients to understand the progress they have made so they can clearly understand and celebrate their accomplishments, as well as identify areas that need attention. This process should ensure that clients understand why progress has happened, as well as include a dialogue about any changes that need to occur in the problem-solving process to facilitate continued growth.

THE METHODS USED TO IDENTIFY LEARNING NEEDS FOR CLIENTS

There are six levels of cognition:

1. Knowledge: rote memorization, recognition, or recall of facts
2. Comprehension: understanding what the facts mean
3. Application: correct use of the facts, rules, or ideas
4. Analysis: breaking down information into component parts
5. Synthesis: combination of facts, ideas, or information to make a new whole
6. Evaluation: judging or forming an opinion about the information or situation

Ideally, in order for a client to learn, there should be objectives at each of these levels. Clients may have goals to learn in any of three domains of development:

1. *Cognitive:* mental skills (knowledge)
2. *Affective:* growth in feelings or emotional areas (attitude or self)
3. *Psychomotor:* manual or physical skills (skills)

Assessment of Strengths and Challenges

9

THE METHODS USED TO ASSESS CLIENTS' STRENGTHS AND CHALLENGES

Strength is the capacity to cope with difficulties, to maintain functioning under stress, to return to equilibrium in the face of significant trauma, to use external challenges to promote growth, and to be resilient by using social supports.

There is not a single approach to the assessment of strengths. However, social workers can view all of these areas as strengths or protective factors that can assist clients when they experience challenges. These characteristics can also be abilities that need to be bolstered as a focus of treatment.

1. Cognitive and appraisal skills

- Intellectual/cognitive ability
- Creativity, curiosity
- Initiative, perseverance, patience
- Common sense
- Ability to anticipate problems
- Realistic appraisal of demands and capacities
- Ability to use feedback

2. Defenses and coping mechanisms

- Ability to regulate impulses and affect
- Self-soothing
- Flexible; can handle stressors

3. Temperamental and dispositional factors

- Belief in trustworthiness of others
- Belief in justice
- Self-esteem, self-worth
- Sense of mastery, confidence, optimism
- Ability to tolerate ambiguity and uncertainty
- Ability to make sense of negative events
- Sense of humor
- Lack of hostility, anger, anxiety
- Optimistic, open
- Ability to grieve
- Lack of helplessness
- Responsibility for decisions
- Sense of direction, mission, purpose

4. Interpersonal skills and supports

- Ability to develop/maintain good relationships
- Ability to confide in others
- Problem-solving skills
- Capacity for empathy
- Presence of an intimate relationship
- Sense of security

5. Other factors

- Supportive social institutions, such as church
- Good physical health
- Adequate income
- Supportive family and friends

THE FACTORS USED IN DETERMINING THE CLIENT'S ABILITY TO USE INTERVENTION/TREATMENT

Social workers should not assume that clients are ready or have the skills needed to make changes in their lives. Clients may be oppositional, reactionary, noncompliant, and/or unmotivated. These attitudes or behaviors are often referred to as resistance.

There are indicators that a social worker should use as evidence that a client may be resistant or not ready/able to fully participate in services. These indicators include:

- Limiting the amount of information communicated to a social worker
- Silence/minimal talking during sessions
- Engaging in small talk with a social worker about irrelevant topics

- Engaging in intellectual talk by using technical terms or abstract concepts or asking questions of a social worker that are not related to client issues or problems
- Being preoccupied with past events, instead of current issues
- Discounting, censoring, or editing thoughts when asked about them by a social worker
- False promising
- Flattering a social worker in an attempt to "soften" him or her so client will not to be pushed to act
- Not keeping appointments
- Payment delays or refusals

It is essential to determine the extent to which this resistance or these inabilities are caused by a client, a social worker, and/or the conditions present.

A client may be resistant due to feelings of guilt or shame and may not be ready to recognize or address the feelings and behaviors being brought up by a social worker. Clients may be frightened of change and may be getting some benefit from the problems that they are experiencing.

Social workers may experience a lack of readiness because they have not developed sufficient rapport with clients. There also may not be clear expectations by clients of their role versus those of social workers. Social workers need to use interventions that are appropriate for clients.

Sometimes a lack of readiness or ability is a result of external factors, such as changes in clients' living situations, physical health problems, lack of social support, and/or financial problems.

Whatever the causes, social workers must address these barriers because clients will not make changes until they are ready and able.

THE METHODS USED IN ASSESSING EGO STRENGTHS

Ego strength is the ability of the ego to effectively deal with the demands of the id, the superego, and reality. It is a basis for resilience and helps maintain emotional stability by coping with internal and external stress.

Traits usually considered to be indicators of positive ego strengths include tolerance of pain associated with loss, disappointment, shame, or guilt; forgiveness of others, with feelings of compassion rather than anger; persistence and perseverance in the pursuit of goals; and/or openness, flexibility, and creativity in learning to adapt. Those with positive ego strength are less likely to have psychiatric crises.

Other indicators of positive ego strength include clients:

- Acknowledging their feelings—including grief, insecurity, loneliness, and anxiety
- Not getting overwhelmed by their moods
- Pushing forward after loss and not being paralyzed by self-pity or resentment
- Using painful events to strengthen themselves
- Knowing that painful feelings will eventually fade
- Empathizing with others without trying to reduce or eliminate their pain
- Being self-disciplined and fighting addictive urges
- Taking responsibility for actions
- Holding themselves accountable
- Not blaming others
- Accepting themselves with their limitations
- Setting firm limits even if it means disappointing others or risking rejection
- Avoiding people who drain them physically and/or emotionally

THE INDICATORS OF MOTIVATION AND RESISTANCE

It is critical that a social worker be able to identify indicators of motivation and resistance. It is helpful to detect when clients are eager to modify their behaviors, as well as when they are unlikely to respond to interventions. Building upon motivation and addressing resistance early in the problem-solving process increases the likelihood that real change will take place.

Motivation of clients is essential as a social worker will not be able to assist clients who do not want to be helped. Change requires willingness to engage in different actions, as well as a drive to alter current situations. Motivation must be detected, sustained, and built upon as clients will likely encounter difficulties or setbacks which need to be overcome. Motivated clients are energetic, engaged, and seek feedback, and are open to new ideas and suggestions.

Resistance can take many forms. It can include, but is not limited to, changing the subject, talking about unimportant or unrelated topics, complaining, criticizing, making excuses, blaming others, challenging others, or even being late to or missing appointments. Sometimes resistance is out in the open (overt), such as making public statements, but more often it starts out in a more covert way.

Resistance can also be passive or active. Passive resistance occurs where clients do not take specific actions, though they do not openly express their objections. Active resistance occurs where clients are taking specific and deliberate action to resist the change.

Resistance can also happen on an individual level or by a group that has joined together. People will usually not go to the bother of organizing unless they have serious issues with the change.

Identification of Common Indicators of Risks and Disorders

10

THE EFFECTS OF BODY IMAGE ON SELF-IMAGE

Body image is the way one perceives and relates to his or her body, and how one thinks he or she is seen.

Body image affects nearly everyone from time to time. Body image is not only influenced by the perceptions of others, but by the media and cultural forces as well. Senses are bombarded by an onslaught of mixed messages about how one "should" look or think about his or her body.

Having a healthy body image is a key to well-being, both mentally and physically. A positive body image means that, most of the time, a client has a realistic perception of, and feels comfortable with, his or her looks.

Factors associated with positive body image:

- Acceptance and appreciation of natural body shape and body differences

- Self-worth not tied to appearance

- Confidence in and comfort with body

- An unreasonable amount of time is not spent worrying about food, weight, or calories

- Judgment of others is not made related to their body weight, shape, and/or eating or exercise habits

- Knowing physical appearance says very little about character and value as a person

Factors of negative body image:

- Distorted perception of shape or body parts, unlike what they really are
- Believing only other people are attractive and that body size or shape is a sign of personal failure
- Feeling body doesn't measure up to family, social, or media ideals
- Ashamed, self-conscious, and anxious about body
- Uncomfortable and awkward in body
- Constant negative thoughts about body and comparisons to others

Some possible effects of a negative body image:

- Emotional distress
- Low self-esteem
- Unhealthy dieting habits
- Anxiety
- Depression
- Eating disorders
- Social withdrawal or isolation

THE INDICATORS OF SOMATIZATION

Somatization is the unconscious process by which psychological distress is expressed as physical symptoms. Somatic symptoms often occur as reactions to stressful situations and are not considered abnormal if they occur sporadically. However, some clients experience continuing somatic symptoms and even seek medical care for them.

Persistent somatization is associated with considerable distress and disability. Somatization may lead to overutilization of medical care, including unnecessary medical tests, and even increased hospitalization rates.

Not all somatizing clients are motivated by an unconscious wish to adopt the sick role, as is observed in clients with Factitious Disorder. Clients may vary in their degree of conviction that their symptoms are caused by a physical illness or disease. Clients may also present in multiple ways, including having multiple unexplained somatic symptoms, exhibiting predominantly illness worry or hypochondriacal beliefs, and/or displaying somatization as a manifestation of a variety of mental disorders.

THE INDICATORS OF MALINGERING

Malingering is not considered a mental illness. In the *Diagnostic and Statistical Manual of Mental Disorders*, Fifth Edition *(DSM®-5)*, malingering receives a V code as one of the other conditions that may be a focus of clinical attention. The *DSM-5* defines malingering as intentionally falsely or grossly exaggerating physical or psychological problems. Motivation for malingering is usually external, such as avoiding work, obtaining financial reward, avoiding legal action, and so on.

Malingering varies in intensity, from all symptoms being falsified to some symptoms being falsified or symptoms being exaggerated. Malingering is not easy to diagnose because of the difficulty in gathering external evidence.

Prolonged direct observation can reveal evidence of malingering because it is difficult for a client who is malingering to maintain consistency with the false or exaggerated claims for extended periods. Malingering can be detected by discrepancies between the claimed distress and the objective findings or lack of cooperation during evaluation and in complying with prescribed treatment.

Malingering is different from Factitious Disorder (in which the motive is the desire to occupy a sick role, rather than some form of material gain) and Somatic Symptom and Related Disorders (in which symptoms are not produced willfully).

USE OF THE CURRENT *DIAGNOSTIC AND STATISTICAL MANUAL OF MENTAL DISORDERS* OF THE AMERICAN PSYCHIATRIC ASSOCIATION

The *DSM-5* was published in 2013 and is the current diagnostic framework used by social workers. It has many revisions in content and format from the *DSM-IV-TR*, which was used previously.

The *DSM-5* deleted a separate section for "Disorders Usually First Diagnosed in Infancy, Childhood, or Adolescence" and now lists them in other chapters.

The *DSM-5* replaces the NOS categories with two options: Other Specified Disorder and Unspecified Disorder. The first allows a social worker to specify the reason that the criteria for a specific disorder are not met, whereas the second allows a social worker the option to forgo specification.

The *DSM-5* has discarded the multiaxial system of diagnosis (formerly Axis I, Axis II, and Axis III) and combines the first three axes outlined in past editions of the *DSM* into one axis with all mental and other medical diagnoses.

It has replaced Axis IV with significant psychosocial and contextual features and dropped Axis V (Global Assessment of Functioning, known as GAF).

The World Health Organization's Disability Assessment Schedule (WHODAS) is added to Section III, Emerging Measures and Models, under Assessment Measures.

1. *Neurodevelopmental Disorders*

This is a new chapter.

Intellectual Disabilities
Intellectual Disability (Intellectual Developmental Disorder)
   "Mental retardation" is now Intellectual Disability (Intellectual Developmental Disorder)
      Intelligence quotient (IQ) scores and adaptive functioning are both used in determining a client's ability.

Global Developmental Delay

Unspecified Intellectual Disability (Intellectual Developmental Disorder)

Communication Disorders
Language Disorder

Speech Sound Disorder (previously Phonological Disorder) Childhood-Onset Fluency Disorder (Stuttering)

Social (Pragmatic) Communication Disorder
   This is a new condition that has impaired social verbal and non-verbal communication.

Unspecified Communication Disorder

Autism Spectrum Disorder
Autism Spectrum Disorder
   Autism Spectrum Disorder incorporates Asperger Disorder, Childhood Disintegrative Disorder, and Pervasive Developmental Disorder Not Otherwise Specified (PDD-NOS).

Attention-Deficit/Hyperactivity Disorder
Attention-Deficit/Hyperactivity Disorder
   Must appear by age 12.

Other Specified Attention-Deficit/Hyperactivity Disorder

Unspecified Attention-Deficit/Hyperactivity Disorder

Specific Learning Disorder
Specific Learning Disorder

Motor Disorders (new subcategory)
Developmental Coordination Disorder

Stereotypic Movement Disorder

Tic Disorders
  Tourette's Disorder
  Persistent (Chronic) Motor or Vocal Tic Disorder
  Provisional Tic Disorder
  Other Specified Tic Disorder
  Unspecified Tic Disorder

Other Neurodevelopmental Disorders
Other Specified Neurodevelopmental Disorder

Unspecified Neurodevelopmental Disorder

2. *Schizophrenia Spectrum and Other Psychotic Disorders*

Schizophrenia (all subtypes of Schizophrenia were deleted— paranoid, disorganized, catatonic, undifferentiated, and residual)

Schizotypal (Personality) Disorder
  Delusional Disorder (has new criteria and is no longer separate from Shared Delusional Disorder)

Brief Psychotic Disorder

Schizophreiform Disorder

Schizoaffective Disorder
  Requires a major mood episode.

Substance/Medication-Induced Psychotic Disorder

Psychotic Disorder Due to Another Medical Condition

Catatonia
  Requires 3 of a total of 12 symptoms. Catatonia may be a specifier for Depressive, Bipolar, and Psychotic disorders; part of another medical condition; or of another specified diagnosis.

Catatonia Associated With Another Mental Disorder (Catatonia Specifier)

Catatonic Disorder Due to Another Medical Condition

Unspecified Catatonia

Other Specified Schizophrenia Spectrum and Other Psychotic Disorders

Unspecified Schizophrenia Spectrum and Other Psychotic Disorder

3. *Bipolar and Related Disorders*

New specifier "with mixed features" can be applied to Bipolar I Disorder, Bipolar II Disorder, Bipolar Disorder NED (Not Elsewhere Defined, previously called "NOS"/Not Otherwise Specified). Anxiety symptoms are a specifier (called "anxious distress") added to Bipolar Disorder and to Depressive Disorders (but are not part of the bipolar diagnostic criteria).

Bipolar I Disorder

Bipolar II Disorder Cyclothymic Disorder

Substance/Medication-Induced Bipolar and Related Disorder Bipolar and Related Disorder Due to Another Medical Condition Other Specified Bipolar and Related Disorder (allowed for particular conditions)

Unspecified Bipolar and Related Disorder

4. *Depressive Disorders*

Anxiety symptoms are a specifier (called "anxious distress"). The bereavement exclusion was removed.

Disruptive Mood Dysregulation Disorder (DMDD; this is a new disorder for children up to age 18 years)

Major Depressive Disorder, Single and Recurrent Episodes (new specifier "with mixed features" can be applied)

Persistent Depressive Disorder (previously Dysthymia)

Premenstrual Dysphoric Disorder (new disorder)

Substance/Medication-Induced Depressive Disorder

Depressive Disorder Due to Another Medical Condition

Other Specified Depressive Disorder

Unspecified Depressive Disorder

5. *Anxiety Disorders*

Requirement that clients "must recognize that their fear and anxiety are excessive or unreasonable" is removed. The duration of at least 6 months now applies to everyone (not only to children).

Separation Anxiety Disorder (previously a Disorder of Early Onset)

Selective Mutism (previously a Disorder of Early Onset)

Specific Phobia

Social Anxiety Disorder (Social Phobia)

Panic Disorder (it is separated from Agoraphobia)

Panic Attack (Specifier; applies to all *DSM-5* diagnoses)

Agoraphobia

Generalized Anxiety Disorder

Substance/Medication-Induced Anxiety Disorder

Anxiety Disorder Due to Another Medical Condition

Other Specified Anxiety Disorder

Unspecified Anxiety Disorder

6. *Obsessive-Compulsive and Related Disorders*

Obsessive-Compulsive Disorder

Body Dysmorphic Disorder (new criteria were added that describes repetitive behaviors or mental acts that may arise with perceived defects or flaws in physical appearance)
> A specifier was expanded to allow for good or fair insight, poor insight, and "absent insight/delusional" (i.e., complete conviction that obsessive-compulsive disorder beliefs are true).

Hoarding Disorder (new disorder defined as a persistent difficulty discarding or parting with possessions due to a perceived need to save the items and distress associated with discarding them)
> A specifier was expanded to allow for good or fair insight, poor insight, and "absent insight/delusional" (i.e., complete conviction that obsessive-compulsive disorder beliefs are true).

Trichotillomania (Hair-Pulling Disorder; was moved from "Impulse-Control Disorders Not Elsewhere Classified.")

Excoriation (Skin-Picking) Disorder (new disorder)

Substance/Medication-Induced Obsessive-Compulsive and Related Disorder (new disorder)

Obsessive-Compulsive and Related Disorder Due to Another Medical Condition (new disorder)

Other Specified Obsessive-Compulsive and Related Disorder (new disorder)
> Includes body-focused repetitive behavior disorder (behaviors like nail biting, lip biting, and cheek chewing, other than hair pulling and skin picking) or obsessional jealousy.

Unspecified Obsessive-Compulsive and Related Disorder (new disorder)

7. *Trauma- and Stressor-Related Disorders*

Separate criteria were added for children 6 years old or younger.

Reactive Attachment Disorder (was previously a subtype – emotionally withdrawn/inhibited)

Disinhibited Social Engagement Disorder (indiscriminately social/disinhibited was previously a subtype, but now a separate disorder)

Posttraumatic Stress Disorder (criteria were modified and now has four clusters)

Acute Stress Disorder (criteria were modified)

Adjustment Disorders (moved, and now recognized as a stress-response syndrome)

Other Specified Trauma- and Stressor-Related Disorder

Unspecified Trauma- and Stressor-Related Disorder

8. *Dissociative Disorders*

Dissociative Identity Disorder (the criteria were expanded to include "possession-form phenomena and functional neurological symptoms")

It is made clear that "transitions in identity may be observable by others or self-reported"; criterion was also modified for clients who experience gaps in recall of everyday events—not only trauma.

Dissociative Amnesia (Dissociative Fugue became a specifier)

Depersonalization/Derealization Disorder (previously Depersonalization Disorder)

Other Specified Dissociative Disorder

Unspecified Dissociative Disorder

9. *Somatic Symptom and Related Disorders*

Somatoform Disorders are now called Somatic Symptom and Related Disorders. Somatization Disorder, Hypochondriasis, Pain Disorder, and Undifferentiated Somatoform Disorder were deleted. They are defined by positive symptoms, and the use of medically unexplained symptoms is minimized, except in the cases of Conversion Disorder and Pseudocyesis (false pregnancy). People with chronic pain can now be diagnosed with Somatic Symptom Disorder With Predominant Pain; or Psychological Factors That Affect Other Medical Conditions; or an Adjustment Disorder.

Somatic Symptom Disorder (Somatization Disorder and Undifferentiated Somatoform Disorder were combined to become Somatic Symptom Disorder, a diagnosis that no longer requires a specific number of somatic symptoms).

Illness Anxiety Disorder

Conversion Disorder (Functional Neurological Symptom Disorder; criteria were changed)

Psychological Factors Affecting Other Medical Conditions (new disorder)

Factitious Disorder

Other Specified Somatic Symptom and Related Disorder

Unspecified Somatic Symptom and Related Disorder

10. *Feeding and Eating Disorders*

Pica (criteria now refer to clients of any age)

Rumination Disorder (criteria now refer to clients of any age)

Avoidant/Restrictive Food Intake Disorder (previously "Feeding Disorder of Infancy or Early Childhood" and the criteria were expanded)

Anorexia Nervosa (criteria changed and there is no longer a requirement of amenorrhea)

Bulimia Nervosa (requirements were changed from "at least twice weekly for 6 months" to "at least once weekly over the last 3 months")

Binge-Eating Disorder (new disorder)

Other Specified Feeding or Eating Disorder

Unspecified Feeding or Eating Disorder

11. *Elimination Disorders*

Enuresis

Social worker needs to rule out medical reasons for bed-wetting—infection, physiological abnormalities.

Encopresis

Involves repeated passage of feces in inappropriate places, causing embarrassment, and client may avoid situations that lead to embarrassment—camp or sleepovers.

Other Specified Elimination Disorder

Unspecified Elimination Disorder

12. *Sleep–Wake Disorders*

"Sleep Disorders Related to Another Mental Disorder" and "Sleep Disorders Related to a General Medical Condition" were deleted.

Insomnia Disorder (previously Primary Insomnia) Hypersomnolence Disorder

Narcolepsy

Breathing-Related Sleep Disorders

Obstructive Sleep Apnea Hypopnea (new disorder)

Central Sleep Apnea (new disorder)

Sleep-Related Hypoventilation (new disorder)

Circadian Rhythm Sleep–Wake Disorders
Includes advanced sleep phase syndrome, irregular sleep–wake type, and non-24-hour sleep–wake type. Jet lag was removed.

Parasomnias

Non-Rapid Eye Movement Sleep Arousal Disorders

Sleepwalking Sleep Terrors Nightmare Disorder

Rapid Eye Movement Sleep Behavior Disorder (a separate disorder instead of being listed under "Dyssomnia Not Otherwise Specified")

Restless Legs Syndrome (a separate disorder instead of being listed under "Dyssomnia Not Otherwise Specified")

Substance/Medication-Induced Sleep Disorder

Other Specified Insomnia Disorder

Unspecified Insomnia Disorder

Other Specified Hypersomnolence Disorder Unspecified Hypersomnolence Disorder Other Specified Sleep–Wake Disorder Unspecified Sleep–Wake Disorder

13. *Sexual Dysfunctions*

DSM-5 has sex-specific sexual dysfunctions. Sexual Aversion Disorder was deleted. Sexual Dysfunctions (except Substance-/Medication-Induced Sexual Dysfunction) now require a duration of approximately 6 months and more exact severity criteria. Subtypes for all disorders include only "lifelong versus acquired" and "generalized versus situational."

Two subtypes were deleted: "Sexual Dysfunction Due to a General Medical Condition" and "Due to Psychological Versus Combined Factors."

Delayed Ejaculation

Erectile Disorder

Female Orgasmic Disorder

Female Sexual Interest/Arousal Disorder (for females, Sexual Desire and Arousal Disorders are combined into this single disorder)

Genito-Pelvic Pain/Penetration Disorder (a new diagnosis, combines Vaginismus and Dyspareunia)

Male Hypoactive Sexual Desire Disorder

Premature (Early) Ejaculation

Substance/Medication-Induced Sexual Dysfunction

Other Specified Sexual Dysfunction

Unspecified Sexual Dysfunction

14. *Gender Dysphoria* (It is now its own category)

Separate criteria for children, adolescents, and adults that are appropriate for varying developmental states are added. Subtypes of Gender Identity Disorder based on sexual orientation were deleted. Among other wording changes, Criterion A and Criterion B (cross-gender identification and aversion toward one's gender) were combined. Gender Dysphoria is a new diagnostic class with revised criteria to better characterize the experiences in children, adolescents, and adults.

Gender Dysphoria

Other Specified Gender Dysphoria

Unspecified Gender Dysphoria

15. *Disruptive, Impulse-Control, and Conduct Disorders*

Oppositional Defiant Disorder (there are three types: angry/irritable mood, argumentative/defiant behavior, and vindictiveness; the Conduct Disorder exclusion is deleted; the criteria were also changed, with a note on frequency requirements and a measure of severity)

Intermittent Explosive Disorder (a specifier was added for people with limited "prosocial emotion," showing callous and unemotional traits)

Conduct Disorder

Antisocial Personality Disorder

Pyromania

Kleptomania

Other Specified Disruptive, Impulse-Control, and Conduct Disorder Oppositional Defiant Disorder, Conduct Disorder, and Disruptive Behavior Disorder Not Otherwise Specified became Other Specified and Unspecified Disruptive Disorder, Impulse-Control, and Conduct Disorders.

Unspecified Disruptive, Impulse-Control, and Conduct Disorder

16. *Substance-Related and Addictive Disorders*

Substance Abuse and Substance Dependence have been combined into the single Substance Use Disorders specific to each substance of abuse.

"Recurrent legal problems" was deleted and "craving or a strong desire or urge to use a substance" was added to the criteria.

The threshold of the number of criteria that must be met was changed. Severity from mild to severe is based on the number of criteria endorsed.

New specifiers were added for early and sustained remission along with new specifiers for "in a controlled environment" and "on maintenance therapy."

Substance-Related Disorders

Substance Use Disorders

Substance-Induced Disorders

Substance Intoxication and Withdrawal

Substance/Medication-Induced Mental Disorders

Alcohol-Related Disorders

Alcohol Use Disorder

Alcohol Intoxication

Alcohol Withdrawal

Other Alcohol-Induced Disorders

Unspecified Alcohol-Related Disorder

Caffeine-Related Disorders

Caffeine Intoxication

Caffeine Withdrawal (new disorder)

Other Caffeine-Induced Disorders

Unspecified Caffeine-Related Disorder

Cannabis-Related Disorders

Cannabis Use Disorder

Cannabis Intoxication

Cannabis Withdrawal (new disorder)

Other Cannabis-Induced Disorders

Unspecified Cannabis-Related Disorder

Hallucinogen-Related Disorders
Phencyclidine Use Disorder
Other Hallucinogen Use Disorder
Phencyclidine Intoxication
Other Hallucinogen Intoxication
Hallucinogen Persisting Perception Disorder
Other Phencyclidine-Induced Disorders
Other Hallucinogen-Induced Disorders
Unspecified Phencyclidine-Related Disorder
Unspecified Hallucinogen-Related Disorder

Inhalant-Related Disorders
Inhalant Use Disorder
Inhalant Intoxication
Other Inhalant-Induced Disorders
Unspecified Inhalant-Related Disorder

Opioid-Related Disorders
Opioid Use Disorder
Opioid Intoxication
Opioid Withdrawal
Other Opioid-Induced Disorders
Unspecified Opioid-Related Disorder

Sedative-, Hypnotic-, or Anxiolytic-Related Disorders
Sedative, Hypnotic, or Anxiolytic Use Disorder
Sedative, Hypnotic, or Anxiolytic Intoxication
Sedative, Hypnotic, or Anxiolytic Withdrawal
Other Sedative-, Hypnotic-, or Anxiolytic-Induced Disorders
Unspecified Sedative-, Hypnotic-, or Anxiolytic-Related Disorder

Stimulant-Related Disorders
Stimulant Use Disorder
Stimulant Intoxication
Stimulant Withdrawal
Other Stimulant-Induced Disorders
Unspecified Stimulant-Related Disorder

Tobacco-Related Disorders (new category of disorders)

Tobacco Use Disorder

Tobacco Withdrawal

Other Tobacco-Induced Disorders

Unspecified Tobacco-Related Disorder

Other (or Unknown) Substance-Related Disorders

Other (or Unknown) Substance Use Disorder

Other (or Unknown) Substance Intoxication

Other (or Unknown) Substance Withdrawal

Other (or Unknown) Substance-Induced Disorders

Unspecified Other (or Unknown) Substance-Related Disorder

Non-Substance-Related Disorders

Gambling Disorder (new disorder)

17. *Neurocognitive Disorders*

Delirium

Other Specified Delirium

Unspecified Delirium

Major and Mild Neurocognitive Disorders
> Dementia and Amnestic Disorder became Major or Mild Neurocognitive Disorder (Major NCD or Mild NCD).
> > New separate criteria are now presented for Major or Mild NCD due to various conditions.

Major Neurocognitive Disorder

Mild Neurocognitive Disorder

Major or Mild Neurocognitive Disorder Due to Alzheimer's Disease

Major or Mild Frontotemporal Neurocognitive Disorder

Major or Mild Neurocognitive Disorder With Lewy Bodies

Major or Mild Vascular Neurocognitive Disorder

Major or Mild Neurocognitive Disorder Due to Traumatic Brain Injury

Substance/Medication-Induced Majoror Mild Neurocognitive

Disorder (new disorder)

Major or Mild Neurocognitive Disorder Due to HIV Infection

Major or Mild Neurocognitive Disorder Due to Prion Disease

Major or Mild Neurocognitive Disorder Due to Parkinson's Disease

Major or Mild Neurocognitive Disorder Due to Huntington's Disease

Major or Mild Neurocognitive Disorder Due to Another Medical Condition

Major or Mild Neurocognitive Disorder Due to Multiple Etiologies

Unspecified Neurocognitive Disorder (new disorder)

Personality Disorders

Personality Disorders are associated with ways of thinking and feeling that significantly and adversely affect how a client functions in many aspects of life.

A personality disorder is an enduring pattern of inner experience and behavior that deviates from the expectations of a client's culture. The pattern is manifested in cognition, affect, interpersonal functioning, and/or impulse control.

Personality Disorders previously belonged on a different axis than almost all other disorders, but they are now with all mental and other medical diagnoses.

General Personality Disorder

Cluster A: Odd and Eccentric

Schizoid Personality Disorder

Introverted, withdrawn, solitary, emotionally cold, and distant; absorbed with own thoughts and feelings and fearful of closeness and intimacy with others.

Paranoid Personality Disorder

Interpreting the actions of others as deliberately threatening or demeaning; untrusting, unforgiving, and prone to angry or aggressive outbursts.

Schizotypal Personality Disorder

A pattern of peculiarities—odd or eccentric manners of speaking or dressing; strange, outlandish, or paranoid beliefs; display signs of "magical thinking."

Cluster B: Dramatic, emotional, and erratic

Antisocial Personality Disorder

Impulsive, irresponsible, and callous; history of legal difficulties; belligerent and irresponsible behavior; aggressive and even violent relationships; no respect for others.

Borderline Personality Disorder

Unstable in interpersonal relationships, behavior, mood, and self-image; abrupt and extreme mood changes; stormy interpersonal relationships; fluctuating self-image; self-destructive actions.

Narcissistic Personality Disorder

Exaggerated sense of self-importance; absorbed by fantasies of unlimited success; seek constant attention; oversensitive to failure.

Histrionic Personality Disorder
  Behave melodramatically or "over the top," constantly displaying an excessive level of emotionality; attention seeking.

Cluster C: Anxious and fearful
Avoidant Personality Disorder
  Hypersensitive to rejection and unwilling to become involved with others unless sure of being liked; avoidance of social events or work that involves interpersonal contact.

Dependent Personality Disorder
  Pattern of dependent and submissive behavior; relying on others to make personal decisions; require excessive reassurance and advice.

Obsessive-Compulsive Personality Disorder
  Conscientious, with high levels of aspiration; strive for perfection; never satisfied with achievements.

Other Personality Disorders

Personality Change Due to Another Medical Condition.

Other Specified Personality Disorder

Unspecified Personality Disorder

18. *Paraphilic Disorders*

  New specifiers "in a controlled environment" and "in remission" were added to criteria for all Paraphilic Disorders.
  Disorder added to names to distinguish between behavior and disorder. Must have both qualitative criteria and negative consequences to have the disorder and be diagnosed.

Voyeuristic Disorder

Exhibitionistic Disorder

Frotteuristic Disorder

Sexual Masochism Disorder

Sexual Sadism Disorder

Pedophilic Disorder

Fetishistic Disorder

Transvestic Disorder

Other Specified Paraphilic Disorder

Unspecified Paraphilic Disorder

19. *Other Mental Disorders*

Other Specified Mental Disorder Due to Another Medical Condition
Unspecified Mental Disorder Due to Another Medical Condition

Other Specified Mental Disorder

Unspecified Mental Disorder

20. *Medication-Induced Movement Disorders and Other Adverse Effects of Medication*

21. *Other Conditions That May Be a Focus of Clinical Attention*

PSYCHOPATHOLOGY

Psychopathology refers to either the study of mental illness or the manifestation of behaviors that may be indicative of mental illness or psychological impairment.

In the 16th and 17th centuries, bizarre behavior associated with mental illness was believed to be acts of evil spirits, demons, or the devil. To remedy this, many individuals suffering from mental illness were tortured in an attempt to drive out demons. When the torturous methods failed to return individuals to sanity, they were typically deemed eternally possessed and were executed.

By the 18th century, mental illness was viewed differently. It was during this time period that "madness" began to be seen as an illness beyond the control of an individual rather than the act of a demon. Because of this, thousands of people were confined to asylums where medical forms of treatment began to be investigated.

Today, the medical model is a driving force in the diagnosing and treatment of psychopathology.

There is a general consensus that psychopathology is influenced by the milieus in which clients are socialized and the cultural experiences to which they have been exposed. The magnitude of cultural influences on psychopathology is not fully known. Certainly definitions of aberrant behavior vary between cultural groups.

Many different professions, including social work, are involved in studying and/or treating mental illness or psychopathology.

THE SYMPTOMS OF MENTAL AND EMOTIONAL ILLNESS

There are many diverse symptoms of mental and emotional illness across the life course. Symptoms can vary depending on the particular disorder, circumstances, and other factors. Mental and emotional illness can affect attitudes, thoughts, and behaviors. Emotional symptoms include feeling sad, angry, confused fearful, worried, or guilty and are often accompanied by an inability to concentrate. Clients may also withdraw from friends and activities, show significant tiredness, have low energy, and/or exhibit sleeping problems. Mental and emotional illness can also be characterized by detachment from reality (delusions), paranoia or hallucinations, alcohol or drug abuse, major changes in eating habits, and/or suicidal thinking. Mental and emotional illness may also manifest as physical problems such as stomach pain, back pain, headache, and/or other unexplained aches and pains.

There are some terms and concepts that a social worker should be familiar with when making assessments and/or diagnoses.

1. *Comorbid*: existing with or at the same time; for instance, having two different illnesses at the same time

2. *Contraindicated*: not recommended or safe to use (a medication or treatment that is contraindicated would not be prescribed because it could have serious consequences)

3. *Delusion*: false, fixed belief despite evidence to the contrary (believing something that is not true)

4. *Disorientation*: confusion with regard to person, time, or place

5. *Dissociation*: disturbance or change in the usually integrative functions of memory, identity, perception, or consciousness (often seen in clients with a history of trauma)

6. *Endogenous depression*: depression caused by a biochemical imbalance rather than a psychosocial stressor or external factors

7. *Exogenous depression*: depression caused by external events or psychosocial stressors

8. *Folie a deux*: shared delusion

9. *Hallucinations*: hearing, seeing, smelling, or feeling something that is not real (auditory most common)

10. *Hypomanic*: elevated, expansive, or irritable mood that is less severe than full-blown manic symptoms (not severe enough to interfere with functioning and not accompanied by psychotic symptoms)

11. *Postmorbid*: subsequent to the onset of an illness

12. *Premorbid*: prior to the onset of an illness

13. *Psychotic*: experiencing delusions or hallucinations

THE SYMPTOMS OF NEUROLOGIC AND ORGANIC PROCESSES

Neurologic and organic symptoms are those that are caused by disorders that affect part or all of the nervous system or are biologically based. These symptoms can vary greatly. For example, the nervous system controls many different body functions. Symptoms can, but do not have to, be associated with pain, including headache and back pain. Neurologic symptoms can also include muscle weakness or lack of coordination, abnormal sensations in the skin, and disturbances of vision, taste, smell, and hearing.

They may be minor (such as a foot that has fallen asleep) or life threatening (such as coma due to stroke).

Some Common Neurologic Symptoms

Pain

- Back pain
- Neck pain
- Headache
- Pain along a nerve pathway (as sciatica)

Muscle malfunction

- Weakness
- Tremor (rhythmic shaking of a body part)
- Paralysis
- Involuntary (unintended) movements (such as tics)
- Clumsiness or poor coordination
- Muscle spasms

Changes in sensation

- Numbness of the skin
- Tingling or a "pins-and-needles" sensation
- Hypersensitivity to light touch
- Loss of sensation for touch, cold, heat, or pain

Changes in the senses

- Disturbances of smell and taste
- Partial or complete loss of vision
- Double vision
- Deafness
- Ringing or other sounds originating in the ears (tinnitus)

Other symptoms

- Vertigo
- Loss of balance
- Slurred speech (dysarthria)

Changes in consciousness

- Fainting
- Confusion or delirium
- Seizures (ranging from brief lapses in consciousness to severe muscle contractions and jerking throughout the body)

Changes in cognition (mental ability)

- Difficulty understanding language or using language to speak or write (aphasia)
- Poor memory
- Inability to recognize familiar objects (agnosia) or familiar faces (prosopagnosia)
- Inability to do simple arithmetic (acalculia)

Organic brain syndrome is a term used to describe physical disorders that impair mental function. The most common symptoms are confusion; impairment of memory, judgment, and intellectual function; and agitation. Disorders that cause injury or damage to the brain and contribute to organic brain syndrome include, but are not limited to, alcoholism, Alzheimer's disease, Fetal Alcohol Spectrum Disorders (FASDs), Parkinson's disease, and stroke.

Elderly clients are at high risk for depression as well as cognitive disorders, the latter of which can be chronic (as in Dementia) or acute (as in Delirium). Some patients have both affective (mood) and cognitive disorders. Clarifying the diagnosis is the first step to effective treatment, but this can be particularly difficult because elderly clients often have medical comorbidities that can contribute to cognitive and affective changes.

	Delirium	Dementia	Depression
Alertness	Altered level of consciousness; alertness may fluctuate	May vary	May vary
Motor behavior	Fluctuates; lethargy or hyperactivity	May vary	Psychomotor behavior may be agitated or unaffected
Attention	Impaired and fluctuates	Usually normal	Usually normal, but may be distractible
Awareness	Impaired, reduced	Clear	Clear
Course	Acute; responds to treatment	Chronic, with deterioration over time	Chronic; responds to treatment
Progression	Abrupt	Slow but stable	Varies
Orientation	Fluctuates in severity; usually impaired	May be impaired	May be selective disorientation
Memory	Recent and immediate impaired	Recent and remote impaired	Selective or patchy impairment
Thinking	Disorganized, distorted, incoherent; slow or accelerated	Difficulty with abstraction; thoughts impoverished; difficulty finding words; poor judgment	Intact, but may voice hopelessness and self-depreciation
Instrumental activities of daily living (IADL)	May be intact or impaired	May be intact early; impaired ADLs as disease progresses	May be intact or impaired
Stability	Variable, hour-to-hour	Fairly stable	Some variability
Emotions	Irritable, aggressive, fearful	Labile, apathetic, irritable	Flat, unresponsive, or sad; may be irritable
Activities of daily living (ADL)	May be intact or impaired	May be intact early, impaired as disease progresses	May neglect basic self-care

THE SYMPTOMS OF SUBSTANCE ABUSE AND OTHER ADDICTIONS

Some people are able to engage in behaviors or use substances without abusing them and/or becoming addicted.

There are signs when clients are addicted to behaviors and/or substances are being abused. These include, but are not limited to, indications that the behavior or substance use is:

- Causing problems at work, home, school, and in relationships
- Resulting in neglected responsibilities at school, work, or home (i.e., flunking classes, skipping work, neglecting children)
- Dangerous (i.e., driving while on drugs, using dirty needles, having unprotected sex, binging/purging despite medical conditions)
- Causing financial and/or legal trouble (i.e., arrests, stealing to support shopping, gambling, or drug habit)
- Causing problems in relationships, such as fights with partner or family members or loss of old friends
- Creating tolerance (more of the behavior or substance is needed to produce the same impact)
- Out of control or causing a feeling of being powerless
- Life-consuming, resulting in abandoned activities that used to be enjoyed
- Resulting in psychological issues such as mood swings, attitude changes, depression, and/or paranoia

Signs of Drug Use

- *Marijuana*: glassy, red eyes; loud talking, inappropriate laughter followed by sleepiness; loss of interest, motivation; weight gain or loss
- *Cocaine*: dilated pupils; hyperactivity; euphoria; irritability; anxiety; excessive talking followed by depression or excessive sleeping at odd times; may go long periods of time without eating or sleeping; weight loss; dry mouth and nose
- *Heroin*: contracted pupils; no response of pupils to light; needle marks; sleeping at unusual times; sweating; vomiting; coughing; sniffling; twitching; loss of appetite

INDICATORS OF SEXUAL DYSFUNCTION

Sexual dysfunction is a problem associated with sexual desire or response. Many issues can be included under the term *sexual dysfunction*. For example, for men, sexual dysfunction may include erectile dysfunction and premature or delayed ejaculation. For women, sexual dysfunction may refer to pain during sexual intercourse.

Problems may be caused by psychological factors, physical conditions, or a combination of both. It is essential that a medical examination be the first step in treating sexual dysfunction in order to identify medications or medical conditions that are the causes of the problems. Many of the symptoms can be addressed medically. However, sexual dysfunction can also be due to childhood sexual abuse, depression, anxiety, stressful life events, and/or other psychological issues. Treatment may also be needed to assist with coping with the signs and symptoms; these include, but are not limited to:

- Premature or delayed ejaculation in men
- Erectile disorder or dysfunction (not being able to get or keep an erection)
- Pain during sex
- Lack or loss of sexual desire
- Difficulty having an orgasm
- Vaginal dryness

THE DYNAMICS AND INDICATORS OF NEGLECT AND PHYSICAL, PSYCHOLOGICAL, AND SEXUAL ABUSE

There are various forms of neglect and abuse: **neglect** (failing to meet physical, emotional, or other needs); **physical abuse** (infliction of physical injury); **psychological abuse** (emotional/verbal/mental injury); and **sexual abuse** (inappropriate exposure or sexual contact, activity, or behavior without consent).

Different forms of abuse occur separately, but are often seen in combinations. Psychological abuse almost always accompanies other forms of abuse.
There is no single cause of abuse.

- *Stressors*: history of abuse; isolated with lack of social supports; low sense of self-competence and self-esteem; financial problems
- *Poor skills*: rigid, authoritarian; low IQ; poor self-control; poor communication, problem-solving, and interpersonal skills
- *Family issues*: marital discord, imbalanced relationship with marital partner (dominant or noninvolved); domestic violence; substance abuse

The victim is often blamed for the abuse by the perpetrator.

Physical abuse is defined as nonaccidental trauma or physical injury caused by punching, beating, kicking, biting, or burning. It is the most visible form of abuse because there are usually physical signs.

With a child, physical abuse can result from inappropriate or excessive physical discipline.

Indicators of physical abuse include:

- Unexplained bruises or welts on the face, lips, mouth, torso, back, buttocks, or thighs, sometimes reflecting the shape of the article used to inflict them (electric cord, belt buckle, etc.)
- Unexplained burns from a cigar or cigarette, especially on soles, palms, back, or buttocks—sometimes patterned like an electric burner, iron, or similar
- Unexplained fractures to the skull, nose, or facial structure
- Unexplained lacerations or abrasions to the mouth, lips, gums, eyes, and/or external genitalia

Behavioral indicators include being wary of individuals (parent or caretaker if a child is being abused) and behavioral extremes (aggressiveness or withdrawal), as well as fear related to reporting injury.

Psychological abuse is sustained, repetitive, and inappropriate behavior aimed at threatening, isolating, discrediting, belittling, teasing, humiliating, bullying, confusing, and/or ignoring. Psychological abuse/neglect can be seen in constant criticism, belittling, teasing, ignoring or withholding of praise or affection, and placing excessive or unreasonable demands, including expectations above what is appropriate.

It can impact intelligence, memory, recognition, perception, attention, imagination, and moral development. Individuals who have been psychologically abused are likely to be fearful, withdrawn, and/or resentful, distressed, and despairing. They are likely to feel unloved, worthless, and unwanted, or only valued in meeting another's needs.

Those who are victims of psychological abuse and neglect often:

- Avoid eye contact and experience deep loneliness, anxiety, and/or despair
- Have a flat and superficial way of relating, with little empathy toward others
- Have a lowered capacity to engage appropriately with others
- Engage in bullying, disruptive, or aggressive behaviors toward others

■ Engage in self-harming and/or self-destructive behaviors (i.e., cutting, physical aggression, reckless behavior showing a disregard for self and safety, drug taking)

Sexual abuse can sometimes be detected by physical or anatomical signs/injuries associated with the genital and rectal areas. Behavioral signs include any extreme changes in behavior, including regression, fears and anxieties, withdrawal, sleep disturbances, and/or recurrent nightmares. If the victim is a child, he or she may also show an unusual interest in sexual matters or know sexual information inappropriate for his or her age group. Sexual promiscuity, sexual victimization, and prostitution can also be signs.

Some factors influencing the effect of sexual abuse include:

■ Age of the victim (at time of abuse and time of assessment)
■ Extent and duration of sexual abuse
■ Relationship of offender to victim
■ Reaction of others to the abuse
■ Other life experiences

Immediately after disclosing the abuse, an individual is at risk for:

■ Disbelief by others (especially if victim is a child or perpetrator is a spouse/partner of an adult)
■ Being rejected by others
■ Being blamed for the abuse and the consequences of disclosing the sexual abuse

For a child, one of the most significant factors contributing to adjustment after sexual abuse is the level of parental support.

Some of the effects of sexual abuse can be:

■ Aversive feelings about sex; overvaluing sex; sexual identity problems; and/or hypersexual behaviors
■ Feelings of shame and guilt or feeling responsible for the abuse, which are reflected in self-destructive behaviors (such as substance abuse, self-mutilation, suicidal ideation and gestures, and acts that aim to provoke punishment)
■ Lack of trust, unwillingness to invest in others; involvement in exploitive relationships; angry and acting-out behaviors
■ Perceived vulnerability and victimization; phobias; sleep and eating problems

THE CHARACTERISTICS OF PERPETRATORS OF ABUSE AND NEGLECT

Many individuals with these characteristics do not commit acts of abuse. However, some factors are more likely to be present in those who commit abusive acts. Thus, having one of these risk factors does not mean that an individual will become an abuser, but an abuser is likely to have one or more of these risk factors.

A past history of violent behavior is the best predictor of future violence. Each prior act of violence increases the chance of future episodes of violence. In addition, those who suffered some form of abuse as children are more likely to be perpetrators of abuse as adults.

Risk factors include:

1. History of owning weapons and using them against others

2. Criminal history; repetitive antisocial behavior

3. Drug and alcohol use (substance use is associated with the most violent crimes)

4. Psychiatric disorder with coexisting substance abuse

5. Certain psychiatric symptoms such as psychosis, intense suspiciousness, anger, and/or unhappiness

6. Personality disorders (Borderline and Antisocial Personality disorders)

7. History of impulsivity; low-frustration tolerance; recklessness; inability to tolerate criticism; entitlement

8. Angry affect without empathy for others—high anger scores associated with increased chance of violence

9. Environmental stressors: lower socioeconomic status or poverty; job termination

A social worker should take all reports of abuse and all threats for harm seriously.

A social worker can distinguish between static and dynamic risk factors.

Static risk factors: such as past history of violent behavior or demographic information.

Dynamic risk factors: factors that can be changed by interventions such as change in living situation, treatment of psychiatric symptoms, abstaining from drug and alcohol use, access to weapons, and so on. Each client presents with a unique set of risk factors that require an individualized plan.

Interventions to reduce dynamic risk factors include:

■ Pharmacological interventions
■ Substance use treatment
■ Psychosocial interventions
■ Removal of weapons
■ Increased level of supervision

THE INDICATORS OF CLIENT DANGER TO SELF AND OTHERS

Social workers are often called upon to assess the risks of clients to themselves and others. Such assessments are not easy as there are no indicators that definitively predict whether a client will act on his or her feelings or desires to hurt himself or herself. A social worker must review all assessment data in order to determine the appropriate level of care and treatment plan. Such assessment must include examining risk and protective factors, as well as the presence of behavioral warning signs. Such an assessment may include examining:

■ Frequency, intensity, and duration of suicidal or violent thoughts
■ Access to or availability of method(s)
■ Ability or inability to control suicidal/violent thoughts
■ Ability *not* to act on thoughts
■ Factors making a client feel better or worse
■ Consequences of actions
■ Deterrents to acting on thoughts
■ Whether client has been using drugs or alcohol to cope
■ Measures a client requires to maintain safety

In situations where a client is seen to be a danger to self or others, a social worker may limit a client's right to self-determination and seek involuntary treatment such as commitment to an inpatient setting. If a client is deemed to be a danger to an identifiable third party, a social worker should consider this as a "duty to warn" situation (under the Tarasoff decision) and notify the authorities, as well as the party in danger.

There are risk factors that must be considered in any assessment because they are linked to dangerousness to others.

Risk Factors

■ Youth who become violent before age 13 generally commit more crimes, and more serious crimes, for a longer time; these youth exhibit a pattern of escalating violence throughout childhood, sometimes continuing into adulthood.

■ Most highly aggressive children or children with behavioral disorders do not become serious violent offenders.

■ Serious violence is associated with *drugs, guns, precocious sex, and other risky behaviors.*

■ *Ininquent peers and gang membership are two of the most powerful predictors of violence.*

Some Protective Factors

■ Effective programs combine components that address both *individual risks and environmental conditions;* building individual skills and competencies; changes in peer groups

■ Interventions that target *change in social context* appear to be more effective, on average, than those that attempt to change individual attitudes, skills, and risk behaviors

■ Effective and appropriate clinical care for mental, physical, and substance abuse disorders

■ Easy access to a variety of clinical interventions and support; that is, medical and mental health care relationships

■ Restricted access to highly lethal methods

■ Family and community support

■ Learned coping and stress reduction skills

Some Behavioral Warning Signs

■ Drug and alcohol use

■ Marked personality changes

■ Angry outbursts

■ Preoccupation with killing, war, violence, weapons, and so forth

■ Isolation from others

■ Obtaining guns or other lethal methods

There are risk factors that must be considered in any assessment because they are linked to risk of suicide.

Risk Factors

■ History of previous suicide attempt (*best predictor of future attempt;* medical seriousness of attempt is also significant)

■ Lives alone; lack of social supports

■ Presence of psychiatric disorder—depression (feeling hopeless), anxiety disorder, personality disorder (*A client is also at greater risk after being discharged from the hospital or after being started on antidepressants because he or she may now have the energy to implement a suicide plan.*)

■ Substance abuse

■ Family history of suicide

■ Exposure to suicidal behavior of others through media/peers

■ Losses—relationship, job, financial, social

■ Presence of firearm or easy access to other lethal methods

Some Protective Factors

■ Effective and appropriate clinical care for mental, physical, and substance use disorders

■ Easy access to a variety of clinical interventions and support; that is, medical and mental health care

■ Restricted access to highly lethal methods

■ Family and community support

■ Learned coping and stress reduction skills

■ Cultural and religious beliefs that discourage suicide and support self-preservation

Some Behavioral Warning Signs

■ Change in eating and sleeping habits

■ Drug and alcohol use

■ Unusual neglect of personal appearance

■ Marked personality change

■ Loss of interest in pleasurable activities

■ Not tolerating praise or rewards

■ Giving away belongings

■ Isolation from others

■ Taking care of legal and other issues

■ Dramatic increase in mood (might indicate a client has made a decision to end his or her life)

■ Verbalizes threats to commit suicide or feelings of despair and hopelessness
   ■ "I'm going to kill myself."

- "I wish I were dead."
- "My family would be better off without me."
- "The only way out for me is to die."
- "It's just too much for me to put up with."
- "Nobody needs me anymore."

THE METHODS USED TO ASSESS THE CLIENT'S COMMUNICATION SKILLS

Social workers must involve clients in every aspect of treatment. In order to do so, social workers must assess clients' communication skills and determine effective methods to gather needed information, as well as to ensure that clients understand data that is presented to them. Thus, the expressive and receptive communication of clients must be considered.

Communication can be verbal and nonverbal, so an assessment of clients' communication skills must involve both. Role-playing is a good way to assess and enhance clients' communication skills. It also allows a social worker to see if there is congruence between nonverbal and verbal communication.

As many clients may have experienced trauma, it is essential that social workers understand how such experiences may impact on clients' communication styles and patterns. Much of communication is also cultural and should be viewed within the context of clients' backgrounds and experiences.

Silence is a form of communication and should be considered by a social worker when used by a client.

Social workers should understand how to communicate with clients who are upset and angry, as well as how some wording choices and tones can be upsetting to clients based on their ethnic backgrounds and/or past experiences, such as victimization.

THE USE OF OBSERVATION TO ASSESS CLIENT INTERACTIONS

Although most information that a social worker uses during assessment comes from the social work interview, direct observation of interactions between family members and the client's nonverbal behavior can produce a lot of information about emotional states and interaction patterns.

Social workers also may use observation as part of a macro-level intervention in order to assess the extent of a problem/issue, driving and restraining forces for change, key policy influencers, and community members who can work as part of a task group for reform.

When functioning as an observer, a social worker can take many roles, including complete participant (living the experience as a participant), participant as observer (interacting with those who are participating), observer as participant (limited relationship with others participating—primarily observer), or complete observer (removed from activity—observer only). Observation is also a method used in scientific inquiry to collect data.

THE WAYS IN WHICH THE CLIENT'S BEHAVIOR WITH A SOCIAL WORKER IS REPRESENTATIVE OF HIS/HER RELATIONSHIP PATTERNS

The social worker–client relationship is a social microcosm where clients' interpersonal, behavioral, and conditioned patterns of perceiving and feeling are manifested. This relationship allows social workers to see for themselves the interaction patterns and methods of communication that have caused difficulties for clients in their everyday lives.

Social workers should use various intervention techniques to assist clients in identifying distorted perceptions and communication patterns and replacing them with healthy, more constructive ones.

For example, social workers who observe that clients have poor boundaries with them and/or engage in behaviors that interfere with productive interactions during the problem-solving process can use limit setting. Limit setting can be facilitative because clients do not feel safe or accepted in a completely permissive environment. In addition, it is important for clients to learn the importance of appropriate boundaries.

Social workers may also observe in the helping relationship that clients are not assertive. Thus, they may use assertiveness training to teach clients how to express their positive and negative feelings and to stand up for their rights in ways that will not alienate others.

Learning self-observation skills and awareness of personal preferences, as well as assuming personal responsibility, are important components of the assertiveness training process.

One of the best ways that a social worker can assist a client when observing a maladaptive behavior is by modeling, along with role-play and reinforcement, to produce behavioral change.

Social workers and clients should view the therapeutic environment as a place to learn and practice new skills and relationship patterns that can be used outside of this setting with others.

COMMON PSYCHOTROPIC AND NONPSYCHOTROPIC PRESCRIPTIONS AND OVER-THE-COUNTER MEDICATIONS AND THEIR SIDE EFFECTS

Psychotropic medications affect brain chemicals associated with mood and behavior. Psychotropic drugs are prescribed to treat a variety of mental health problems and typically work by changing the amounts of important chemicals in the brain called neurotransmitters. Psychotropic drugs are usually prescribed by psychiatrists, though other physicians and professionals may be allowed to prescribe them in certain jurisdictions. Psychotropic drugs may be needed to treat disorders such as Schizophrenia or Bipolar Disorder, but are often combined with other supports, such as that from family and friends, therapy, lifestyle changes, and other treatment protocols, to ensure healthy everyday living.

Antipsychotics

Used for the treatment of Schizophrenia and mania

Typical
Haldol (haloperidol)

Haldol Decanoate (long-acting injectable)

Loxitane (loxapine)

Mellaril (thioridazine)

Moban (molindone)

Navane (thiothixene)

Prolixin (fluphenazine)

Serentil (mesoridazine)

Stelazine (trifluoperazine)

Thorazine (chlorpromazine)

Trilafon (perphenazine)

Atypical
Abilify (aripiprazole)

Clozaril (clozapine)

Geodon (ziprasidone)

Risperdal (risperidone)

Seroquel (quetiapine)

Zyprexa (olanzapine)

With Clozaril, there is an increased risk of agranulocytosis that requires blood monitoring.

Some antipsychotics are available in injectable forms that are useful for clients who are noncompliant with oral medications.

Tardive dyskinesia (abnormal, involuntary movements of the tongue, lips, jaw, and face, as well as twitching, snakelike movement of the extremities, and occasionally the trunk) may result from taking high doses of antipsychotic medications over a long period of time. Symptoms may persist indefinitely after discontinuation of these medications. Thus, antipsychotic use should be closely monitored and prescribed at low doses, if possible.

Antimanic Agents (Mood Stabilizers)

Used for the treatment of Bipolar Disorder

Depakene (valproic acid, sodium divalproex), Depakote sprinkles

Lamictal (lamotrigine)

Lithium (lithium carbonate), Eskalith, Lithobid

Tegretol (carbamazepine), Carbatrol

Topamax (topiramate)

There is a small difference between toxic and therapeutic levels (narrow therapeutic index) that necessitates periodic checks of blood levels of lithium. Also, there is a need for periodic checks of thyroid and kidney functions because lithium can affect the functioning of these organs.

Antidepressants

Used for the treatment of depression

Selective Serotonin Reuptake Inhibitors (SSRIs)
Celexa (citalopram)

Lexapro (escitalopram)

Luvox (fluvoxamine)

Paxil (paroxetine)

Prozac (fluoxetine)

Zoloft (sertraline)

Tricyclics

Anafranil (clomipramine)

Asendin (amoxapine)

Elavil (amitriptyline)

Norpramin (desipramine)

Pamelor (nortriptyline)

Aventyl Sinequan (doxepin)

Surmontil (trimipramine)

Tofranil (imipramine)

Vivactil (protriptyline)

Monoamine Oxidase Inhibitors (MAOIs)

Nardil (phenelzine)

Parnate (tranylcypromine)

There are dietary restrictions of foods that contain high levels of tyramine (generally food that has been aged). Foods to avoid may include beer, ale, wine (particularly Chianti), cheese (except cottage and cream cheese), smoked or pickled fish (herring), beef or chicken liver, summer (dry) sausage, fava or broad bean pods (Italian green beans), and yeast vitamin supplements (brewer's yeast).

Others

Effexor (venlafaxine)

Desyrel (trazodone) Remeron (mirtazapine)

Serzone (nefazodone)

Wellbutrin (bupropion), Zyban

Antianxiety Drugs

Used for the treatment of Anxiety and Panic disorders

Ativan (lorazepam)

Buspar (buspirone)

Klonopin (clonazepam)

Valium (diazepam) Xanax (alprazolam)

There is a high abuse potential of these drugs and they can be dangerous when combined with alcohol/illicit substances. It is critical to look for sights of impaired motor or other functioning.

Stimulants

Used for the treatment of Attention-Deficit/Hyperactivity Disorder

Adderall (amphetamine, mixed salts)

Concerta (methylphenidate, long acting) Dexedrine (dextroamphetamine), Dextrostat

Dexedrine Spansules (dextroamphetamine, long acting)

Metadate (methylphenidate, long acting), Ritalin SR

Ritalin (methylphenidate), Methylin

Nonpsychotropic Prescriptions

The vast majority of Americans take at least one prescription medication, with more than half of Americans taking two or more. Commonly prescribed include the following medications.

Advair Diskus is a prescription used to treat asthma and chronic obstructive pulmonary disease (COPD).

Crestor is a lipid-lowering agent taken orally.

Cymbalta is a selective serotonin and norepinephrine reuptake inhibitor (SNRI) for oral administration.

Diovan is used to treat heart disease or heart failure.

Hydrocodone/acetaminophen is the most popular painkiller used to treat moderate to severe pain. Hydrocodone, a narcotic analgesic, relieves pain through the central nervous system, and it also is used to stop or prevent coughing. This drug can become habit-forming when used over an extended period of time.

Lantus is a sterile solution of insulin glargine for use as a subcutaneous injection for diabetes.

Levothyroxine sodium is used to treat hypothyroidism, a condition where the thyroid gland does not produce enough of the thyroid hormone. This drug also is used to treat thyroid cancer and to help shrink an enlarged thyroid gland.

Lisinopril (which used to be sold under the brand names Zestril and Prinivil) is a high blood pressure medication. Its main function is to block chemicals in the body that trigger the tightening of blood vessels. Lisinopril also is used to help treat heart failure.

Lyrica is used to control seizures, as well as treat nerve pain and fibromyalgia.

Metoprolol, the generic version of Lopressor, is used to treat high blood pressure and also helps reduce the risk of repeated heart attacks. Metoprolol also treats heart failure and heart pain or angina.

Nexium is used to treat symptoms of gastroesophageal reflux disease (GERD) and other conditions involving excessive stomach acid.

Simvastatin (generic Zocor) is prescribed to treat high cholesterol and is typically recommended in conjunction with diet changes. This drug is believed to have a variety of benefits including helping to prevent heart attacks and strokes.

Synthroid is a prescription, man made thyroid hormone that is used to treat hypothyroidism.

Ventolin solution is used in inhalers for asthma.

Vyvanse is used to treat hyperactivity and impulse control disorders.

Micro Practice and Social Work Relationships (18%)

Application of Theories, Methods, and Processes to Micro Systems

11

THE PROBLEM-SOLVING MODEL

The problem-solving approach is based on the belief that an inability to cope with a problem is due to some lack of motivation, capacity, or opportunity to solve problems in an appropriate way. Clients' problem-solving capacities or resources are maladaptive or impaired.

The goal of the problem-solving process is to enhance client mental, emotional, and action capacities for coping with problems and/or making accessible the opportunities and resources necessary to generate solutions to problems.

A social worker engages in the problem-solving process via the following steps:

1. Engaging
2. Assessing (includes a focus on client strengths and not just weaknesses)
3. Planning
4. Intervening
5. Evaluating
6. Terminating

THE CRISIS INTERVENTION/TREATMENT APPROACH

A state of crisis is time limited. Brief intervention during a crisis provides maximum therapeutic effect. Crisis intervention is a process of actively influencing the psychosocial functioning of clients during a period of disequilibrium or crisis. The goals are to alleviate stress and mobilize psychological capabilities and social resources.

The goals of crisis intervention are to (a) relieve the impact of stress with emotional and social resources, (b) return a client to a previous level of functioning (regain equilibrium), (c) help strengthen coping mechanisms during the crisis period, and (d) develop adaptive coping strategies.

Crisis intervention focuses on the here-and-now, is time limited (most crises last from 4 to 6 weeks), is directive, and requires high levels of activity and involvement from a social worker. A social worker sets specific goals and tasks in order to increase a client's sense of mastery and control.

TASK-CENTERED PRACTICE

A task centered approach aims to quickly engage clients in the problem-solving process and to maximize their responsibility for treatment outcome. In this modality, the duration of treatment is usually limited due to setting constraints, limitations imposed by third-party payers, or other reasons. Thus, at the outset, the expectation is that interventions from learning theory and behavior modification will be used to promote completion of a well-defined task to produce measurable outcomes. The focus is on the "here and now." This type of practice is often preferred by clients because they are able to see more immediate results.

The problem is partialized into clearly delineated tasks to be addressed consecutively (assessment leads to goals, which lead to tasks). A client must be able to identify a precise psychosocial problem and a solution confined to a specific change in behavior or a change of circumstances. A client must also be willing to work on the problem. It is essential that a social worker and client establish a strong working relationship quickly. A social worker's therapeutic style must be highly active, empathic, and sometimes directive in this approach.

Assessment focuses on helping a client identify the primary problem and explore the circumstances surrounding the problem. Specific tasks are expected to evolve from this process. Consideration is given to how a client would ideally like to see the problem resolved. Termination, in this modality, begins almost immediately upon the onset of treatment.

BEHAVIORAL APPROACHES

Behavioral approaches suggest that personality is a result of interaction between the individual and the environment. Behavioral theorists study observable and measurable behaviors, rejecting theories that take internal thoughts and feelings into account.

These approaches represent the systematic application of principles of learning to the *analysis and treatment of behaviors*. Behaviors determine feelings. Thus, changing behaviors will also change or eliminate undesired feelings. The goal is to modify behavior.

The focus is on *observable behavior*—a target symptom, a problem behavior, or an environmental condition, rather than on the personality of a client.

There are two fundamental classes of behavior: respondent and operant.

1. Respondent: involuntary behavior (anxiety, sexual response) that is automatically elicited by certain behavior. A stimulus elicits a response.

2. Operant: voluntary behavior (walking, talking) that is controlled by its consequences in the environment.

The best-known applications of behavior modification are sexual dysfunction, phobic disorders, compulsive behaviors (i.e., overeating, smoking), and training of persons with intellectual disabilities and/or Autism Spectrum Disorder.

It is impractical for those using behavior modification to observe behavior when clients are not in residential inpatient settings offering 24-hour care. Thus, social workers train clients to observe and monitor their own behaviors. For example, clients can monitor their food intake or how many cigarettes they smoke. Client self-monitoring has advantages (i.e., inexpensive, practical, and therapeutic) and disadvantages (i.e., clients can collect inadequate and inaccurate information or can resist collecting any at all).

There are several behavioral paradigms.

A. RESPONDENT OR CLASSICAL CONDITIONING (Pavlov): Learning occurs as a result of pairing previously neutral (conditioned) stimulus with an unconditioned (involuntary) stimulus so that the conditioned stimulus eventually elicits the response normally elicited by the unconditioned stimulus.

Unconditioned Stimulus ⟶ Unconditioned Response
Unconditioned Stimulus + Conditioned Stimulus ⟶ Unconditioned Response
Conditioned Stimulus ⟶ Conditioned Response

B. OPERANT CONDITIONING (B. F. Skinner): Antecedent events or stimuli precede behaviors, which, in turn, are followed by consequences. Consequences that increase the occurrence of the behavior are referred to as reinforcing consequences; consequences that decrease the occurrence of the behavior are referred to as punishing consequences. Reinforcement aims to increase behavior frequency, whereas punishment aims to decrease it.

Antecedent ⟶ Response/Behavior ⟶ Consequence

Operant Techniques:

1. **Positive reinforcement**: Increases probability that behavior will occur—praising, giving tokens, or otherwise rewarding positive behavior.

2. **Negative reinforcement**: Behavior increases because a negative (aversive) stimulus is removed (i.e., remove shock).

3. **Positive punishment**: Presentation of undesirable stimulus following a behavior for the purpose of decreasing or eliminating that behavior (i.e., hitting, shocking).

4. **Negative punishment**: Removal of a desirable stimulus following a behavior for the purpose of decreasing or eliminating that behavior (i.e., removing something positive, such as a token or dessert).

Specific Behavioral Terms:

1. **Aversion therapy**: Any treatment aimed at reducing the attractiveness of a stimulus or a behavior by repeated pairing of it with an aversive stimulus. An example of this is treating alcoholism with Antabuse.

2. **Biofeedback**: Behavior training program that teaches a person how to control certain functions such as heart rate, blood pressure, temperature, and muscular tension. Biofeedback is often used for attention deficit hyperactivity disorder (ADHD) and panic/anxiety disorders.

3. **Extinction**: Withholding a reinforcer that normally follows a behavior. Behavior that fails to produce reinforcement will eventually cease.

4. **Flooding**: A treatment procedure in which a client's anxiety is extinguished by prolonged real or imagined exposure to high-intensity feared stimuli.

5. **In vivo desensitization**: Pairing and movement through anxiety hierarchy from least to most anxiety provoking situation; takes place in "real" setting.

6. **Modeling**: Method of instruction that involves an individual (the model) demonstrating the behavior to be acquired by a client.

7. **Rational emotive therapy (RET)**: A cognitively oriented therapy in which a social worker seeks to change a client's irrational beliefs by argument, persuasion, and rational reevaluation and by teaching a client to counter self-defeating thinking with new, nondistressing self-statements.

8. **Shaping**: Method used to train a new behavior by prompting and reinforcing successive approximations of the desired behavior.

9. **Systematic desensitization**: An anxiety-inhibiting response cannot occur at the same time as the anxiety response. Anxiety-producing stimulus is paired with relaxation-producing response so that eventually an anxiety-producing stimulus produces a relaxation response. At each step, a client's reaction of fear or dread is overcome by pleasant feelings engendered as the new behavior is reinforced by receiving a reward. The reward could be a compliment, a gift, or relaxation.

10. **Time out**: Removal of something desirable—negative punishment technique.

11. **Token economy**: A client receives tokens as reinforcement for performing specified behaviors. The tokens function as currency within the environment and can be exchanged for desired goods, services, or privileges.

THE SELECTION OF THEORETICAL APPROACHES TO MEET CLIENT NEED

Social workers must have a sound theoretical base. Theories bring together explanations, including current research findings, which clearly should influence which strategies or interventions are chosen when working with clients. However, there may be reluctance by some social workers to embrace theory and research as they are considered to be irrelevant, obscure, abstract, and untranslatable in terms of direct practice. The split between theory and practice is detrimental as theory can bring benefits and clarity to practice situations. For example, a social worker who has a client who is moving from one foster home to another may find it useful to draw upon Bowlby's theory of attachment to understand the feelings and behaviors that may accompany this move.

Educating clients about social work theories can help them understand their situations and realize that they are not alone. Using newfound knowledge to solve existing problems and resolve future dilemmas helps empower clients, giving them the ability to solve their own difficulties. There is a sense of confidence and resilience that accompanies clients' knowledge acquisition.

PSYCHOTHERAPIES

Psychotherapy aims to treat clients with mental disorders or problems by helping them understand their illness or situation. Social workers use verbal techniques to teach clients strategies to deal with stress, unhealthy thoughts, and dysfunctional behaviors. Psychotherapy helps clients manage their symptoms better and function optimally in everyday life.

Sometimes, psychotherapy alone may be the best treatment for a client, depending on the illness and its severity. Other times, psychotherapy is combined with the use of medication or a psychopharmacological approach.

There are many kinds of psychotherapy, so social workers must determine which is best to meet a client's need. A social worker should not use a "one size fits all approach" or a particular type of psychotherapy because it is more familiar or convenient. Some psychotherapies have been scientifically tested more than others for particular disorders.

For example, cognitive behavioral therapy (CBT), a blend of cognitive and behavioral therapy, is used for depression, anxiety, and other disorders. CBT is a hands-on, practical approach to problem solving. Its goal is to change patterns of thinking or behavior that are responsible for clients' difficulties, and thereby change the way they feel. CBT works by changing clients' attitudes and their behavior by focusing on the thoughts, images, beliefs, and attitudes that are held (cognitive processes) and how these relate to behavior, as a way of dealing with emotional problems.

This approach is active, collaborative, structured, time limited, goal-oriented, and problem-focused. This approach lends itself to the requirements posed by managed care companies, including brief treatment, well-delineated techniques, goal and problem-oriented, and empirically supported evidence of its effectiveness.

Steps in Cognitive Restructuring

Assist clients in:

1. Accepting that their self-statements, assumptions, and beliefs determine or govern their emotional reaction to life's events

2. Identifying dysfunctional beliefs and patterns of thoughts that underlie their problems

3. Identifying situations that evoke dysfunctional cognitions

4. Substituting functional self-statements in place of self-defeating thoughts

5. Rewarding themselves for successful coping efforts

Dialectical behavior therapy (DBT), a form of CBT developed by Marsha Linehan, was developed to treat people with suicidal thoughts and actions. It is now also used to treat people with Borderline Personality Disorder. A social worker assures a client that his or her feelings are valid and understandable, but coaches him or her to understand that they are unhealthy or disruptive and a balance must be achieved. A client understands that it is his or her personal responsibility to change the situation.

Some psychotherapies are effective with children and adolescents and can also be used with families.

SHORT-TERM INTERVENTIONS/TREATMENTS

The growing need for time limited treatment, fueled by the widening influence of managed care in the behavioral health field, has produced a renewed focus on short-term therapy. Short-term interventions vary greatly in their duration.

Research has suggested that it may be a social worker's and client's views on the time of treatment that are more important than the duration of treatment itself, although sometimes these approaches are used because of organizational or financial constraints. In other instances, clients are choosing them over open-ended approaches. Although some have been wary of the effectiveness of these techniques to instill long-lasting change, they are being used more broadly than ever before. Some short-term interventions include a psychodynamic model, a crisis intervention model, or a cognitive behavioral model.

Although psychoanalysis is often thought of as long term, this was not the case with Freud's early work; psychoanalysis did not start out this way. There are a number of short-term psychodynamic approaches that focus on the belief that childhood experiences are the root of adult dysfunction.

CLIENT ADVOCACY

Advocacy by social workers can occur on the micro or macro levels. It is a process for affecting or initiating change either with or on behalf of an individual client or group to (a) obtain services or resources that would not otherwise be provided, (b) modify or influence policies or practices that adversely affect groups or communities, and/or (c) promote legislation or policies that will result in the provision of requisite resources or services.

Social workers in direct practice fight for the rights of clients on a daily basis. Social workers are particularly concerned for those who are vulnerable or are unable to speak up for themselves. Advocacy can occur both within and outside the agency in which a social worker is employed. It can also focus on meeting a specific client's need or the needs of a larger group who are experiencing the same problem. Advocacy can occur on all organizational and governmental levels.

Advocacy can also be performed by social work managers and community organizers/developers. The role of advocacy by these social workers is to persuade others that something needs to be done and to gain support for their view of how systems, such as organizations and communities, should develop and function.

Advocacy focuses on obtaining public support by convincing those who have access to or control of resources (power, financial, etc.) that is essential to make change. Advocacy can result in the acquisition of needed financial resources or, more importantly, the agreement or "buy in" of others to the identified cause.

THE METHODS USED IN WORKING WITH THE UNMOTIVATED OR INVOLUNTARY CLIENT

Social workers often may find themselves providing services to those who did not choose to receive them but instead have to do so as mandated by law, including families in the child protection system, people in the criminal justice system, and so on. Working with involuntary clients can be challenging because they may want to have no contact or may only participate because they feel that they have no other choice.

Often, these situations require social workers to receive peer support or supervision to process struggles encountered, as well as reassert their professionalism, because clients may try to test and exhibit anger at social workers, who represent the mandates placed upon them.

Some methods that can be helpful in working with involuntary clients include:

- Acknowledging clients' circumstances and understanding how they came about given clients' histories
- Listening to clients' experiences in order to try to understand how they feel about intervention
- Engaging in clear communication because involuntary clients struggle to understand what is happening to them
- Making clear what the purpose of the intervention is, what clients have control over and what they do not, what is going to happen next, and what the likely consequences will be if they do not participate
- Assisting at an appropriate pace as progress may be slow
- Building trust, even on the smallest scale, by consistently being honest and up-front about the situation and why a social worker is involved
- Giving clients practical assistance when needed to help them fight for their rights
- Paying attention to what is positive in clients' behavior and celebrating achievements
- Showing empathy and viewing clients as more than the problems that brought them into services

CASE MANAGEMENT

Case management has been defined in many ways. However, all models are based on the belief that clients often need assistance in accessing services in today's complex systems, as well as the need to monitor duplication and gaps in treatment and care.

Although there may be many federal, state, and local programs available, there are often serious service gaps. A client might have a specific need met in one program and many related needs ignored because of the lack of coordination. Systems are highly complex, fragmented, duplicative, and uncoordinated.

Social workers provide case management services to different client populations in both nonprofit and for-profit settings.

The primary goal of social work case management is to optimize client functioning and well-being by providing and coordinating high-quality services, in the most effective and efficient manner possible, to individuals with multiple complex needs (*NASW Standards for Social Work Case Management*, 2013).

Five case management activities are (a) assessment, (b) planning, (c) linking, (d) monitoring, and (e) advocacy.

THE USE OF PERMANENCY PLANNING AS AN INTERVENTION/TREATMENT METHOD

Permanency is not just a process, plan, or placement, nor is it intended to be a relationship that lasts only until a child turns age 18. Rather, permanence is about locating and supporting lifelong connections. For young people in the child welfare system, planning for permanence should be youth-driven, culturally competent, and continuous until the goal of permanency is achieved.

Permanence should bring physical, legal, and emotional safety and security, and allow multiple relationships between youth and caring adults. At the same time, young people in out-of-home care must be given opportunities to learn the life skills necessary to become independent and interdependent adults. Ensuring that young people in foster care have both permanent relationships and life skills for independence are critical for their future well-being.

Permanence can be the result of preservation of the biological family, reunification with the birth family, or legal guardianship/adoption by kin or other caring and committed adults. In addition, it is vital to promote the achievement or maintenance of other lifelong relationships, like siblings, extended family members, mentors/teachers, and childhood relationships.

Efforts to achieve timely permanency must begin with the initial child protective services contact and involve concurrent contingency planning to ensure stability and continuity of relationships if out-of-home placement is needed.

Permanency planning must:

1. Recognize that every young person is entitled to permanent supportive relationships

2. Be driven by youth themselves, recognizing that they are the best source of information about their own strengths and needs

3. Support decision making by youth about their futures

4. Honor the cultural, racial, ethnic, linguistic, and religious/spiritual backgrounds of young people and their families and respect differences in sexual orientation and gender identity

5. Recognize and build upon the strengths and resilience of young people, their parents, their families, and other significant adults

6. Ensure that services and supports are provided in ways that are fair, responsive, timely, and accountable to young people and their families, and do not stigmatize them, their families, or their caregivers

THE PHASES OF INTERVENTION/TREATMENT

Often clients have multiple service needs that must be prioritized. Social workers should consider Maslow's hierarchy of needs when working with clients. Clients will require services that address "deficiency needs" (such as those related to physiological, security, social, and esteem concerns) prior to accessing support to promote their "growth needs" (such as self-actualization).

In addition, making sure that psychological and social issues are not caused, and cannot be subsequently addressed, by medical and/or substance use issues is paramount. Social workers should always address these problems first.

Interventions and services are intended to aid clients in alleviating problems impeding their well-being. The interventions used by social workers and the services available to clients are those that are identified as potentially helpful on the basis of the ongoing assessment of clients.

The selection and prioritization of service needs may be driven by many factors, including client desires and motivation, treatment modality selected, agency setting, available resources, funding and time constraints, and so forth. A social worker should focus on ensuring that service needs chosen are outlined in the intervention or treatment plan and are reevaluated on a regular basis. A social worker should also make sure that the needs are based on an unbiased assessment and client wishes. They should not be solely driven by funding and time constraints.

Social workers should not recommend only services that are familiar or provided by their employing agencies because this is a "cookie cutter" or "one size fits all" approach.

Social work aims to assist with making change on the micro or macro levels to enhance well-being. Despite the level of intervention, the phases or steps that a social worker takes are similar.

Step 1: Engagement with client, group, or community

In *engagement*, a social worker should be actively involved in determining why change is sought, what has precipitated the desire to change now, and the parameters of the helping relationship, including defining the roles of a social worker and the expectations for treatment (what will occur and when it will happen).

Step 2: Assessment of strengths and needs

In *assessment*, essential information is collected upon which to define the problem and solutions, as well as identify collateral contacts from which gaps in data can be collected.

Step 3: Planning or design of intervention

In *planning*, an understanding of the problem is developed. Goals are developed from this understanding in order to provide a direction to help or assist. Specific action plans are developed and agreed upon in order to specify who will do what, what resources will be needed and how they will be used, and timelines for implementation and review.

Step 4: Intervention aimed at making change

In *intervention*, there is active involvement to realize continued progress and sustainable change. Issues that may threaten goal attainment must be addressed. Progress must be tracked and plans and timelines adjusted accordingly.

Step 5: Evaluation of efforts

In *evaluation*, subjective reports, in conjunction with objective indicators of progress, should be used to determine when goals and objectives have been met and whether new goals or objectives should be set.

Step 6: Termination and anticipation of future needs

In *termination*, progress that has been achieved should be reviewed and supports anticipated to be needed in the future should be identified.

THE INDICATORS OF CLIENT READINESS FOR TERMINATION

Readiness for termination may be marked when meetings between a social worker and client seem uneventful and the tone becomes one closer to cordiality rather than challenge, as well as when no new ground has been discovered for several sessions in a row.

In termination, a social worker and client (a) evaluate the degree to which a client's goals have been attained, (b) acknowledge and address issues related to the ending of the relationship, and (c) plan for subsequent steps a client may take relevant to the problem that do not involve a social worker (such as seeking out new services, if necessary).

The process of evaluation helps a client determine if his or her goals have been met and if the helping relationship was beneficial. As a result of the evaluation process, a social worker can become a more effective practitioner and provide better services. *There must always be a method to evaluate the effectiveness of the services received. Evaluation measures, when compared with those taken at baseline, assist in determining the extent of progress and a client's readiness for termination.*

A social worker helps a client cope with the feelings associated with termination. This process may help a client cope with future terminations. By identifying the changes accomplished and planning how a client is going to cope with challenges in the future, a social worker helps a client maintain these changes.

THE METHODS OF CONFLICT RESOLUTION

Management of conflict entails four steps:

1. The recognition of an existing or potential conflict
2. An assessment of the conflict situation
3. The selection of an appropriate strategy
4. Intervention

When previous attempts to resolve a conflict have only escalated the conflict, a useful technique is to structure the interactions between the parties. Structuring techniques include:

1. Decreasing the amount of contact between the parties in the early stages of conflict resolution
2. Decreasing the amount of time between problem-solving sessions
3. Decreasing the formality of problem-solving sessions
4. Limiting the scope of the issues that can be discussed
5. Using a third-party mediator

SMALL GROUP THEORIES

Groupthink is when a group makes faulty decisions because of group pressures. Groups affected by groupthink ignore alternatives and tend to take irrational actions that dehumanize other groups. A group is especially vulnerable to groupthink when its members are similar in background, when the group is insulated from outside opinions, and when there are no clear rules for decision making.

There are eight causes of groupthink:

1. Illusion of invulnerability—creates excessive optimism that encourages taking extreme risks

2. Collective rationalization—members discount warnings and do not reconsider their assumptions

3. Belief in inherent morality—members believe in the rightness of their cause and ignore the ethical or moral consequences of their decisions

4. Stereotyped views of those "on the out"—negative views of the "enemy" make conflict seem unnecessary

5. Direct pressure on dissenters—members are under pressure not to express arguments against any of the group's views

6. Self-censorship—doubts and deviations from the perceived group consensus are not expressed

7. Illusion of unanimity—the majority view and judgments are assumed to be unanimous

8. Self-appointed "mindguards"—members protect the group and the leader from information that is problematic or contradictory to the group's cohesiveness, views, and/or decisions

Group polarization occurs during group decision making when discussion strengthens a dominant point of view and results in a shift to a more extreme position than any of the members would adopt on their own. These more extreme decisions are toward greater risk if individuals' initial tendencies are to be risky and toward greater caution if individuals' initial tendencies are to be cautious.

OTHER INTERVENTION/TREATMENT STRATEGIES

It is also essential that a social worker address cultural and other considerations in treatment or intervention planning. These considerations should include the identification of cross-cultural barriers that may hinder a client's engagement and/or progress in treatment.

Social workers also have an ethical mandate to take information learned when working with individual clients and adapt agency resources to assist others who may have similar needs for language assistance and other cultural considerations.

A social worker should understand and validate each client's norms, beliefs, and values. Areas in treatment or intervention planning that can be greatly influenced by cultural and other factors include identification of client strengths and problems, goals and objectives, and modalities of treatment.

For example, a client's culture can provide him or her with strengths that can be brought to the intervention process. These strengths can include, but are not limited to:

- Supportive family and community relations
- Community and cultural events and activities
- Faith and spiritual/religious beliefs
- Multilingual capabilities
- Healing practices/beliefs
- Participation in rituals (religious, cultural, familial, spiritual, community)
- Dreams and aspirations

A culturally informed intervention plan must be based on a therapeutic relationship in which a client feels safe to explore his or her problems.

Intervention will be most effective when it is consistent with a consumer's culture. A social worker should consider the following given their cultural appropriateness:

- Individual versus group treatment
- Alternative treatment approaches (yoga, aromatherapy, music, writing)
- Medication (western, traditional, and/or alternative)
- Family involvement
- Location/duration of intervention

The *DSM-5* incorporates a greater cultural sensitivity throughout the manual rather than a simple list of culture-bound syndromes.

Different cultures and communities exhibit or explain symptoms in various ways. Because of this, it is important for social workers to be aware of relevant contextual information stemming from clients' cultures, races, ethnicities, religious affiliations, and/or geographical origins so social workers can more accurately diagnose client problems, as well as more effectively treat them.

In the *DSM-5*, specific diagnostic criteria were changed to better apply across diverse cultures. The Cultural Formulation Interview Guide is included to help social workers assess cultural factors influencing clients' perspectives of their symptoms and treatment options. It includes questions about clients' backgrounds in terms of their culture, race, ethnicity, religion, or geographical origin. The interview provides an opportunity for clients to define their distress in their own words and then relate this distress to how others, who may not share their culture, see their problems.

Micro Intervention Techniques

12

THE USE OF PARTIALIZING, SUPPORTING, FOCUSING, CLARIFYING, CONFRONTING, INTERPRETING, AND REFLECTING

- *Partializing* is dissecting information or goals into manageable portions so that clients are better able to develop discrete actions or tasks, giving them a sense of efficacy that ultimately leads to goal attainment.

- *Supporting* is showing empathetic understanding of clients' problems and assisting clients in making changes.

- *Focusing* helps clients narrow their attention to concerns or problems that should be prioritized.

- *Clarifying* uses questioning, paraphrasing, and restating to ensure full understanding of clients' ideas and thoughts.

- *Confronting* occurs when social workers call clients' attention to information, observations, and/or issues.

- *Interpreting* shows clients that there are different perspectives and ideas that can help to change negative thinking patterns and promote change.

- *Reflecting* or validating shows empathetic understanding of clients' problems and assists clients in understanding negative thought patterns.

THE TECHNIQUES USED TO MOTIVATE CLIENTS

A motivational approach aims to help clients realize what needs to change and to get them to talk about their daily lives and level of satisfaction with current situations. Social workers want to create doubt that everything is "OK" and help clients recognize consequences of current behaviors or conditions that contribute to dissatisfaction.

It is much easier if clients believe goals can be achieved and life can be different. Sometimes, clients are incapacitated by conditions that need to be addressed first (i.e., depression). Social workers can help clients think of a time when things were better or create a picture of what their lives could look like with fewer stresses.

The role of a social worker is to create an atmosphere that is conducive to change and to increase a client's intrinsic motivation so that change arises from within rather than being imposed from without.

Motivation is a state of readiness or eagerness to change, which may fluctuate from one time or situation to another.

Some additional techniques include:

- Clearly identifying the problem or risk area
- Explaining why change is important
- Advocating for specific change
- Identifying barriers and working to remove them
- Finding the best course of action
- Setting goals
- Taking steps toward change
- Preventing relapse

Empathy is a factor that increases motivation, lowers resistance, and fosters greater long-term behavioral change.

THE TECHNIQUES USED TO DEVELOP CONTRACTS WITH CLIENTS

Based on assessments and in conjunction with clients, social workers engage in planning. The aim of planning is to define clearly the issues and goals for intervention and develop intervention, treatment, or service plans likely to resolve the identified issues and achieve the final goals. There are many social work techniques or skills used to develop contracts with clients. They form the basis of the sequential steps which must take place in planning including, but not limited to the following.

1. *Identify issues and develop hypotheses*
   Social workers must demonstrate to clients that they understand their views of identified topics of concern and work with them to develop explanatory hypotheses. Social workers may identify issues not mentioned during the exploration process.

2. *Outlining scope of work*
   Social workers and clients must jointly agree on the specific problems or issues to address. A commitment must be made that they will work together and will focus primarily on these particular areas.

3. *Establishing goals*
   Following clarification of problems or issues, social workers must encourage clients to participate in establishing goals designed to address and resolve them. Goals should be specific, measurable, action oriented, realistic, and timely.

4. *Developing action plans*
   Sometimes called "intervention plans," "treatment plans," or "service plans," action plans address the questions of who, what, where, when, and especially how social workers and clients will pursue the agreed-upon goals.

5. *Identifying action steps*
   When it is unrealistic and impractical to undertake simultaneously all the actions needed to accomplish particular goals, social workers must engage clients in identifying small action steps or tasks that are likely to contribute to goal accomplishment.

6. *Planning for evaluation*
   Social workers and clients must identify means to measure progress toward goal attainment.

7. *Summarizing the contract*
   Social workers must concisely review with clients all the essential elements of the intervention, treatment, or service agreement. The contract specifies problem(s) to be worked on; the goals to reduce the problem(s); client and worker roles in the process; the interventions or techniques to be employed; the means of monitoring progress; stipulations for renegotiating the contract; and the time, place, fee, and frequency of meetings.

THE TECHNIQUES USED TO CLARIFY THE RESPONSIBILITIES OF THE CLIENT

Central to the provision of high quality, respectful, and compassionate services is the acknowledgment that both social workers and clients are responsible for the change process, each with unique but complementary roles. During the initial stage of the problem-solving process, engagement, it is critical that social workers and clients review the rights of clients and the responsibilities of both parties.

For example, clients have the right to be treated by social workers with courtesy, dignity, and respect for their individuality. They should not be subjected to any form of discrimination on the basis of race, ethnicity, national origin, color, sex, sexual orientation, gender identity or expression, age, marital status, political belief, religion, immigration status, or mental or physical disability. Clients' privacy must be respected, and confidentiality of records and other protected health information must be maintained according to legal and ethical standards. Clients have the right to refuse treatment or care, as well as voice concerns or recommendations aimed at improving services.

Clients also have responsibilities in the problem-solving process. They should openly share the concerns that caused them to seek treatment, and provide, to the extent possible, information that social workers need in order to assist them. To the degree possible, clients should work to understand their situations and problems, develop agreed upon treatment goals, and engage in treatment. They should keep scheduled appointments and be open to the receipt of feedback. Lastly, clients should tell social workers about changes in their lives, especially situations that compromise health and safety.

THE USE OF GOAL SETTING

A social worker and client work together to develop a contract (intervention or service plan), including an agreement on its implementation or the activities used to help a client attain his or her goals. Modification of the contract may be required as new information about a client's situation emerges and/or as the situation changes.

When clients seek to attain their goals, changes may need to be made to themselves, groups, families, and/or systems in the larger environment. This choice of targets is an even more complex issue than it first appears since the process of changing one system may bring about changes in others.

Change Strategies

- *Modify systems:* The decision to help a client on a one-to-one basis or in the context of a larger system must take into consideration a client's preferences and previous experiences, as well as the degree to which a client's problem is a response to forces within the larger system and whether the client's change can be readily attained by a change in the larger system.

- *Modify individual thoughts:* A social worker may teach a client how to problem solve and alter his or her self-concepts by modifying self-defeating statements. A social worker may also make interpretations that can increase a client's understanding about the relationship between events in his or her life.

■ *Modify individual actions:* A social worker may use behavior modification techniques such as reinforcement, punishment, modeling, role-playing, and/or task assignments. *Modeling and role-modeling are very effective methods for teaching. They should be used whenever possible.*

■ Thoughts can be modified by feedback from others and behaviors can be modified through the actions of others in a system (by altering reinforcements).

■ A social worker can also *advocate* for a client and seek to secure a change in a system on his or her behalf.

■ A social worker can be a *mediator* by helping a client and another individual or system to negotiate with each other so that each may attain their respective goals.

THE TECHNIQUES USED TO TEACH SKILLS TO CLIENTS

Social workers assist clients in realizing how their lives can improve and/or how they can learn from mistakes that they have made. The techniques that social workers employ are a form of informal or didactic teaching.

For example, social workers may help clients see:

■ How their histories have shaped them

■ Needs associated with medical and/or behavioral health conditions

■ Developmental issues related to various phases across the life span

■ The workings of systems in which they operate

■ Ways of coping in various situations

A social worker must use the problem-solving process to teach clients skills needed to make changes in their lives.

In addition, social workers may collaborate with or inform clients of colleagues who may also assist with more formal teaching, such as learning to read, obtaining a driver's license, and so on.

THE DIFFERENTIAL USE OF INTERVENTION/ TREATMENT TECHNIQUES

A social worker uses both subjective and objective data throughout the problem-solving process. For example, in assessment, a social worker must understand the "facts" related to a client's situation (objective data), but also how those "facts" are perceived by the client through descriptions of his or her feelings, experiences, and perceptions (subjective data). It is not the objective facts that determine whether an event is traumatic, but a subjective emotional experience of the event. Thus, having a client describe the meaning of an event to him or her is critically important.

Treatment plans are often developed and progress is often assessed based upon subjective and objective data gathered by a social worker. For example, in health care, a SOAP format is often used.

S (Subjective):

The subjective component is a client's report of how he or she has been doing since the last visit and/or what brought a client into treatment.

O (Objective):

In health care, the objective component includes vital signs (temperature, blood pressure, pulse, and respiration), documentation of any physical examinations, and results of laboratory tests. In other settings, this section may include other objective indicators of problems such as disorientation, failing school, legal issues, and so forth.

A (Assessment):

A social worker pulls together the subjective and objective findings and consolidates them into a short assessment.

P (Plan):

The plan includes what will be done as a consequence of the assessment.

Lastly, in evaluation, subjective reports of a client, in conjunction with objective indicators of progress, should be used to determine when goals or objectives have been met and whether new goals or objectives should be set. Client self-monitoring (subjective data) is a good way to involve a client so he or she can see and track progress himself or herself.

CLIENT SELF-MONITORING TECHNIQUES

Clients are encouraged to pay attention to any subtle shift in feelings. Clients frequently keep thought or emotion logs that include three components: (a) disturbing emotional states, (b) the exact behaviors engaged in at the time of the emotional states, and (c) thoughts that occurred when the emotions emerged. In cognitive behavioral therapy, homework is often done between sessions to record these encounters. This homework involves client self-monitoring, which is central to this approach.

THE USE OF TIMING IN INTERVENTION/TREATMENT

The use of timing in social work interventions is critical. Both verbal expressions and nonverbal communication by a social worker, if timed appropriately, can cause a client to feel joined with a social worker, resulting in a stronger therapeutic alliance that can lead to enhanced outcomes. However, the same expressions or communication at the wrong time can result in a client thinking that a social worker is not aligned or relating to a his or her experiences.

Social workers must examine cues provided by clients to determine the appropriateness of communication styles and strategies, as well as when clients are ready to move forward in the problem-solving process. In addition, sometimes a social worker must reassess, with a client, the continued appropriateness of an agreed upon intervention because factors have made it no longer feasible or desirable.

Maslow's hierarchy of needs can help identify which client problems need immediate attention and should be prioritized for intervention first.

THE TECHNIQUE OF ROLE-PLAY

Role-playing is a teaching strategy that offers several advantages. Role-playing in social work practice may be seen between supervisor and supervisee or social worker and client.

In all instances, role-playing usually raises interest in a topic as clients are not passive recipients in the learning process. In addition, role-playing teaches empathy and understanding of different perspectives as clients take on the role of another, learning and acting as that individual would in the specified setting. In role-playing, participation helps embed concepts. Role-playing gives clarity to information that may be abstract or difficult to understand.

The use of role-playing emphasizes personal concerns, problems, behavior, and active participation. It improves interpersonal skills, improves communication skills, and enhances communication.

Role-playing activities can be divided into four stages:

1. Preparation and explanation of the activity

2. Preparation of the activity

3. Role-playing

4. Discussion or debriefing after the role-play activity

ROLE-MODELING TECHNIQUES

Role-modeling emphasizes the importance of learning from observing and imitating and has been used successfully in helping clients acquire new skills, including those associated with assertiveness.

Role-modeling works well when it is combined with role-play and reinforcement to produce lasting change.

There are different types of modeling, including live modeling, symbolic modeling, participant modeling, or covert modeling.

Live modeling refers to watching a real person perform the desired behavior.

Symbolic modeling includes filmed or videotaped models demonstrating the desired behavior. Self-modeling is another form of symbolic modeling in which clients are videotaped performing the target behavior.

In participant modeling, an individual models anxiety-evoking behaviors for a client and then prompts the client to engage in the behavior.

In covert modeling, clients are asked to use their imagination, visualizing a particular behavior as another describes the imaginary situation in detail.

Models in any of these forms may be presented as either a coping or a mastery model. The coping model is shown as initially fearful or incompetent, and then is shown as gradually becoming comfortable and competent performing the feared behavior. The mastery model shows no fear and is competent from the beginning of the demonstration.

THE TECHNIQUES USED FOR FOLLOW-UP

Discharge may occur for a variety of reasons; for example, a client may have met his or her goals or no longer needs the services; decides not to continue to receive them from a particular social worker or in general; and/or requires a different level of care. In addition, when a social worker leaves an agency, a client may continue to receive the same service from this agency, but from another worker. Although this is not a "discharge" from services, it involves careful planning and standards that need to be followed to ensure continuity of care and prevent gaps in service.

The *NASW Code of Ethics* (1999) provides some guidance with regard to discharge or terminations, as well as aftercare and follow-up services.

Social workers should terminate services to clients and professional relationships with them when such services and relationships are no longer required or no longer serve client needs or interests (*NASW Code of Ethics, 1999—1.16 Termination of Services*).

Social workers should take reasonable steps to avoid abandoning clients who are still in need of services. Social workers should withdraw services

Termination of Services (handwritten margin note)

precipitously only under unusual circumstances, giving careful consideration to all factors in the situation, and taking care to minimize possible adverse effects. Social workers should assist in making appropriate arrangements for continuation of services when necessary (*NASW Code of Ethics, 1999—1.16 Termination of Services*).

Social workers in fee-for-service settings may terminate services to clients who are not paying an overdue balance if the financial contractual arrangements have been made clear to a client, if a client does not pose an imminent danger to self or others, and if the clinical and other consequences of the current nonpayment have been addressed and discussed with a client (*NASW Code of Ethics, 1999—1.16 Termination of Services*).

Social workers should not terminate services to pursue a social, financial, or sexual relationship with a client (*NASW Code of Ethics, 1999—1.16 Termination of Services*).

Social workers who anticipate the termination or interruption of services to clients should notify clients promptly and seek the transfer, referral, or continuation of services in relation to client needs and preferences (*NASW Code of Ethics, 1999—1.16 Termination of Services*).

Social workers who are leaving an employment setting should inform clients of appropriate options for the continuation of services and of the benefits and risks of the options (*NASW Code of Ethics, 1999—1.16 Termination of Services*).

It is unethical to continue to treat clients when services are no longer needed or in their best interests.

Another standard that is relevant to termination of services (*NASW Code of Ethics, 1999—1.15 Interruption of Services*) mandates that social workers should make reasonable efforts to ensure continuity of services in the event that services are interrupted by factors such as unavailability, relocation, illness, disability, or death.

Social workers must involve clients and their families (when appropriate) in making their own decisions about follow-up services or aftercare. Involvement must include, at a minimum, discussion of client and family preferences (when appropriate).

Social workers are often responsible for coordination of clients' follow-up services when needed.

A return of clients to services quickly may suggest either that they did not receive needed follow-up services or that these services were inadequate. Termination may have occurred prematurely.

Clients who are at high risk for developing problems after services have ended should receive regular assessments after discharge to determine whether services are needed or discharge plans are being implemented as planned.

STRESS MANAGEMENT TECHNIQUES

Stress is a psychological and/or physical reaction to life events, with most people experiencing it regularly in their own lives. When a life event is seen as a threat, it signals the release of hormones aimed at generating a response. This process has been labeled the "fight-or-flight" response.

Once the threat is gone, clients should return to typical relaxed states, but this may not happen if other threats are presented immediately thereafter. Thus, stress management is important because it provides tools to deal with threats and minimize the impacts of psychological and/or physical reactions.

The first step in stress management is for clients to monitor their stress levels and identify their stress triggers. These can be major life events, but also those associated with day-to-day life, such as job pressures, relationship problems, or financial difficulties. Positive life events, such as getting a job promotion, getting married, or having children, also can be stressful.

The second step in stress management is to assist clients in identifying what aspects of a situation they can control. Clients can make these changes, as well as benefit from stress-reduction techniques, such as deep breathing, exercise, massage, tai chi, or yoga, to manage those aspects of a situation that cannot be altered. Maintaining a healthy lifestyle is essential to helping manage stress.

Stress will always be a part of life, but assisting clients to manage it can increase their ability to cope with challenges and enhance their psychological and/or physical well-being.

LIMIT SETTING

Clients of all ages are frequently desperate for an environment with consistent boundaries. For this reason, it is helpful if social workers can learn limit-setting skills. Limit setting is facilitative as clients do not feel safe or accepted in a completely permissive environment.

In addition, although compassion is important for a social worker, it is important to maintain a client–social worker relationship. Understanding boundaries and being able to maintain those boundaries with clients are essential.

THE PROCESS USED TO REFER CLIENTS FOR SERVICES

There are important steps, as well as ethical concerns, that must be taken when referring clients for services.

Step 1: Clarifying the Need or Purpose for the Referral
Social workers should refer clients to other professionals when the other professionals' specialized knowledge or expertise is needed to

serve clients fully or when social workers believe that they are not being effective or making reasonable progress with clients and additional service is required *(NASW Code of Ethics, 1999—2.06 Referral for Services).*

Step 2: Researching Resources

When making a referral, it is critical that a social worker refers to a competent provider, someone with expertise in the problem that a client is experiencing. When researching resources, a client's right to self-determination should be paramount. In addition, if a client is already receiving services from an agency, it may be advisable to see if there are available services provided by this agency in order to avoid additional coordination and fragmentation for a client.

Step 3: Discussing and Selecting Options

Social workers are prohibited from giving or receiving payment for a referral when no professional service is provided by the referring social worker *(NASW Code of Ethics, 1999—2.06 Referral for Services).*

Step 4: Planning for Initial Contact

Social workers may want to work with a client to prepare for the initial meeting. Preparation may include helping a client to understand what to expect or reviewing needs and progress made so that it can be discussed with the new provider.

Step 5: Initial Contact

Social workers who refer clients to other professionals should take appropriate steps to facilitate an orderly transfer of responsibility. Social workers who refer clients to other professionals should disclose, with clients' consent, all pertinent information to the new service providers *(NASW Code of Ethics, 1999—2.06 Referral for Services).*

Step 6: Follow Up to See If Need Was Met

Social workers should always follow up to ensure that there was not a break in service and that the new provider is meeting a client's needs.

THE APPROACHES TO FAMILY THERAPY

Social workers use a variety of techniques to work with families. Family therapy treats the family as a unified whole, a system of interacting parts in which change in any part affects the functioning of the whole. The family is the unit of attention for diagnosis and treatment. Social roles and interpersonal interaction are the focus of treatment. Real behaviors and communication that affect current life situations are addressed. The goal is to interrupt the circular pattern of pathological communication and behaviors and replace it with a new pattern that will sustain itself without the dysfunctional aspects of the original pattern.

Key clinical issues include:

- Establishing a contract with the family
- Examining alliances within the family
- Identifying where power resides
- Determining the relationship of each family member to the problem
- Seeing how the family relates to the outside world
- Assessing the influence of family history on current family interactions
- Ascertaining communication patterns
- Identifying family rules that regulate patterns of interaction
- Determining the meaning of the presenting symptom in maintaining family homeostasis
- Examining flexibility of structure and accessibility of alternative action patterns
- Finding out about sources of external stress and support

The following are some types of family therapy.

Strategic Family Therapy

In strategic family therapy, a social worker initiates what happens during therapy, designs a specific approach for each person's presenting problem, and takes responsibility for directly influencing people.

It has roots in structural family therapy and is built on communication theory.

It is active, brief, social worker-centered, directive, and task-centered. Strategic family therapy is more interested in creating change in behavior than change in understanding.

Strategic family therapy is based on the assumption that families are flexible enough to modify solutions that do not work and adjust/develop. There is the assumption that all problems have multiple origins; a presenting problem is viewed as a symptom of, and a response to, current dysfunction in family interactions.

Therapy focuses on problem resolution by altering the feedback cycle or loop that maintains the symptomatic behavior. A social worker's task is to formulate the problem in solvable, behavioral terms and to design an intervention plan to change the dysfunctional family pattern.

Concepts/Techniques

- Pretend technique—encourage family members to "pretend" and encourage voluntary control of behavior
- First-order changes—superficial behavioral changes within a system that do not change the structure of the system
- Second-order changes—changes to the systematic interaction pattern so the system is reorganized and functions more effectively
- Family homeostasis—families tend to preserve familiar organization and communication patterns—resistant to change
- Relabeling—changing the label attached to a person or problem from negative to positive so the situation can be perceived differently and it is hoped that new responses will evolve
- Paradoxical directive or instruction—prescribe the symptomatic behavior so a client realizes he or she can control it; uses the strength of the resistance to change in order to move a client toward goals

Structural Family Therapy

This approach stresses the importance of family organization for the functioning of the group and the well-being of its members. A social worker "joins" (engages) the family in an effort to restructure it. Family structure is defined as the invisible set of functional demands organizing interaction among family members. Boundaries and rules determining who does what, where, and when are crucial in three ways.

1. Interpersonal boundaries define individual family members and promote their differentiation and autonomous, yet interdependent, functioning. Dysfunctional families tend to be characterized by either a pattern of rigid enmeshment or disengagement.

2. Boundaries with the outside world define the family unit, but boundaries must be permeable enough to maintain a well-functioning open system, allowing contact and reciprocal exchanges with the social world.

3. Hierarchical organization in families of all cultures is maintained by generational boundaries, the rules differentiating parent and child roles, and rights and obligations.

Restructuring is based on observing and manipulating interactions within therapy sessions, often by enactments of situations as a way to understand and diagnose the structure and provide an opportunity for restructuring.

Bowenian Family Therapy

Unlike other models of family therapy, the goal of this approach is not symptom reduction. Rather, a Bowenian-trained social worker is interested in improving the intergenerational transmission process. Thus, the focus within this approach is consistent whether a social worker is working with an individual, a couple, or the entire family. It is assumed that improvement in overall functioning will ultimately reduce a family member's symptomatology. Eight major theoretical constructs are essential to understanding Bowen's approach. These concepts are differentiation, emotional system, multigenerational transmission, emotional triangle, nuclear family, family projection process, sibling position, and societal regression. These constructs are interconnected.

Differentiation is the core concept of this approach. The more differentiated, the more a client can be an individual while in emotional contact with the family. This allows a client to think through a situation without being drawn to act by either internal or external emotional pressures.

Emotional fusion is the counterpart of differentiation and refers to the tendency for family members to share an emotional response. This is the result of poor interpersonal boundaries between family members. In a fused family, there is little room for emotional autonomy. If a member makes a move toward autonomy, it is experienced as abandonment by other members of the family.

Multigenerational transmission stresses the connection of current generations to past generations as a natural process. Multigenerational transmission gives the present a context in history. This context can focus a social worker on the differentiation in the system and on the transmission process.

An emotional triangle is the network of relationships among three people. Bowen's theory states that a relationship can remain stable until anxiety is introduced. However, when anxiety is introduced into the dyad, a third party is recruited into a triangle to reduce the overall anxiety. It is almost impossible for two people to interact without triangulation.

The nuclear family is the most basic unit in society and there is a concern over the degree to which emotional fusion can occur in a family system. When forming relationships outside of the nuclear family, clients tend to pick mates with the same level of differentiation.

Sibling position is a factor in determining personality. Where a client is in birth order has an influence on how he or she relates to parents and siblings. Birth order determines the triangles that clients grow up in.

Societal regression, in contrast to progression, is manifested by problems such as the depletion of natural resources. Bowen's theory can be used to explain societal anxieties and social problems because Bowen viewed society as a family, as an emotional system complete with its own multigenerational transmission, chronic anxiety, emotional triangles, cutoffs, projection processes, and fusion and differentiation struggles.

USE OF CLIENTS' STRENGTHS

The strengths perspective is based on the assumption that clients have the *capacity to grow, change, and adapt* (**humanistic approach**). Clients also have the knowledge that is important in defining and solving their problems (clients or families are experts about their own lives and situations); they are resilient and survive and thrive despite difficulties.

Strength is any ability that helps an individual (or family) to confront and deal with a stressful life situation and to use the challenging situation as a stimulus for growth. Individual strengths include, but are not limited to, cognitive abilities, coping mechanisms, personal attributes, interpersonal skills, or external resources. Families may have other strengths such as kinship bonds, community supports, religious connections, flexible roles, strong ethnic traditions, and so on.

Strengths vary from one situation to another and are contextual. What may be an appropriate strength or coping mechanism in one situation may not be appropriate in another. Ideally, in a given situation, a client selects an appropriate way to cope by drawing from a repertoire of coping mechanisms or strengths. The appropriateness of a particular coping mechanism may vary according to life course stage, developmental tasks, kinds of stressors, situation, and so on. Having a variety of coping mechanisms and resources enables flexibility in the way a client copes with stresses.

The strengths perspective focuses on understanding clients (or families) on the basis of their strengths and resources (internal and external) and mobilizing the resources to improve their situations. There is a systematic assessment of all the strengths and resources available to meet desired goals.

Methods to enhance strengths include:

- Collaboration and partnership between a social worker and client
- Creating opportunities for learning or displaying competencies
- Environmental modification—environment is both a resource and a target of intervention

The concept of resilience has deep roots in social work, though there is a lack of agreement as to whether a resilience theory exists or resiliency is a concept that describes a set or series of person-in-environment interactions. Research related to resiliency focuses on understanding why clients do not only survive, but thrive from negative, stressful life events or trauma. Understanding what helps them function and grow in the context of adversity can assist social workers to incorporate this knowledge into the development of new interventions.

COUPLES/INTERVENTION/TREATMENT APPROACHES

There are often reasons that couples experience problems including, but not limited to:

- Retriggering emotional trauma and not repairing it
- An inability to bond or reconnect after hurting or doing damage to one another
- Lack of skills or knowledge

Many treatment techniques are used with individuals that can be adapted in work with couples, including the following:

Behavior modification—Successful couples' counseling methods will address and attempt to modify any dysfunctional behavior so that couples can change the way individuals behave with each other.

Insight-oriented psychotherapy—A good deal of time is spent studying interactions between individuals in order to develop a hypothesis concerning what caused individuals to react to each other in the way they do.

There are also specific couples therapy approaches including the *Gottman method*, which is based on the notion that healthy relationships are ones in which individuals know each other's stresses and worries, share fondness and admiration, maintain a sense of positiveness, manage conflicts, trust one another, and are committed to one another.

The Gottman method focuses on conflicting verbal communication in order to increase intimacy, respect, and affection; removes barriers that create a feeling of stagnancy in conflicting situations; and creates a heightened sense of empathy and understanding within relationships.

With all approaches, there are actions that a social worker can take to facilitate effective couples treatment.

For example, when developing a collaborative alliance with each person, a social worker should validate the experience of each and explore each person's reservations about engaging in couples therapy. In addition, when developing an alliance with the couple as a unit, a social worker can reframe individual problems in relationship terms and support each person's sense of himself or herself as being part of a unit, as well as a separate individual.

GROUP DYNAMICS

People clearly behave differently when they are part of a group. For example, when presented with danger alone, individuals will act, but they often do not act in a group because they think others will take the responsibility (known as "diffusion of responsibility").

When in groups, individuals also take on various roles, including the "energizer" who prods the group to action or decision and the "encourager" who praises, agrees with, and accepts the contribution of the others.

When leading groups, a social worker should understand the ways in which the group context influences individual actions and determine the roles that individuals have taken within groups. This knowledge is critical so that a social worker can determine the techniques that are needed to make change and where the locus of the change effort should lie (i.e., by focusing primarily on the individual, the larger group, or both).

In addition, when facilitating a task or psychotherapeutic group, a social worker may be called upon to remind the group of its goals and rules and confront relationships that may be interfering with the overall purpose of the group.

Social workers can use the following questions to assess the functioning of a group:

- Is there satisfaction by members about participation?
- Have members' ideas and thoughts been listened to by others?
- Have members been open in their willingness to share thoughts and ideas?
- Have members treated one another in a respectful manner?
- Have members been supportive of one another?
- Has the group made decisions with regard to its functioning?
- Has the group acknowledged any problems or concerns?
  - If so, has the group worked to correct or address them?
- Has the group regularly evaluated its effectiveness?

THE APPROACHES TO SOCIAL GROUP WORK

Group work is a method of working with two or more people for personal growth, the enhancement of social functioning, and/or for the achievement of socially desirable goals.

Social workers use their knowledge of group organization and functioning to affect the performance and adjustment of individuals. Individuals remain the focus of concern and the group is the vehicle of growth and change.

A social worker takes on different roles throughout the group process, which has a beginning, middle, and end.

Beginning
A social worker identifies the purpose of the group and his or her role. This stage is characterized as a time to convene, to organize, and to set

a plan. Members are likely to remain distant or removed until they have had time to develop relationships.

Middle
Almost all of the group's work will occur during this stage. Relationships are strengthened as a group so that the tasks can be worked on. Group leaders are usually less involved.

End
The group reviews its accomplishments. Feelings associated with the termination of the group are addressed.

THE APPROACHES TO GROUP PSYCHOTHERAPY

A therapeutic group provides a unique microcosm in which members, through the process of interacting with each other, gain more knowledge and insight into themselves for the purpose of making changes in their lives.

The goal of the group may be a major or minor change in personality structure or changing a specific emotional or behavioral problem.

A social worker helps members come to agreement regarding the purpose, function, and structure of a group.

A group is the major helping agent.

Individual self-actualization occurs through:

- Release of feelings that block social performance
- Support from others (not being alone)
- Orientation to reality and check out own reality with others
- Reappraisal of self

Some types of groups include:

- Groups centered on a shared problem
- Counseling groups
- Activity groups
- Action groups
- Self-help groups
- Natural groups
- Closed versus open groups
- Structured groups
- Crisis groups
- Reference groups (similar values)

Psychodrama is a treatment approach in which roles are enacted in a group context. Members of the group recreate their problems and devote themselves to the role dilemmas of each member.

THE DIFFERENTIAL USE OF GROUP PROCESS

There are some advantages to participation in group therapy that individual treatment does not provide. The group process serves as a support network and a sounding board for clients. Through the group process, clients hear specific ideas for improving difficult situations or circumstances from others who are going through similar challenges. Group members' opinions are often highly respected as they come with the credibility of having experienced similar issues.

Regularly talking and listening to others also helps clients put their own problems in perspective. Clients may feel that they are the only ones struggling, but they learn, through the group process that they are not. The ability to see and hear others like themselves indicates to clients that they are not alone and, thereby, reduces stigma and isolation.

Diversity is another important benefit of group therapy. Clients have different personalities and backgrounds and look at situations in different ways. By seeing how others address problems, clients are afforded new strategies for facing their own concerns.

Observing maladaptive behavior in others also may help clients see the effects of their own similar behavior. Discussing problems in a group may make it easier for clients to discuss their feelings with others, such as friends and family members, outside of the group. Group interaction helps develop healthy social interaction skills. Members can observe the social and coping skills of others who may serve as positive role models. Role-playing is also feasible in the group context.

THE TECHNIQUES FOR DEVELOPING AND MAINTAINING GROUP COHESION

Despite the differences in goals or purposes, all groups have common characteristics and processes.

Groups help through:

- Instillation of hope
- Universality
- Altruism
- Interpersonal learning
- Self-understanding and insight

Factors affecting group cohesion include:

- Group size
- Homogeneity: similarity of group members
- Participation in goal and norm setting for group
- Interdependence: being dependent on one another for achievement of common goals
- Member stability: frequent change in membership results in less cohesiveness

Contraindications for a group include a **client** who is **in crisis, suicidal**, compulsively needy for attention, actively psychotic, and/or paranoid.

THE PROCESS OF CO-THERAPY

Co-therapy or conjoint therapy is psychotherapy conducted with more than one social worker present. This format is more common in group and family therapy.

Co-therapy is often used as a teaching or supervision method in which one of the social workers is modeling therapeutic skills for the other. In this model of co-therapy, the social workers do not have equal power or authority, which can be problematic and lead to role conflict. For clients, co-therapists should have equal standing, which is not possible when one is the supervisor of the other and a hierarchical relationship exists between them. However, advantages for the supervisor–supervisee include having the supervisor able to observe performance firsthand and becoming immediately aware of performance issues or concerns.

When working with heterosexual couples, co-therapy is often done with male and female social work teams. This model gives each client an individual therapist, not a "shared one," as well as a therapy team for the couple. With two social workers there is more opportunity and flexibility for clinical attention to be given individually or as a unit. Using this approach also helps prevent "triangulation" (a client feeling that there is two against one), which is often gender based. It also provides the modeling of healthy relationship skills, as well as the opportunity for one social worker to be a clinical observer while the other is directing and managing a session. Lastly, a second social worker can be useful to manage a crisis should it arise.

THE CONCEPT OF CONGRUENCE IN COMMUNICATION

Communication can be verbal and nonverbal, so an assessment of clients' communication skills must involve both. Role-playing is a good way to assess and enhance clients' communication skills. It also allows a social worker to see if there is congruence between nonverbal and verbal communication.

Congruence is the matching of awareness and experience with communication. It is essential that a client is able to express himself or herself and that this communication is reflective of his or her feelings. Congruence is essential for the vitality of a relationship and to facilitate true helping as part of the problem-solving process.

THE METHODS USED IN SUMMARIZING COMMUNICATION

Summarization seeks to bring together the important points of a discussion and to give a client and social worker awareness of the progress made. It can give a client a sense that a social worker understands and/or brings a sense of closure. It omits irrelevant information and organizes pertinent aspects of the interaction. It allows a social worker and a client to leave an interaction with the same ideas in mind and provides a sense of closure at the completion of a discussion. Summarizing can be done periodically throughout the discussion or only at its close. But no matter who does it or how frequently it occurs, summarization is a valuable intervention technique.

During summarization, a social worker and a client strive to grasp the significance of what has been said, to formulate the meaning of the information, and to achieve new understandings. Summarization is helpful in pulling together what seems to be disorganized or unrelated material.

There are a variety of summarization approaches. A social worker can summarize the content and essential feelings expressed at any point or at the end of an interaction. A social worker can ask a client to review what he or she has accomplished or the status of the presenting problem. Lastly, a social worker and a client may jointly look at what has been achieved.

Summarization statements can include a social worker saying, "Have I got this correct . . . ?" "You have said that . . . ," and/or "During the past hour, you and I have discussed . . . ."

VERBAL AND NONVERBAL COMMUNICATION TECHNIQUES

In order to facilitate change through the problem-solving process, a social worker must use various verbal and nonverbal communication techniques to assist clients to understand their behavior and feelings. In addition, to ensure clients are honest and forthcoming during this process, social workers must build trusting relationships with clients. These relationships develop through effective verbal and nonverbal communication. Social workers must be adept at using both forms of communication successfully, as well as understanding them, because verbal and nonverbal cues will be used by clients throughout the problem-solving process. Insight into their meaning will produce a higher degree of sensitivity to clients' experiences and a deeper understanding of their problems.

There are many verbal and nonverbal communication methods, including:

- *Active listening*, in which social workers are sitting up straight and leaning toward clients in a relaxed and open manner. Attentive listening can involve commenting on clients' statements, asking open-ended questions, and making statements that show listening is occurring.

- *Silence* by social workers, which can show acceptance of clients' feelings and promotes introspection or time to think about what has been learned.

- *Questioning* using open- and closed-ended formats to get relevant information in a nonjudgmental manner.

- *Reflecting or validating* to show empathetic understanding of clients' problems. These techniques can also assist clients in understanding negative thought patterns.

- *Paraphrasing and clarifying* by social workers to rephrase what clients are saying in order to join together information. Clarification uses questioning, paraphrasing, and restating to ensure full understanding of clients' ideas and thoughts.

- *Reframing* by social workers shows clients that there are different perspectives and ideas that can help to change negative thinking patterns and promote change.

- Exhibiting *desirable facial expressions*, which include direct eye contact if culturally appropriate, with warmth and concern reflected through varied facial expressions.

- Using *desirable postures or gestures*, which include appropriate arm movements and attentive gestures.

TECHNIQUES THAT ELICIT THE UNDERLYING MEANING OF COMMUNICATION

In communication, there are two types of content, manifest and latent. *Manifest content* is the concrete words or terms contained in a communication, whereas *latent content* is that which is not visible, the underlying meaning of words or terms.

Relying just on the manifest content to understand client experiences or problems may result in *not* really understanding their meaning to individuals.

There are social work techniques such as *clarifying, paraphrasing, confronting,* and *interpreting* that can assist social workers in developing a better understanding of the meaning of clients' communication.

In addition, therapeutic techniques, such as psychoanalysis, focus on the hidden meaning of fantasies or dreams.

THE METHODS USED TO OBTAIN AND PROVIDE FEEDBACK

Social workers interface with professionals and others in order to achieve the best possible outcomes for clients. Feedback is essential in order to learn what works and what can be done better.

There is no single method for social workers to seek feedback. Many factors may impact on how such feedback is solicited and incorporated into practice. However, there are some important principles that social workers should adhere to when obtaining or providing feedback.

1. Feedback may be either verbal or nonverbal, so social workers must make efforts to see what clients are trying to convey verbally or via their behavior and nonverbal cues in order to see whether interventions should be altered.

2. When social workers involve consultants or others in the feedback process related to client care, clients should provide consent.

3. Social workers should ask for feedback in difficult circumstances—not just when circumstances appear neutral or positive. It can be tempting only to ask for feedback from people who will say something positive. Sometimes, the best learning can be from those who will be critical. Talking through difficult feedback in supervision is important.

4. Feedback is especially critical at key decision points (such as when transferring or closing cases).

5. It is important to guard against influencing people to respond in a particular way; this influence may be unintentional, because a social worker may have more influence or power than the individual from whom feedback is sought.

6. Confidentiality should be respected if the informant wants it.

7. Always be clear about why feedback is needed and what will be done with the information.

8. Documentation of feedback is essential.

9. Be aware that the feedback may be very different depending upon when it is solicited. It is critical to realize how recent events may have influenced information received. Getting feedback repeatedly at several different times may be needed to see if responses differ.

10. A social worker must make sure that the communication method is appropriate. For a younger person, texting, e-mail, or an online questionnaire may work, whereas a face-to-face conversation may be needed for others. The language should be jargon-free and issues such as language, culture, and disability may affect the ways in which people both understand and react to requests for feedback. A social worker may want to use closed-ended questions and/or open ones to capture needed data.

Dynamics of the Social Worker–Client Relationship

13

THE PROCESS OF ENGAGEMENT IN SOCIAL WORK PRACTICE

The beginning of the problem-solving process includes activities of a social worker and a client to be helped that are directed at (a) *becoming engaged with each other (engagement)*, (b) assessing a client's situation in order to select appropriate goals and the means of attaining them (assessment), and (c) planning how to employ these means (planning). During engagement, the limits to confidentiality must be explicitly stated at the beginning of this stage.

It is important to consider how a client feels about coming for help and to deal with any negative feelings a client may feel (particularly if a client is involuntarily seeking help). A social worker must be willing to discuss these feelings openly, because very little in a client can be changed until negative feelings are addressed. If a social worker is empathic with a client, it may be possible to find a common ground between what a client wishes and what a social worker can legitimately do.

A social worker and a client establish a therapeutic alliance in which a client views himself or herself as an ally of a social worker. A working alliance or a willingness by a client to work with a social worker should be established. A working alliance is sometimes referred to as a treatment alliance.

A social worker should express hopefulness that change can occur.

Resistance may occur during this stage. If clients are resistant to engage, social workers should clarify the process or specify what will happen and discuss this ambivalence.

THE SOCIAL WORKER'S ROLE IN THE CHANGE PROCESS

People generally like to give advice. It gives them the feeling of being competent and important. Hence, social workers may easily fall into this inappropriate role without taking into account the abilities, the fears, and the interests of clients and/or their circumstances.

Social workers should also not be insensitive to clients' resistance. When a client does not claim any difficulties, is unable or refuses to talk, explains that it is someone else's fault, and/or denies what has happened, a social worker may try to argue or in other ways exert pressure. This response tends to increase a client's resistance. This approach does nothing for a client.

A social worker may also confuse the situation and hinder clarification of the problem. In an effort to establish a relationship, a social worker may overpraise or fail to confront a client. A client must look at his or her own role in the situation and recognize his or her own limitations.

Social worker roles in the problem-solving process include consultant, advocate, case manager, catalyst, broker, mediator, facilitator, instructor, mobilizer, resource allocator, and so on.

THE CONCEPT OF EMPATHY

Empathic understanding involves being nonjudgmental, accepting, and genuine.

Empathic Communication

- Establishes rapport with clients—empathic communication is one means of bridging the gap between a social worker and client
- *Starts where a client is* and stays attuned to a client throughout the encounter (being perceptive to changes in frame of mind)
- Increases the level at which clients explore themselves and their problems
- Responds to a client's nonverbal messages (a social worker can observe body language and make explicit a client's feelings)
- Decreases defensiveness and engages a client in processing and testing new information
- Defuses anger that represents obstacles to progress

Empathic responding encourages more rational discussion and sets the stage for problem solving. For those clients who have learned to cope with feelings of helplessness and frustration by becoming angry and/or violent, an empathic response may be the first step in engaging in helping relationships.

THE CONCEPT OF A HELPING RELATIONSHIP

The therapeutic process calls for several basic conditions.

There must be trust with a social worker. Unless this condition exists, facts will be withheld and there will be no real exploration of problems. Trust grows as clients talk about themselves and their circumstances, revealing things they do not ordinarily disclose, and discovering that social workers do not condemn them. Trust does not come quickly.

There must be recognition that *the therapeutic process is a joint exploration.* Both a social worker and client must be willing to examine problems, attitudes, and feelings.

There must be listening on both sides. However, a social worker must listen more than a client does. There is no movement when a social worker is doing all the talking and a client listens passively. A social worker must behave in a manner that makes it easier for a client to speak freely by listening attentively, by *accepting what is said in a nonjudgmental manner*, and by giving occasional support or encouragement.

A social worker may be encouraging by simply repeating reflectively or paraphrasing what a client has said. A social worker may, without other comment, say, "Tell me more," or show acceptance when a client reveals ideas, attitudes, or behaviors that are generally viewed unfavorably. A social worker may also point out that other persons also have such attitudes or make similar mistakes. By assisting a client to speak more freely, a social worker not only furthers mutual exploration of the problem, but also frees a client of anxieties that stand in the way of readiness to accept suggestions. A social worker is also obligated to respect the confidence a client has placed in him or her and to refrain from sharing the information with others.

THE USE OF ACCEPTANCE

The aim of helping varies with different situations. The purpose is to assist a client to develop new skills. The intent may be to stimulate or to bolster the self-confidence of a client. Again, a client may have requested assistance to think through a problem or to make a decision. In a helping relationship, a social worker is trying to constructively assist a client—that is, to have an impact on or to influence his or her thinking and acting. The influence is further presumed to be in the direction of increasing the autonomy, understanding, effectiveness, and skill of a client.

Helping is distinguished from the more common concepts of advice giving, reprimanding, or punishing. These often involve threats and seldom result in more than outward conformity or superficial change. They generally do not increase strength or willingness and ability to carry responsibility.

The core of the helping process is the relationship between a social worker and a client.

The relationship between a social worker and a client is expressed through *interaction*. This interaction is commonly thought of in terms of *verbal communication*, which is natural, because the greater part of treatment consists of talking. However, *nonverbal behavior* is also very important. Body posture, gestures, facial expressions, eye movements, and other reactions often express feelings and attitudes more clearly than do spoken words. It is often for these reasons that a social worker must be aware of his or her own feelings, attitudes, and responses, as well as those of a client, if he or she is to understand what is taking place and be of assistance.

THE METHODS USED TO CLARIFY THE ROLE OF THE SOCIAL WORKER

Roles consist of a set of rules or norms that function to guide behavior. Roles specify what goals should be pursued, what tasks must be accomplished, and how to behave in a given situation. Role theory views day-to-day social behavior as individuals carrying out their defined roles.

Problems can arise when a client is not clear on a social worker's role. Initial clarification should be made during engagement and should be discussed during the therapeutic process if the role of a social worker changes.

THE PRINCIPLES OF RELATIONSHIP BUILDING

A social worker cannot be useful in helping others unless he or she understands and is willing to accept the difficulties that all human beings encounter in trying to meet their needs. A social worker must know that the potential for all the weaknesses and strengths known to humanity exists at some level in every person. Social workers must also understand that human beings become more capable of dealing with their problems as they feel more adequate. Social workers recognize positive, as well as negative, aspects of a client, which will influence efforts to change and successful achievements of goals.

The interaction between a social worker and a client both involves and is affected by the relationship between the two persons. Human beings act in terms of their feelings, attitudes, and understandings; hence, these must be taken into account and explored if the helping process is to result in change. Both a social worker and a client have objectives; a social worker's perceived objective is to be of assistance. *Clarification and definition of these objectives often become important parts of the helping process.* Both a social worker and a client have a degree of power (i.e., ability to influence the situation and the results).

PROFESSIONAL OBJECTIVITY IN THE SOCIAL WORKER–CLIENT RELATIONSHIP

Social worker communication should not be burdened with emotional investment; instead, social workers should be interested, genuinely concerned, and encouraging, while neither condemning nor praising.

The relationship between a social worker and a client must be productive, and must have certain characteristics. There must be *mutual acceptance and trust*. A client must feel he or she is understood and valued as a person, though his or her performance may be unsatisfactory. *If a client feels judged, he or she will not speak freely*, and his or her response will be to find ways to defend himself or herself and his or her acts.

A social worker accepts and understands a client's problems, recognizes the demands and the requirements of the situation, and assists a client to examine alternatives and potential consequences. A social worker does not tell a client what he or she should do. Only a client can and will decide, because he or she acts upon his or her feelings, insights, and/or understanding of himself or herself and the problem.

THE CONCEPT OF TRANSFERENCE AND COUNTERTRANSFERENCE

Transference refers to redirection of a client's feelings for a significant person to a social worker. Transference was first described by Sigmund Freud, who acknowledged its importance for a better understanding of a client's feelings.

Transference is often manifested as an erotic attraction toward a social worker, but can be seen in many other forms such as rage, hatred, mistrust, parentification, extreme dependence, or even placing a social worker in an esteemed status.

When Freud initially encountered transference in his therapy with clients, he felt it was an obstacle to treatment success. But what he learned was that the analysis of the transference was actually the work needed to be done. The focus in psychoanalysis is, in large part, a social worker and a client recognizing the transference relationship and exploring the relationship's meaning.

Since the transference between a client and a social worker happens on an unconscious level, a social worker doing psychoanalysis uses transference to reveal unresolved conflicts a client has with childhood figures.

Countertransference is defined as redirection of a social worker's feelings toward a client or, more generally, as a social worker's emotional entanglement with a client. A social worker's recognition of his or her own countertransference is nearly as critical as understanding a client's transference.

Not only does this help a social worker regulate his or her emotions in the therapeutic relationship, but it also gives a social worker valuable insight into what a client is attempting to elicit in him or her.

For example, a social worker who is sexually attracted to a client must understand this as countertransference and look at how a client may be eliciting this reaction. Once it has been identified, a social worker can ask a client what his or her feelings are toward a social worker, and/or explore how they relate to unconscious motivations, desires, or fears.

THE COMPONENTS OF THE SOCIAL WORKER–CLIENT RELATIONSHIP

A social worker–client relationship is an emotional or connecting bond. The relationship is the communication bridge whereby messages pass over the bridge with greater or lesser difficulty, depending on the nature of the emotional connection or alliance.

A positive relationship is an important tool of helping. Social workers must create a warm, accepting, trustworthy, and dependable relationship with clients.

In working with a client, a social worker must convey a sense of respect for a client's individuality, as well as his or her right and capacity for *self-determination* and for being fully involved in the helping process from beginning to end.

The most consistent factor associated with beneficial outcomes of a helping relationship is a positive relationship between a social worker and a client, but other factors, such as a social worker's competence and the motivation and involvement of a client, are also influential.

THE USE OF THE SOCIAL WORKER–CLIENT RELATIONSHIP AS AN INTERVENTION/TREATMENT TOOL

The primary mission of the social work profession is to enhance human well-being and help meet the basic human needs of all people, with particular attention to the needs and empowerment of people who are vulnerable, oppressed, and living in poverty (*NASW Code of Ethics, 1999—Preamble*).

Empowerment aims to ensure a sense of control over well-being and that change is possible. A social worker can help to empower individuals, groups, communities, and institutions.

On an individual level, social workers can engage in a process with a client aimed at strengthening his or her self-worth by making a change in life that is based on his or her desires (self-determination).

To facilitate empowerment, a social worker should:

- Establish a relationship aimed at meeting a client's needs and wishes such as access to social services and benefits or to other sources of information

- Educate a client to improve his or her skills, thereby increasing the ability for self-help

- Help a client to secure resources, such as those from other organizations or agencies, as well as natural support networks, to meet needs

- Unite a client with others who are experiencing the same issues if and when needed to enable social and political action

Social workers should also use an empowerment process with groups, communities, and institutions so they may gain or regain the capacity to meet human needs, enhance overall well-being and potential, and provide individuals control over their lives to the extent possible.

A social worker needs many skills that focus on the activation of resources, the creation of alliances, and the expansion of opportunities in order to facilitate empowerment.

THE EFFECTS OF THE CLIENT'S DEVELOPMENTAL LEVEL ON THE SOCIAL WORKER–CLIENT RELATIONSHIP

Social workers' ability to understand clients' developmental levels is essential in order to effectively assist them. Chronological age is often a poor predictor of abilities. Instead in-depth assessments of physical, cognitive, social, emotional, psychological, spiritual, and cultural well-being should be conducted to understand limits and capabilities in these areas. This information will help social workers devise appropriate, informed communication, socialization, and intervention strategies that are developmentally appropriate. A good grasp of clients' developmental levels keeps clients from becoming frustrated, discouraged, oppositional, and/or uncooperative as techniques that require greater insight and/or advanced communication skills are used inappropriately.

Many clients also have long trauma histories which may impede growth or even cause regression in developmental functioning. Clients may be resistant to trust the seemingly good intentions of social workers. Clients may also be using regression as a defense mechanism, causing their functioning to have reverted back to that achieved by them in earlier developmental stages.

Given the problems or crises facing them, clients may need simple concrete explanations, rather than abstract techniques. They may be distracted by their situations and thus appear to be functioning at lower cognitive levels than would be expected or demonstrated in the past. Clients are not "pretending," and social workers can help by providing tangible examples and using simple, direct communication strategies.

THE INFLUENCE OF THE SOCIAL WORKER'S OWN VALUES ON THE SOCIAL WORKER–CLIENT RELATIONSHIP

Social workers must recognize values that may *inhibit* the therapeutic relationship.

1. **Universalism—There is one acceptable norm or standard for everyone** *versus* there are other valid standards that have been developed by people that they have determined to be most useful to them.

2. **Dichotomous "either-or" thinking; differences are inferior, wrong, bad** *versus* differences are just different and coexist.

3. **Heightened ability/value on separating, categorizing, numbering, "left-brain"** *versus* "right-brain" or "whole picture." Mental activity is highly valued to the exclusion of physical and spiritual experiences. Persons are studied in isolation, not as part of a group or interrelated with their environment.

4. **High value on control, constraint, restraint** *versus* value on flexibility, emotion/feelings, expressiveness, spirituality. What cannot be controlled and definitively defined is deemed nonexistent, unimportant, unscientific, or deviant/inferior. Reality is defined with the assumption of objectivity; subjective reality is viewed as invalid because it cannot be consistently replicated by many people.

5. **Measure of self comes from outside, and is only in contrast to others** *versus* value comes from within—you are worthwhile because you were born, and you strive to live a life that is in harmony with others and the environment. Worth is measured by accumulation of wealth or status (outside measures)—therefore, one can only feel good if one is better than someone else, or accumulates more than someone else, or has a higher status.

6. **Power is defined as "power over" others, mastery over environment** *versus* "power through" or in harmony with others; by sharing power, power can be expanded, and each becomes more powerful.

THE DYNAMICS OF POWER AND TRANSPARENCY IN THE HELPING RELATIONSHIP

Social workers have power and privileges associated with their roles, titles, and education. Being conscious of these privileges is critical because there is a responsibility to challenge hierarchical assumptions and power dynamics inherent in social worker–client relationships. Social workers should use egalitarian and collaborative approaches that give clients choices, decision-making power, and opportunities for honest feedback.

If social workers are transparent and honest about their positions of privilege, they help to undercut the power differentials. Transparency about the process and intent of social work interventions is essential. Role expectations should be discussed and power differences should be acknowledged.

Transparency and power are linked. If clients are not informed about what is going to occur in each stage of the problem-solving process and do not understand the theoretical models which help explain their situations, they cannot be full participants in the change process. Thus, transparency or the provision of all available information is the underpinning of the therapeutic relationship. If social workers deliberately withhold observations or knowledge from clients, they are reinforcing the power differential which inherently exists and disempowering clients. This is not helpful to clients or in accordance with the values of social work practice.

THE DYNAMICS OF DIVERSITY IN THE HELPING RELATIONSHIP

Culture, race, and ethnicity are strongly linked to values. *A social worker's self-awareness about his or her own attitudes, values, and beliefs about cultural differences and a willingness to acknowledge racial and cultural differences are critical factors* in working with diverse populations. A social worker is responsible for bringing up and addressing issues of cultural difference with a client and is also ethically responsible for being culturally competent by obtaining the appropriate knowledge, skills, and experience.

Social workers should:

1. Move from being culturally unaware to aware of their own heritage and the heritage of others

2. Value and celebrate differences of others rather than maintaining an ethnocentric stance

3. Have an awareness of personal values and biases and how they may influence relationships with clients

4. Demonstrate comfort with racial and cultural differences between themselves and clients

5. Have an awareness of personal and professional limitations

6. Acknowledge their own racial attitudes, beliefs, and feelings

THE DYNAMICS OF DOMESTIC VIOLENCE AND OTHER VIOLENCE IN THE HELPING RELATIONSHIP

According to most literature on domestic violence, traditional marital/ couples therapy is not appropriate in addressing abuse in the family. It puts victims in greater danger of further abuse.

Medical needs and safety are priorities. Social workers should consider domestic violence in the context of Maslow's hierarchy of needs.

In working with a victim of abuse, *trust* is a major issue in establishing a therapeutic alliance.

Application of Evidence-Based Practices

14

THE TECHNIQUES USED TO EVALUATE A CLIENT'S PROGRESS

Evaluating progress is a critical part of the problem-solving process. Examining with a client what has occurred and what still needs to occur involves him or her in treatment decisions.

Evaluation methods can be simple or complex. They can rely on quantitative information that shows data on reductions in target behaviors, health care improvements, or psychiatric symptom increases, and/or qualitative information in which a client and/or social worker subjectively report on progress made in various areas.

When evaluating progress, a social worker and client should gather all needed information and identify factors that helped or hindered progress. Goals outlined in the contract should be modified, if needed, based upon the outcome of the evaluation.

Social workers should assist clients to understand the progress they have made so they can clearly understand and celebrate their accomplishments as well as identify areas that need attention. This process should ensure that clients understand why progress has happened, as well as include a dialogue about any changes that need to occur in the problem-solving process to facilitate continued growth.

TECHNIQUES USED TO MEASURE THE EFFECTIVENESS OF THE SOCIAL WORK INTERVENTION

Goal-attainment scaling (GAS) was first used to evaluate the effectiveness of mental health treatments, but has now been expanded for use with a wide variety of populations and in multiple service delivery areas. Client outcomes for each goal are specified, with the worst to the best possible outcomes noted. These outcomes become a Likert-type scale for each client to assess his or her progress. For example, a 5-point scale can be constructed with response choices consisting of an outcome much better than expected (+2), an outcome somewhat better than expected (+1), an outcome as expected (0), an outcome somewhat worse than expected (-1), and an outcome much worse than expected (-2).

The specific actions or tasks aimed at achieving these outcomes can also be rated using a similar method called task-achievement scaling (TAS). The effort toward task achievement, the timeliness of task achievement, and/or the steps taken/progress made toward task achievement are all aspects that can be rated and evaluated.

GAS and TAS are easy, low-cost evaluation techniques, though there are problems with both reliability and validity that threaten their utility.

UTILIZATION OF RESEARCH RESULTS IN PRACTICE

The promotion of evidence-based research within social work is widespread. Evidence-based research gathers evidence that may be informative for clinical practice or clinical decision making. It also involves the process of gathering and synthesizing scientific evidence from various sources and translating it to be applied to practice.

The use of evidence-based practice places the well-being of clients at the forefront, desiring to discover and use the best practices available. The use of evidence-based practice requires social workers to only use services and techniques that were found effective by rigorous, scientific, empirical studies—that is, outcome research.

Social workers must be willing and able to locate and use evidence-based interventions. In areas in which evidence-based interventions are not available, social workers must still use research to guide practice. Applying knowledge gleaned from research findings will assist social workers in providing services informed by scientific investigation and lead to new interventions that can be evaluated as evidence-based practices.

When reading and interpreting experimental research findings, social workers must be able to identify independent variables (or those that are believed to be causes) and dependent variables (which are the impacts or results). In many studies, the independent variable is the treatment provided and the dependent variable is the target behavior that is trying to be changed. The reliability and validity of research findings should also be assessed.

> *Reliability* (dependability, stability, consistency, predictability): Can you get the same answer repeatedly?
>
> *Validity* (accuracy): Is what is believed to be measured actually being measured or is it something else?
>> External validity: Can the results be generalized?
>> Internal validity: Is there confidence in cause and effect?

APPLYING EVIDENCE-BASED PRACTICES TO CURRENT PROGRAMS

The results of research and statistical analyses are only as useful as the extent to which they can be accurately and confidently interpreted. The issue of accurate and confident interpretation is at the center of determining validity. Validity is the degree to which correct inferences can be made from research. There are two types of validity—**internal and external**.

Internal validity is the *confidence that one thing* (the independent variable) *causes another* (the dependent variable). In social work research, the intervention or treatment is often the independent variable.

There are threats or events other than the independent variable (or believed cause) that may have caused changes to the dependent variable (the results). A social worker critiquing research should look to see if these and other factors were present that could have influenced the results.

Some Threats to Internal Validity

- *History*—a client's attitudes or behaviors changed due to other events occurring in his or her life or society that did not relate to the intervention

- *Maturation*—a client's attitudes or behaviors changed because of natural maturational occurrences in the life course and not due to the intervention

- *Selection biases*—there were preexisting differences between clients who received the intervention and those who did not, causing differential outcomes

- *Testing*—exposure to repeated testing, not the intervention, influenced a client's behavior

- *Statistical regression*—extreme attitudes and behaviors tend to systematically drift to the mean rather than remain stable or become more extreme, so changes were due to statistical regression rather than intervention effects

- *Instrumentation*—use of revised or alternate scales and instruments caused differential results rather than the intervention itself causing the noted changes

- *Mortality or attrition*—sometimes those who dropped out of treatment were different in some way than those who remained and these differences, rather than the intervention, caused the outcomes

External validity is the ability to *generalize* findings to other settings, populations, and so on. When critiquing relevant research, a social worker should determine the characteristics of the sample used and the conditions under which the research was conducted. It may not be possible to achieve the same results if the intervention was used with those who were older or younger than the study sample or in an urban, suburban, or rural setting different than the one chosen. A social worker should be able to identify issues or threats that limit the potential generalizability of the findings so that additional research can be conducted to determine whether similar results can be achieved with varying populations and in diverse settings.

Macro Practice (18%)

Research Methods and Design **15**

THE METHODS OF DATA COLLECTION

Qualitative research usually involves collecting information through unstructured interviews, observation, and/or focus groups. Data can be collected from a single individual at a time or multiple people in group settings. Qualitative data collection methods are usually very time consuming, so they are confined to smaller samples than usually found in quantitative approaches. Quantitative research mainly collects data through the input of responses to research instruments containing questions (i.e., such as questionnaires). Information can be input either by the respondents themselves (e.g., online or mail survey) or social workers can input data (e.g., phone surveys or interviews). Methods for distributing surveys are via postal mail, phone, website, or in person. However, newer technologies have created additional delivery options, including through wireless devices such as smartphones.

Social workers can also do research using secondary data, which is information that has already been collected for other purposes. Use of existing data is efficient since time and money associated with data collection are spared. However, the completeness of existing data, as well as its reliability, may be a concern as sound research practices covering its collection may not have been used.

THE DIFFERENCE BETWEEN QUANTITATIVE AND QUALITATIVE DATA

Evaluation/research methods can be classified as either qualitative or quantitative. In qualitative evaluations, data are collected through observations and/or interviews. Findings are generated via identification of themes in the language used and content contained in the communication observed or generated.

Quantitative evaluations are conducted by making numerical comparisons and statistical inferences. If both qualitative and quantitative methods are used, social workers are using a mixed-method approach to evaluation/research.

DATA ANALYSIS PROCEDURES

Data analysis procedures begin with preparation that involves cleaning the data, checking it for accuracy, coding it for analysis, developing a database, and entering the data into the computer.

Once entered into the computer, *descriptive statistics* are used to describe the basic features of the data. They provide simple summaries about the sample and the measures. Together with simple graphics analysis, they form the basis of virtually every quantitative analysis of data. Descriptive statistics describe what the data shows.

Inferential statistics are used to answer research questions or test models or hypotheses. In many cases, the conclusions from inferential statistics extend beyond the immediate data. For instance, inferential statistics determine the probability that an observed difference between groups is a dependable one or one that might have happened by chance.

In most research, analyses include both descriptive and inferential statistics. Social workers must balance the level of detail that is included in a research report with the need to avoid overwhelming readers and missing the highlighting of major findings. If too much detail is included, readers may not be able to pick out the key results. Analysis details are appropriately relegated to appendices, reserving only the most critical analysis summaries for the body of the report itself.

THE METHODS USED TO EVALUATE RESEARCH INSTRUMENTS

Social workers should not simply use research instruments because they are available or have been used commonly in the past. Poor instrument selection can threaten the efficacy of a study. Spending time critically reviewing possible instruments is essential. Factors to consider include instrument length and complexity, research aims, sensitivity, specificity, reliability, validity, and ethical issues.

Often, the time to complete instruments takes away from program participation. In addition, clients are taxed by presenting problems and may not have the ability to devote extensive attention to instrument completion. Language barriers or literacy may also be issues. Thus, shorter and simpler instruments are always preferred. The aim is to develop and/or use instruments that gather the needed information in as short a time as possible. Instrument instructions and layout also need to be straightforward.

Ensuring that instruments are collecting data needed to meet research aims is paramount. When using existing surveys, there is a greater risk that questions do not truly measure what is intended as they may have been constructed to assess similar, but not exactly the same, constructs. A careful review of instruments must be done to ensure that all variables are measured accurately and that question wording captures the information that is essential to answer research questions of interest.

The level of measurement is also important. A dichotomous (yes/no) variable does not produce much sensitivity or variability, whereas a ratio measure may reduce reliability. A balance needs to be reached between measuring variables at the highest levels of measurement and concerns about reliability. The number of response choices for Likert-type scales must be weighed in light of this needed balance.

Instruments should be reliable and valid—detecting real change and not measurement errors, as well as assessing the constructs being studied. Reliability and validity testing can take a lot of time and effort. Thus, social workers often look to use existing instruments that have been extensively tested as they may not have the resources to do reliability and/or validity testing themselves.

Lastly, ethical issues must be examined. Social workers should only gather necessary information. Extraneous data that is not needed to answer research questions should not be included in instruments. Ensuring that clients cannot be identified is critical if the data collection is not anonymous. All data collected must be confidential, even when identities of client participants are known.

THE METHODS USED TO ASSESS RELIABILITY AND VALIDITY IN SOCIAL WORK RESEARCH

Reliability in social work research concerns the ability to get consistent assessments or data by reducing random errors associated with its collection. There are four main methods to assess reliability.

- *Interrater or Interobserver Reliability*
  Assesses the degree to which different raters/observers give consistent estimates of the same phenomenon

■ *Test–Retest Reliability*
Assesses the consistency of a measure from one time to another.

■ *Parallel Forms Reliability*
Assesses the consistency of the results of two tests constructed in the same way from the same content domain

■ *Internal Consistency Reliability*
Assesses the consistency of results across items within a test

Validity is the degree to which what is actually being measured actually is what is claimed to be measured. It attempts to minimize systematic errors that may yield reliable results but do not actually assess the constructs of interest. There are different means to assess validity.

■ *Face Validity*
Examines whether the assessments "on their face" measure the constructs

■ *Content Validity*
Examines whether all of the relevant content domains are covered

■ *Criterion-Related Validity (including predictive, concurrent, convergent, and discriminant validities)*
Examines whether constructs perform as anticipated in relation to other theoretical constructs

 ■ *Predictive validity* assesses whether constructs predict what they should theoretically be able to predict.
 ■ *Concurrent validity* assesses whether constructs distinguish between groups that they should be able to distinguish between.
 ■ *Convergent validity* assesses the degree to which constructs are similar to (converge on) other constructs to which they should be similar.
 ■ *Discriminant validity* assesses the degree to which constructs are different from (diverge away from) other constructs to which they should be dissimilar.

SOCIAL WORK RESEARCH DESIGNS

Social work research needs a design or a structure before data collection or analysis can commence. The function of a research design is to ensure that the evidence or data collected enables the research questions to be answered. Research design is different from the method by which data are collected. Many research methods texts confuse research designs with methods. It is not uncommon to see research design treated as a mode of data collection rather than as a logical structure of the inquiry.

Research design is a blueprint, with the research problem determining the type of design used. Research design will:

1. Identify the research problem clearly and justify its selection

2. Review previously published literature associated with the problem area

3. Clearly and explicitly specify hypotheses (i.e., research questions) central to the problem selected

4. Effectively describe the data that will be necessary for an adequate test of the hypotheses and explain how such data will be obtained

5. Describe the methods of analysis that will be applied to the data in determining whether or not the hypotheses are true or false.

Types of Research

There are three broad types of research—*experimental, quasi-experimental,* and *pre-experimental.* Randomized experiments, also called experimental, are the most rigorous. When randomization of subjects or groups is neither practical nor feasible, quasi-experimental approaches can be used. Quasi-experimental research uses intervention and comparison groups, but assignment to the groups is nonrandom. Pre-experimental studies contain intervention groups only and lack comparison/control groups, making them the weakest.

Single-Subject Research

Single-subject research aims to determine whether an intervention has the intended impact on a client, or on many clients who form a group. The most common single-subject research is *pre–post test* or *single-case study* (AB) in which there is a comparison of behavior before treatment (baseline; denoted by an "A") and behavior after the start of treatment (intervention; denoted by a "B"). The *reversal or multiple baseline* (ABA or ABAB) is also commonly used.

In single-subject research, a client is used as his or her own control. The focus differs from experimental research, which looks at the average effect of an intervention between groups of people.

Single-subject research is ideal for studying the behavioral change a client exhibits as a result of some treatment. When done correctly and carefully, single-subject research can show a causal effect between the intervention and the outcome.

The flexibility, simplicity, and low cost of single-subject research are also beneficial. It can be more flexible and easier to plan because it is usually smaller in scale than experimental research.

Attempts should be made to maximize both internal and external validity. Internal validity addresses the extent to which causal inferences can be made about the intervention and the targeted behavior. External validity addresses how generalizable those inferences are to the general population. Due to the small number of study participants, single-subject research tends to have poor external validity, limiting the ability to generalize the findings to a wider audience.

It is important to remember that, in some cases, it would be unethical to withdraw treatment if clients would be put at risk for harm. Also, in a crisis, treatment would not be delayed in an effort to obtain baseline data.

APPROPRIATE USE OF STATISTICAL DATA

Social workers engaged in research or the evaluation of services should discuss collected information only for professional purposes and only with people professionally concerned with this information (*NASW Code of Ethics, 1999—5.02 Evaluation and Research*).

Social workers should report evaluation and research findings accurately. They should not fabricate or falsify results and should take steps to correct any errors later found in published data using standard publication methods (*NASW Code of Ethics, 1999—5.02 Evaluation and Research*).

Social workers who report evaluation and research results should protect participants' confidentiality by omitting identifying information unless proper consent has been obtained authorizing disclosure (*NASW Code of Ethics, 1999—5.02 Evaluation and Research*).

RESEARCH ETHICS (E.G., INSTITUTIONAL REVIEW BOARDS, USE OF HUMAN SUBJECTS, INFORMED CONSENT)

Social workers have an ethical mandate to monitor and evaluate policies, the implementation of programs, and practice interventions. They also must promote and facilitate evaluation and research to contribute to the development of knowledge. In addition to doing research themselves, social workers must keep current with emerging knowledge relevant to social work and fully use evaluation and research evidence in their professional practice.

When doing research and evaluation, social workers must consider possible consequences and should follow guidelines developed for the protection of evaluation and research participants. Social workers must protect participants from unwarranted physical or mental distress, harm, danger, or deprivation (*NASW Code of Ethics, 1999—5.02 Evaluation and Research*). Appropriate institutional review boards should be consulted.

For example, social workers engaged in evaluation or research should obtain voluntary and written informed consent from participants, when appropriate, without any implied or actual deprivation or penalty for refusal to participate or without undue inducement to participate. Informed consent should include information about the nature, extent, and duration of the participation requested and disclosure of the risks and benefits of participation in the research (*NASW Code of Ethics, 1999—5.02 Evaluation and Research*). When evaluation or research participants are incapable of giving informed consent, social workers should provide an appropriate explanation to the participants, obtain the participants' assent to the extent they are able, and obtain written consent from an appropriate proxy (*NASW Code of Ethics, 1999—5.02 Evaluation and Research*).

Social workers should never design or conduct evaluation or research that does not use consent procedures, such as certain forms of naturalistic observation and archival research, unless rigorous and responsible review of the research has found it to be justified because of its prospective scientific, educational, or applied value and unless equally effective alternative procedures that do not involve waiver of consent are not feasible (*NASW Code of Ethics, 1999—5.02 Evaluation and Research*).

Social workers should inform participants of their right to withdraw from evaluation and research at any time without penalty (*NASW Code of Ethics, 1999—5.02 Evaluation and Research*).

Social workers should take appropriate steps to ensure that participants in evaluation and research have access to appropriate supportive services (*NASW Code of Ethics, 1999—5.02 Evaluation and Research*).

Social workers engaged in evaluation or research should ensure the anonymity or confidentiality of participants and of the data obtained from them. Social workers should inform participants of any limits of confidentiality, the measures that will be taken to ensure confidentiality, and when any records containing research data will be destroyed (*NASW Code of Ethics, 1999—5.02 Evaluation and Research*).

Social workers engaged in evaluation or research should be alert to and avoid conflicts of interest and dual relationships with participants, should inform participants when a real or potential conflict of interest arises, and should take steps to resolve the issue in a manner that makes participants' interests primary (*NASW Code of Ethics, 1999—5.02 Evaluation and Research*).

Program Evaluation and Outcomes $\quad$ **16**

THE METHODS USED TO EVALUATE AGENCY PROGRAMS

Social workers have an ethical mandate to ensure that they are providing the most efficient and effective services possible. They also must do no harm and ensure that the intervention provided enhances the well-being of clients.

These goals require the evaluation of practice. Routine practice evaluation by social workers can enhance treatment outcomes and agency decision making, planning, and accountability.

There are two main types of evaluations—*formative* and *summative*. Formative evaluations examine the process of delivering services, whereas summative evaluations examine the outcomes.

Formative evaluations are ongoing processes that allow for feedback to be implemented during service delivery. These types of evaluations allow social workers to make changes as needed to help achieve program goals. Needs assessments can be viewed as one type of formative evaluation.

Summative evaluations occur at the end of services and provide an overall description of their effectiveness. Summative evaluation examines outcomes to determine whether objectives were met. Summative evaluations enable decisions to be made regarding future service directions that cannot be made during implementation. Impact evaluations and cost-benefit analyses are types of summative evaluations.

ASSESSMENT/DIAGNOSIS INSTRUMENTS USED TO EVALUATE SOCIAL WORK PRACTICE

Program evaluation is the systematic assessment of the processes and/or outcomes of a program with the intent of furthering its development and improvement. There are many types of program evaluation including, but not limited to, the following.

■ A **cost-benefit analysis** determines the financial costs of operating a program as compared with the fiscal benefits of its outcomes. A *cost-benefit ratio* is generated to determine whether, and the extent to which, the costs exceed the benefits. Program decisions can be made to eliminate or modify the program (by reducing program expenditures) based upon the findings.

■ A **cost-effectiveness analysis** is similar to a cost-benefit analysis, but distinct. *It considers the benefits that are not measured in monetary terms,* such as illnesses prevented and/or lives saved. It does not produce a cost-benefit ratio, but may focus on the most financially efficient way to achieve a defined outcome or the cost for producing a specific nonmonetary outcome.

■ An **outcome assessment** is the process of determining whether a program has achieved its intended goal(s). It involves collecting evidence through assessment, analyzing the data, and then *using the findings to make programmatic changes if needed.* It is an iterative process with continual feedback loops.

THE EFFECTS OF PROGRAM EVALUATION FINDINGS ON SERVICES

One of the most significant benefits that a program evaluation communicates is the need to make service improvements. Some examples of improvements that may need to be made include:

■ Eliminating services that do not achieve program outcomes

■ Adding services that are better designed to achieve outcomes

■ Acquiring more adequate resources to support effective services

■ Targeting a different group of participants to receive services

Evaluation findings should be viewed and communicated as an opportunity to make programs better. Evaluation results that indicate the need for improvement should not be communicated as an indictment of the failure of a program. Program evaluation findings should be viewed with an excitement about the possibilities of developing an even stronger set of service offerings and improving already successful efforts. An action plan aimed at improvement should be developed, based on evaluation results, and communicated widely to key stakeholders.

ACCREDITATION AND PROGRAM REVIEWS

Administrative reviews, such as annual reviews from public and private social service organizations, are critical to the fulfillment of the social work mission. They provide accountability to the public about the number of people served, the services delivered, and how funds were allocated. They also may be used by social workers to document unmet needs that should be addressed.

Social workers may be required to engage in grant monitoring, evaluations, program inspections, and accreditation reviews. While each of these reviews serves a different purpose, they all require social workers to use critical thinking/analysis to help clients directly or indirectly.

DETERMINATION OF APPROPRIATE EVALUATION TOOLS

Evaluation often involves the collection of qualitative data (such as interviews and narrative stories) and quantitative data such as numeric survey ratings. Though pre-experimental in nature, quantitative evaluations commonly focus on the collection of pre- and postdata that can document level of change in knowledge, attitudes, skills, motivations, and behaviors. There is often no control or comparison group against which changes can be compared.

A common qualitative technique includes collecting narrative information ("success stories") as a part of program follow-up to determine if behavioral changes were realized among participants.

Often, evaluators must decide if they will collect their own data in order assess the effectiveness of services or if they will use existing information.

When collecting new data, there are many decisions to make throughout the process. For example, survey tool construction or survey item adaptation from existing sources is often completed during the planning phase of program evaluation. A challenge in selecting tools and methods for program evaluation is that there are various tradeoffs in decisions related to using preexisting tools versus creating unique ones. Other decisions about tools for program evaluation efforts include what types of software to use for data analysis and whether to use online or mobile devise data collection.

When deciding whether to design a new data collection tool or use an existing one, there are several criteria to consider. If implementing an evidence-based program with a valid and reliable evaluation tool, it is advisable to *use an existing tool* because it will add to the knowledge base of the profession and costly resources for tool development and testing are not needed.

However, if the program is not exactly like others, it may be best to *adapt an existing instrument* to fit the goals and audience. If none of these options work, a social worker will be required to *create an evaluation tool.*

Some important tips to remember when designing or evaluating evaluation tools include:

- Request only the information needed for the evaluation
- Make evaluation questions clear
- Explain the reason for the evaluation clearly
- Get the data or information in a way that is usable
- Pretest wording, flow, layout, instructions, delivery, and coding/ analysis

Record-Keeping and Reporting

17

WRITTEN COMMUNICATION SKILLS

Written documentation is a vital part of professional social work practice. Social workers need to use written communications for letter writing, e-mails, case notes, minute taking, and reports.

In order to ensure that all communications are written in a professional manner that will assist clients, social workers should ensure that:

- The purpose of the written communication is clear and concise
- Arguments and opinions are logical, with recommendations well-supported
- Client confidentiality is addressed ethically
- Grammar is correct
- Assessments and recommendations are not based on assumptions or generalizations
- The format is clear and headings are appropriate
- The content is easily understood
- Jargon is not included
- Person-first language is used
- Language is culturally appropriate
- Content is based on value-free, objective descriptions

Written communications of social workers may be harmful to clients if they are not prepared correctly with care and skill. Social workers should understand the "audience" for each document that is prepared and ensure that they are written so that they can be used effectively.

CASE RECORDING AND RECORD-KEEPING

The proper documentation of client services is paramount to competent practice. Without proper case recording or record-keeping the quality of service may be compromised, the continuity of service may be disrupted, there may be misinterpretation that can cause harm, client confidentiality may be breached, and a client's confidence in the integrity of a social worker may be impacted.

In addition to client harm, a social worker, as well as his or her agency if applicable, may be at risk of liability due to malpractice, negligence, and/or breach of confidentiality.

Some important "rules" about case recording include that it is:

- A clear, accurate, and unbiased representation of the facts
- A written record of all decisions
- Free of value judgments and subjective comments
- Timely

It should also include only information that is directly relevant to the delivery of services.

The release and storage of case recordings is also critical. Social workers must make sure that records are not released without proper client consent and that they are properly stored both during and following the termination of services. Records should be maintained for the number of years required by state statutes and regulations and relevant contracts.

THE USE OF APPROPRIATE DOCUMENTATION AND CORRESPONDENCE IN SERVICE DELIVERY

Recording in social work is the process of putting in writing and keeping relevant information about a client and his or her problem(s), intervention(s), and progress, as well as the social, economic, and health factors contributing to his or her situation.

The social work record should also emphasize a client's strengths and solutions for making change. There are many types of recordings related to assessment and service delivery, and their use depends upon factors such as agency requirements, a social worker's theoretical base, and the type of intervention employed.

Recording involves reviewing, selecting, analyzing, and organizing information that documents what has been discovered and done to ameliorate client problems.

Recording helps social workers make practice decisions based on documented subjective and objective information; assists with administrative functions by documenting levels of service and client outcomes; informs supervision aimed at enhancing social workers' skills in order to improve client goal attainment; and is used to evaluate client progress toward short-term and long-term goals.

Thus, recording provides accountability to a client, organization, funder, regulator, and/or others about the services delivered and the reasons that the services were needed; organizes information gathered during all parts of the problem-solving process; and notes all relevant data for future social work involvement and continuity of care.

THE MANAGEMENT OF AGENCY/PRACTICE RECORDS

Documentation in social work practice is critical because it forms the basis of assessment, planning, intervention, and evaluation of services. It is used to memorialize what has occurred and to hold social workers accountable for their services to clients, third-party payers, employers, and others. It also is used for supervision to ensure that clients receive the most effective and efficient services possible. Social workers should always document services appropriately and must never tamper with or alter records to mislead, omit, or falsify information.

There are many issues with regard to the management of practice records, including, but not limited to, that they have sufficient and credible content, they are prepared and stored correctly, and they are protected and accessed only by those who are authorized to do so. It is essential that there are written protocols with regard to the management of practice records and that these protocols are reviewed and revised regularly. Training on these protocols should be regularly conducted so that social workers know what is expected and how to address routine situations as well as those that are not anticipated, such as the receipt of a subpoena or court order.

Management of practice records must be in accordance with federal laws, state laws, and agency policies. Funders may also have requirements with regard to necessary documentation and/or the retention of records. Social workers should be knowledgeable about standards related to practice records that appear in the *NASW Code of Ethics (1999)*.

The protection of confidential information also requires great care. Social workers should know the exceptions to confidentiality and how to handle practice records when working with court-ordered clients or those who are involved in divorce or child custody proceedings. Social workers who are providing treatment to children whose parents are divorced should be aware of legal custody determinations and the respective rules that govern release of information in these arrangements.

Program Development and Service Delivery Systems

18

THE TYPES OF SERVICE DELIVERY PROGRAMS/SYSTEMS

Social work aims to solve problems in human relationships and empower clients so they can improve their well-being. To achieve this goal, social workers must engage in interactions at three different system levels—micro, mezzo, and macro.

Micro

At the micro level of intervention, social workers concentrate on helping clients solve their problems. These problems may relate to difficulties with partners/spouses, children, other family members, coworkers, and/or neighbors. At the micro level, social workers help clients to access needed services from other agencies, as well as provide direct support and counseling. This type of social work intervention is often the focus of clinical practice in social work and clients can include individuals, couples, and/or families.

Mezzo

The second level of intervention for social workers is that which is mezzo (also known as meso). Mezzo interventions apply to larger groups or communities. At the mezzo intervention level, social workers attempt to make connections between the micro and macro levels.

Macro

The third level of intervention for social workers is macro. This level stresses the importance of economic, historical, sociopolitical, and environmental influences on client well-being and functioning. Social workers determine how these factors can facilitate growth and/or create problems for clients.

Social workers are charged with making systems-level changes that can lead to opportunities and/or reducing barriers. Macro interventions can include creating or changing policies, procedures, regulations, and laws. They are aimed at not only assisting individual clients, but others who are experiencing the same difficulties. The focus of social work to engage in broader macro-level changes is what distinguishes it from other allied professions.

THE METHODS USED TO CLARIFY THE BENEFITS AND LIMITATIONS OF RESOURCES

Social workers must respect the rights to self-determination of clients. In order for clients to make informed decisions, it is critical that they understand the range of services available and be informed about any opportunities they have to obtain services from other service providers. Clients should also understand their right to be referred to other professionals for assistance, as well as their right to refuse services and possible consequences of such refusals. Clients must also understand any limitations that may impact accessing some services or benefits, such as the need for medical necessity criteria to be met.

Throughout the problem-solving process, social workers should be assisting clients to access available resources, as well as create new ones if they do not exist or are not appropriate. In order for clients to choose between alternative resources, social workers must review the advantages and disadvantages of using each.

THE METHODS USED TO INTERPRET AND COMMUNICATE POLICIES AND PROCEDURES

Social workers are often called upon to develop and/or communicate policies and procedures. There is no one method for doing so, but there are elements that need to be remembered in order to ensure that these tasks are done in a manner that is consistent with the values and principles of the profession and maximizes client benefit.

1. Policies and procedures are essential to ensure that individuals have a clear understanding of expectations and proper ways of conducting activities. However, there are always instances in which exceptions

may need to be made. A social worker must recognize that "one size does not fit all" and have ways to evaluate alternatives when needed.

2. Policies and procedures should be clear and concise, and communicated in a manner that facilitates understanding. They should be broadly communicated so all are clear about the expectation. Copies of the policies and procedures should be available for reference if needed.

3. Policies and procedures should always support actions that are in the best interest of clients. Social workers have the mandate to challenge those that are not. They should be tailored to the service setting as well as client needs, and should not be "packaged procedures" that fail to take cultural and other differences into account.

4. Training on policies and procedures should be available and routinely attended as part of a process of self-development.

5. Policies and procedures need to be reviewed periodically—not just when there is a problem. Regular review will ensure that changes within and outside an agency are considered and modifications to the policies and procedures are made accordingly.

6. Effective policies and procedures are "owned" by all those asked to follow them. Feedback on what is working and not working is essential. Their development must be based on the experiences of social workers and clients who are expected to adhere to them.

THE DEVELOPMENT OF PROGRAMS AND SERVICES TO MEET COMMUNITY NEEDS

Community development is a tenet of the social work profession. Strong communities play a protective role in human development. Community development is focused on improving the lives of community members. Ensuring that communities have the programs and services needed requires social workers to be integrative, comprehensive, collaborative, participatory, and strengths and asset focused. Social workers must focus on the present needs of communities with an eye toward the future. Social workers will need to assume the roles of facilitator, enabler, mediator, broker, coordinator, and mobilizer. Each role supports the key goal of building the capacity of communities to help members achieve their goals.

THE METHODS USED TO ESTABLISH SERVICE NETWORKS OR COMMUNITY RESOURCES

The need for services to not be duplicative and to complement one another is central to meeting client needs. Social workers are often called upon to assist with developing or navigating service networks and creating community resources where they are lacking. Integrating services takes sustained effort and hard work. Though the concept of service integration may seem simple, it is not, and it usually involves several administrative and operational strategies. Strong leadership and sound management are critical.

In order to effectively meet client needs, organizations are increasingly recognizing collaborations, networks, alliances, and/or partnerships. There are two distinct network forms—*mandated network arrangements* and *self-organizing networks.*

Within each of these forms, there may be a lead organization or a model in which all organizations share decision-making power. The former is often associated with a centralized structure, whereas the latter is more indicative of a decentralized one. Networks can also have strong and weak arrangements in which the parameters of integration are either highly regulated or not.

The willingness and ability of social service organizations to form networks often depends on organizational size, resource dependency, and collaborative experience.

THE EFFECTS OF AGENCY POLICIES, REGULATION, AND FUNCTION ON SERVICE DELIVERY

Client functioning must be viewed using a "person-in-environment" perspective. The "rules" that govern society are critical to the way in which the environment is structured, operates, and changes. They can both facilitate and hinder client functioning across time. Social workers can think of clients as part of a larger system with many layers of influence. Clients are most immediately impacted by their families, who are members of neighborhoods and communities. However, each of these contextual influences—families, neighborhood, and communities—are affected by state, national, and international forces such as policies, procedures, regulations, and laws. They dictate who may be eligible for programs, the amount of funding received, and/or which programs are established or eliminated.

Their influence is dynamic because, using a systems perspective, changes to any one "rule" impact all others. The creation or modification of a societal "rule" also impacts on individuals, and vice versa.

At different times, state, national, and international forces may be more or less prominent. For example, international policies may influence U.S. businesses and communities because multinational corporations make decisions about job location, outsourcing, and other restructuring. In addition, international unrest may restrict travel to other countries. Thus, policies, procedures, regulations, and laws at different levels interact with one another and can create both the opportunities and the barriers for clients in their family units, neighborhoods, and communities.

Social workers must be aware of this dynamic and the relationship of "rules" on client functioning as well as their own professional practice to ensure that they are delivering effective and efficient services to clients in accordance with existing rules and best practices.

THE METHODS OF CONDUCTING A NEEDS ASSESSMENT

A needs assessment is a systematic process for determining and addressing gaps between current and desired conditions. It examines strengths and weaknesses of a community, agency, and/or program with the aim of improvement. There are multiple methods for conducting needs assessments and they may be conducted by consultants, staff, and/or volunteers internal or external to the organization.

First, information is collected about a community, agency, and/or program. This data may be collected via focus groups, key informant interviews, community meetings, or through the administering of surveys. In addition, including existing data sources can be time and cost effective.

Using information gathered, social workers must decide what needs are being met and what resources exist in addition to the needs that are not being addressed. There are several methods for determining need—including assessing perceived, expressed, and/or relative needs. *Perceived needs* are defined by what clients think about their needs, with the standard set by each client. *Expressed needs* are defined by the number of clients who have sought help, thus taking action to address their problems. A major weakness of using expressed needs is that not all who need help seek it. *Relative needs* are concerned with equity—comparing the needs of clients with the goal of ranking them.

ESTABLISHING PROGRAM OBJECTIVES AND OUTCOMES

The terms "mission," "goals," "objectives," and "outcomes" are often used interchangeably without being clearly defined.

A *mission statement* is a general, concise statement outlining the purpose guiding the practices of an organization. Outcomes eventually flow from the mission statements of an agency. *Goals* are broad, general statements of what the program intends to accomplish. Goals describe broad outcomes and concepts expressed in general terms (e.g., clear communication, problem-solving skills). Goals should provide a framework for determining the more specific objectives of a program and should be consistent with the mission of the agency. A single goal may have many specific subordinate objectives.

Objectives are brief, clear statements that describe the desired outcomes. They are distinguished from goals by the level of specificity. Goals express intended outcomes in general terms and objectives express them in specific terms.

Outcomes may be knowledge, abilities (skills), and/or attitudes (values, dispositions) that have been obtained. Outcomes are *achieved* results.

Interdisciplinary Collaboration

19

ELEMENTS OF A CASE PRESENTATION

When a social worker communicates with others in order to ensure comprehensive and complete care for clients, he or she completes a case presentation. Case presentations are also used in professional development and learning to provide input into options for treatment and to ensure services are being delivered effectively and efficiently.

There is no universal format for a case presentation in social work practice. However, there are some standard elements, including:

- Identifying data (demographics, cultural considerations)
- History of the presenting problem (family history)
- Significant medical/psychiatric history (diagnoses)
- Significant personal and/or social history (legal issues, academic or work problems, crisis and safety concerns)
- Presenting problem (assessment, mental status, diagnosis)
- Impressions and summary (interview findings)
- Recommendations (treatment plan and intervention strategies, goals, theoretical models used)

Content areas can be added or eliminated based on the reasons for the case presentation and input sought. Information for a case presentation is usually information that a social worker has obtained directly from a client during an interview and/or observation, as well as that collected from collateral contacts, other professionals, and/or case records.

THE RANGE OR EXPERTISE OF PROFESSIONS OTHER THAN SOCIAL WORK

Social workers should maintain access to professional case consultation. Often, this consultation may be from qualified professionals in other disciplines. Each discipline has its own set of assumptions, values, and priorities; in order to ensure that the assessment of a client's problems considers all possible root causes (including medical) and that all needs of a client are met, a social worker should consult with experts in other fields and refer a client to them when needed.

Social workers often work together with others from various professions. This is known as an interdisciplinary approach. Some interdisciplinary teams interface daily, whereas others may only meet periodically.

Sometimes social workers form interdisciplinary relationships that do not constitute team practice, but are nevertheless necessary for effective service. These relationships may be with legal or educational professionals.

Social work knowledge is influenced by, and in turn influences, other disciplines, including family studies, medicine, psychiatry, sociology, education, and psychology.

THE USE OF COLLATERALS TO OBTAIN RELEVANT INFORMATION

Social workers often use collateral sources—family, friends, other agencies, physicians, and so on—as informants when collecting information to effectively treat clients. These sources can provide vital information because other professionals or agencies may have treated a client in the past. Family members and friends may also provide important information about the length or severity of issues or problems.

It is essential that a social worker get a client's informed consent prior to reaching out to collateral sources. However, they can be a valuable source of data to supplement that obtained directly from a client and to provide contextual or background information that a client may not know.

THE APPROACHES USED IN CONSULTATION

Social workers are often called upon to seek consultation for a problem related to a client, service, organization, and/or policy. Consultation is the utilization of an "expert" in a specific area to assist with developing a solution to the issue. Consultation is usually time limited and the advice of the consultant can be used by a social worker in the problem-solving process. While a consultant does not have any formal authority over a social worker, he or she has informal authority as an "expert." However, a social worker is not required to follow the recommendations of a consultant.

Four things are critical in consultation:

1. Defining the purpose of the consultation
2. Specifying the consultant's role
3. Clarifying the nature of the problem
4. Outlining the consultation process

Social workers should seek the advice and counsel of colleagues whenever such consultation is in the best interests of clients, but should only do so from colleagues who have demonstrated knowledge, expertise, and competence related to the subject of the consultation (*NASW Code of Ethics, 1999—2.05 Consultation*).

When seeking consultation, social workers need to get the permission of clients if any identifying or specific information will be shared. In addition, social workers should only disclose information that is absolutely necessary when interacting with consultants.

Social workers may also provide consultation. They should have the appropriate knowledge and skill to do so and should follow all ethical standards, including avoiding conflicts of interest and maintaining boundaries (*NASW Code of Ethics, 1999—3.01 Supervision and Consultation*).

When social workers and those from other disciplines come together to discuss client issues or plans for the future, these meetings are often referred to as case conferences. Today, case conferences are often done remotely instead of face-to-face. All applicable ethical standards, particularly those related to confidentiality, must be strictly adhered to when social workers participate in case conferences.

THE USE OF NETWORKING

The importance of networking has been stressed heavily in business, but it has received far less attention in social work practice. This void is interesting as it is critical to the effective delivery of services. Networking involves building relationships with other professionals who share areas of interest. It is about creating a community around common interests and building alliances. It is also about creating opportunities to work with others toward the achievement of mutual goals.

Although networking in business is a way to attract patrons/customers or to get jobs, it has a broader and more altruistic focus in social work.

For example, learning about others who do similar or complementary work can result in a sharing of resources and expertise that could be beneficial to clients by keeping the cost of services contained and/or increasing the skills of practitioners. Learning about the skills of others and establishing professional relationships through networking can also provide resources for clients who may need referrals to other professionals.

Networking helps improve social skills and the ability to relate to others in a variety of settings. It puts social workers "out there" so that others can be aware of the important work that they do. Educating others about social problems is an important part of making systematic changes. Lastly, networking can identify individuals who would be good candidates for jobs. Recruiting qualified individuals into the agencies where social workers are employed results in clients receiving quality care.

THE PROCESS FOR INTERDISCIPLINARY COLLABORATION

Interdisciplinary collaboration is a rewarding, yet challenging, social work activity. Collaboration, a learned skill that can be improved through practice, is a vehicle for improving services for all clients. It means working with others for the betterment of a client. Collaborative teams are more likely to develop important new and innovative approaches to dealing with problems.

Collaboration goes beyond people sitting around a table. It includes pre-meeting work (i.e., making telephone calls), how members typically conduct themselves (i.e., being friendly), and how meetings proceed (i.e., choosing to ignore minor irritations in order to get on with the agenda).

Social workers must understand their own styles and focus on their behavior as part of a group, rather than on how others should change.

Collaboration involves strong interpersonal communication and group process skills, as well as the ability to understand the perspectives of others. It can be discrete (distinct or separate; limited to a single occurrence or action) or continuous (ongoing or repetitive).

The following list provides some guidelines that can be helpful when social workers participate in such collaboration.

1. Social workers should clearly articulate their roles on interdisciplinary teams.

2. Social workers should understand the roles of professionals from other disciplines on these teams.

3. Social workers should seek and establish common ground with these professionals, including commonalities in professional goals.

4. Social workers should acknowledge the differences within the field and across other disciplines.

5. Social workers should address conflict within teams so that it does not interfere with the collaborative process and the teams' outcomes.

6. Social workers should establish and maintain collegial relationships.

There are also ethical guidelines that must be followed when social workers are part of interdisciplinary collaboration (*NASW Code of Ethics, 1999—2.03 Interdisciplinary Collaboration*).

1. Social workers who are members of an interdisciplinary team should participate in and contribute to decisions that affect the well-being of clients by drawing on the perspectives, values, and experiences of the social work profession. Professional and ethical obligations of the interdisciplinary team as a whole and of its individual members should be clearly established.

2. Social workers for whom a team decision raises ethical concerns should attempt to resolve the disagreement through appropriate channels. If the disagreement cannot be resolved, social workers should pursue other avenues to address their concerns consistent with client well-being.

THE METHODS USED TO COORDINATE SERVICES BETWEEN SERVICE PROVIDERS OR AGENCIES

Fragmentation presents one of the biggest service delivery challenges for clients and those who are assisting them, such as social workers. Clients can fall through the cracks because the connections between services are either absent or problematic or needed services are missing altogether.

The purpose of coordinating services for clients is to improve outcomes. The assumption is that collaborative activity can facilitate access to services, reduce unnecessary duplication of effort, and produce a more effective and efficient social service system.

Social workers are uniquely positioned to coordinate services.

One method of coordination is *integration of services*, in which services are combined and provided simultaneously. Such an approach is often used with mental health and substance use interventions that are combined within a primary treatment relationship or service setting.

Another method of coordination is *wrap-around services*, in which multiple providers and services may overlap in some ways but are not combined to the same degree as integrated services.

A third method of coordination is *case management* or care coordination. Although there are many models of these two concepts, the aim of most is linking a client to needed services.

In addition, "roundtables" or interdisciplinary team approaches are useful in ensuring that all professionals are brought together to stay informed of total client care and work together to avoid fragmentation and/or duplication.

THE MULTIDISCIPLINARY TEAM APPROACH

A multidisciplinary team is a group of individuals from different disciplines, each with unique skills and perspectives, who work together toward a common purpose or goal.

The benefits of this approach are well documented. Multidisciplinary teams are often seen as advantageous to clients because they do not have the burden of navigating multiple service systems and communicating to multiple professionals involved in their care. Multidisciplinary teams also can have increased positive outcomes and be cost effective.

A multidisciplinary approach can also have benefits for social workers because they:

1. Provide peer support, especially when working with stressful problems associated with involuntary service delivery, violence, suicide, and so forth

2. Allow for work to be assigned across multiple professionals

3. Fulfill professional goals by ensuring all aspects of a client's biopsychosocial–spiritual–cultural care are delivered

4. Create cross-fertilization of skills between professionals

5. Facilitate decision making related to all aspects of client care, which can lead to increased job satisfaction

6. Streamline work practices by sharing of information

THE USE OF INFORMAL AND FORMAL POWER STRUCTURES

It is essential for social workers to understand sources of power in order to access them for the betterment of the community. Organizing community members to focus these sources of power on the problem(s) and mobilizing resources to assist is critical.

- *Coercive:* power from control of punishment
- *Reward:* power from control of rewards
- *Expert:* power from superior ability or knowledge

- *Referent:* power from having charisma or identification with others who have power
- *Legitimate:* power from having legitimate authority
- *Informational:* power from having information

THE USE OF ADVOCACY AMONG AGENCIES AND DISCIPLINES

Advocacy is one of social workers' most important tasks. Social workers may advocate when working with an individual client to ensure that his or her needs are met. However, social workers have an ethical mandate to make systematic changes to address the problems experienced by groups of individuals who are vulnerable and/or who are unable to speak for themselves.

Social workers may engage in advocacy by convincing others of the legitimate needs and rights of members of society. Such work can occur on the local, county, state, or national levels. Some social workers are even involved in international human rights and advocacy for those in need in other countries.

Fundamental to social work is advocating to change the factors that create and contribute to problems.

Sometimes advocacy can be achieved by working through the problem-solving process as it relates to a problem, including acknowledging the problem, analyzing and defining the problem, generating possible solutions, evaluating each option, implementing the option of choice, and evaluating the outcomes.

In other instances, social workers may engage in obtaining legislative support or using the media to draw attention to a concern.

In all instances, social workers should be working with clients to have their voices heard and should not be speaking for them. The goal of social work advocacy is to assist clients to strengthen their own skills in this area. Social workers may assist by locating sources of power that can be shared with clients to make changes.

Policy Analysis and Advocacy

20

INTERPRETING LEGISLATION TO CLIENTS

Regardless of setting, there is a strong chance that social workers will be required to analyze and interpret statutes for clients. For example, clients may want to determine whether laws apply to them and/or their situations.

Statutory interpretation is not easy because the meaning and wording of legislation is often unclear or ambiguous. It is critical to read laws closely and in their entirety. Social workers must keep in mind that their initial understanding of statutes may not be the correct or only plausible interpretations of them.

Statutory language may not have directly considered the exact situations currently encountered. Changing times may find that old statutes do not address or consider new issues which were not present when legislation was passed.

When interpreting legislation, it is critical to examine primary sources such as statutory definitions, case law, and administrative regulations for how terms and provisions should be interpreted and applied. When primary sources are not sufficient, social workers need to rely on dictionaries, legal encyclopedias, and legislative history documents to assist in interpretation.

Clients often are not familiar with or comfortable in the legal arena. Thus, social workers must explain the latent meaning of legislative content so that clients can understand how laws apply to them and their circumstances. Understanding legal requirements and the ramifications for not complying with them are essential to ensuring clients can make informed choices.

THE IMPACT OF SOCIAL WELFARE LEGISLATION ON SOCIAL WORK PRACTICE

Social workers should be fully informed of existing laws, policies, practices, and procedures that impact or govern service delivery.

Social workers are also expected to keep up-to-date with new public laws and policies.

Many laws affect social work practice. Although social workers may not be responsible for implementing these pieces of legislation, they provide protections or programs that are critical to those served.

Some relevant federal legislation is listed in chronological order in the following list.

1. *Title VI of the Civil Rights Act of 1964* states that no person shall "on the grounds of race, color, or national origin, be excluded from participation in, denied the benefits of, or be subjected to discrimination under any program or activity receiving federal financial assistance." It desegregated all schools and public buildings and required all agencies that receive federal funds to terminate discriminatory hiring practices. Social workers are charged with challenging discriminatory practices and upholding the belief of equal rights for all.

2. The *Older Americans Act (OAA) of 1965* offers services to older Americans. It established the Administration on Aging, which empowers the federal government to distribute funds to the states for supportive services for individuals over the age of 60. The Administration achieves its aim by awarding grants to states, which pass them along to local Area Agencies on Aging (AAA). Some programs target vulnerable older adults who need help staying in their homes. Other programs provide access services, in-home services, community services, caregiver services, and opportunities for volunteer work.

3. The *Child Abuse Prevention and Treatment Act of 1974* is key legislation for addressing child abuse and neglect. It has been amended several times and provides federal funding to states in support of prevention, assessment, investigation, prosecution, and treatment activities; it also provides grants to public agencies and nonprofit organizations for demonstration programs and projects.

4. The *Family Educational Rights and Privacy Act (FERPA) of 1974* protects the privacy of educational records. The law applies to all schools that receive funds under an applicable program of the United States Department of Education. FERPA gives parents certain rights with respect to their children's education records. These rights transfer to the student when he or she reaches the age of 18 or attends a school beyond the high school level. Prior to 18, parents have the right to

inspect and review a student's education records maintained by the school. Schools are not required to provide copies of records unless, for reasons such as great distance, it is impossible for parents to review the records. Schools may charge a fee for copies. Parents also have the right to request that a school correct records that they believe to be inaccurate or misleading. If the school decides not to amend the record, the parent or eligible student then has the right to a formal hearing. After the hearing, if the school still decides not to amend the record, the parent has the right to place a statement with the record setting forth his or her view about the contested information. Generally, schools must have written permission from the parent in order to release any information from a student's education record, though there are some exceptions related to the student's care.

5. The *Education for Handicapped Children Act of 1975* guarantees a free, appropriate public education to all children with disabilities between the ages of 3 and 21. Children receiving such services should be provided with Individual Educational Plans (IEPs) that are revised annually. A team composed of a social worker, teacher, administrator, and other relevant school personnel typically create the IEP. The parents, and often the child, also participate. The IEP includes goals, means of attaining goals, and ways of evaluating goal attainment. A child who has an IEP must also be educated in the "least restrictive environment." Thus, the child should either spend part or all of his or her time in a regular classroom or in an environment that is as close to this as possible while still leading to the attainment of the educational goals. Services that are needed, such as speech therapy and others related to educational goals, are provided at no extra cost to the family.

6. *Indian Child Welfare Act of 1978* gives American Indian/Native American/Indigenous nations or organizations jurisdiction over child welfare cases that involve an American Indian/Native American/Indigenous child in order to protect the integrity of American Indian/Native American/Indigenous families. The law specifies a hierarchical procedure for placement of an American Indian/Native American/Indigenous child: (a) verify the ethnic and tribal identity of the child; (b) allow tribal jurisdiction over case; (c) if tribe rejects jurisdiction, placement with family member or; (d) if that is impossible, placement with family of the same tribe. The last resort is placing the child in a home with a family that is not American Indian/Native American/Indigenous.

7. The *Adoption Assistance and Child Welfare Act of 1980* focuses on family preservation efforts to help keep families together and children out of foster care or other out-of-home placements. This law also focuses on family reunification or adoption if a child is removed from a home. The act requires courts to review child welfare cases more regularly and mandates that states make "reasonable efforts" to keep families

together via prevention and family reunification services. States are also required to develop reunification and preventive programs for foster care and assure that children in nonpermanent settings are seen at least every 6 months. An adoption subsidy reimbursed by the federal government is also provided through this law for children with complex needs or disabilities.

8. The *Americans with Disabilities Act (ADA) of 1990* is civil-rights legislation that prohibits discrimination on the basis of disability. It has been amended and affords similar protections as the Civil Rights Act of 1964 for discrimination based on race, religion, sex, national origin, and other characteristics. Unlike the Civil Rights Act of 1964, the ADA also requires covered employers to provide reasonable accommodations to employees with disabilities and imposes accessibility requirements on public accommodations. ADA disabilities include both mental and physical conditions. A condition does not need to be severe or permanent to be a disability.

9. The *Patient Self-Determination Act (PSDA) of 1991* introduced a new set of federal requirements intended to implement advance directive policies at all health care facilities that receive federal funding through Medicaid and Medicare programs. The Act specified that these facilities must inform clients of their rights to make decisions concerning their own health care, ask and document whether a client has an advance directive, and provide education for staff and the community.

Advance directives are a legal way of indicating that a person has given the legal rights to a designated person to make decisions on his or her behalf about continuation of support measures should the individual be incapable physically or mentally of making wants known.

The purpose of advance directives is to respond to judicial decisions that have been made indicating that if a person has not told someone of his or her wishes, in case of severe physical injury, the decision to remove a person from life supports or to place the person on life supports cannot be made. Therefore, it has become increasingly imperative that people indicate their wishes and identify individuals that they designate to make these decisions if needed.

Advance directives have been paired with *living wills* to give people control over what happens to them in a severe illness or injury. A living will allows individuals to retain some control over what happens at the end of their lives, even if the individuals are then no longer competent to make personal choices for terminal care, while they are still healthy and at a time when there is no doubt of their mental competence.

10. The *Family and Medical Leave Act (FMLA) of 1993* requires covered employers to provide up to 12 weeks of unpaid, job-protected leave to "eligible" employees for certain family and medical reasons with

continuation of group health insurance coverage under the same terms and conditions as if the employee had not taken leave.

11. The *Multiethnic Placement Act of 1994 (MEPA)* and its subsequent amendments, prohibits agencies from refusing or delaying foster or adoptive placements because of a child's or foster/adoptive parent's race, color, or national origin and prohibits agencies from considering race, color, or national origin as a basis for denying approval as a foster and/or adoptive parent. It also requires agencies to diligently recruit a diverse base of foster and adoptive parents to better reflect the racial and ethnic makeup of children in out-of-home care.

12. The *Violence Against Women Act (VAWA) of 1994* has improved the criminal justice response to violence against women by strengthening federal penalties for repeat sex offenders and creating a federal "rape shield law," which is intended to prevent offenders from using victims' past sexual conduct against them during a rape trial; keeping victims safe by requiring that a victim's protection order will be recognized and enforced in all state, tribal, and territorial jurisdictions; increasing rates of prosecution, conviction, and sentencing of offenders by helping communities develop dedicated law enforcement and prosecution units and domestic violence dockets; training law enforcement officers, prosecutors, victim advocates, and judges; and ensuring access to the services needed by victims to achieve safety and rebuild their lives.

13. The *Personal Responsibility and Work Opportunity Reconciliation Act of 1996 (PRWORA)* was considered to be a fundamental shift in both the method and goal of federal cash assistance to the poor. It added a workforce development component to welfare legislation, encouraging employment among the poor. PRWORA instituted Temporary Assistance for Needy Families (TANF), which became effective July 1, 1997. TANF replaced the Aid to Families With Dependent Children (AFDC) program, which had been in effect since 1935, and also supplanted the Job Opportunities and Basic Skills (JOBS) Training Program of 1988. It also imposed a lifetime 5-year limit on the receipt of benefits.

14. The *Health Insurance Portability and Accountability Act (HIPAA) of 1996* (HIPAA) provides individuals with access to their medical records and more control over how their personal health information is used and disclosed. It represents a uniform, federal floor of privacy protections for individuals across the country. State laws providing additional protections are not affected by HIPAA, which took effect on April 14, 2003.

15. The *Patient Protection and Affordable Care Act of 2010 (ACA)* expands access to insurance, increases protections, emphasizes prevention and wellness, improves quality and system performance, expands the

health workforce, and curbs rising health care costs. Key provisions of the ACA that intend to address rising health costs include providing more oversight of health insurance premiums and practices; emphasizing prevention, primary care, and effective treatments; reducing health care fraud and abuse; reducing uncompensated care to prevent a shift onto insurance premium costs; fostering comparison shopping in insurance exchanges to increase competition and price transparency; implementing Medicare payment reforms; and testing new delivery and payment system models in Medicaid and Medicare.

16. The *Workforce Innovation and Opportunity Act of 2014 (WIOA)* reauthorizes the Workforce Investment Act (WIA) of 1998 with several key changes in areas such as Workforce Development Boards structure; One-Stop Operations; Job-Driven Training for Adults and Dislocated Workers; and Integrated Performance and Youth Services.

SOCIAL POLICY PROCESSES AND ANALYSIS

Policy analysis is a systematic approach to solving problems through policies.

It involves identifying the problem, developing alternatives, assessing the impacts of the alternatives (such as conducting a cost/benefit analysis), selecting the desired option, designing and implementing the policy, and evaluating the outcomes.

Critical to social policy analysis is the identification of alternative policy options and the evaluation of these alternatives. Analyses include developing an understanding of who "wins" and who "loses." Some of the values upon which alternatives are weighed include equity, efficiency, and liberty.

The policy analysis field has become more diversified; thus, it is highly influenced by theories from other fields. Often there are many stakeholders involved, such as federal, state, and local government agencies, community leaders, and clients, all of which will bring in their own set of values. Thus, the chosen approach will be influenced by who participates.

LEGISLATIVE ADVOCACY

Social work is unique in its dual focus on assisting clients on an individual level while also working to change the policies that adversely impact them. The personal troubles of clients are linked to the public policies which can help to prevent or address them. Social workers are charged with working and helping individuals and their families directly, but also working within decision-making bodies to promote these policies.

In order to shape public policy, social workers must be knowledgeable about the political environment in order to shape public policy based upon the core values of the profession. As there are always competing interest groups who would like to influence policymakers in their favor, political advocacy is seen as an important and necessary social work skill.

Advocacy can be defined as attempting to influence public policy through education, lobbying, or political pressure. Social workers are often called upon to educate the general public, as well as public policymakers, about the nature of problems, what legislation is needed to address problems, and the funding required to provide services or conduct research.

THE METHODS OF ADVOCACY FOR POLICY AND/OR PROCEDURAL CHANGE

Social policy is influenced by many factors, such as the following.

Knowledge/Innovation

Knowledge and innovation create new opportunities to change, as well as information that current practices may need to be reformed. Technological advances are often drivers of changes in policy.

Social, Political, and Economic Conditions/Resources

Good policies are often not adopted because they are proposed without the social, political, or economic resources to move them through the policy process and/or implement them.

Social norms change over time and foster or impede social policy development or revision.

Political and/or economic conditions can also promote or hinder the creation and/or revision of policy, as well as whether policy alternatives are suggested or considered for adoption.

Legal Issues/Laws

Understanding how new policies will influence or interact with existing laws is essential. Policies may not be supported if they are believed to negatively impact on existing policies that are seen as beneficial.

Institutional Influences

The structure of institutions, such as government agencies, private sector organizations, and so on, can also impact the ability to influence and efficiently or effectively implement social policies. Sometimes policies are so complex or integrated into the practices of complex institutional systems that it is difficult to understand them; therefore, change is less likely.

External Influences

The media and other external influences can be very influential. Media can be used to call attention to a problem. More media coverage of one policy alternative may influence its support by virtue of being more familiar. Public opinion is a very salient influence as to whether policies will be proposed and/or adopted.

Social workers who want to promote certain social policies must be aware of these influences and use methods to support policies as they relate to these areas. Similarly, social workers can decrease the desirability of policies by creating barriers or removing positive influences in these areas.

Problems are also often associated with policy implementation. Policies may not be clearly communicated, leaving implementers and others at a loss as to how to follow them in order to achieve the intended goals. Negative attitudes of service personnel, lack of resources to carry out policies, and/or the conflict with previously established procedures or structures can also be obstacles to implementation.

THE METHODS OF ADVOCACY FOR RESOURCES TO MEET CLIENT NEEDS

Social workers struggle with many issues related to meeting the needs of clients. Needs often exceed available resources, thus requiring social workers to advocate on clients' behalf. Advocacy is taking an active, direct role on behalf of clients in need of help. It is bringing about action or change in policies, laws, and practices of influential individuals, groups, and institutions. It involves many people working together toward a shared vision of change. In order to advocate for resources to meet client needs, a social worker must:

- **Educate** about the gap between service availability and demand
- **Raise awareness** that the problem is important and needs to be addressed
- **Influence others** about the importance of the issue
- **Develop coalitions and networks** to efficiently use available resources
- **Convince legislators and private funders** to allocate money for services
- **Evaluate existing services** to ensure resources are being used in the most effective and efficient manner

THE METHODS OF ADVOCACY FOR POLICIES AND SERVICES SENSITIVE TO ETHNIC AND CULTURAL DIFFERENCES

Advocacy serves many purposes, including ensuring that policies and services are sensitive to ethnic and cultural differences. The timeline for advocacy varies, but most advocacies involve both long- and short-term thinking.

Some of the most powerful advocacy methods are led by clients affected by the problem or issue. However, it is very important to receive permission from clients affected by the problem if social workers use their stories or testimonials in advocacy work.

Policies and services that are sensitive to ethnic and cultural differences should:

- Acknowledge culture as a predominant force in shaping behaviors, values, and institutions
- Acknowledge and accept that cultural differences exist and have an impact on service delivery
- Recognize that diversity within cultures is as important as diversity among cultures
- Respect the unique, culturally defined needs of various client populations
- Recognize that concepts such as "family" and "community" are different for various cultures and even for subgroups within cultures
- Recognize that diversity enhances the human experience for all

Advocacy action steps related to ensuring ethnic and cultural sensitivity are similar to those in other areas and include:

1. Defining the scope of the problem (i.e., the lack of existing ethnic and cultural competence)
2. Building support for the problem through coalition building
3. Creating an advocacy plan, including identifying legislative strategies to address the initial concern(s)
4. Implementing and modifying the plan to change policies and/or create services
5. Evaluating the advocacy efforts

THE METHODS OF ADVOCACY FOR POLICIES TO END DISCRIMINATORY PRACTICES

Fighting discrimination is a basic tenet in the *Code of Ethics (1999)*. There are many strategies, including formal and informal actions, that a social worker can take to advocate against discriminatory practices.

First, a social worker must educate those responsible for such policies when they are detected. Though not acceptable, discriminatory practices may result from a lack of knowledge by those responsible for their construction and/or implementation. Policymakers may not realize that the policies are differentially affecting people based on of race, ethnicity, national origin, color, sex, sexual orientation, gender identity or expression, age, marital status, political belief, religion, immigration status, or mental or physical disability.

A social worker may also want to bring discriminatory practices to the attention of rights or advocacy organizations. These entities may have more success in fighting against detected discrimination because they are able to bring together people who are adversely affected by the policies. They also may be more familiar with legal and other protections and have more expertise and resources to take more formal action.

A social worker can also directly fight discriminatory practices legally. However, this is often expensive and time consuming and requires extensive legal knowledge.

It should be noted that, the social worker does not need to choose only one of these methods but can try them consecutively or simultaneously. The social worker should also consider using media to call attention to the situation. The threat of exposing unfair practices can often cause elicit modifications in policy.

THE POLICY IMPLICATIONS OF RESEARCH FINDINGS

Because policymakers seek and prefer to use information from trusted sources, research findings are very useful for informing policy. Research findings on local, state, and federal programs are particularly useful to legislators. Resources are scarce, and allocations of funds are made based upon evaluation outcomes, so ensuring that services are efficient and effective is critical. Social Workers should also ensure that research agendas are driven by issues and problems facing clients and that research designs and recommendations are based on the core principles of the profession.

Research findings must be timely and communicated clearly. Policymakers often have to digest a lot of information and are not subject-matter experts in the areas in which they must make decisions. Thus, to influence policymakers' decisions, report findings should be free of jargon and must be presented in a manner that a lay person can understand and digest quickly. Implications of research findings should be explicit so policymakers do not have to speculate about them.

Finding sources of information based on accurate, concise, relevant research is often problematic for policymakers. Research articles in academic journals are not easily understandable or readily available.

Theories and Methods of Social Change

21

PRIMARY, SECONDARY, AND TERTIARY PREVENTION STRATEGIES

There are three major types of prevention strategies—primary, secondary, and tertiary. Optimally, all three types are needed to create comprehensive strategies of prevention and protection.

Primary Prevention

The goal is to protect people from developing a disease, experiencing an injury, or engaging in a behavior in the first place.
   Examples:

- Immunizations against disease
- Education promoting the use of automobile passenger restraints and bicycle helmets
- Screenings for the general public to identify risk factors for illness
- Controlling hazards in the workplace and home
- Regular exercise and good nutrition
- Counseling about the dangers of tobacco and other drugs

Since successful primary prevention helps avoid the disease, injury, or behavior and its associated suffering, cost, and burden, it is typically considered the most cost-effective.

Secondary Prevention

Secondary prevention occurs after a disease, injury, or illness has occurred and aims to slow its progression or limit its long-term impacts. It is often implemented when asymptomatic but risk factors are present. It also may focus on preventing reinjury.

Examples:

- Telling those with heart conditions to take daily, low-dose aspirin
- Screenings for those with risk factors for illness
- Modifying work assignments for injured workers

Tertiary Prevention

Tertiary prevention focuses on managing complicated, long-term diseases, injuries, or illnesses. The goal is to prevent further deterioration and maximize quality of life because disease is now established and primary prevention activities have been unsuccessful. However, early detection through secondary prevention may have minimized the impact of the disease.

Examples:

- Pain management groups
- Rehabilitation programs
- Support groups

THE CONCEPT OF CITIZEN PARTICIPATION

Community participation is critical in social work practice. Community participation informs others about needed changes that must occur. Policies, programs, and services that were effective or appropriate previously may have become inappropriate or ineffective.

Community participation also creates relationships and partnerships among diverse groups who can then work together but may not usually do so.

Community participation puts decision-making power partly or wholly with the community, ensuring that individuals will remain interested and involved over time.

When engaging in community-based decision making, individuals will typically go through various stages.

Orientation stage—This is the stage in which community members may meet for the first time and start to get to know each other.

Conflict stage—Disputes, little fights, and arguments may occur. These conflicts are eventually worked out.

Emergence stage—Community members begin to see and agree on a course of action.

Reinforcement stage—Community members finally make a decision and justify why it was correct.

Community members are far more likely to buy into policy that has been created with their participation. Their support over time will lead to permanent change.

Community participation energizes the community to continue to change in positive directions. Once involved in a successful change effort, community members see what they can accomplish collectively and take on new challenges.

Lastly, community members must inform policy makers and planners of the real needs of the community, so that the most important problems and issues can be addressed. They must also provide information about what has been tried before and worked or not worked.

COMMUNITY ORGANIZATION AND DEVELOPMENT METHODS

Community organizing is focused on harnessing the collective power of communities to tackle issues of shared concern. It challenges government, corporations, and other power-holding institutions in an effort to tip the power balance more in favor of communities.

Community organization enhances participatory skills of local citizens by working with and not for them, thus developing leadership with particular emphasis on the ability to conceptualize and act on problems. It strengthens communities so they can better deal with future problems; *community members can develop the capacity to resolve problems.*

COMMUNITY RESOURCES

Social work is often a challenging yet rewarding career. Social workers are responsible for helping individuals, families, and groups of people to cope with problems in order to improve their lives. Though social workers may deliver some services directly, such as teaching skills or counseling, they will often serve as liaisons between different agencies or resources to ensure that client needs are met. Thus, social workers must become familiar with existing community resources.

Community resources are assets that can help meet certain needs for for those in their vicinity. These assets can be people, places, structures, or services. Many things can serve as community resources. A park can be a community resource for clients who want to meet others or engage in recreational activities, and churches are community resources that can assist with meeting spiritual and support needs. When considering these resources, social workers should include those that are generic in addition to those that serve a particular client group or address specialized problems.

Conducting a community resource inventory is essential if social workers are to effectively assist individual clients and determine what gaps exist. These voids will serve as areas for community development efforts to be led by social workers.

COMMUNITY OUTREACH AND ADVOCACY

Working with large groups takes special planning and skills by a social worker. Some critical factors in working with large groups are as follows.

Establishing a common goal—Everyone in the group should have some common ground—whether it is the desire to take action or sharing views on an issue. Finding the common goal and bringing the group back to it when differences arise is essential.

Committing to consensus building—Consensus requires commitment, patience, tolerance, and a willingness to put the group first. In a large group, there may be more disagreement and conflict. Using a consensus model, disagreement can be used as a tool for helping to build cohesiveness.

Sufficient time—All decision-making techniques need enough time if the quality of decision is going to be good. Work with large groups will take longer so that all viewpoints can be heard and consensus can be reached.

Clear process—It is essential that the group has a shared understanding of the process and what to expect. Ground rules should be agreed upon by the group as its first consensus-building task.

Good facilitation and active participation—There may be a need to have more than one facilitator help with managing a large group. In addition, using techniques so that all can be heard, but are not fighting for attention, will be essential. Activities that keep group members engaged will need to be incorporated into group sessions.

There are a number of large scale intervention methods, such as a *World Café* where people with an interest in a topic or issues are brought together for a meeting. The host explains the purpose and logistics. There are then progressive rounds of conversations by smaller subgroups that move between small tables, exploring questions that matter and connecting diverse perspectives. A facilitator listens for patterns and insights that are shared with the larger group for validation.

SOCIAL PLANNING METHODS

Social planning is defined as the process by which a group or community decides its goals and strategies relating to societal issues. It is not an activity limited to government, but includes activities of the private sector, social movements, professions, and other organizations focused specifically on social objectives.

Models of social planning in social work practice include those that are based on community participation. Rather than planning "for" communities, social workers as planners engage "with" community members. Social planning does not merely examine sociological problems that exist, but also includes the physical and economic factors that relate to societal issues.

All issues confronting those who are served by social workers are really human or social issues. Social workers can help facilitate the process of planning through all stages: organizing community members; data gathering related to the issue—including identifying economic, political, and social causes; problem identification; weighing of alternatives; policy/program implementation; and evaluation of effectiveness.

THE IMPACT OF SOCIAL INSTITUTIONS ON SOCIETY

Many social institutions exist within our society. They have many functions including satisfying clients' basic needs, defining and promoting dominant social values, defining and promoting roles, creating permanent patterns of social behavior, and supporting other social institutions.

The five basic institutions are family, religion, government, education, and economics.

Some of the functions of each of these institutions include the following.

Family

- To control and regulate sexual behavior
- To provide for new members of society (children)
- To provide for the economic and emotional maintenance of individuals
- To provide for primary socialization of children

Religion

- To provide solutions for the unexplained
- To support the normative structure of the society

- To provide a psychological diversion from unwanted life situations
- To sustain the existing class structure
- To promote and prevent social change

Government

- To create norms via laws and enforce them
- To adjudicate conflict via the courts
- To provide for the welfare of members of society
- To protect society from external threats

Education

- To transmit culture
- To prepare for jobs and roles
- To evaluate and select competent individuals
- To transmit functional skills

Economics

- To provide methods for the production and distribution of goods and services
- To enable individuals to acquire goods and services that are produced

THE THEORIES OF SOCIAL CHANGE

One of the most important values of the social work profession is social justice.

Social workers promote social justice and social change with and on behalf of clients who are individuals, families, groups, organizations, and/or communities.

Social workers should engage in social and political action that seeks to ensure that all people have equal access to the resources, employment, services, and opportunities they require to meet their basic human needs and to develop fully. Social workers should be aware of the impact of the political arena on practice and should advocate for changes in policy and legislation to improve social conditions in order to meet basic human needs and promote social justice (*NASW Code of Ethics, 1999–6.04 Social and Political Action*).

Administration and Management

22

THE IMPACT OF AGENCY POLICY AND PROCEDURES ON SOCIAL WORK PRACTICE

The context of social work practice clearly has a profound influence on the quality and standards of professional activities and the ability of social workers to practice ethically and effectively. Social work takes place in a wide variety of settings, including, but not limited to, private practices, public sector organizations (government), schools, hospitals, correctional facilities, and private not-for-profit agencies.

To meet the needs of clients, social workers must have work environments that support ethical practice and are committed to standards that promote good quality services. A positive working environment is created where the values and principles of social workers are reinforced in agency policies and procedures.

To achieve this aim, employers must understand social work practice and provide supervision, workload management, and continuing professional development consistent with best practices.

Policies setting out standards of ethical practice should be written and clear. Social workers should never be required to do anything that would put at risk their ability to uphold ethical standards, including those in the areas of confidentiality, informed consent, and safety and risk management.

The public, including clients, should be regularly informed of agency policies and procedures and provided with information about how to raise concerns or make complaints. Policies that do not tolerate dangerous, discriminatory, and/or exploitative behavior must be in place so that social workers and their clients are safe from harm.

The adoption and implementation of policies and procedures on workload and caseload management contribute greatly to the provision of quality services to clients. In addition, policies and procedures for confidential treatment and storage of records should be established.

Continuing professional development and further training enable social workers to strengthen and develop their skills. Orientation and other relevant training provided to social workers upon hire and when assuming other jobs within the setting are essential.

Good quality, regular social work supervision by professionals who have the necessary experience and qualifications in social work practice is a critical tool to ensure service quality.

Rates of pay for social workers need to be comparable with similar professionals, and the skill and qualifications of social workers must be recognized, while ensuring services are affordable to clients.

LEADERSHIP AND MANAGEMENT TECHNIQUES

There are many different definitions of leadership and management, with little consensus about the differences between the two terms. However, there is agreement that successful organizations need both good leadership and management. Some suggest that leadership can be viewed as a subset of management because a leadership role is inherent in a management position. Leadership is related to being focused on the future, dealing with uncertainty and instability, and prospectively considering the ways in which organizational operations need to change. Leadership also includes initiating, sustaining, and helping to maintain a certain amount of momentum through the change process. Leaders must be attentive to and help to balance stability and change. Management, on the other hand, focuses on efficiency, effectiveness, and planning.

Social work leaders need management skills and social work managers need leadership skills in order to be effective. The skill sets of leaders focus on inspiration, transformation, empowerment, trust, innovation, and creativity whereas managers are concerned with performance, planning, accountability, monitoring, evaluation, cooperation, and teamwork. Managers must govern resources and oversee the tensions between controlling, rationing, and providing needed services.

There is typically little distinction between managers and leaders because leaders are often appointed to management positions. Thus, managers and leaders within organizations are usually the same individuals.

TIME MANAGEMENT APPROACHES

Time management is planning and consciously controlling the amount of time spent on specific activities, especially to increase effectiveness, efficiency, or productivity. Though time management initially focused on business or work activities, it is now increasingly used to control personal activities as well.

Most time management approaches focus on creating conducive or effective environments, modifying behaviors, setting priorities, and/or reducing time spent on nonpriorities.

The approaches to time management have evolved. Initially, approaches consisted of checklists and notes to recognize the demands on time. These then evolved into calendars and appointment books that focused on looking ahead to anticipate future events. The third approach, often used today, examines efficiency with the focus on prioritizing, planning, controlling, and taking steps toward a goal.

The last approach requires the categorization of daily activities by importance and urgency. Those activities that are urgent and important can be stressful and require immediate action; those who deal with these exclusively will think they are just "putting out fires." Activities that are not urgent or important require little or no attention, and time spent on these activities will result in feelings of disengagement. Activities that are urgent but not important often take up a lot of attention but tend to yield little difference or progress. The last grouping—those things that are important but not urgent—are likely to be put aside yet are critical to personal fulfillment. Time management should include minimizing time spent on activities that are not important and ensuring those that are not urgent but are important, such as building relationships, recreation and leisure, and so on, are also prioritized.

FORMAL AND INFORMAL ORGANIZATIONAL STRUCTURE

Organizations have formal structures, even if they are only loosely adhered to. Organizations have informal structures as well. There are times when the informal structures conflict with the formal ones, making it important to understand the difference between them.

Formal structure refers to the official hierarchy and lines of authority. Formal structure is built on division of labor and functional processes and structures. A typical organizational chart illustrates the formal structure. The hierarchical organization begins at the top with the most senior leader and cascades down to subordinate managers and employees below top-level managers. There are job titles, financial obligations, and clear lines of authority for each box on the organization chart. It is deliberately impersonal and is often criticized for not accounting for the interactions and communication which take place informally in organizations.

Informal structure refers to the relationship between people in organizations based on personal attitudes, emotions, likes, dislikes, and so on. These relationships are not developed according to procedures and regulations laid down in the formal structure. This structure is not preplanned but develops spontaneously. These associations may be among employees on the same level of the hierarchy or on different levels.

Informal structures influence productivity and job satisfaction.

Employees rely on the informal structure if the formal structure has stopped being effective, which often happens as an organization grows or changes but does not reevaluate its hierarchy or formal structure.

THE ELEMENTS OF CASELOAD MANAGEMENT

Caseload management outlines the kind and volume of work undertaken by social workers and/or their supervisees. The number of clients—individuals or families—is not usually a good indication of the actual work involved.

Although there is no set criteria by which to determine caseload sizes, there are some factors that contribute to determining the time needed to be spent on delivery services.

First, the *complexity of client problems*, including the number of other professionals with which a social worker will need to interface, is directly related to the time that must be spent on assisting clients.

Second, the *risk associated with client situations* can be an indicator of service intensity needed. Clients who are in crisis or at-risk for instability require a lot of contact by a social worker. High-risk situations also take a lot of emotional energy by social workers. Self-care is essential, and a social worker needs to have time in his or her schedule to attend to any presenting client issues that need immediate attention these issues are often unforeseen and rapidly changing, causing anxiety for all involved.

Lastly, a social worker may have to travel appreciable distances to work with a particular individual or family. *Travel time and paperwork required* must be considered in deciding appropriate caseload sizes.

There may be other criteria that should also be considered in caseload management. These criteria may be related to *the nature of client problems, characteristics of clients, organizational issues*, and so on. Once the relevant areas have been determined, formal or informal processes may be used to decide the appropriate size and makeup of caseloads. A formal process can involve a consistent and clear weighting system of each client situation. Caseload decisions may be based on ensuring *equitable distributions* based on time required and/or complexity of client circumstances or *proportional distributions* based on social workers' levels of experience and expertise.

Examining the composition of caseloads can help to define areas of professional development needed by social workers. It can also help to examine potentially stressful situation that may lead to burnout.

THE USE OF DELEGATION AS A TECHNIQUE

Delegation is the on-going process by which a supervisor gives responsibilities and authority to another for assigned tasks. Delegation has value for the supervisor, supervisee, and agency as a whole.

Supervisors often have many roles and responsibilities, each of which involves demands on their time. Delegation of responsibilities allows the organization to achieve more because it provides opportunities for supervisors to split up essential responsibilities and activities within agencies.

Delegating routine work relieves leaders of stress associated with these tasks and gives them more time to work on critical job duties. Thus, delegation decreases burnout by avoiding overwhelming supervisors.

Delegation also allows supervisees more responsibility, increasing the leadership credibility of supervisors while garnering the respect and loyalty of those provided with the extra authority. Delegation exposes supervisees to new skills and gives them the opportunity to develop themselves and achieve their goals. Delegation makes them more versatile and more important parts of organizational teams.

Delegation shows supervisees that they are trusted and that supervisors have confidence in them. Having interesting and challenging work feels good, and being trusted to complete jobs raises self-esteem. Having strong self-esteem can motivate supervisees to accomplish organizational goals. With new responsibility and authority, supervisees use their own initiative and their imagination to solve agency problems that may not have been recognized.

Thus, delegation increases organizational efficiency, enhances worker flexibility, and builds teamwork by providing employees with opportunities to interface with others with whom they do not normally work. Delegation also more effectively balances workloads and keeps employees interested and motivated by demonstrating that talents will be used to the utmost regardless of their official positions within organizations.

THE METHODS USED TO PLAN AND ASSIGN WORK TO STAFF

When it comes to managing staff tasks, there are a number of methods that can be used. Social workers will need to make decisions in regard to planning work, assigning tasks, ensuring implementation, and evaluating whether the job has been done in a timely and effective manner.

A major decision that social workers must consider is whether to assign work to staff believed to be best able to do the jobs accurately and efficiently or to divide tasks among different employees to spread out the workload. There are advantages and disadvantages with each approach. If tasks are assigned to individuals believed to be most competent to complete them, it is likely that social workers will get those with the skill sets to do the jobs correctly; however, supervisors may be come overreliant on a small group of employees. In addition, always using staff who will complete work satisfactorily does not help to assess the strengths of others and develop their skills further.

Spreading the work around may be a more equitable approach and ensure that there is time to get the work done as it will not fall on the shoulders of a small number of staff. However, the problems with this method is that the people best suited to a task may not be doing it, leading to problems with quality.

When assigning work to others, social workers must evaluate the work completed ensure that it has been done correctly.

THE CONCEPTS OF AUTHORITY AND RESPONSIBILITY

While used interchangeably, authority and responsibility have significantly different meanings. *Authority* is the power to make decisions that guide the actions of others. These decisions may relate to the allocation of resources or whether to act/not act in a given situation. Authority can be assigned by one person to another and may be granted based upon position within an organization. Authority is critical in management positions as they are responsible for the operations of organizations.

Responsibility is the obligation to perform an assigned duty. When assigned a task by a supervisor, a social worker has the responsibility to complete it. Like authority, responsibility can be assigned to another person. However, the essence of responsibility is to be dutiful. It usually originates from a superior-subordinate relationship.

Social workers must always ensure that they use their authority and complete tasks for which they are responsible in a manner that puts clients' interests first.

The greatest authority can be found at the top of an organizational chart while responsibility, or the execution of duties assigned by supervisors, is often more prevalent at the bottom.

THE MODELS FOR INTERPRETING AGENCY POLICIES AND PROCEDURES TO STAFF

An organization should have policies in place to explain how it will deal with issues when they arise and to show that it operates in a fair and consistent way toward all employees and clients. Orientation is a good way of making policies known to new employees, but they also need to be systematically reinforced in a variety of contexts.

Though most employees are, to some extent, aware of an organization's mission when being hired, precise details of that mission should be spelled out and distributed to staff.

All employers should have copies of general policies regarding employee conduct, including guidelines on what is considered appropriate behavior between employees, employees and supervisors, and employees and clients.

Venues that allow staff to ask questions about agency policies and procedures are also essential. Staff may be unclear about how and in what circumstances agency policies apply or the finer points of procedures. These venues may be part of routine supervisory sessions or other gatherings with agency leadership. Employees should always have the opportunity to voice their concerns about policies and procedures that adversely affect service provision or outcomes and should take advantage of these opportunities in a proactive and professional manner.

THE COMPONENTS OF A COLLEGIAL AND POSITIVE WORK ENVIRONMENT

Work environments influence the quality of services provided to clients. Although there are no agreed upon definitions of work environment or conditions, the terms are related to factors present in employment settings that influence work processes and outcomes as well as employee well-being. Healthy work environments impact organizational functionality, employee satisfaction, work-family balance, staff development, and so on. Burnout and turnover can be reduced when a collegial and positive work environment exists.

There can be many elements that relate to the quality of a work environment, including employment terms, work performed, and cultural or physical conditions present. Employment terms can include wages and benefits paid, number of hours worked, scheduling, and so on. Work performed relates to both the quality and quantity of the tasks to be completed. Cultural and physical conditions include the degree to which social work values are respected and promoted, autonomy is allowed, health and safety are ensured, professional development and supervision are available, and so on.

FISCAL MANAGEMENT TECHNIQUES

Human service organizations need to be accountable in the recording and reporting of their financial transactions. Financial management refers to planning for, acquiring, allocating, controlling, and recording/reporting of financial and material resources, as well as the evaluation of methods used to achieve these aims. Financial management involves the following activities/techniques:

- **Planning**—the short- and long-term strategies used to ensure fiscal solvency
- **Acquisition**—the gathering of human, material and economic resources through such means as fundraising, grant writing, contractual arrangements, fees, purchase of merchandise, and so on

- **Allocation**—the distribution of resources internally (such as to specific departments) or externally (such as by contracting outside organization or using consultants)
- **Internal control**—the establishment of standardized policies and procedures relating to all transactions and events involving monetary items (including the use of generally accepted accounting principles and adherence to contractual obligations)
- **Recording/reporting**—the use of a manual, automated, or computerized system to list and classify all transactions of a fiscal nature in journals and ledgers to generate statements and reports
- **Evaluating**—the periodic review of financial activities to assess their efficiency and effectiveness at meeting the goal of financial accountability

Social work administrators need to be knowledgeable about financial management techniques because they are responsible for the oversight and operations of their programs. This responsibility includes overseeing fiscal staff and fiscal operations.

THE BUDGETARY PROCESS

A budget is a plan that outlines an entity's financial and operational goals. There are some similarities and differences between the budgetary processes of public entities such as federal, state, and local governments and the private social service organizations in which most social workers are employed. Understanding how budgets are developed and adopted in both the public and private sectors is critical.

Budgeting is forecasting by the government about its expenditures and revenues for a specific period of time. The budget process for the federal government of the United States involves both the executive and legislative branches of government. The president submits a budget to Congress, which then passes legislation to appropriate and authorize the funds to be spent. In state government, the governor, who is the leader of the executive branch, proposes a budget to the legislature, which then has an opportunity to modify it before voting to adopt the budget and appropriate funds. In a nonprofit agency, the executive director usually constructs the proposed budget and then works with a board of trustees to refine and adopt it.

The most reliable budgets yield the best fiscal results and are income based. *Income-based budgeting* establishes targets on realistic expectations and only includes reliable income in the budget. Expenses must be lower than the total dependable income total.

Incremental budgeting begins with prior year totals and builds the subsequent year's budget by calculating percentage increases or decreases.

Zero-based budgeting starts from scratch every year, examining the assumptions every year and allocating resources to the most important mission activities.

When looking at expenditures, it is necessary to distinguish between fixed and variable costs. *Fixed costs* are not ordinarily affected by the number of projects, programs, or clients served. Examples of fixed costs include permanent full-time staff, office rent, and payments on long-term loans. *Variable costs* are usually project-oriented and are more adjustable. *Semi-variable costs* are in between—they must occur, but can be modified (e.g., short-term rental versus purchasing equipment or engaging part-time temporary help rather than hiring full-time permanent staff).

The key to a successful budget is the generation of income. *Reliable revenue* can be counted upon from year-to-year and would include examples such as, dependable annual foundation gifts or government grants for general operating and long-standing contracts with government agencies or other entities. During a recession, many revenue sources that have traditionally been dependable may become less so, moving these items from reliable toward transient. *Transient revenue* is income generated from one-time program offerings or financial gifts such as a bequest. Transient revenue can be useful for single capital purchases but cannot be counted on to sustain organizational operations over time.

GOVERNANCE STRUCTURES

Governance concerns those structures, functions, processes, and customs that exist within an organization to ensure it operates in a way that achieves its objectives, and does so in an effective and transparent manner. It is a framework of accountability to clients, stakeholders, and the wider community, within which organizations make decisions and control their functions and resources to achieve their objectives.

Good governance adds value by improving the performance of an organization through more efficient management, more strategic and equitable resource allocation and service provision, and other improvements that lend themselves to improved outcomes and impacts.

Social workers should advocate within and outside their agencies for adequate resources to meet clients' needs and for resource allocation procedures that are open and fair (*NASW Code of Ethics, 1999—3.07 Administration*). When not all clients' needs can be met, an allocation procedure should be developed that is nondiscriminatory, appropriate, and consistent. Social workers should take reasonable steps to ensure that adequate agency or organizational resources are available to provide appropriate staff supervision and that the working environment for which they are responsible is consistent with and encourages compliance with the *NASW Code of Ethics (1999)*.

THE METHODS USED FOR STRATEGIC PLANNING

The goal of strategic planning is to develop a consistent vision for guiding an organization's actions, decision making, and resource allocation. There are various models of strategic planning, each with their own methods. It is important for social workers to choose the one that best fits their organizational needs.

Vision/goals-based strategic planning is usually carried out by top-level management and is ideal for agencies that have not done a lot of strategic planning in the past. It focuses on identifying organizational vision, mission, and goals that are used to create specific action plans. These plans are monitored and updated as needed.

Issues-based planning is done in instances where there are very limited resources, significant issues are present, and/or little success in or "buy in" for strategic planning. It identifies the current, major issues facing the organization and brainstorms ideas to address them. Chosen alternatives serve as the basis of a plan that will be monitored and updated.

An *alignment model* ensures strong consistency between an organization's mission and its resources. This model is useful for organizations that need to fine-tune strategies or find out why existing strategies are not working. The essential aim is identifying what is working well and what needs adjustment.

Organic or real-time planning is an alternative to traditional strategic planning processes which are sometimes considered too linear. They involve ongoing and "real time" dialogue about what processes are needed to arrive at the organization's vision.

EMPLOYEE RECRUITMENT, TRAINING, RETENTION, PERFORMANCE APPRAISAL, EVALUATION, AND DISCIPLINE

Employment and human resources law can be very complicated. Social work administrators should be familiar with federal, state, and local regulations. They must ensure that human service organizations operate legally and they must make ethical decisions with regard to employee recruitment, training, retention, performance appraisal, evaluation, and discipline. Social work administrators must also ensure that employment policies and practices are not discriminatory based on race, ethnicity, national origin, color, sex, sexual orientation, gender identity or expression, age, marital status, political belief, religion, immigration status, or mental or physical disability.

Employee recruitment can be difficult as it involves finding the best candidates for positions. Bad recruitment practices may lead to unqualified people being selected. Although there is no perfect method for hiring, it is best to start well in advance of a hiring need. A pool of candidates should be recruited using a detailed job description and an established background check policies. Interviews should use standard questioning which complies with legal and ethical standards.

Once hired, employees need to be initially trained and should receive ongoing development opportunities to ensure that they have the skills needed to fulfill the mission of an organization. There are several options for training and education related to employees' official duties. These include doing training within an agency or having employees go to other entities to be trained. Training may be paid solely by an employer or an employee, or split between the two parties. In addition, time spent in training may be compensated by an employer or not, depending upon the policy of an agency.

Once employees are hired and trained, retaining them should also be a top priority. Many good retention practices are inexpensive to implement. Employee retention is positively linked to career development opportunities and a chance to advance within an agency, opportunities for regular feedback and recognition, flexible work schedules that recognize the need for work/life balance, and good salaries and benefits.

Employee performance should be periodically evaluated to ensure that employees are meeting expected standards, as well as to inform them of their status. Performance appraisal should be both formal and informal so that employees can get immediate feedback if they are doing something good or bad. Positive reinforcement is a powerful force for employees who are doing a good job. For problem employees, specific work-quality issues can be pointed out. Evaluations should make employees feel empowered, not micromanaged. After employees have been evaluated, goals for development, and/or improvement should be established.

Sometimes discipline, including termination, becomes necessary. Social work administrators must be knowledgeable about both laws and agency policies that impact disciplinary actions. When employees have performed illegal acts, termination is justified. Breaking agency policies can also be grounds for termination. However, there are situations where termination can be considered "wrongful" or inappropriate, such as when an employee is fired for reporting wrongdoing or for taking time off when covered by the Family Medical Leave Act (FMLA).

Supervision and Consultation

23

THE STAGES OF PROFESSIONAL DEVELOPMENT

Professions enjoy a high social status, regard, and esteem conferred upon them by society. This high esteem arises primarily from the higher social function of their work, which is regarded as vital to society as a whole and, thus, being special and valuable in nature. All professions involve technical, specialized, and highly skilled work, often referred to as "professional expertise." Training for this work involves obtaining degrees and professional qualifications (i.e., licensure), without which entry to the profession is barred. Training also requires regular updating of skills through continuing education.

Professional development refers to skills and knowledge attained for effective service delivery and career advancement. Professional development encompasses all types of learning opportunities, ranging from formal coursework and conferences to informal learning opportunities situated in practice. There are a variety of approaches to professional development, including *consultation, coaching, communities of practice, mentoring, reflective supervision, and technical assistance.*

Social workers often go through various stages of professional development, including:

1. Orientation and job induction
2. Autonomous worker
3. Member of a service team (independence to interdependence)
4. Development of specialization
5. Preparation to be a mentor or supervisor

THE EDUCATIONAL COMPONENTS, TECHNIQUES, AND METHODS OF SUPERVISION

There are three components of supervision—administrative, educational, and supportive. *Administrative supervision* aims to ensure that a social worker is accountable to the public as well as to his or her organization's policies. The major responsibility is to make sure that the work is performed in an acceptable manner. *Educational supervision* establishes a learning alliance between a supervisor and a social worker with the aim of teaching new skills or refining existing ones. *Supportive supervision* is focused on increasing performance by decreasing job-related stress that interferes with functioning.

For a social worker to learn job-related material and develop as a skilled professional, he or she must make appropriate and effective use of educational supervision. The educational component of supervision is concerned with teaching a social worker what he or she needs to know in order to do his or her job and helping him or her through the learning process. In essence, the educational component relates to the transmission of knowledge, skills, attitudes, and values needed by social workers.

In order for learning to occur, a supervisee must be cooperative (willing to work and learn new skills), willing to follow directions (initially doing what is told until able to complete routines without direction), and knowledgeable (about agency procedures). A supervisee also must show initiative (seeking out learning opportunities and applying new knowledge) and accepting of criticism (trying to improve and accepting feedback when it is justified and constructive).

Supervisors also have responsibilities in educational supervision. They must provide education and training (formal and informal opportunities to ensure supervisees have the knowledge and skills needed to do their jobs competently) and feedback (explanations on what is going well and what needs improvement). Identifying the learning needs of supervisees should be done at hire and regularly thereafter. Changes in the field must always be considered. Lastly, supervisors should be aware of supervisees' learning styles and ensure that education is delivered via methods that are most effective. There are three main cognitive learning styles: visual (uses visual objects such as graphs and charts to learn), auditory (retains information through hearing and speaking), and kinesthetic (likes to use hands-on approaches to acquire knowledge).

THE MODELS OF GROUP SUPERVISION

Social workers' learning and continued development typically is fostered through concurrent use of individual and group supervision. Group supervision is unique in that growth is aided by the interactions occurring between groups members. Social workers do not function in isolation, so groups become natural venues to accomplish professional socialization and to increase learning. Supervision in groups provides an opportunity for social workers to experience mutual support, share common experiences, solve complex tasks, learn new behaviors, participate in skills training, and increase interpersonal competencies and insight.

The benefit of group supervision is the interaction of the supervisees. Collaborative learning is a pivotal benefit, with social workers having opportunities to be exposed to a variety of cases, interventions, and approaches to problem solving in a group. By viewing and being viewed and actively giving and receiving feedback, social workers' opportunities for experimental learning are expanded. Thus, group supervision is a valuable social modeling experience. From a relationship perspective, group supervision provides an opportunity to interact with peers in a way that encourages self-responsibility and increases mutuality between supervisor and supervisee. Groups allow members to be exposed to the cognitive processes of other social workers at various levels of development. Lastly, hearing the success and the frustrations of other social workers gives members a more realistic model by which they can critique themselves and build confidence.

Group supervision sessions can be theme-centered, case-centered, and/or worker-centered. *Theme-centered* sessions include discussions around topics such as self-disclosure or use of a particular modality. *Case-centered* sessions involve brainstorming about a particular client situation for which a member would like collegial input. Lastly, *work-centered* sessions are avenues to share issues related to work and discover ways to deal with work-related stress.

The supervisor may take a very active role in a group or may act more as a facilitator, allowing most of the learning to take place through supervisee interactions. However, a supervisor should be responsible for establishing the structure and format, as well as selecting group members. During group sessions, a supervisor should also summarize and reflect what occurs in a group, validating observations with and involving all supervisees present.

THE MODELS OF PEER SUPERVISION AND CONSULTATION

Peer supervision differs from more traditional forms of supervision because it does not require the presence of a more qualified professional in the process. Peer supervision usually refers to reciprocal arrangements in which peers work together for mutual benefit. Peer supervision is based on the use of feedback to assist with self-directed learning and evaluation.

Some of the benefits of peer supervision include increased access/frequency of supervision, reciprocal learning through the sharing of experiences, increased skills and responsibility for self-assessment, and decreased dependency on expert supervisors. Peer supervision can play a valuable role in giving more people more access to more supervision, which in turn impacts on the quality of service to clients.

There are several models of peer supervision, based on theoretical orientations that are discussed in the following text.

Psychodynamic Model This model focuses on human interactions and examines the relationship between a social worker and a client. This approach can use video or audio recordings to look at the interactions between a social worker and a client.

Developmental Model This model focuses on how treatment goes through stages such as the beginning, middle, and end. It can be applied as a client and social worker go through the problem-solving process together.

Role-Centered Model This model examines the social worker–client relationship through the tenets of social role theory. Group members are assigned roles or characters to pay attention to during the presentation of a case. These roles can be chosen and assigned by a group supervisor, supervisee presenter, or other group members. Perspectives include a social worker, a client, a client's significant other, client nonverbal behaviors, the problem-solving process, and/or theoretical perspectives. Group members discuss a case from their assigned roles or perspectives.

In addition, peer supervision models may vary according to the size of the group—with only two social workers providing input to and supporting each other on one end of the continuum to much larger groups on the other.

Other factors that impact on models of peer supervision include goals or focus of the group, structure, and learning models (formal versus informal, didactic [role-playing/experiential learning/reflective practice] versus case presentation, leadership structure, and member roles).

In order for peer supervision to be effective, those participating must create an environment of openness and be nonjudgmental. In addition, it should occur regularly and be scheduled—not just happen "on the fly." Social workers must also engage in self-reflection and be self-directed learners. They should not dominate the group's time or give advice because all members are equal in these models.

THE METHODS USED TO IDENTIFY LEARNING NEEDS AND DEVELOP LEARNING OBJECTIVES FOR SUPERVISEES

Supervision is an essential way in which social workers acquire knowledge and skills needed for professional practice. It is often the bridge between the classroom and the field. Supervision is necessary to improve client care, develop professionalism, and maintain ethical standards in the field. Supervision has also become the cornerstone of quality improvement and assurance.

Quality supervision is founded on a positive supervisor–supervisee relationship that promotes client welfare and the professional development of the supervisee. A supervisor is a teacher, coach, consultant, mentor, evaluator, and administrator. *Ultimately, effective supervision ensures that clients are competently served.* Supervision ensures that social workers continue to increase their skills, which in turn increases service effectiveness.

Some of the skills that social work supervisors must have in order to effectively teach supervisees include the ability to:

- Identify learning needs and styles
- Write learning goals and objectives
- Devise instructional strategies to accommodate needs and learning styles
- Present material in a didactic manner, using modeling
- Match learning styles to developmental levels (e.g., provide more instruction to junior supervisees and use guided discovery for those who are senior)
- Explain the rationales for interventions
- Evaluate supervisees learning
- Give constructive feedback to supervisees

Learning needs of supervisees may result from gaps in knowledge about practice modalities; effective communication strategies; setting, funding, or legal requirements; self-care strategies; and so on. Social work supervisors should be knowledgeable about the skills supervisees acquired from previous professional training and experience, as well as gaps in learning, such as those related to diagnostic assessment and treatment; ethical standards of practice; state and federal laws and rules; record-keeping; cultural competence; methods for establishing treatment relationships with clients; methods for including family members in clients' treatment when appropriate; communication with other professionals in developing diagnosis and treatment plans and assuring continuity of care; and so on. Lastly, social work supervisors should solicit input from supervisees about what they view as their greatest learning needs and develop learning objectives to meet these needs in partnership with supervisees. Identifying learning needs and developing learning objectives is a collaborative process between social work supervisors and supervisees.

TRANSFERENCE AND COUNTERTRANSFERENCE WITHIN SUPERVISORY RELATIONSHIPS

Transference and countertransference within supervisory relationships can be a parallel process of what is occurring between a social worker and a client. The transference occurs when a social worker recreates, within a supervisory relationship, a presenting problem and emotions occurring in a therapeutic relationship. Countertransference occurs when a supervisor responds to a social worker in the same manner that a social worker responds to a client. Thus, a supervisory interaction replays, or is parallel with, a social worker–client interaction. In essence, the processes at work in the relationship between a social worker and a client are reflected in the relationship between a social worker and his or her supervisor.

Parallel process is an unconscious identification with a client and can be used as an important part of the supervisory process. Examining it will assist a social worker and his or her supervisor in identifying issues that exist in a therapeutic relationship and allow for techniques to resolve these issues to be identified and discussed.

THE SOCIAL WORKER'S RESPONSIBILITY TO SEEK AND RECEIVE APPROPRIATE SUPERVISION

The short-term objectives of supervision are to increase a social worker's capacity to work more effectively, to provide a work context conducive to productivity, and to help a social worker take satisfaction in his or her work. *The ultimate objective is to assure the delivery of the most effective and efficient client services.*

Social workers who are administrators should take reasonable steps to ensure that adequate agency or organizational resources are available to provide appropriate staff supervision.

Competence is essential for ethical social work practice and social workers must be competent in the services that they are providing (*NASW Code of Ethics, 1999–1.04 Competence*). In order to be competent, they must keep abreast of new developments in the field and obtain supervision.

Social workers should provide services and represent themselves as competent only within the boundaries of their education, training, license, certification, consultation received, supervised experience, or other relevant professional experience (*NASW Code of Ethics, 1999–1.04 Competence*).

Social workers should provide services in substantive areas or use intervention techniques or approaches that are new to them only after engaging in appropriate study, training, consultation, and supervision from people who are competent in those interventions or techniques (*NASW Code of Ethics, 1999–1.04 Competence*).

When generally recognized standards do not exist with respect to an emerging area of practice, social workers should exercise careful judgment and take responsible steps (including appropriate education, research, training, consultation, and supervision) to ensure the competence of their work and to protect clients from harm (*NASW Code of Ethics, 1999–1.04 Competence*).

If a supervisor needs to talk with a social worker about a problem situation, he or she should meet privately with the social worker to discuss the matter.

STUDENT/SUPERVISEE CHARACTERISTICS AND SUITABILITY FOR THE PROFESSION

Social workers come from all kinds of backgrounds and exhibit a wide range of personality profiles and social lifestyles. They come to choose the profession for many different reasons. Some have a strong convictions in regard to altruism or the desire to help, whereas others have a commitment to social justice or ensuring that policies are fair and just. Some individuals enter social work due to religious convictions, having been helped by services in the past, and/or having a relative in the field. Whatever the reason for the initial interest, social workers must undergo rigorous educational and experience requirements to ensure that they are suitable for the profession.

Professional suitability is defined as a good understanding of social work knowledge, skills, and values and the ability to display of appropriate behaviors in given practice situations. The assessment and screening processes of professional suitability begin at admission to a social work program, continue throughout coursework and fieldwork, and carry on after graduation. Assessing and screening suitability for social work practice is essential to ensure that only suitable individuals are allowed to enter and remain in the profession of social work.

There are no universal tools or methods to assess and screen for professional suitability. Social work has developed a unique set of professional values and goals of practice. Fundamental is the belief in the intrinsic worth and dignity of every human being and a commitment to the values of acceptance, self-determination, and respect of individuality. The fundamental values and goals of practice characterize the professional identity of social worker and provide a blueprint for supervisors to assess suitability for practice.

Areas for evaluation include possession of essential knowledge, skills, and values for use in social work; development of capacity for establishing and sustaining purposeful working relationships; development of social consciousness; ability to think critically and analytically; and knowledge of practice environments. Supervisees must demonstrate self-awareness, commitment to social work values, knowledge of the profession, good interpersonal skills, respect for others, desire to learn, and maintenance of a nonjudgmental attitude in order to be effective. Assessing suitability of supervisees is essential to promoting high standards of practice and protecting the interests of clients.

THE USE OF CASE RECORDING/DOCUMENTATION FOR PRACTICE EVALUATION OR SUPERVISION

Case records are often an excellent source of information for evaluating the impacts of services. They are existing sources of data, so there is no additional cost or time associated with their collection. However, there are a few limitations. If looking at records completed by multiple workers, there may be inconsistencies in recording styles or detail that may impact on the evaluation. Also, information of interest may not be contained in the records; evaluations would need to be limited to only information that is explicitly stated, which may not reflect all progress that has been made.

In addition, the opinions about how a client views both the process and outcome of service delivery are also critical and may not be fully captured in the record. Ensuring that a client's views are the center of any practice evaluation is critical. Thus, a social worker may want to use the case record as one source of information but include others that can help to ensure that all aspects of a client's care, including satisfaction with services, are included.

Social workers engaged in formal evaluation beyond that used to determine individual client progress should obtain voluntary and written informed consent from clients regarding the use of their records without any penalty for refusal to participate or undue inducement to participate (*NASW Code of Ethics, 1999—5.02 Evaluation and Research*).

Review of case records by supervisors is also essential. This review will ensure that a social worker is documenting properly and recording information in an unbiased manner. Clients must understand and consent to supervisory review of records.

When reviewing information, supervisors should adhere to the same standards of confidentiality as a social worker. The supervisor should not review the records unless it is for the betterment of a client, and only within the supervisory context to ensure the quality of services. If the supervisor is a consultant, a client must consent unless there is a compelling need for such disclosure.

Risk Management

24

SYSTEMS OF INTERNAL CONTROLS THAT MINIMIZE RISK FOR CLIENTS, WORKERS, AND THE AGENCY

Internal controls are systematic measures (such as reviews, checks and balances, and procedures) instituted by a human service organization to deliver services in an orderly and efficient manner; appropriately manage its assets and resources; deter and detect errors, abuse, fraud, and theft; produce reliable and timely management information; and adhere to established policies and procedures. Internal controls are put in place to help ensure that human service organizations achieve their objectives.

Most internal controls can be classified as preventive or detective. *Preventive controls* are designed to avoid errors or irregularities from occurring, such as having managers approve expense requests to prevent inappropriate expenditures. *Detective controls* are designed to identify an error or irregularity after it has occurred. These controls are performed on a routine basis to identify issues that pose potential risks in a timely manner. A detective control can be having managers review expenditure and other fiscal reports to assure that they accurately reflect the financial transactions of the agency.

Many circumstances may compromise the effectiveness of an internal control structure, including inadequate segregation of duties, inappropriate access to assets, inadequate knowledge of agency policies, procedures which lack substance, absence of monitoring of control overrides, and so on.

Internal controls can be, but do not have to be, costly. Sometimes there is no out-of-pocket cost to establish an adequate control—for example, creating segregation of duties such as having voided receipts approved by someone (preferably a manager) other than the person preparing the receipts. The ramifications of poor internal controls are serious, as causing a loss of good will and poor public relations when it is discovered that organizations did not safeguard funds properly or follow established protocols and required policies.

THE METHODS TO CREATE, IMPLEMENT, AND EVALUATE POLICIES AND PROCEDURES THAT MINIMIZE RISK FOR CLIENTS, WORKERS, AND THE AGENCY

Social workers should create, implement, and evaluate policies that minimize risk for clients, workers, and practice settings. One critical feature of implementing a comprehensive risk management strategy is conducting a comprehensive ethics audit. An ethics audit entails examining risks through the following steps:

1. Appointing a committee or task force of concerned and informed staff and colleagues

2. Gathering information from agency documents, interviews with staff and clients, accreditation reports, and other sources to assess risks associated with client rights; confidentiality and privacy; informed consent; service delivery; boundary issues; conflicts of interest; documentation; client records; supervision; staff development and training; consultation; client referral; fraud; termination of services; professional impairment; misconduct, or incompetence; and so on

3. Reviewing all collected information

4. Determining whether there is no risk, minimal risk, moderate risk, or high risk in each area

5. Preparing action plans to address each risk, paying particular attention to policies that need to be created to prevent risk in the future and steps needed to mitigate existing risk

6. Monitoring policy implementation and progress made toward reducing existing risk, as well as ensuring that procedures adhere to social work's core ethical principles as outlined in the *Code of Ethics (1999)*

Risk management is an ongoing process and must consist of preventive strategies as well as corrective actions that result from audits done routinely or in response to particular concerns or complaints.

THE SOCIAL WORKER'S RESPONSIBILITIES TO RESPOND TO CLIENT AND/OR COMMUNITY CONCERNS

Feelings and emotions exert a powerful influence on clients' behaviors and often play a critical role in their problems. Voluntary clients often enter into services with openness and hope that they will explore both their concerns and accompanying feelings. However, involuntary clients have not actively sought out services from the social workers who aim to help them. To respond effectively to both client groups, social workers must be able to address a broad spectrum of concerns and emotions. In addition, social workers must possess a rich vocabulary that accurately reflects both client emotions and the intensity of those emotions. For example, involuntary clients may express anger and frustration as their primary concerns when having to meet with social workers. Being able to communicate with clients using a broad emotional vocabulary allows social workers to convey their understanding and compassion for what clients are experiencing. "Starting where the client is" reminds social workers of the need to immediately respond to and address client concerns. Acknowledging clients' emotions and expressions about these emotions are the basis of the social worker–client relationship and central to providing assistance.

Social workers must remember that client concerns may be communicated by facial features, gestures, and/or body posture. Social workers should be sensitive to these nonverbal messages and changes in clients' nonverbal expression. Being pensive or showing discomfort when speaking can indicate areas of concern that need to be acknowledged and addressed. Often the issues that clients verbally express as concerns are only a hint at their problems or are masking their actual troubles.

Lastly, social workers must remember that clients' concerns may not be the situations that drove them to seek or receive services and may be very different than what superficially appear to be their issues. Social workers must not only respond to clients' concerns, but uncover and solicit them. Clients often will not feel comfortable being honest about their concerns until they feel that social workers are both empathetic and trustworthy.

THE POLICY IMPLICATIONS OF RISK MANAGEMENT

Complaints filed against social workers fall into two categories: those that allege that social workers carried out their duties incorrectly or not in accordance with the proper ways set forth by the profession (acts of commission); and those that allege that social workers failed to act as per the standards of care of the profession (acts of omission).

In order to mitigate risk in these areas, social workers should have established policies and procedures that outline the steps that prudent professionals would follow in performing duties and making sound decisions. These policies include:

- *Consulting colleagues*—Social workers should seek advice from those with specialized expertise and knowledge and document the use of such consultation. Risk management committees should be used whenever available to assist in dealing with presenting issues and problems.

- *Obtaining supervision*—Social workers should use supervisors in their work settings to assist with complicated circumstances. When such supervision is not available on the job, social workers should seek outside supervision, adhering to ethical standards, state laws, and agency policies in regard to its provision.

- *Reviewing the* Code of Ethics—The *Code of Ethics (1999)* provides ethical principles which must be upheld at all times. Risk management strategies should follow all ethical mandates. These standards also provide guidance when social workers are uncertain about the course of action most appropriate to balance client risk with their duty to do no harm.

- *Reading regulations, laws, and policies*—There are many rules that govern professional practice. Social workers must be aware of licensing regulations; federal, state, and local laws; and agency/funder policies to ensure compliance. Breaching these tenets can have negative implications for both social workers and their clients.

- *Consulting relevant literature*—Understanding best practices and basing decisions on what has been done successfully by others in the past greatly minimizes the opportunity for adverse outcomes. Social workers should stay abreast of new developments in the fields and make decisions after consulting relevant resource documents.

- *Hiring legal representation when needed*—Preventing and/or managing risk sometimes requires social workers to seek the advice of attorneys. Lawyers can review agency policies and procedures to ensure that they are sound and do not violate clients' legal rights. Lawyers also can assist in understanding legal options in instances in which clients' rights have been infringed upon.

- *Documenting decision-making steps*—Central to the management of risk is good documentation. Policies and procedures aimed at reducing or mitigating risk should be available, clear, and culturally appropriate.

METHODS TO MANAGE CRITICAL INCIDENTS, INCLUDING DEBRIEFING FOR CLIENTS AND STAFF

Clients and staff involved with, or exposed to, critical incidents can experience a range of emotional responses. These responses can lead to trauma and negatively impact on well-being and productivity, causing methods to manage these incidents—with the goal of minimizing their effects—to emerge.

A critical incident is any event that may cause strong emotional reactions that could interfere with ability to function. Critical incident stress debriefing (CISD) is a strategy that immediately intervenes following a traumatic event to eliminate or at least reduce delayed stress reactions. Social workers who are trained in this intervention can work with clients and staff in either groups or individually to have them share their thoughts and feelings about the critical incident and help them in making sense of the trauma. In addition to providing reassurance and support, resources and information regarding practical coping skills should also be offered. Ideally, debriefing can be conducted on or near the site of the precipitating event.

Debriefing typically occurs one to three days following the traumatic event. Debriefing responses are often recommended as standard practice in many schools, workplaces, and other settings.

Values, Boundaries, and Ethics

25

THE EFFECTS OF DIFFERENCES IN VALUES INFLUENCED BY CULTURE, POLITICAL BELIEFS, RACE, ETHNICITY, GENDER, AGE, DISABILITY, SEXUAL ORIENTATION, GENDER IDENTITY, AND RELIGION/SPIRITUALITY

Values are linked to both behaviors and attitudes. For example, extrinsic values—such as wealth or preservation of public image—tend to influence our levels of personal well-being. In general, the esteem of others or pursuit of material goods seem to be the major drivers for the majority of people, even if more inherently rewarding motivations and self-direction values seem to provide more self-satisfaction.

It is common to see people segmented into distinct groups or dichotomies based upon their values.

People who hold strong traditional values are more likely to observe national holidays and customs. Stronger achievement values are associated with stress-related behaviors (such as taking on too many commitments).

However, values are not the sole determinant of behavior. In fact, actions can at times be fairly divergent from dominant values. For example, despite proenvironmental and prosocial values, people may not always protect either the environment or the interest of others.

Aspects of society may constrain people from expressing the intrinsic values they hold. Education, the media, and social pressures are likely to influence the kinds of values seen as relevant to particular situations.

Given the impact of values on actions, it is important for social workers to look at what influences values and how they develop and change over time.

INTRINSIC WORTH AND VALUE OF THE INDIVIDUAL

The social work profession is based on the belief that every person has dignity and worth. It is essential that social workers respect this value and treat everyone in a caring and respectful fashion. Social workers should also be mindful of individual differences and cultural and ethnic diversity.

Social workers should promote clients' right to self-determination and act as a resource to assist clients to address their own needs. Social workers have a dual responsibility to clients and to the broader society and must resolve any conflicts that arise due to this dual mandate in a socially responsible and ethical manner.

PROFESSIONAL BOUNDARY ISSUES

Many standards speak to the professional boundaries that social workers should maintain with clients. These include those related to sexual relationships, physical contact, and sexual harassment.

The standards that govern social work practice address the use of physical contact with clients. Setting clear, appropriate, and sensitive boundaries that govern physical contact is essential for professional practice (NASW Code of Ethics, 1999–1.10 Physical Contact). Social workers should not engage in physical contact with clients when there is a possibility of psychological harm to a client as a result of the contact (such as cradling or caressing clients).

Physical contact or other activities of a sexual nature with clients are clearly not allowed by social workers.

Social workers should under no circumstances engage in sexual activities or sexual contact with current clients, whether such contact is consensual or forced (NASW Code of Ethics, 1999–1.09 Sexual Relationships).

Social workers should not engage in sexual activities or sexual contact with clients' relatives or other individuals with whom clients maintain a close personal relationship when there is a risk of exploitation or potential harm to a client. Sexual activity or sexual contact with clients' relatives or other individuals with whom clients maintain a personal relationship has the potential to be harmful to a client and may make it difficult for a social worker and client to maintain appropriate professional boundaries. Social workers— not their clients, their clients' relatives, or other individuals with whom a client maintains a personal relationship—assume the full burden for setting clear, appropriate, and culturally sensitive boundaries (NASW Code of Ethics, 1999–1.09 Sexual Relationships).

Social workers should not engage in sexual activities or sexual contact with former clients because of the potential for harm to the former clients. If social workers engage in conduct contrary to this prohibition, or claim that an exception to this prohibition is warranted because of extraordinary circumstances, it is social workers—not their clients—who assume the full burden of demonstrating that the former client has not been exploited, coerced, or manipulated, intentionally or unintentionally *(NASW Code of Ethics, 1999–1.09 Sexual Relationships)*.

Social workers should not provide clinical services to individuals with whom they have had a prior sexual relationship. Providing clinical services to a former sexual partner has the potential to be harmful to the individual and is likely to make it difficult for a social worker and individual to maintain appropriate professional boundaries *(NASW Code of Ethics, 1999–1.09 Sexual Relationships)*.

In addition, social workers should not sexually harass clients, including sexual advances, sexual solicitation, requests for sexual favors, and other verbal or physical conduct of a sexual nature *(NASW Code of Ethics, 1999–1.11 Sexual Harassment)*.

DUAL RELATIONSHIPS

Social workers must ensure that they do not engage in dual or multiple relationships that may impact on the treatment of clients. The standards related to this area provide guidelines that can assist social workers if such relationships emerge *(NASW Code of Ethics, 1999—1.06 Conflicts of Interest)*.

Social workers should be alert to and avoid conflicts of interest that interfere with the exercise of professional discretion and impartial judgment. Social workers should inform clients when a real or potential conflict of interest arises and take reasonable steps to resolve the issue in a manner that makes clients' interests primary and protects clients' interests to the greatest extent possible. In some cases, protecting clients' interests may require termination of the professional relationship with proper referral of clients *(NASW Code of Ethics, 1999—1.06 Conflicts of Interest)*.

Social workers should not take unfair advantage of any professional relationship or exploit others to further their personal, religious, political, or business interests *(NASW Code of Ethics, 1999—1.06 Conflicts of Interest)*.

Social workers should not engage in dual or multiple relationships with clients or former clients in which there is a risk of exploitation or potential harm to a client. In instances when dual or multiple relationships are unavoidable, social workers should take steps to protect clients and are responsible for setting clear, appropriate, and culturally sensitive boundaries. Dual or multiple relationships occur when social workers relate to clients in more than one relationship, whether professional, social, or business. Dual or multiple relationships can occur simultaneously or consecutively *(NASW Code of Ethics, 1999—1.06 Conflicts of Interest)*.

[handwritten margin note: What is a dual relationship]

When social workers provide services to two or more people who have a relationship with each other (e.g., couples, family members), social workers should clarify with all parties which individuals will be considered clients and the nature of social workers' professional obligations to the various individuals who are receiving services. Social workers who anticipate a conflict of interest among the individuals receiving services or who anticipate having to perform in potentially conflicting roles (e.g., when a social worker is asked to testify in a child custody dispute or divorce proceedings involving clients) should clarify their role with the parties involved and take appropriate action to minimize any conflict of interest (*NASW Code of Ethics, 1999—1.06 Conflicts of Interest*).

In addition, social workers engaged in evaluation or research should be alert to and avoid conflicts of interest and dual relationships with participants, should inform participants when a real or potential conflict of interest arises, and should take steps to resolve the issue in a manner that makes participants' interests primary (*NASW Code of Ethics, 1999—5.02 Evaluation and Research*).

IDENTIFICATION AND RESOLUTION OF ETHICAL DILEMMAS

What is an ethical dilemma

An ethical dilemma is a predicament in which a social worker must decide between two viable solutions that seem to have similar ethical value. Sometimes two viable ethical solutions can conflict with each other. Social workers should be aware of any conflicts between personal and professional values and deal with them responsibly.

In instances where social workers' ethical obligations conflict with agency policies or relevant laws or regulations, they should make a responsible effort to resolve the conflict in a manner that is consistent with the values, principles, and standards expressed in the *Code of Ethics*.

In order to resolve this conflict, ethical problem-solving is needed.

Essential Steps in Ethical Problem Solving

1. Identify ethical standards, as defined by the professional *Code of Ethics*, that are being compromised (always go to the *Code of Ethics* first—do not rely on supervisor or coworkers)

2. Determine whether there is an ethical issue or dilemma

3. Weigh ethical issues in light of key social work values and principles as defined by the *Code of Ethics*

4. Suggest modifications in light of the prioritized ethical values and principles that are central to the dilemma

5. Implement modifications in light of prioritized ethical values and principles

6. Monitor for new ethical issues or dilemmas

ETHICAL AND LEGAL ISSUES

While there is an overlap in the ethical and legal requirements for social work practice, the two mandates are not the same and at times conflict with one another. For example, the law does not fully address all ethical issues that a social worker may face. For example, something might be legal but unethical or ethical but illegal.

Legal practices refer to processes and policies to abide by laws dictated by government, such as the protection of electronic health records. Ethical practices refer to behavioral guidelines that result from personal morals and values, as well as standards of conduct that are set by social work professionals for those who are practicing within the field. The relationship between ethical and legal issues can fall within four distinct quadrants—those behaviors that are (a) ethical and legal; (b) not ethical, but legal; (c) legal, but not ethical; and (d) not legal and not ethical.

Relationship Between Ethical and Legal Conduct Examples

Legal?	Ethical?	
	Yes	**No**
Yes	Treating a client with dignity and respect Reporting suspected child abuse	Having an intimate or sexual relationship with an adult client Borrowing money from a client
No	Engaging in civil disobedience to draw attention to social injustice Failing to submit court-ordered information to protect client safety	Releasing confidential client health care information Physically or sexually assaulting a client

MEDICAL ISSUES

Ethical concerns in health care are common. Nearly every medical issue has ethical implications—for clients, for health care and other service providers, and for social workers.

Some of the biggest health care challenges bring with them ethical dilemmas. For example, there is an overall challenge of, and tension between, balancing health care quality and safety with efficiency. There is an ongoing debate about whether limited resources should be used to provide the most efficient services, allowing a greater number of clients to be served, or the most effective services, allowing a smaller number of clients to have all of their needs met.

Providing access to basic medical care also remains a concern. Although the ability to receive basic care is seen as a hallmark of a civilized society, there are still questions about the implementation of current laws that still have many people unable to access health care.

A shortage of health care professionals can also be seen as a problem. As a larger percentage of society ages, we see an increasing shortage of those trained and able to provide services for this population. While many enter the "helping professions," there is a sustainability issue because they often leave their fields due to constant ethical conflicts and workplace demands that burn them out.

End-of-life issues also grow in importance as the population ages. The entire decision-making process, as well as the financing that pays for end-of-life care, will be the basis of further debates and discussions. As life expectancy increases, there is a dilemma emerging around the ability to keep up with the needs of the older population given the need to care for others. For example, shortages of critical medications and donor organs in the future may raise issues about how they are allocated.

ETHICAL ISSUES IN SUPERVISION AND MANAGEMENT

Social workers must follow all ethical standards when providing and receiving supervision, as well as engaging in management tasks. These include, but are not limited to, those regarding commitment to clients, self-determination, informed consent, competence, cultural competence and social diversity, conflicts of interest, privacy and confidentiality, access to records, sexual relationships, physical contact, sexual harassment, derogatory language, payments, clients who lack decision-making capacity, and interruption or termination of services.

Social workers who provide supervision should have the necessary knowledge and skill to supervise or consult appropriately, and they should do so only within their areas of competence. They should also evaluate supervisees' performance in a manner that is fair and respectful *(NASW Code of Ethics, 1999–3.01 Supervision and Consultation)*. Social workers who are in managerial roles should take reasonable steps to ensure that adequate agency resources are available to provide appropriate staff supervision *(NASW Code of Ethics, 1999–3.07 Administration)*.

Social workers who provide supervision are responsible for setting clear, appropriate, and culturally sensitive boundaries. They should not engage in any dual or multiple relationships with supervisees when there is a risk of exploitation of or potential harm to the supervisee *(NASW Code of Ethics, 1999–3.01 Supervision and Consultation)*.

Social workers in managerial roles should advocate within and outside their agencies for adequate resources to meet clients' needs and ensure resource allocation procedures are open, fair, and nondiscriminatory. Social work managers should ensure that working environments are consistent with the *NASW Code of Ethics* and eliminate conditions which are not *(NASW Code of Ethics, 1999–3.07 Administration)*.

Confidentiality

26

LEGAL AND ETHICAL ISSUES REGARDING CONFIDENTIALITY, INCLUDING ELECTRONIC INFORMATION

Social workers should respect clients' right to privacy. Social workers should not solicit private information from clients unless it is essential to providing services or conducting social work evaluation or research. Once private information is shared, standards of confidentiality apply (*NASW Code of Ethics, 1999–1.07 Privacy and Confidentiality*).

Social workers may disclose confidential information when appropriate with valid consent from a client or a person legally authorized to consent on behalf of a client (*NASW Code of Ethics, 1999–1.07 Privacy and Confidentiality*).

Social workers should protect the confidentiality of all information obtained in the course of professional service, except for compelling professional reasons. The general expectation that social workers will keep information confidential does not apply when disclosure is necessary to prevent serious, foreseeable, and imminent harm to a client or other identifiable person. In all instances, social workers should disclose the least amount of confidential information necessary to achieve the desired purpose; only information that is directly relevant to the purpose for which the disclosure is made should be revealed (*NASW Code of Ethics, 1999–1.07 Privacy and Confidentiality*).

Social workers should inform clients, to the extent possible, about the disclosure of confidential information and the potential consequences, when feasible, before the disclosure is made. This applies whether social workers disclose confidential information on the basis of a legal requirement or client consent (*NASW Code of Ethics, 1999–1.07 Privacy and Confidentiality*).

[handwritten note in margin: If you have to disclose make sure its least amount possible]

Social workers should discuss with clients and other interested parties the nature of confidentiality and limitations of clients' right to confidentiality. Social workers should review with clients' circumstances where confidential information may be requested and where disclosure of confidential information may be legally required. This discussion should occur as soon as possible in a social worker–client relationship and as needed throughout the course of the relationship (*NASW Code of Ethics, 1999–1.07 Privacy and Confidentiality*).

[margin note: discussion should happen ASAP]

When social workers provide counseling services to families, couples, or groups, social workers should seek agreement among the parties involved concerning each individual's right to confidentiality and obligation to preserve the confidentiality of information shared by others. Social workers should inform participants in family, couples, or group counseling that social workers cannot guarantee that all participants will honor such agreements (*NASW Code of Ethics, 1999–1.07 Privacy and Confidentiality*).

Social workers should inform clients involved in family, couples, marital, or group counseling of a social worker's, employer's, and agency's policy concerning a social worker's disclosure of confidential information among the parties involved in the counseling (*NASW Code of Ethics, 1999–1.07 Privacy and Confidentiality*).

[margin note: agency policy]

Social workers should not disclose confidential information to third-party payers unless clients have authorized such disclosure (*NASW Code of Ethics, 1999–1.07 Privacy and Confidentiality*).

Social workers should not discuss confidential information in any setting unless privacy can be ensured. Social workers should not discuss confidential information in public or semipublic areas such as hallways, waiting rooms, elevators, and restaurants (*NASW Code of Ethics, 1999–1.07 Privacy and Confidentiality*).

Social workers should protect the confidentiality of clients during legal proceedings to the extent permitted by law. When a court of law or other legally authorized body orders social workers to disclose confidential or privileged information without a client's consent and such disclosure could cause harm to a client, social workers should request that the court withdraw the order or limit the order as narrowly as possible or maintain the records under seal, unavailable for public inspection (*NASW Code of Ethics, 1999–1.07 Privacy and Confidentiality*).

A subpoena and court order are not the same. When receiving a subpoena, a social worker should respond and claim privilege, but not turn over records unless the court issues a subsequent order to do so. As stated, when a social worker gets a court order, he or she should try to limit its scope and/or ask that the records be sealed.

[margin note: respond w/out records]

Social workers should protect the confidentiality of clients when responding to requests from members of the media (*NASW Code of Ethics, 1999–1.07 Privacy and Confidentiality*).

Social workers should protect the confidentiality of clients' written and electronic records and other sensitive information. Social workers should take reasonable steps to ensure that clients' records are stored in a secure location and that clients' records are not available to others who are not authorized to have access *(NASW Code of Ethics, 1999–1.07 Privacy and Confidentiality).*

Social workers should take precautions to ensure and maintain the confidentiality of information transmitted to other parties through the use of computers, electronic mail, facsimile machines, telephones and telephone answering machines, and other electronic or computer technology. Disclosure of identifying information should be avoided whenever possible *(NASW Code of Ethics, 1999–1.07 Privacy and Confidentiality).*

Social workers should transfer or dispose of clients' records in a manner that protects clients' confidentiality and is consistent with state statutes governing records and social work licensure *(NASW Code of Ethics, 1999–1.07 Privacy and Confidentiality).*

Social workers should take reasonable precautions to protect client confidentiality in the event of a social worker's termination of practice, incapacitation, or death *(NASW Code of Ethics, 1999–1.07 Privacy and Confidentiality).*

Social workers should not disclose identifying information when discussing clients for teaching or training purposes unless a client has consented to disclosure of confidential information *(NASW Code of Ethics, 1999–1.07 Privacy and Confidentiality).*

Social workers should not disclose identifying information when discussing clients with consultants unless a client has consented to disclosure of confidential information or there is a compelling need for such disclosure *(NASW Code of Ethics, 1999–1.07 Privacy and Confidentiality).*

Social workers should protect the confidentiality of deceased clients consistent with the preceding standards *(NASW Code of Ethics, 1999–1.07 Privacy and Confidentiality).*

If a client sues a social worker, a social worker has the right to defend himself/herself and may need to release client information as part of this defense. A social worker should limit this disclosure only to information required for defense.

Confidentiality of a minors' records can be challenging, especially if a parent wants access to them and/or consents to their release. Social workers must be knowledgeable about ethical standards and laws that relate to the protection and release of minors' records. Parents may have access to these records depending upon the age of the minor and the type of treatment or setting. Social workers treating minors with parents who may have joint or limited custody must also be aware of the rights of all parties to access and/ or consent to their release.

THE USE OF CLIENT RECORDS

Social workers should provide clients with reasonable access to their records. Social workers who are concerned that clients' access to their records could cause serious misunderstanding or harm to a client should provide assistance in interpreting the records and consultation with a client regarding the records. Social workers should limit clients' access to their records, or portions of their records, **only in exceptional circumstances when there is compelling evidence that such access would cause serious harm to a client**. Both clients' requests and the rationale for withholding some or all of the record should be documented in clients' files (NASW Code of Ethics, 1999–1.08 Access to Records).

When providing clients with access to their records, social workers should take steps to protect the confidentiality of other individuals identified or discussed in such records.

ETHICAL AND LEGAL ISSUES REGARDING MANDATORY REPORTING OF ABUSE

Social workers are required to disclose confidential information, sometimes against a client's wishes, to comply with mandatory reporting laws. Laws not only require social workers to report suspected cases of abuse and neglect, but there can be varying levels of civil and criminal liability for failing to do so.

This mandate causes ethical issues for social workers who have a commitment to their clients' interests as well as a responsibility to the larger society.

The majority of all reports of abuse and/or neglect came from professionals, including medical personnel, law enforcement agents, educators, lawyers, and social workers.

THE PROCESS OF OBTAINING INFORMED CONSENT

In instances when clients are not literate or have difficulty understanding the primary language used in the practice setting, social workers should take steps to ensure clients' comprehension. This may include providing clients with a detailed verbal explanation or arranging for a qualified interpreter or translator whenever possible (NASW Code of Ethics, 1999–1.03 Informed Consent).

In instances when clients lack the capacity to provide informed consent, social workers should protect clients' interests by seeking permission from an appropriate third party, informing clients consistent with clients' level of understanding. In such instances, social workers should seek to ensure that the third party acts in a manner consistent with the clients' wishes and interests.

Social workers should take reasonable steps to enhance such clients' ability to give informed consent *(NASW Code of Ethics, 1999–1.03 Informed Consent)*.

Social workers who provide services via electronic media (such as computer, telephone, radio, and television) should inform recipients of the limitations and risks associated with such services *(NASW Code of Ethics, 1999–1.03 Informed Consent)*.

Social workers should obtain clients' informed consent before audiotaping or videotaping clients or permitting observation of services to clients by a third party *(NASW Code of Ethics, 1999–1.03 Informed Consent)*.

When social workers act on behalf of clients who lack the capacity to make informed decisions, social workers should take reasonable steps to safeguard the interests and rights of those clients *(NASW Code of Ethics, 1999–1.14 Clients Who Lack Decision-Making Capacity)*.

In order to obtain informed consent, social workers must use clear and understandable language related to service purpose, risks, limits due to third-party payers, time frame, and right of refusal or withdrawal. If the client lacks capacity or is a minor, informed **consent** must be obtained by a responsible third party and **assent** must be obtained from the client.

Mitchell

Self-Determination

27

THE CIRCUMSTANCES UNDER WHICH CLIENTS HAVE THE RIGHT TO REFUSE SERVICE

Social workers should provide services to clients only in the context of a professional relationship based, when appropriate, on valid informed consent. Social workers should use clear and understandable language to inform clients of the purpose of the services, risks related to the services, limits to services because of the requirements of a third-party payer, relevant costs, reasonable alternatives, clients' right to refuse or withdraw consent, and the time frame covered by the consent. Social workers should provide clients with an opportunity to ask questions (*NASW Code of Ethics, 1999–1.03 Informed Consent*).

In instances when clients are receiving services involuntarily, social workers should provide information about the nature and extent of services and about the extent of clients' right to refuse service (*NASW Code of Ethics, 1999–1.03 Informed Consent*).

INDIVIDUAL, GROUP, ORGANIZATION, AND COMMUNITY SELF-DETERMINATION

Self-determination is a professional ideology, an interrelated set of values and ideas related to freedom and autonomy. It refers to the belief that individuals, groups, organizations, and communities should be allowed to make choices freely. Central to self-determination is the process of gaining control over events, outcomes, and resources. Self-determination is linked with empowerment as the latter is a process of increasing personal, interpersonal, or political power so that individuals can take action to improve their lives.

Empowerment is necessary in order to give clients real (rather than perceived) influence over the quality of their lives and conditions that affect them.

If clients are allowed free, independent choice, they must recognize and discuss the power differential that exists between social workers and clients. Clients are subject to pressures and the social work relationship is often conceived within a structure of authority. Thus, the degree to which self-determination in its purest sense is possible is debatable. However, focusing on outcomes that clients value (whenever they do not compromise the rights of others) promotes self-determination.

THE LIMITATIONS OF SELF-DETERMINATION

Social workers respect and promote the right of clients to self-determination and assist clients in their efforts to identify and clarify their goals. Social workers may limit clients' right to self-determination when, in a social workers' professional judgment, clients' actions or potential actions pose a serious, foreseeable, and imminent risk to themselves or others (*NASW Code of Ethics, 1999–1.02 Self-Determination*).

CLIENTS' RIGHTS AND GRIEVANCE PROCEDURES

Social workers have always recognized that clients have rights with regard to the provision of services. Throughout the profession's history, social workers have especially understood the fundamental importance of clients' rights. These rights form the basis of the *Code of Ethics* and include those related to confidentiality, self-determination, informed consent, nondiscriminatory practices, and so on. Deceased clients also have rights, such as those to confidentiality. In addition, when social workers act on behalf of clients who lack the capacity to make informed decisions, social workers are charged with taking reasonable steps to safeguard the interests and rights of those clients.

Social workers should be clear about clients' rights and provide clients with clear information about them. Informing clients about their rights is important ethically and can also help prevent ethical complaints and lawsuits filed by clients who allege that social workers violated their rights. Ideally, social workers and their agencies should develop clear, understandable summaries of client rights.

Clients have the right to challenge or appeal decisions and actions with which they disagree, including those which they feel violate their rights. Social workers should inform clients about their right to file grievances and about relevant procedures to do so.

Professional Responsibilities for Ethical Practice

28

THE SOCIAL WORKER'S ETHICAL RESPONSIBILITY AS A PROFESSIONAL

As professionals, social workers have duties that relate to ensuring competence and not condoning discrimination. They also have to ensure that their private activities do not interfere with their professional practice. Social workers should never engage in fraud or deception and must monitor their well-being for potential impairment. Lastly, social workers should never take credit for the work of others or misrepresent their credentials.

- **Competence**—Social workers should only accept responsibility or employment if competent or with the intention to acquire the necessary competence. They should keep abreast of current knowledge and use it in practice (*NASW Code of Ethics, 1999—4.01 Competence*).

- **Discrimination**—Social workers should not practice, condone, facilitate, or collaborate with any form of discrimination on the basis of race, ethnicity, national origin, color, sex, sexual orientation, gender identity or expression, age, marital status, political belief, religion, immigration status, or mental or physical disability (*NASW Code of Ethics, 1999—4.02 Discrimination*).

- **Private Conduct**—Social workers should not permit their private conduct to interfere with their ability to fulfill their professional responsibilities (*NASW Code of Ethics, 1999—4.03 Private Conduct*).

- **Dishonesty, Fraud, and Deception**—Social workers should not participate in, condone, or be associated with dishonesty, fraud, or deception (*NASW Code of Ethics, 1999—4.04 Dishonesty, Fraud and Deception*).

- **Impairment**—Social workers should not allow their own problems to interfere with their professional judgment and performance and should take immediate remedial action if they do in order to protect clients (*NASW Code of Ethics, 1999—4.05 Impairment*).

- **Misrepresentation**—Social workers should distinguish personal from professional actions and represent the official position of an organization when speaking on behalf of it. Social workers' professional qualifications should be accurately represented and social workers should correct any errors of their credentials by others (*NASW Code of Ethics, 1999—4.06 Misrepresentation*).

- **Solicitations**—Social workers should not solicit potential clients who, because of their circumstances, are vulnerable to undue influence, manipulation, or coercion. Social workers should not solicit clients' testimonial endorsements (*NASW Code of Ethics, 1999—4.07 Solicitations*).

- **Acknowledging Credit**—Social workers should only take credit for work they have actually performed and to which they have contributed. Social workers should honestly acknowledge the work of and the contributions made by others (*NASW Code of Ethics, 1999—4.08 Acknowledging Credit*).

THE SOCIAL WORKER'S ETHICAL RESPONSIBILITY TO BROADER SOCIETY

The mission of social work is to enhance human well-being and help meet basic human needs. Social work focuses on individual well-being in a social context, attending to the environmental forces that create and contribute to problems. Social workers have several ethical mandates to the broader society, including promoting social justice and social change.

- **Social Welfare**—Social workers should promote the general welfare of society and advocate for living conditions conducive to meeting basic human needs (*NASW Code of Ethics, 1999—6.01 Social Welfare*).

- **Public Participation and Emergencies**—Social workers should facilitate informed participation by the public in shaping social policies and institutions, as well as provide appropriate professional services in public emergencies to the greatest extent possible (*NASW Code of Ethics, 1999—6.02 Public Participation and 6.03—Public Emergencies*).

  Provide assistance in emergency situations

- **Social and Political Action**—Social workers should engage in social and political action that seeks to ensure that people have equal access to and expanded choice for needed resources. Social workers should promote conditions that encourage respect for cultural and social diversity *(NASW Code of Ethics, 1999—6.04 Social and Political Action).*

THE SOCIAL WORKER'S ETHICAL RESPONSIBILITIES TO THE SOCIAL WORK PROFESSION

Maintaining the integrity of the social work profession is paramount. Clients come to social workers with trust that they will act in clients' best interests. Social workers must uphold the ethical standards of the profession and advance its values and mission. Lastly, social workers must continue to contribute to the social work knowledge base so that service provision can meet the highest standards of practice.

- **Integrity of the Profession**—Social workers should protect, enhance, and improve the integrity of the profession through appropriate study and research, active discussion, and responsible criticism of the profession. Social workers should engage in teaching, research, consultation, service, legislative testimony, presentations in the community, and participation in their professional organizations. Social workers should seek to contribute to the profession's literature and to share their knowledge at professional meetings and conferences *(NASW Code of Ethics, 1999—5.01 Integrity of the Profession).*

- **Evaluation and Research**—Social workers should monitor and evaluate policies, program implementation, and practice interventions. Social workers should promote and facilitate evaluation and research—according to ethical standards—to contribute to the development of knowledge *(NASW Code of Ethics, 1999—5.02 Evaluation and Research).*

THE SOCIAL WORKER'S ETHICAL RESPONSIBILITIES IN PRACTICE SETTINGS

Social workers have ethical responsibilities within the settings in which they work. These obligations relate to their duties as supervisors, administrators, and/or employees. Some of these standards relate to interactions with coworkers and others address client communications.

- **Supervision and Consultation**—Social workers providing supervision or consultation should have necessary knowledge and skills, operate within areas of competence, set clear appropriate and culturally-sensitive boundaries, not engage in dual or multiple relationships, and evaluate performance fairly and respectfully (*NASW Code of Ethics, 1999—3.01 Supervision and Consultation*).

- **Education and Training**—Social workers serving as educators, field instructors or trainers should have necessary knowledge and skills, set clear appropriate and culturally-sensitive boundaries, not engage in dual or multiple relationships, and evaluate performance fairly and respectfully. Clients should be informed when services are provided by students (*NASW Code of Ethics, 1999—3.02 Education and Training*).

[handwritten margin note: Clients to be informed when working w/ students]

- **Performance Evaluation**—Social workers should be fair and considerate when evaluating the performance of others (*NASW Code of Ethics, 1999—3.03 Performance Evaluation*).

- **Client Records**—Social workers should make sure that records are accurate and reflect provided services, as well as provide sufficient and timely documentation when providing services. *Only information relevant to services should be included* in records and privacy should be protected. Storage after termination should allow for access (*NASW Code of Ethics, 1999—3.04 Client Records*).

- **Billing**—Social workers should establish and maintain billing practices that are accurate and reflect services provided (*NASW Code of Ethics, 1999—3.05 Billing*).

- **Client Transfer**—Social workers should carefully decide before agreeing to provide services to new clients, as well as discuss with them the benefits and risks of receiving services from new service providers. Social workers should discuss with clients whether consultation with previous service providers is in their best interest (*NASW Code of Ethics, 1999—3.06 Client Transfer*).

- **Administration**—Social work administrators should advocate for adequate resources, with fair allocation procedures, to meet client needs. Adequate organizational resources should also be available to provide appropriate staff supervision. Working conditions should be consistent with the *Code of Ethics* and social work administrators should eliminate those which are not (*NASW Code of Ethics, 1999—3.07 Administration*).

- **Continuing Education and Staff Development**—Social work administrators and supervisors should arrange for staff to have continuing education and staff development (*NASW Code of Ethics, 1999—3.08 Continuing Education and Staff Development*).

- **Commitments to Employers**—Social workers should honor commitments made to employers and improve employment policies to ensure that they are consistent with the *Code of Ethics*. Preventing and eliminating discrimination is essential. Social workers should be good stewards of agency resources and not have student interns in settings with unfair personnel practices (*NASW Code of Ethics, 1999—3.09 Commitments to Employers*).

■ **Labor-Management Disputes**—Social workers may engage in organized action, including the formation of and participation in labor unions, to improve services to clients and working conditions. Labor disputes should be guided by professional values, ethical principles, and ethical standards (*NASW Code of Ethics, 1999—3.10 Labor-Management Disputes*).

THE SOCIAL WORKER'S ETHICAL RESPONSIBILITIES TO COLLEAGUES

Social workers have ethical mandates with regard to the treatment of colleagues. These standards include those related to interactions (respect, confidentiality, collaboration, disputes), collaborations and referrals, sexual relationships and harassment, and impairment and incompetence, as well as how to address unethical conduct of colleagues if detected.

■ **Respect**—Social workers should treat colleagues with respect and avoid unwarranted criticism of them when communicating with others. Cooperation with colleagues must occur to serve the well-being of clients (*NASW Code of Ethics, 1999—2.01 Respect*).

■ **Confidentiality**—Social workers should protect confidential information shared by colleagues unless mandated to report the information (*NASW Code of Ethics, 1999—2.02 Confidentiality*).

■ **Interdisciplinary Collaboration**—Social workers who are members of interdisciplinary teams should participate in and contribute to decisions to ensure they positively impact the well-being of clients. If ethical conflicts arise, attempts should be to resolve them to promote client well-being (*NASW Code of Ethics, 1999—2.03 Interdisciplinary Collaboration*).

■ **Disputes**—Social workers should not advance their own interests when disputes between colleagues and employers occur. Clients should not be engaged in or exploited disputes between social workers and their colleagues (*NASW Code of Ethics, 1999—2.04 Disputes Involving Colleagues*).

■ **Consultation**—Social workers should use consultation from those with demonstrated knowledge, expertise, and competence when it is in clients' best interest. Client information disclosed should be the least amount needed to achieve the purpose of the consultation (*NASW Code of Ethics, 1999—2.05 Consultation*).

■ **Referrals**—Social workers should make referrals, which are orderly, to other professionals when specialized knowledge is needed to serve clients, additional service is required, or progress is not being made. All pertinent information should be disclosed to these professionals with clients' consent. *Fee splitting (giving or receiving payment for referrals) is prohibited (NASW Code of Ethics, 1999—2.06 Referral for Services).*

- **Sexual Relationships**—Social workers should not engage in sexual activities with supervisees, students, trainees, or colleagues who are under their professional oversight or other colleagues where there is a potential for a conflict of interest *(NASW Code of Ethics, 1999—2.07 Sexual Relationships).*

- **Sexual Harassment**—Social workers should not sexually harass supervisees, students, trainees, or colleagues *(NASW Code of Ethics, 1999—2.08 Sexual Harassment).*

- **Professional Impairment and Incompetence**—Social workers aware of impairment or incompetence of a colleague that interferes with practice effectiveness should *consult with the colleague first to assist him or her in taking remedial actions* and then go through other appropriate channels if adequate steps are not taken by the colleague *(NASW Code of Ethics, 1999—2.09 Impairment of Colleagues and 2.10 Incompetence of Colleagues).*

- **Unethical Conduct**—Social workers should take adequate measures to discourage, prevent, expose, and correct unethical conduct of colleagues. Social workers should be knowledgeable about policies and procedures to address such conduct. Social workers should try to resolve issues with the colleague first when feasible and likely to be productive. Social workers should defend and assist colleagues unjustly charged with unethical conduct *(NASW Code of Ethics, 1999—2.11 Unethical Conduct of Colleagues).*

Practice Test

170 Question Practice Test

This practice test contains 170 questions; however, remember that your score on the actual examination will be based on 150 questions because 20 items are being piloted. As you won't know which items will be scored and determine whether or not you pass, you will need to complete all 170 questions. Thus, this practice test has 170 questions so that you can see the length of time that it takes you to complete an equivalent number of questions. Although the questions in each domain or area are in random order on this practice test, as they are on the actual examination, there is a similar distribution of questions from each section as will appear on your actual examination.

Human Development, Diversity, and Behavior in the Environment

31 Questions

Micro Assessment and Planning

37 Questions

Micro Practice and Social Work Relationships

31 Questions

Macro Practice

31 Questions

Professional Values and Ethics

40 Questions

The best way to use this practice test is as a mock examination, which means:

a. Take it AFTER you have completed your studying—do not memorize answers to these questions;

b. Do not apply the answers to these questions to the actual examination because you may miss subtle differences that are present in each question that can determine the correct from the incorrect answer;

c. Take it in its entirety during a 4-hour block of time to show yourself that you can finish in the allotted time period for the examination;

d. Do not look up the answers until you are completely finished with the entire practice test; and

e. Do not worry if you get incorrect answers. Remember, this examination is not one in which you are going to get them all correct. **The number of questions that you have to get correct generally varies from 93 to 106 of the 150 scored items.**

1. Which of the following is NOT a secondary prevention strategy?

   A. Regular screenings of those with risk factors for an illness or disease
   B. Regular exercise and good nutrition
   C. Modification of work assignments for those who are injured
   D. Taking low doses of aspirin for those with heart conditions

2. All of the following may be viewed as indicators of resistance EXCEPT:

   A. A client engaging in small talk about irrelevant topics during a session
   B. A client who limits the amount of information communicated to a social worker during treatment
   C. A client who is silent during appointments
   D. A client who was originally referred by another person

3. A client abruptly stopped coming to sessions after 6 weeks. He calls the social worker and asks for a copy of his record about a month later. There is nothing in the record that is harmful to the client, but the social worker refuses to give it to him. In this situation, the social worker's actions are:

   A. Ethical because the client did not terminate with the social worker prior to not coming anymore
   B. Ethical because the request must come in writing and include the reason that a copy of the record is needed
   C. Unethical because the social worker has a duty to give the client a copy of his record in this situation
   D. Unethical because the social worker has a duty to give the client a copy of his or her record under all circumstances

4. When a social worker has direct knowledge of a social work colleague's impairment that interferes with effective practice, the social worker should FIRST:

   A. Design a short-term intervention to stabilize the situation
   B. Notify the agency director so that employee assistance services can be accessed
   C. Report the situation to the social work licensing board
   D. Consult with that colleague when feasible and assist the colleague in taking remedial action

5. A client is extremely upset because her 14-year-old son is not helping around the house, independently doing his homework, or arriving to school on time. The son states that his mother watches over him too closely and does not give him needed privacy. This problem is best understood as:

   A. A communication problem
   B. Role discomplementarity

    C. Progressive discipline

    D. Developmental processes

6. Which of the following is NOT true about conflict theory?

    A. Constant competition between groups forms the basis for the ever-changing nature of society

    B. Society is fragmented into groups that compete for social and economic resources

    C. Social order is maintained by those with the greatest political, economic, and social resources

    D. There is a strong emphasis on consensus and conformity

7. A client has just been fired from his job and is focusing solely on the stress associated with the financial challenges that he is facing. Using a systems approach, the social worker can expect the client's unemployment to:

    A. Result in a negative impact on the client's financial well-being

    B. Affect other areas of the client's life, such as her physical and mental health

    C. Cause him the client to be worried about finding another job

    D. Build resiliency that can be used to deal with other life crises

8. Which of the following medications is NOT typically prescribed for the treatment of Attention-Deficit/Hyperactivity Disorder?

    A. Adderall

    B. Ritalin

    C. Dexedrine

    D. Tofranil

9. A client has dilated pupils, appears jittery, and complains that he "just needs to get some sleep." The client is MOST likely using which of the following substances?

    A. Cocaine

    B. Heroin

    C. Marijuana

    D. Painkillers

10. According to the Tarasoff decision, social workers must:

    A. Notify both the authorities and intended victims of imminent danger

    B. Seek inpatient hospitalization if dangerousness exists

    C. Notify only the intended victims of imminent danger

    D. Identify the risk factors that are linked to dangerousness to others

11. Which of the following is NOT associated with low-ego strength?

    A. Viewing challenges as something to avoid
    B. Feeling overwhelmed by reality
    C. Finding new ways to deal with struggles
    D. Using wishful thinking or fantasies

12. In couples development, which of the following stages describes when partners try to please each other; place few demands on one another; and begin initially bonding on cognitive, emotional, physical, and behavioral levels?

    A. Practicing
    B. Rapprochement
    C. Mutual interdependence
    D. Symbiosis

13. Which of the following is NOT one of the therapeutic advantages of injectable antipsychotic medications?

    A. They reduce medication noncompliance because they are needed less frequently than oral medications
    B. They are less likely to be used for suicide or result in overdose because the dosing is controlled
    C. They are associated with decreased hospitalizations due to symptom relapses
    D. They are less expensive than oral medications

14. When making level of care determinations, which criterion is primarily used in behavioral health settings?

    A. Capitation
    B. Medical necessity
    C. Managed risk
    D. Diagnostic groupings

15. A client has made substantial progress in treatment and has achieved all established goals. When the social worker speaks to the client about discharge, the client states that he does not want to stop seeing the social worker because he is worried about her future needs. As there are no additional treatment goals, the social worker agrees to see the client pro bono for the next 6 months or until the client feels comfortable. The social worker's actions are:

    A. Ethical since there is no fee for the sessions
    B. Not ethical since there are no new treatment goals
    C. Ethical since the client does not feel ready to end treatment
    D. Not ethical because termination decisions are the responsibility of the social worker

16. Which of the following is an objective outcome that might be associated with a foster care program?

   A. Proportion of children served who are reunified with their biological families
   B. Satisfaction of foster parents with the program
   C. Perceived safety of children
   D. Number of children served in the program

17. All of the following are associated with Borderline Personality Disorder EXCEPT:

   A. Poor impulse control
   B. Control of aggressive drives
   C. Dichotomous thinking
   D. Emotional dysregulation

18. Which of the following is the FIRST goal of assisting clients who have suffered a life crisis?

   A. Helping them to develop coping skills to deal with similar crises in the future
   B. Identifying the cause of the crisis in order to prevent it from reoccurring in the future
   C. Assisting them to establish a sense of equilibrium and return to prior levels of functioning
   D. Linking them with others who have experienced a similar crisis to and can provide a network of support

19. A social worker suspects that a child receiving services from her agency is being psychologically abused and neglected. She discusses the reasons for her belief and her serious concerns about the child's home environment with her social work supervisor. After a lengthy conversation, the social work supervisor does not agree with the social worker and tells the social worker to monitor the situation for a while before deciding whether to make a report to the child protection agency. The social worker should:

   A. Make an anonymous report to the child protection agency
   B. Contact the child protection agency immediately while informing the supervisor of the need to do so
   C. Make another appointment to speak to the supervisor and try to collect additional information that supports the social worker's concerns
   D. Continue to collect information and follow-up regularly with the supervisor to seek direction

20. A social worker is seeing a family for therapy. During a session, the 17-year-old daughter states that her father molested her when she was

6 years old. She says that it happened twice and has not occurred since that time. The father confirms the daughter's account and says that he is remorseful about his actions. He assures the social worker and his family that it will never happen again. In this situation, the social worker should:

A. Not contact the child protection agency given the length of time that has occurred since the incidents

B. Not contact the child protection agency because these were isolated incidents and the father realizes the inappropriateness of his actions

C. Contact the child protection agency after telling the family of the need to do so because the social worker is a mandated reporter

D. Contact the child protection agency, but do not tell the family in order to preserve the therapeutic relationship

21. A client recently started a new job and reports fighting with his boss. The boss tells the client repeatedly that he is not "doing what he is supposed to," but the client claims that he does everything that the boss asks. In order to BEST understand the situation, the social worker should:

A. Recommend that the client speak to the boss's supervisor to request assistance with mediating the situation

B. Ask the client to explain his work responsibilities as they relate to the official job description and his boss's feedback

C. Explore with the client his underlying feelings about being criticized by his boss and its impact on his job performance

D. Assess why the client initially accepted this position and his willingness to complete the required tasks

22. Which of the following contains thoughts, feelings, desires, and memories of which a client has no awareness, even though they influence his or her daily life?

A. Preconscious
B. Conscious
C. Superego
D. Unconscious

23. A client whose husband is very controlling has used newly learned assertiveness skills in the home. She reports that her husband is reacting by placing more restrictions on her actions. Which of the following is the BEST explanation for the husband's actions?

A. The husband's behavior is caused by a suprasystem
B. The husband is trying to reject homeostasis
C. The husband's behavior is attributable to negative entropy
D. The husband is trying to maintain homeostasis

24. After an assessment is completed, what follows according to the problem-solving process?

   A. Intervention
   B. Evaluation
   C. Planning
   D. Engagement

25. A client shows a social worker a large tattoo on his arm dedicated to his mother who recently died. He begins to cry and states that it always makes him very emotional when he sees it because it reminds him of her bravery in fighting her illness. The tattoo is a form of:

   A. Symbolization
   B. Substitution
   C. Sublimation
   D. Splitting

26. Which of the following is NOT true about the relationship between research and policy in social work practice?

   A. There must be a reciprocal relationship between research and policy with each informing the other
   B. Policymakers need to receive full research articles and reports so that they can make informed decisions
   C. Policy decisions must be based on research findings to ensure that scarce resources are efficiently allocated
   D. Policymakers and researchers often have different professional backgrounds, causing communication challenges

27. A social worker who is a director of a residential substance abuse facility sees a former client who left the program about 5 years ago at a community event. The former client tells the social worker that he has always been attracted to her and would like to go on a date with her now that he has left the program and is no longer in need of services. The social worker, who also has romantic feelings toward the client, should:

   A. Accept his invitation—it is ethical based on the length of time that he has been out of services
   B. Accept his invitation as the professional code of ethics does not address relationships with former clients
   C. Decline his invitation as it is unethical to date him until more time passes following his leaving the program
   D. Decline his invitation—it is unethical to date him at all given these circumstances

28. Which of the following BEST describes the benefit of peer supervision in social work practice?

    A. It is less expensive than individual supervision
    B. It can occur as needed, anytime and anywhere
    C. It is a reciprocal learning relationship aimed at skill acquisition
    D. It does not require "experts" in the field

29. Which of the following is NOT a "Deficiency Need" according to Maslow?

    A. Self-actualization
    B. Safety
    C. Esteem
    D. Physiological

30. Which of the following is the MOST important factor in choosing an appropriate intervention or treatment strategy?

    A. It is currently being used by a social worker to assist clients with similar problems
    B. It results from the biopsychosocial–spiritual–cultural assessment of a client
    C. It is approved as medically necessary by third-party payers
    D. It is not constrained by agency practices and/or time limits for treatment

31. A social worker is asked to determine the need for a new parenting support group within his agency. In order to determine how many people might be interested, the social worker looks at existing case files to identify the number of clients with children who cite childrearing difficulties on their intake applications. What is the PRIMARY concern of using this data collection method to determine need?

    A. Clients who could benefit from this group may not be identified
    B. Informed consent procedures are not being used to select service recipients
    C. Clients outside of the agency should have been surveyed
    D. The need for a service should be based on subjective assessments, not empirical data

32. Which of the following is NOT true about data analysis in social work practice?

    A. It is a sequential process which begins with cleaning the data and checking it for accuracy
    B. It involves using either descriptive or inferential statistics

    C. It involves a balance between generating too little and too much information

    D. It is usually performed electronically by a computer once the data is coded and entered

33. According to the family life cycle, which of the following is NOT generally a task in families with young children?

    A. Adjusting to children taking a more central role in family maintenance

    B. Adopting and developing parenting roles

    C. Assisting children to develop peer relationships

    D. Realigning relationships with families of origin to include parenting and grandparenting roles

34. Which of the following is TRUE about risk factors for violence?

    A. They are present only at the individual level

    B. They predict with certainty who will engage in aggressive acts

    C. They are positively associated with protective factors to predict violence

    D. They increase the likelihood that a community will be affected by, or a client will be a perpetrator of, violence

35. A social worker is reviewing intake paperwork received for a new 65-year-old client. It states that she is currently taking Paxil after being switched from Zoloft. The client is MOST likely diagnosed with which of the following?

    A. Insomnia Disorder

    B. Schizoaffective Disorder

    C. Major Depressive Disorder

    D. Antisocial Personality Disorder

36. A social worker receives a call from a former girlfriend who is now married and is having trouble dealing with the recent death of her mother. The former girlfriend would like to see the social worker for counseling. The social worker has not seen the former girlfriend in more than 10 years. The social worker should:

    A. Begin treatment immediately because more than a decade has passed since the presence of an intimate relationship

    B. Gather more information about why the former girlfriend wants the social worker to provide therapy

    C. Contact the social work licensing board to determine if regulation prohibits this treatment

    D. Inform the former girlfriend that the social worker cannot treat her

37. Which of the following is the MOST important function of service networks?

    A. Service networks share resources that strengthen their member agencies
    B. Service networks increase ease of service billing because payments are managed centrally
    C. Service networks reduce duplication and increase integration of client services
    D. Service networks increase agency referrals because they have a single point of entry

38. When clients sue social workers for malpractice, social workers fulfill their ethical obligations by:

    A. Not releasing any information about treatment, including whether clients were even served
    B. Providing all information obtained during treatment so the court can get a complete picture of clients' concerns, issues, and problems
    C. Not responding to the courts because the information is privileged
    D. Releasing only information related to the nature of the lawsuit

39. Social workers are allowed to terminate services when:

    A. They wish to pursue social relationships with clients
    B. They are leaving employment settings to pursue other opportunities
    C. They believe that clients are making poor choices that negatively affect their well-being
    D. They are owed money for services even if the consequences for nonpayment have not been discussed

40. In the *DSM-5*, the global functioning of a client should be determined using the:

    A. Global Assessment of Functioning Scale (GAF)
    B. World Health Organization Disability Assessment Schedule (WHODAS)
    C. Myers–Briggs Type Indicator
    D. Thematic Apperception Test

41. Which of the following is NOT a diagnostic criterion in the *DSM-5* for Gambling Disorder?

    A. Lying to conceal gambling
    B. Loss of relationship, job, or opportunity due to gambling
    C. Legal problems associated with gambling
    D. Preoccupation with gambling

42. Which of the following diagnoses is MOST likely to be given as the result of mental status examinations?

    A. Delirium
    B. Schizophrenia
    C. Oppositional Defiant Disorder
    D. Avoidant Personality Disorder

43. A social worker is worried that he does not have all the necessary information to make a practice decision, so he uses multiple sources to collect data. This approach is known as:

    A. Cooptation
    B. Triangulation
    C. Social exchange
    D. Twinning

44. A social worker is asked to do a case presentation for her supervisor. She presents basic demographic information, client and family history, and the presenting problem. The supervisor would consider this presentation to be:

    A. Satisfactory because it contains all information needed to develop a treatment plan
    B. Satisfactory because it should only include objective data
    C. Unsatisfactory because it does not contain the social worker's impressions and treatment recommendations
    D. Unsatisfactory because it should only include information on the client and not the client's family

45. A social worker employed in a hospital is using a SOAP documentation format. Which of the following is NOT usually included in this record?

    A. A plan of care
    B. Insurance coverage limits
    C. Assessment of the client's current needs
    D. Subjective reports of client well-being

46. Which BEST describes the role of a social worker when engaged in crisis intervention?

    A. Short-term support focused on restoring clients' psychological capacities
    B. Long-term support to ensure clients will be able to address all aspects of trauma
    C. Passively involved through acting as a resource for any concerns or problems
    D. Highly involved and focused on meeting the clients' basic needs

47. A social worker is a facilitator of a group for clients diagnosed as having anorexia nervosa. Over several weeks, clients talk about their diverse backgrounds, including their varied early childhood experiences. The social worker comments that this disorder is caused by many different factors. The concept mentioned by the social worker is:

    A. Homeostasis
    B. Equifinality
    C. Subsystems
    D. Diagnostic-related groups

48. An elderly client has been diagnosed with a terminal illness and wants to make sure that his financial affairs are in order. He would like to divide his assets equally among his children upon his death. The client is worried that choosing one of his children to serve as executor of his estate will be a burden. The social worker volunteers to take on this role as long there is no financial compensation. The social worker is acting:

    A. Ethically as there is no financial remuneration for this responsibility
    B. Unethically since it was the social worker who suggested assuming this role and not at the client's initial request
    C. Unethically as it represents a dual relationship between the client and the social worker
    D. Ethically as it helps the client has self-determination about how his assets will be divided after his death

49. A social worker is seeing a 69-year-old client who is a former cigarette smoker and has chronic obstructive pulmonary disease (COPD), which makes it hard to breathe. She takes several medications, including one to regulate her blood pressure. Her primary prevention needs include:

    A. Participation in a support group for others with COPD
    B. Monitoring her blood pressure to modify her medications as needed
    C. Reducing strenuous activity that causes heavy breathing
    D. Receiving an annual influenza immunization

50. Which is the MOST important reason that self-monitoring is used as a social work technique?

    A. Clients are the most reliable sources of information
    B. It is an effective and efficient data collection method, saving time and money
    C. It allows clients to better understand the causes and frequency of the problem behaviors
    D. It is based on the principles of self-determination

51. A social worker receives a referral to provide case management to a family who just came to the United States from another country and

needs to be linked to services to meet their basic needs. The 13-year-old daughter in the family speaks English in addition to her native language, which is exclusively spoken by the parents. The social worker, who only understands and speaks English, accepts the referral. This action is:

A. Ethical because the daughter will be available to translate for the parents
B. Unethical because the social worker has not determined if the daughter is willing to translate
C. Ethical because the services are time-limited and nonclinical in nature
D. Unethical because the social worker cannot speak to or understand all family members

52. A recognition that all people who could benefit from assistance do not seek help implies that using which type of need is NOT adequate justification for program development?

A. Relative
B. Perceived
C. Expressed
D. Absolute

53. Tardive dyskinesia is a side effect of taking antipsychotic medications that affects which of the following?

A. Nervous system
B. Circulatory system
C. Respiratory system
D. Muscular system

54. A social worker in an agency setting who determines that an ethical dilemma exists should select an appropriate course of action based on:

A. Past practices
B. Agency policies and procedures
C. Funding requirements
D. Social work values and principles

55. A client reports to a social worker that he is having problems with his wife because he feels that she does not care about him. The social worker discovers that this belief stems from her perceived distraction when the husband is talking. The social worker challenges this thought and helps him replace it with an alternative one that she "does care, but just has a lot of other demands for her attention." The approach used by the social worker is:

A. Operant conditioning
B. Cognitive behavioral therapy

    C. Classical conditioning

    D. Ego psychology

56. A man is seeing a social worker because he is struggling to "find himself" since his children became adults and left the family home. He feels that his job has become mundane and he is feeling "bored with life." This client is MOST likely in which stage of psychosocial development?

    A. Generativity versus stagnation

    B. Industry versus inferiority

    C. Initiative versus guilt

    D. Intimacy versus isolation

57. A social worker observes that a client is having trouble communicating with her husband, so she often confides in her sister-in-law about her fears and concerns, hoping that the sister-in-law will be able to assist. The sister-in-law finds that she is increasingly "in the middle" of the problems that exist between her brother and his wife. This situation is known as:

    A. Joining

    B. Differentiation

    C. Familial regression

    D. Triangulation

58. A married couple comes in to see a social worker because they are having problems in their relationship. They report feeling disconnected and having little intimacy. The husband admits that his drinking recently caused him to be fired from his job and he is currently unemployed. The wife reports that she is fearful of her husband because he often is loud when he drinks and spends a lot of time out of the house. They have not had sex for several months and are behind in their mortgage payments. The FIRST issue that the social worker should help the couple address is:

    A. The couple's lack of emotional intimacy

    B. The wife's absence from the home

    C. The husband's alcohol use

    D. The couple's financial problems

59. Which of the following is NOT true about normal and abnormal client behavior?

    A. There are many influences on client behavior including individual, interpersonal, institutional, and community factors

    B. Client behavior should not be viewed through an ecological perspective

C. There are many theoretical perspectives which help explain client behavior

D. Client behavior can be explained using social constructivism

60. A hospital social worker is charged with completing a biopsychosocial–spiritual–cultural assessment on a client upon admission. In the biological section of the assessment, the social worker lists the client's current medications, weight, height, blood pressure, and subjective assessment of well-being. The social worker then moves on to the psychological section of the assessment. When the social worker's supervisor looks at the biological section, it will be viewed as:

A. Complete because it gives critical information about the client's current physical well-being

B. Accurate and useful in understanding the current functioning of the client

C. Incorrect because it should contain only objective data and not subjective information

D. Incomplete because it does not contain the client's current medical problems and history, including developmental milestones

61. A social worker, who has been court-ordered to release information about a client, feels strongly that providing this information will place the client and the client's family in grave danger. The social worker refuses to comply with the court order. In this situation, the actions by the social worker are:

A. Illegal and unethical

B. Legal, but unethical

C. Illegal, but ethical

D. Legal and ethical

62. When engaging in structural family therapy, social workers may use which of the following techniques to understand and diagnose structures that maintain families' dysfunctional interactions?

A. Collateral information

B. Journaling

C. Enactments

D. Confrontation

63. When working with an involuntary client, which of the following actions is likely to be MOST effective during engagement?

A. Reviewing the court order so the client understands why services are mandated

B. Discussing mandates of confidentiality as per the *Code of Ethics*

C. Explaining the professional standards to be upheld by the social worker

D. Listening to the client to understand his or her feelings and current situation

64. A social worker is seeing a client in private practice. The client has not paid the social worker for many weeks, accumulating a substantial balance, despite receiving and acknowledging the social worker's payment policy. The social worker has told the client repeatedly that he will be terminated if he does not pay his bill and decides to do so at the next session. The client comes into this session visibly upset and crying because he doesn't think "he can go on" without the social worker. The social worker tells the client that he can come back to see her once the balance is paid. The actions of the social worker are:

A. Ethical because the social worker has given the client notice of the nonpayment consequences, as well as the payment policy

B. Ethical because the social worker is allowing the client to return when the balance is paid

C. Unethical because the *Code of Ethics* does not allow termination based upon nonpayment of services

D. Unethical because the client may be a danger to himself

65. A school social worker is employed part-time in a mental health agency. A mother brings her daughter into the agency and asks that the social worker provide counseling because she has been impressed by the social worker's ability to "relate to" her daughter in school. The school social worker has taken the lead in developing her daughter's Individual Education Plan (IEP) and meets with the daughter regularly in school to assess her progress. In this situation, the social worker should:

A. Complete only the intake and assessment of the daughter at the mental health agency before proceeding to determine whether she could benefit from seeing the school social worker in this alternate setting

B. Serve the daughter in both settings because this will ensure continuity of treatment outside of the school setting

C. Ask another social worker to be the primary treating professional in the mental health agency and agree to be a consultant as needed to provide information on problems or issues in school

D. Not serve the daughter in the mental health agency because this poses a conflict of interest

66. In which of the following situations could it be ethical for a social worker to breach privilege?

A. A social worker needs to tell a client's family about poor choices being made

B. An insurance company is suing a client for fraud and needs behavioral health information

C. A social worker is contacted by the police who are investigating a crime that may have been committed by a client

D. A client is suing a social worker and information is needed for the social worker's defense

67. A social work supervisor is asked by a supervisee in her agency for a written recommendation for a graduate program in a related discipline. The supervisor agrees to provide it. In this situation, the supervisor's actions are:

A. Unethical because writing this recommendation for a supervisee creates a potential conflict of interest or dual relationship

B. Ethical since the supervisor would be aware of the supervisee's strengths and learning needs

C. Unethical since the graduate program is not in social work, but in a related field

D. Ethical because it would benefit the agency to have employees with higher academic credentials

68. A social worker asks her current clients to write testimonial endorsements to assist with attracting others to her private practice. These requests are:

A. Ethical because clients can decide whether they will write them

B. Ethical if she agrees not to identify them by name

C. Unethical because she did not also solicit former clients

D. Unethical because they are vulnerable due to their circumstances

69. Which of the following are predominantly used by younger people to define themselves?

A. Social roles

B. Emotional relationships

C. Intellectual abilities

D. Personal characteristics

70. During the first session, a client becomes very upset and hostile about his need to seek treatment. He blames others for his situation and yells in a loud manner. In order to facilitate the problem-solving process, the social worker should FIRST:

A. Listen to the client as he explains his concerns

B. Tell the client that he needs to calm down in order for the social worker to best understand his issues

C. Develop a plan to help him deal with his anger and blaming of others

D. Assess why the client is so upset and unwilling to accept responsibility for his problems

71. Which of the following would be an UNETHICAL use of identifying client data?

    A. Releasing information to a targeted victim under duty to warn
    B. Notifying child protective services of suspected neglect
    C. Seeking assistance from a supervisor or consultant concerning critical treatment issues
    D. Using it in a grant application for emergency funding following significant budget cuts

72. Social work intervention with offenders is MOST effective when focused on:

    A. Dynamic risk factors
    B. Genetic predispositions to violence
    C. Static risk factors
    D. Arrest records and past legal involvement

73. While meeting with a client and her child, a social worker becomes suspicious of markings on the child's arms and legs. After asking the client about them, the social worker believes that they are the result of physical abuse in the home. In order to appropriately address the situation, the social worker should FIRST:

    A. Inform the client of the need to make a report to the child protection agency
    B. Wait for the client to leave the office
    C. Gather information about the length and severity of the abuse
    D. Interview the child alone to see if the suspicion of abuse is corroborated

74. In instances in which clients lack the capacity to provide informed consent, social workers must do all of the following, according to the *Code of Ethics*, EXCEPT:

    A. Seek permission from appropriate third parties
    B. Help identify appropriate third parties for full guardianship of clients
    C. Inform clients consistent with their understanding
    D. Ensure third parties act in a manner consistent with clients' interests and wishes

75. A couple comes to see a social worker because they feel that they have suffered discrimination. They are blind and would like to adopt a child, but have been told by an adoption agency that it is not possible because of their visual impairments. They are distraught, but do not think that they will be able to fight the agency bias. In order to BEST assist this couple, the social worker should:

    A. Assist them to identify other methods to become parents
    B. Help them cope with their disappointment with being denied

C. Support them in fighting the agency bias
D. Connect them with others who have experienced similar discrimination

76. Which of the following BEST describes most older adults with regard to their typical mental functioning?

A. They continue to learn, but may experience declines in memory skills
B. They are at their peak with regard to problem-solving and mental processes
C. They do not learn and may experience declines in memory skills
D. They are not able to acquire new skills or solve problems

77. A client reports to a social worker that she was often criticized by her parents when she was in elementary and middle school and now has poor self-esteem and doubts her abilities. According to Erickson's stages of psychosocial development, the client experienced a crisis in which of the following stages?

A. Identity versus role confusion
B. Generativity versus stagnation
C. Industry versus inferiority
D. Integrity versus despair

78. A social worker believes that there may be an ethical dilemma in his agency. According to steps in ethical problem solving, the social worker should FIRST consult:

A. His supervisor
B. The *Code of Ethics*
C. The policies and procedures of the agency
D. A colleague who has worked in the agency longer

79. A social worker is charged with evaluating the effectiveness of a mental health outpatient treatment program. He constructs an evaluation strategy that consists of collecting data on the quality of services by holding focus groups with current clients so that they can relay their firsthand experiences. In addition, he uses existing agency data to compute the proportion of clients who have been rehospitalized since admission. The social worker is conducting what type of evaluation?

A. Qualitative
B. Quantitative
C. Quasi-experimental
D. Mixed method

80. Which of the following is an example of a role reversal?

    A. A 14-year-old boy told by his mother that he has to work to financially contribute to household expenses
    B. A 13-year-old girl physically and emotionally taking care of her father who was permanently injured in an accident
    C. A 10-year-old boy yelling at his mother that she is not doing enough work around the house
    D. A 12-year-old girl staying out later than allowed by her parents

81. Which of the following is a protective factor for dangerousness to others?

    A. Violence at an early age
    B. Drug and/or alcohol use
    C. Clinical services for physical and behavioral care
    D. Exposure to violent acts

82. Therapy sessions conducted by social workers in an agency are frequently audiotaped for review by their supervisors. These tapes are destroyed upon client terminations and are used only for supervisory purposes, not shared with others outside the agency. The standard consent form used by the agency states that social workers will receive supervision and client information may be disclosed with supervisors to ensure service quality. In order to avoid making clients feel uncomfortable, taping is not discussed with them, but consent forms are read by the social worker to clients who sign them. The audiotaping of these sessions is:

    A. Ethical because it is done as part of supervision to ensure service quality
    B. Unethical because clients should receive the names of the supervisors before signing the consent forms
    C. Unethical because informed consent for audiotaping has not been obtained
    D. Ethical because the tapes are destroyed upon termination

83. A social worker finds that she has a lot in common with a client. The client suggests seeing another professional because the client feels she "would be a better friend than client." The social worker agrees, but states that she cannot have contact with the client for several months after termination to allow time for the client to get engaged in treatment with a new social worker. The social worker's actions are:

    A. Ethical since there will be several months after the ending of the therapeutic relationship before contact occurs
    B. Unethical because the time period after termination, but before contact occurs, is not long enough

C. Ethical since it respects the client's self-determination
D. Unethical because the social worker cannot terminate services for this reason

84. After several months of treating a client, a social worker learns that the client goes to the same church as the social worker. The social worker continues to go to the church, seeing the client occasionally across the room. The social worker has no contact with the client at church. This situation is:

A. Unethical since a referral should have been made to another social worker once this issue was discovered
B. Ethical because the conflict was not known initially and has been minimized by avoiding contact
C. Unethical because the social worker should have started attending another church
D. Ethical since religious participation is not considered in the evaluation of dual relationships

85. A client is having trouble achieving a treatment goal, so the social worker breaks it down into small successive steps and rewards the client after achieving each one. This behavioral technique is known as:

A. Shaping
B. Biofeedback
C. Modeling
D. Flooding

86. All of the following are methods to address resistance during engagement EXCEPT:

A. Clarifying what will occur in treatment
B. Instilling hope that change is possible
C. Explaining the limits of confidentiality
D. Partializing action steps so clients can make incremental progress toward change

87. A social worker regularly refers clients to a colleague because he has expertise in treating Substance-Related and Addictive Disorders. The colleague is very appreciative of the social worker's confidence in his abilities and offers his season football tickets each time a referral is received. The social worker takes the tickets so as not to "hurt his feelings," but donates them to a local charity. The social worker's actions are:

A. Ethical because the tickets are donated to charity
B. Unethical because the social worker should not accept the tickets

C. Ethical because there is no additional cost to the colleague because he has already purchased season tickets

D. Unethical because the social worker should only refer clients to practitioners that she does not know

88. A man is court-ordered to receive an evaluation by a social worker. Although initially agreeable to participating, the client states at the conclusion of his meetings with the social worker that he "changed his mind" and wished that he had never agreed to be interviewed. He asks the social worker not to release any information to the court. The social worker should:

A. Respect the client's wishes and not provide any information to the court

B. Inform the court that the client rescinded his consent and ask the court to advise the social worker of next steps

C. Complete the evaluation based on all of the information gathered

D. Release only notes from the meetings and not complete a formal evaluation based on the wishes of the client

89. A social worker advises a 16-year-old client who has often been bullied in public by a group of peers to walk away each time such an incident occurs in the future. In the past, the boy would often cry when teased, causing his peers to laugh at his reaction. The social worker is hoping to reduce the teasing through:

A. Systematic desensitization

B. Aversion therapy

C. Extinction

D. Time out

90. Which of the following is TRUE of youth who are not heterosexual and/or gender conforming?

A. They go through different developmental stages than their peers

B. They are challenged to develop identities with few role models

C. They are not more at risk for social isolation and poor self-image than their peers

D. They are not at greater risk for mental and physical health complications compared with their peers

91. An agency is required by its funder to make extensive modifications to its human resource policies. The agency director is worried about the financial health of the agency and reports that the agency does not have the money to hire someone to complete this task. The social worker's wife is a human resource manager at a large corporation and agrees

to work with the agency for a few weeks at a deeply discounted rate to help meet the requirements. According to the *Code of Ethics*, this situation is:

A. Ethical because the wife is being hired as a consultant and is not an employee of the agency
B. Ethical because the agency has no other means to fulfill the funding requirement
C. Unethical because it represents a conflict of interest
D. Unethical because the wife is charging for her services

92. A client in crisis comes to a social worker for critically needed services. The social worker decides to use a single-subject design to determine service efficacy. Which of the following is most appropriate in determining the internal validity of these services?

A. ABAB
B. BAB
C. AB
D. A

93. Which of the following is NOT part of termination in social work practice?

A. Identifying other issues that may need to be addressed in the future
B. Reviewing accomplishments that occurred during treatment
C. Anticipating how to address subsequent reoccurrences of the problem
D. Recognizing loss on the part of the client and social worker

94. A social worker is completing an intake with a family who recently immigrated from another country. They are in need of basic resources such as rental and nutrition assistance. The children appear neat and clean. The social worker observes the mother mixing a small amount of alcohol into her infant's bottle and is told that this "soothes" the child as she is teething. During the intake, the family discloses that they do not believe in Western medicine and think sickness is caused by the presence of evil demons. They report that they spend much of their day engaged in prayer and meditation because one of their children is gravely ill. In order to BEST assist this family, the social worker should:

A. Prioritize them for services provided by the agency
B. Respect their cultural traditions and work with the family to prioritize their needs
C. Inform them that it is necessary to get the child protection agency involved and contact the agency immediately
D. Seek consultation to learn more about the cultural practices of this family

95. A client reports that he was just diagnosed with Hodgkin's disease. This cancer is associated with which of the major body systems?

    A. Lymphatic
    B. Circulatory
    C. Digestive
    D. Endocrine

96. A social worker in a mental health agency is very upset by the passage of legislation that, in his opinion, will be detrimental to some of his clients. He is asked by an advocacy organization to join a protest that he does on his own time and without identifying his employer. His agency director is very upset by his participation because the board of directors of the mental health agency supported this legislation. The social worker's actions are:

    A. Unethical because the social worker is considered a representative of his employer
    B. Ethical because he acted as a private individual
    C. Unethical because he should have gotten permission from his agency director first
    D. Ethical because he is allowed to take any and all actions in instances where policies are considered detrimental to clients

97. A client in a group facilitated by a social worker has a red face and appears visibly upset when he talks about his current relationship with his family. When the social worker states that he can see how the client is not happy about his current situation based upon his physical symptoms, the client says, "Everything is fine." The client is MOST likely exhibiting:

    A. Lack of congruence in communication
    B. Denial of his underlying psychic conflict
    C. Desire to please the social worker
    D. Symptomatology of a psychiatric diagnosis

98. A social worker receives a request for detailed treatment summaries from a client's insurance company. In the correspondence, it is made clear that the insurance company will cease funding for treatment unless they are received immediately. In order to best serve the client, the social worker should:

    A. Prepare the summaries, but review them with the client and get his or her approval before sending
    B. Write to the insurance company and ask why they are needed
    C. Send only the diagnosis and prognosis, citing confidential mandates
    D. Send the treatment summaries as soon as possible so that funding for treatment will not stop

99. A social worker is working with a family who has become homeless after a fire destroyed their home. The 10-year-old daughter begins to use "baby talk" and suck her thumb, behaviors she had not displayed before the fire. The mother also reports that the daughter now constantly wants to sit on her lap and clings to her side when they go out in public. The daughter is MOST likely using the defense mechanism of:

    A. Undoing
    B. Reaction formation
    C. Regression
    D. Splitting

100. Which of the following is NOT a limitation of using existing case records as the basis for practice evaluations?

    A. Records may not contain consistent and/or complete information
    B. There is no additional time or cost associated with their use
    C. Evaluations have to be limited to only topics contained in the case records
    D. The client's opinions about service quality are not considered

101. What is the PRIMARY goal of permanency planning?

    A. Living in stable and long-term homes
    B. Including all parties in case conferencing
    C. Improving educational outcomes
    D. Ensuring treatment decisions are individually based

102. A man comes to see a social worker because he is sexually attracted to those of the same gender and is deeply distressed by the thought that he may be homosexual. The feelings experienced by this client are:

    A. Ego alien
    B. Ego-syntonic
    C. Coping skills
    D. Fixations

103. Which of the following personality disorders is clustered with Antisocial Personality Disorder in a grouping characterized by dramatic, emotional, and erratic behavior?

    A. Schizoid Personality Disorder
    B. Narcissistic Personality Disorder
    C. Obsessive-Compulsive Personality Disorder
    D. Paranoid Personality Disorder

104. A social worker in a substance abuse treatment facility is attracted to one of her supervisees and asks him out on a date. After several months of dating, they get married and the supervisee finds a job at another agency. The behavior of the social worker is:

A. Unethical because she engaged in a dual relationship with a supervisee
B. Ethical since the supervisee found another job once they were married
C. Unethical because the relationship led to marriage
D. Ethical because the sexual contact prohibition only applies to social workers and clients

105. Which of the following is TRUE about using collateral sources during assessment in the social work problem-solving process?

A. Collateral sources should not include family and friends of clients as they cannot provide objective assessments
B. Collateral sources should only validate data which has been collected from clients, not provide other information of which clients are not aware
C. Client consent is not needed when assessing information from collateral sources
D. Prior providers are important collateral sources as they know what services have been effective and ineffective in the past

106. An increased risk of agranulocytosis is associated with which of the following medications?

A. Clozaril
B. Lexapro
C. Lithium
D. Xanax

107. A client reports that she is very upset by her 17-year-old daughter's behavior. She has not been completing her homework and is showing up late for her classes. The client reports that she recently took away the daughter's cell phone until her behavior changes. Which of the following behavioral techniques is the mother using?

A. Positive reinforcement
B. Negative reinforcement
C. Positive punishment
D. Negative punishment

108. In order to ethically obtain informed consent, social workers must use clear and understandable language to review all of the following EXCEPT:

A. Agency mission
B. Service purpose and risks
C. Limits due to third-party payers
D. Right to refuse or withdraw from services

109. Which of the following is NOT true about a task-centered approach in social work practice?

    A. There is no assessment phase
    B. It is highly structured and time-limited
    C. Termination usually begins in the first session
    D. The client takes a very active role in making change

110. Which of the following is TRUE with regard to confidentiality in group work?

    A. Group members have the same protection of confidentiality that they receive in individual counseling
    B. Group members have a legal duty not to disclose information that is shared
    C. Social workers can discuss information shared in groups with others because it is not confidential
    D. Social workers cannot guarantee to group members that information disclosed in groups will be kept confidential because it may be disclosed by other members

111. A social worker develops a survey instrument to assess client well-being. The social worker has clients complete this new survey, as well as one that is currently being used by the agency to reliably measure the same construct. The social worker then compares the consistency of the findings produced by these two separate tests. This social worker is using which of the following methods to assess the reliability of the new survey instrument?

    A. Test–retest
    B. Interrater
    C. Parallel forms
    D. Internal consistency

112. A client tells a social worker that she "feels like a failure" because she cannot seem to meet the multiple daily demands of working and parenting. The social worker states that "many people in your situation experience the same feelings." The technique used by the social worker is known as:

    A. Validating
    B. Reflecting
    C. Paraphrasing
    D. Clarifying

113. Which of the following statements about social work interviews is NOT true?

    A. They aim to serve the best interest of clients
    B. They are uniform in nature in order to collect consistent information on all clients

C. They can be informational, diagnostic, or therapeutic

D. They focus on collecting important information to be used in the problem-solving process

114. A client tells a social worker that he "can't stand it anymore," but does not believe that he can make needed changes in his life. He engages with the social worker in the discussions about what his life would be like without his problem behaviors. The client is MOST likely at which stage of change?

A. Contemplation

B. Precontemplation

C. Preparation

D. Maintenance

115. Which of the following statements is TRUE about research ethics in social work?

A. A client does not need a separate informed consent process for research participation and service receipt if they are done by the same agency

B. Naturalistic observation is a preferred method for social work research as it does not require a consent procedure

C. Social workers do not have an ethical mandate to promote and facilitate research

D. Social workers must ensure that a research participant has access to supportive services

116. Which of the following perspectives on human behavior is based on the belief that clients have the capacity to change themselves and actions are driven by a desire for growth, personal meaning, and competence?

A. Humanistic

B. Developmental

C. Psychodynamic

D. Rational choice

117. A client shows up for the initial session with a coworker. The BEST response for a social worker is to:

A. Tell the client that confidentiality policies preclude the coworker from sitting in on sessions, so the coworker should sit in the waiting area until the session is over

B. Have the coworker also complete the intake paperwork and releases because the coworker is regarded as a client if he or she sits in on the initial session

    C. Complete an assessment in the waiting area to determine why the client brought the coworker to the session and the appropriateness of him or her being there

    D. Leave it up to the client to determine the extent to which the coworker attends or participates in sessions

118. What is the BEST definition of empowerment?

    A. Helping clients obtain services needed to solve their problems

    B. Providing clients with training and education to improve their coping skills

    C. Assisting clients to realize that they have strengths and resources to solve their own problems

    D. Developing a relationship with clients based on mutual respect and trust

119. Which BEST describes what the *Code of Ethics* states about social and political action by social workers?

    A. Social and political action is strictly prohibited by social workers

    B. Social workers should only engage in social and political action if they are not compensated for these activities

    C. Social workers should engage in social and political action that seeks to ensure that clients have equal access to and expanded choice for needed resources

    D. Social and political action must be done by all clients in order to change the conditions that have contributed to their problems

120. Which of the following is NOT an indicator of ego strength?

    A. Taking responsibility for actions

    B. Dealing with mood changes

    C. Accepting limitations and being accountable

    D. Blaming others

121. Which of the following are stages of group development in sequential order?

    A. Preaffiliation, differentiation, intimacy, power and control, and separation/termination

    B. Differentiation, power and control, preaffiliation, intimacy, and separation/termination

    C. Preaffiliation, power and control, intimacy, differentiation, and separation/termination

    D. Differentiation, preaffiliation, power and control, intimacy, and separation/termination

122. A client tells a social worker that she was denied housing based upon her ethnic/racial background. She feels hopeless and depressed due to this discrimination, despite having found alternative housing. She states that she "would not like this treatment to happen to others," but she does not think "anything will change." Treatment goals for the client should focus on:

    A. Determining whether the alternative housing located is safe and affordable
    B. Referring her to a psychiatrist to see if antidepressant medication needs to be prescribed
    C. Helping her cope with the hopelessness and depression experienced
    D. Assisting her to fight the housing discrimination

123. Which of the following is the BEST definition of referent power?

    A. It is derived from position within an organization
    B. It is derived from interpersonal relationships and charisma, as well as connections with those in leadership positions
    C. It results from possessing knowledge or expertise that is highly valued
    D. It arises from the ability to influence the allocation of incentives, including salary increments, positive appraisals, and/or promotions

124. Which of the following is TRUE about transference in social work practice?

    A. It is a conscious process
    B. It does not have any therapeutic value
    C. It is always sexual in nature
    D. It is more likely with clients with certain personality features

125. A client who reports that she repeatedly feels the urge to physically strike her child when angry tells the social worker that she is having trouble moving her arm. The client is MOST likely exhibiting the defense mechanism of:

    A. Introjection
    B. Reaction formation
    C. Conversion
    D. Projective identification

126. An agency is concerned with the recidivism of its clients and hires a consultant to provide recommendations about service modifications that may have to occur. The consultant has a doctorate and extensive experience in the field. After several weeks, the consultant generates a

report advising of service changes that, in the social worker's professional opinion, would be detrimental to clients. The social worker should:

A. Implement them because the consultant is an "expert" in the field
B. Not implement them, citing the reasons for the concerns
C. Speak to the agency director and let him or her decide whether or not to implement them
D. Have another consultant examine the report to see if he or she concurs with the recommendations

127. What is the PRIMARY difference between common and statutory law?

A. Common law is voluntary and does not need to be followed whereas statutory law requires compliance
B. Common law governs federal rules while statutory law applies to state policies
C. Statutory law is time-limited, requiring revision or readoption at specified intervals while common law can be in effect for an indefinite period
D. Statutory law is made by a legislative body whereas common law is made by judges

128. The following do not violate state laws when performed outside the social work context, but are unethical when engaged in by a social worker EXCEPT:

A. Writing a recommendation for a current adult client
B. Dating a current adult client
C. Borrowing money from a current adult client
D. Having a business relationship with a current adult client

129. A client comes in to see a social worker because she is having multiple issues on her job. During the initial session, she tells the social worker that she "can't wait for advice on how to fix the problems." In this situation, the social worker should:

A. Ignore the client's comment
B. Remember to speak to the client about her role in the treatment process once rapport has been established
C. Ask the client why she feels that the social worker's advice would be so valuable
D. Clarify what will happen in treatment and the responsibilities of both the client and social worker with regard to change

130. Which of the following is NOT true about the Substance-Related and Addictive Disorders in the *DSM-5*?

A. Substance use and substance abuse are combined into a single continuum measured from severe to mild

B. Drug craving has been added and legal problems have been eliminated from the diagnostic criteria

C. Caffeine use disorder is included as a new disorder

D. Gambling disorder is the sole disorder under a new category of non-substance-related disorders

131. Which of the following is NOT true of attachment and bonding?

   A. Attachment and bonding are best viewed separately from a client's culture because the theoretical approaches are universal

   B. Some theories of connectedness are understood within an evolutionary context

   C. Attachment can be viewed as a set of learned behaviors involving both classical and operant conditioning

   D. Insecure attachment systems have been linked to psychiatric disorders and aberrant behaviors

132. A school social worker asks the parents of a boy who is Asian to come in for a conference because he has been experiencing problems at school. These problems include not obeying rules and deliberately annoying others. The grandparents of the boy come to the meeting with the parents. Their presence MOST likely can be viewed by the social worker as an indication that:

   A. The boy is having problems at home and the grandparents are needed by the parents to assist with the behaviors

   B. The grandparents are an important part of the boy's support system and should be incorporated into the treatment plan

   C. The parents lack the skills needed to make changes in the boy's behavior and they have shifted the responsibility for change to the grandparents

   D. The boy will only listen to the grandparents and they will be needed in the treatment process in order for him to stop the behaviors in school

133. A client tells a social worker that he has been screamed at by his boss on a daily basis for the last month. He is very angry, but has not said anything for fear of being fired. He also reports that he is having problems with his wife and children because he has not been able to control his temper in the last few weeks at home. This client's behavior is MOST likely represented by which of the following defense mechanisms?

   A. Displacement

   B. Incorporation

   C. Denial

   D. Compensation

134. Which is the PRIMARY reason for filing court-ordered legal documents "under seal"?

 A. It prevents the submission of any information that can be used for prosecution
 B. It allows sensitive information not to become public record
 C. It avoids the need to issue a subpoena for the same information
 D. It expedites the legal process, minimizing adverse impacts due to delays

135. The social worker ends a family session with, "During the last hour, each of you has had a chance to discuss your frustrations with one another and how sometimes your own actions have been perceived by each other as hurtful, though they were not intended to be so." The social worker's statement is MOST likely aimed at:

 A. Clarifying to the family that the social worker is being objective since each member got a chance to talk
 B. Demonstrating that the family members are overreacting to each other's actions because they are not intentional
 C. Summarizing what occurred in the session in order for family members to gain a new understanding of their actions
 D. Praising the family members for their openness and participation in the session

136. Entropy is BEST defined as:

 A. Randomness or disorder in a system, leading to decline
 B. Forward motion, leading toward goal achievement
 C. Specialization in system function and purpose
 D. Openness in a system with good information exchange

137. Which of the following is ETHICAL with regard to consultation in social work practice?

 A. Providing consultants with identifying information about clients without their permission
 B. Only using consultants who social workers judge to have demonstrated competence
 C. Allowing consultants access to all client records so they can decide what is relevant and important to their work
 D. Using family members or close friends who are experts in their fields as interdisciplinary consultants

138. A social worker needs to evaluate the behavior of a client who is living in a group home. The social worker asks two staff to each record the frequency of the behavior independently and to submit their tracking sheets to her without sharing them with one another. The social worker is

using which of the following approaches to ensure reliability of the data collected?

- **A.** Alternate or parallel forms
- **B.** Test–retest
- **C.** Interrater
- **D.** Internal consistency

139. A social worker employed to work with juvenile offenders has developed an innovative program that has yielded very positive outcomes. She approaches the agency director about using the same approach with adult offenders. The director is skeptical about its ability to achieve the same outcomes. The director is expressing concerns about:

- **A.** Internal validity
- **B.** Multicollinearity
- **C.** External validity
- **D.** Measurement error

140. Upon intake, a client states that she "feels like hurting herself, but will be fine." She assures the social worker that she will not act on her feelings. In order to best assist the client, the social worker should FIRST:

- **A.** Conduct a safety assessment
- **B.** Acknowledge the client's feelings and concerns
- **C.** Refer the client to a psychiatrist for a medication evaluation
- **D.** Determine the reasons that have caused the client to feel this way

141. When two or more people share the same delusion or delusional system, it is called:

- **A.** Folie à deux
- **B.** Stereotypic disorder
- **C.** Conversion disorder
- **D.** Comorbid psychosis

142. A social worker is seeing a mother and her 6-year-old child for therapy. They have made substantial progress and the social worker is seeing dramatic improvements in their relationship. During a session, the social worker observes what appear to be burns on the child's neck and arm. She asks the mother about what caused them and the mother's explanation does not seem plausible. The social worker is concerned and feels that physical abuse may have occurred. In order to BEST address this situation, the social worker should:

- **A.** Express her concerns to the mother and ask the mother to come back with the child in a few days so that the social worker can assess the situation

    B. Wait until the mother and child leave the office and contact the child protection agency

    C. Tell the mother that the social worker will need to contact the child protection agency and involve her in making the report immediately

    D. Tell the mother that the social worker will need to report her concerns to the child protection agency in the future if further signs of physical abuse are seen

143. Theories of human development in social work have stressed all of the following EXCEPT:

    A. A systems approach

    B. An ecological orientation

    C. A focus on preventing mental deficiency

    D. A life span perspective

144. A social worker receives a subpoena for a former client's record. The social worker should FIRST:

    A. Respond to the court by claiming privilege

    B. Provide the record because it is for a former client

    C. Send the subpoena and record to the client so he or she can respond to the court

    D. Ignore the subpoena because the information is confidential

145. According to Erikson, psychosocial development follows which sequence of relationship formation?

    A. Attachment-autonomy-intimacy

    B. Intimacy-attachment-autonomy

    C. Autonomy-attachment-intimacy

    D. Intimacy-autonomy-attachment

146. A client reports to a social worker that she is thinking of ending her marriage and would like to get guidance from her priest about her desire. In response to the client's request, the social worker should FIRST:

    A. Determine why the client thinks that speaking to her priest will help

    B. Assess, in conjunction with the client, whether going to her priest will be helpful

    C. Inform the client that this is a good idea as the priest should handle religious/spiritual concerns

    D. Determine what support is needed to prepare the client for this meeting with her priest

147. In social work practice, assent and consent are:

    A. Identical because both give legal authorization to participate in treatment

B. Distinct, with only consent providing legal authorization to participate in treatment

C. Sequential, with consent needed first and assent required later in the problem-solving process

D. Required of all clients, even those who are court-mandated

148. Which of the following is NOT true about feedback in social work practice?

    A. Client consent is not needed if consultation is related to client care

    B. The best insight can often be gained from those who are critical of care

    C. Feedback is especially important at key decision points in service development and implementation

    D. Clarity should always be given about why feedback is needed and what will be done with the information

149. Which of the following is NOT a change to the Neurodevelopmental Disorders listed in the *DSM-5*?

    A. Mental Retardation was renamed Intellectual Disability

    B. Disruptive Mood Dysregulation Disorder was added as a new diagnosis for children up to age 18

    C. Stuttering was renamed Childhood-Onset Fluency Disorder

    D. Autism Spectrum Disorder now encompasses Autistic Disorder, Asperger's Disorder, Childhood Disintegrative Disorder, and Pervasive Developmental Disorder Not Otherwise Specified

150. A social worker is asked by a community governing body to assist with developing youth programs aimed at reducing youth violence, school truancy, vandalism, and drug usage. In order to be most effective, the social worker should FIRST:

    A. Work with the community to prioritize the youth problems to be addressed

    B. Educate community leaders and members about youth programs that have been effective nationally

    C. Collect data on the magnitude of the need that has to be addressed in program design

    D. Determine why youth problems are now seen as a priority for the community governing body

151. A social worker is struggling with treating a client with Pica. This disorder is not common among those served by her agency. The social worker believes that it is in the best interest of the client for her to obtain consultation. A colleague in the agency has shown interest in the situation and agrees to advise because she has known the social worker for many years and they both became employed at the agency

immediately after graduation. In order to best assist the client, the social worker should:

A. Decline the offer in order to find a consultant with more experience in treating this disorder
B. Accept the offer because the colleague is immediately available to assist
C. Accept the offer because the colleague is knowledgeable about the social worker's skills, which may be valuable in making treatment recommendations
D. Decline the offer because it would be a conflict of interest to use a colleague who is employed by the same agency

152. A woman is court-ordered to receive an evaluation and services from an agency. After completing the evaluation, the client stops coming to appointments so the findings are not reviewed with her and services are not rendered. The social worker has been unable to reach her by phone. The court has requested a copy of the evaluation report. In this instance, the social worker should:

A. Send the report and information about the client not coming to appointments to the court
B. Claim privilege and not release the report to the court as it is confidential
C. Request that the court get a signed release from the client prior to submitting it
D. Send the client a registered letter with a copy of the court's request in an effort to motivate her to contact the social worker

153. All of the following are reasons that social workers should seek agency accreditation EXCEPT:

A. Accreditation provides accountability to the public
B. Accreditation justifies higher salaries for agency workers
C. Accreditation involves objective evaluation of agency processes and outcomes
D. Accreditation assists with professional development of agency personnel

154. A couple is seeing a social worker for marriage counseling. After several months, they decide to end their marriage and ask the social worker to make a child custody recommendation to the court because they feel that she is best suited to make suggestions given that she has worked with the couple for so long. The social worker should:

A. Decline because it is not appropriate since they are both current counseling clients

     B. Accept because both clients agree that it would produce the best child custody recommendation

     C. Decline until the social worker is contacted by the court directly

     D. Accept, but with the understanding that further sessions will be needed to collect the information needed by the courts

155. Genetic counseling is most appropriate for all of the following groups EXCEPT:

     A. Couples who have a child with an inherited disorder as identified by newborn screening

     B. Women who have had babies die in infancy and/or multiple miscarriages

     C. New mothers who have suffered postpartum depression

     D. Men who are sexually active with a family history of birth defects

156. Which of the following BEST describes summative evaluation criteria for a prisoner reentry program?

     A. Reincarceration rates

     B. Program satisfaction

     C. Criminal history

     D. Length of services

157. A couple comes in to see a social worker because of their destructive pattern of fighting. The husband complains that his wife is always nagging him to do things around the house and suggests that he will get them done if she just stops complaining. The husband is stating that his behavior will improve if which of the following behavioral techniques is used?

     A. Positive reinforcement

     B. Positive punishment

     C. Negative reinforcement

     D. Negative punishment

158. Which of the following is TRUE about a client who is transgender?

     A. The client is likely to undergo sexual reassignment surgery in the future

     B. The client is likely to be gay or lesbian

     C. The client is likely to be a cross-dresser

     D. The client is likely to experience stigma, bias, and/or discrimination as a result of his or her gender identity

159. A client reports that she is under the surveillance of the police and that they have been following her for days and listening in on her phone

conversations. There is no other evidence to support this belief. The client's report is MOST likely resulting from a:

A. Dissociation
B. Delusion
C. Hallucination
D. Hypomanic state

160. After completing an assessment, a client states that she would like to work on being more assertive at work. In order to best assist the client, the social worker should FIRST:

A. Provide the client with communication strategies aimed at self-expression
B. Assist the client with identifying classes aimed at assertiveness training
C. Gather information on issues at her current and past jobs that have resulted from communication barriers
D. Identify the outcome that she hopes to attain from this behavioral change

161. During the first session, a young woman sobs as she states that she does not think that she will ever get through the recent dissolution of her marriage. She ends by saying that she "is alone and nobody understands how I feel." In order to instill hope, the social worker should:

A. Talk about how she felt the same way during her own divorce and is now happily remarried
B. Assure her that she will have the opportunity to express her feelings and work through them in the coming weeks
C. Refer her to a support group with other women who are going through divorce
D. Evaluate whether she is at risk for self-harm

162. A client is being discharged from an inpatient hospitalization. Upon admission, he slept most of the time, reported extreme despair, and felt hopeless. Several days later, while hospitalized, he appeared jittery and agitated. His speech was rambling and he wandered around the unit, talking to others for hours. He also had trouble sleeping. This client is MOST likely going to be prescribed which of the following medications upon discharge?

A. Lithium
B. Elavil
C. Ativan
D. Haldol

163. In the *DSM-5*, Dysthymia is now called:

A. Persistent Depressive Disorder
B. Major Depressive Disorder

     C. Disruptive Mood Dysregulation Disorder

     D. Substance/Medication-Induced Depressive Disorder

164. A client starts to miss appointments with a social worker after achieving her goals. Prior to these absences, she had very good attendance and had made substantial progress. These missed appointments are MOST likely an indication of:

     A. Readiness to terminate from services

     B. Emergence of a new problem that needs to be addressed

     C. Dissatisfaction with achieved outcomes

     D. Codependency that needs to be addressed as a treatment issue

165. A client has just been diagnosed with Stage 4 cancer and is referred to a pain management group to minimize the discomfort associated with her illness. The provision of this service is BEST represented as which of the following?

     A. Tertiary prevention

     B. Primary prevention

     C. Secondary prevention

     D. Hospice

166. A school social worker is seeing a 14-year-old girl who confides that she is struggling with gender identity issues and is being teased by peers. Several weeks later, the principal asks the social worker what is "going on" with her client because she was involved in an altercation with other students. The principal asks to see her file in order to better understand her issues because she is facing out-of-school suspension for her behavior. The principal thinks that the information contained in the file will help reduce her punishment. The social worker should:

     A. Share the file with the principal since it will potentially assist the client

     B. Refrain from letting the principal see the file, but explain the client's situation

     C. Prepare a written summary of the client's struggles to share with the principal

     D. Tell the principal that the information is confidential and cannot be released

167. If social workers engage in appropriate physical contact with clients, all of the following must be present in the boundaries that govern such contact EXCEPT:

     A. Contact should not occur with those for whom such contact could cause psychological harm

     B. Contact should only occur with adult clients and not children

C. Contact should be culturally sensitive, considering the customs, beliefs, and traditions of clients

D. Rules for the use of contact should be able to be clearly articulated by both social workers and their clients

168. In the *DSM-5*, the "Not Otherwise Specified" diagnostic categories are:

A. Unchanged and still can be used in the same manner
B. Replaced with "Other Specified" and "Unspecified" diagnoses
C. Eliminated completely with no alternative options
D. Expanded to include new diagnostic criteria

169. A social worker is contacted by a man who is very distraught. He is aware that his mother was a client of the social worker because she has recently passed away and he has found bills for services in her belongings. He had little contact with her in the last years of her life as she seemed "to pull away." He is trying to understand her behavior and would like to make an appointment to see the social worker. The social worker should:

A. Reassure the son that his mother's behavior was not related to him in any way
B. Explain to the son that the social worker cannot talk to him about his mother
C. Ask him to put his questions in writing so the social worker can see whether the information can be released
D. Schedule a session to try to assist

170. Which of the following uses "person-first language"?

A. The disabled
B. Individuals with disabilities
C. Disabled people
D. Disabled population

Practice Test

Answers

1. B

Regular exercise and good nutrition are actions that are classified as primary prevention, helping to avoid developing diseases, injuries, and/ or illnesses. The other three response choices are secondary prevention strategies that occur after diseases, injuries, and/or illnesses have developed to mitigate or slow their progression/impacts (see Unit IV—Chapter 21, *Primary, Secondary, and Tertiary Prevention Strategies*).

2. D

All of the options, except the last response choice, are actions taken by a client during treatment. Indicators of resistance can also include engaging in intellectual talk by using technical terms or abstract concepts, asking questions of a social worker that are not related to his or her issues or problems, being preoccupied with past events instead of current issues, false promising, and/or flattering a social worker in an attempt to "soften" him or her so as not to be pushed.

A client who was referred by another person may not necessarily be apprehensive about change, but instead may not have known where to seek help. Behaviors that occur after a client has seen a social worker are better indicators of resistance (see Unit II—Chapter 9, *The Factors Used in Determining the Client's Ability to Use Intervention/Treatment*).

3. C

Social workers should provide clients with reasonable access to their records. Social workers who are concerned that clients' access to their records could cause serious misunderstanding or harm to a client should provide assistance in interpreting the records and consultation with a client regarding the records. Social workers should limit clients' access to their records, or portions of their records, only in exceptional circumstances when there is compelling evidence that such access would cause serious harm to a client.

In this case vignette, there was not a risk of harm due to the release, so the social worker should have provided access; however, information can be withheld in some circumstances, as described, as long as the request and the reason for the denial is documented in the client's file (see Unit V—Chapter 26, *The Use of Client Records*).

4. D

The *Code of Ethics* states social workers who have direct knowledge of a colleague's impairment that is due to personal problems, psychosocial distress, substance abuse, or mental health difficulties that interfere with practice effectiveness should consult with the colleague when feasible and assist the colleague in taking remedial action. Going to the agency director may be appropriate, but only after the social worker has gone to the colleague FIRST (see Unit V—Chapter 28, *The Social Worker's Ethical Responsibility to Colleagues*).

5. B

Role discomplementarity occurs when role expectations are not being met and activities associated with these expectations are not carried out in an expected manner. In this case vignette, the client's belief about what her son should be doing is not consistent with his behavior. In addition, the son is dissatisfied with the fulfillment of the role expectations that he has for his mother. This case vignette solely involves role issues and not communication, discipline, or developmental problems (see Unit I—Chapter 3, *The Effects of Social Role on Relationships*).

6. D

Conflict theory posits that society is fragmented into groups that compete for social and economic resources (B). Social order is maintained by those with the greatest political, economic, and social resources. (C) Inequality exists because those in control of a disproportionate share of society's resources actively defend their advantages.

Conflict theorists challenge the status quo, encourage social change, and believe rich and powerful people force social order on the poor and the weak. This constant competition between groups forms the basis for the ever-changing nature of society (A).

The masses are bound by coercion by those in power. This perspective emphasizes social control, NOT consensus and conformity (D) (see Unit I—Chapter 1, *Conflict Theory*).

7. B

The case vignette requires the social worker to view the unemployment "using a systems approach." Although the job loss is causing financial concerns, it would also have an impact on other aspects of the client's life, such as his physical and mental health. Systems theory indicates that a change to one part of a client's life will impact on others (see Unit I—Chapter 1, *Systems Theory*).

8. D

Adderall, Ritalin, and Dexedrine are stimulants that are used for the treatment of Attention-Deficit/Hyperactivity Disorder. Tofranil is an antidepressant and is used primarily to treat depressive disorders. However, it is also used at times for the treatment of anxiety disorders (see Unit II—Chapter 10, *Common Psychotropic and Non-Psychotropic Prescriptions and Over-the-Counter Medications and Their Side Effects*).

9. A

Cocaine use is indicated by dilated pupils, hyperactivity, euphoria, anxiety, and/or excessive talking.

Heroin use is indicated by contracted pupils, sleeping at unusual times, sweating, vomiting, twitching, and/or loss of appetite. Marijuana use is indicated by glassy, red eyes, inappropriate laughter, and/or loss of interest/motivation. Painkiller addiction is indicated by sleepiness, inattention, constipation, and/or loss of appetite (see Unit II—Chapter 10, *The Symptoms of Substance Abuse and Other Addictions*).

10. A

Since the Tarasoff case in 1974, duty to warn has become an important concept in social work. Being able to protect potential victims from harm and protecting clients from self-harm are ethical obligations. Duty to warn means that social workers must verbally tell intended victims that there is a foreseeable danger of violence. In addition, social workers have a duty to protect, so social workers who determine that their clients present a serious danger of violence to others have an obligation to use reasonable care to protect the intended victims against danger. This may entail police notification or other necessary steps (see Unit II—Chapter 10, *The Indicators of Client Danger to Self and Others*).

11. C

Those with high ego strength approach problems with a sense that they can overcome problems and even grow as a result. They try to find new ways to cope with struggles and handle challenges without losing their sense of self. On the contrary, those with low ego strength view challenges as something to avoid. Reality seems overwhelming and they may try to avoid it through wishful thinking, fantasies, and/or substance use (see Unit II—Chapter 9, *The Methods Used in Assessing Ego Strengths*).

12. D

Couples development follows the stages of Margaret Mahler who chronicled the experiences of parents and children. There are five developmental stages—symbiosis, differentiation, practicing, rapprochement, and mutual interdependence. Symbiosis, the first stage, is when partners are passionate, nurturing, and selflessly attentive to each other's needs (D). They place few demands on one another and create enduring attachment, which is the foundation that allows couples to move to the second stage, differentiation. Differentiation occurs when partners begin to notice annoyances with issues that were previously unnoticed; it is re-emergence of the self in relation to the partner. Practicing, the third stage, is the time when autonomy and individuality become primary (A). Rapprochement, which follows, occurs when openness and vulnerability begin to re-emerge (B); partners feel comfortable with their own individuality in the relationship. The last stage, mutual interdependence, is marked by constancy; each partner is able to value and respect the separateness of the other (C) (see Unit I—Chapter 2, *Models of Couples Development*).

13. D

Clients who receive their antipsychotic medications via injection are more likely to continue their medications than those who take them orally. Since injectable medications are usually only needed once or twice per month, it may be easier to remember these appointments than taking pills several times a day. This consistency in medication compliance may result in fewer hospitalizations and symptom relapses. Those on injectable medications are also less likely to overdose or use their medications for suicide. The cost of the medications is not a therapeutic consideration (see Unit II—Chapter 10, *Common Psychotropic and Non-Psychotropic Prescriptions and Over-the-Counter Medications and Their Side Effects*).

14. B

Medical necessity is a criterion used to determine whether treatments and services are justified as reasonable, necessary, and/or appropriate, based on evidence-based clinical standards of care. Payment for services, as well as whether levels of care are justified, uses medical necessity to assess whether treatment and service requests are "reasonable and necessary" given clients' diagnoses and/or presenting problems (see Unit IV—Chapter 18, *The Methods Used to Clarify the Benefits and Limitations of Resources*).

15. B

The *Code of Ethics* states that it is unethical to continue to treat clients when services are no longer needed. The waiving of cost associated for this treatment is not relevant. Continuing to see the client with no treatment goals is not in the client's best interest. The social worker should have addressed the client's apprehension and nervousness about termination. Central to the termination process is working with the client to anticipate future needs and how to address them. Continuing to see him "just in case" does not assist the client to be autonomous and to practice the coping skills that he has attained during treatment (see Unit III—Chapter 12, *The Techniques Used for Follow-Up*).

16. A

Program evaluation usually relies on both subjective and objective data. The "facts" or objective outcomes include days incarcerated, number of subsequent hospitalizations, and so forth. Subjective information, such as how the "facts" are perceived by clients through descriptions of their feelings, experiences, and perceptions, is equally important. Subjective outcomes often provide valuable information about how the service experience was viewed by those served. The satisfaction of foster parents and perceived safety of children are subjective, not objective, outcomes of a foster care program. The number of children served is not an outcome. The proportion of children reunified is the only objective outcome in the response choices provided (see Unit II—Chapter 8, *The Methods Used to Develop Behavioral Objectives*).

17. B

Clients with Borderline Personality Disorder tend to view the world in black-and-white, all-or-nothing, dichotomous thinking. These polarized thoughts lead to intense emotional reactions that are unable to be regulated. Clients with Borderline Personality Disorder often engage in self-destructive behavior and act impulsively (see Unit II—Chapter 10, *Use of the Current* Diagnostic and Statistical Manual of Mental Disorders *of the American Psychiatric Association*).

18. C

The FIRST goal is to immediately relieve the stress experienced, return clients to previous levels of functioning, and assist them with regaining equilibrium. A social worker may want to work with clients to identify precursors, develop coping skills, and/or link with others for mutual support, but these actions would occur after the crisis has subsided (see Unit III—Chapter 11, *The Crisis Intervention/Treatment Approach*).

19. B

Social workers are mandated reporters. Despite the supervisor's assessment not reaching the same conclusion, the social worker still must make a report because she has "a reasonable suspicion." It would not be appropriate to delay in an effort to collect more information and/or to convince the supervisor of the need. In addition, the social worker should be forthcoming with her supervisor about her actions and not anonymously report (see Unit V—Chapter 26, *Legal and Ethical Issues Regarding Mandatory Reporting of Abuse*).

20. C

Social workers are mandated reporters. In this instance, the social worker should not be making an assessment about these being isolated incidents or the likelihood that they would happen again. The *Code of Ethics* states that clients should be informed whenever possible of such reports. Not telling the family would not be warranted as they are likely to find out that the social worker contacted the child protection agency and will feel betrayed by not having been told that such a report was being made. The social worker should have reviewed the limits of confidentiality with this family upon intake (see Unit V—Chapter 26, *Legal and Ethical Issues Regarding Mandatory Reporting of Abuse*).

21. B

The conflict between the client and his boss focuses on the completion of tasks associated with the job. In order for the client to successfully function in his new employment role, he must start with a clear understanding of what is expected of him by his boss. Disputes, such as the one described, often arise because clients are unclear about role expectations (*role ambiguity*) or have different role expectations than others (*role discomplementarity*). These disputes lead to incompatible or conflicting expectations (*role conflicts*). Thus, determining whether the client's understanding of his duties differ from those in his job description and/or the expectations of his boss would be helpful in understanding whether his problems stem from a lack of clarity or agreement with regard to his role (B).

Obtaining mediation assistance (A) will not help the social worker *understand the situation* as presented in the question. There is no indication that the criticism by his boss is affecting his job performance (C) or that he is unwilling to complete the work (D). Thus, they are not the likely causes of the problem (see Unit I—Chapter 3, *The Effects of Social Role on Relationships*).

22. D

The *unconscious* contains thoughts, feelings, desires, and memories of which clients have no awareness, yet influence every aspect of their day-to-day lives.

The *preconscious* contains all the information outside of a client's attention, but is readily available if needed.

The *conscious* contains all the information that a client is paying attention to at any given time.

The *superego* is the moral component of personality. It causes clients to feel guilty when they go against society's rules (see Unit I—Chapter 1, *Psychoanalytic Theory*).

23. D

A social worker must view a couple or family as a system, with actions of each member affecting the others. Couples and families try to maintain homeostasis or stability in their relationships so that they do not have to change as a result of actions exhibited outside the "norm" of members. This can be problematic if one member of the couple or family is learning new coping skills because others are likely to fight the healthy changes.

The husband is trying to maintain *homeostasis* (D). A *suprasystem* is an entity that is served by a number of component systems organized in interacting relationships. It is a high-level system in which other systems play subsystem roles. It is a way to describe the relationship between systems and is not a cause of the husband's behavior. *Negative entropy* is the exchange of energy and resources between systems that promote growth and transformation. It is an open system and is not the reason for the husband's behavior (see Unit I—Chapter 1, *Family Systems Theory*).

24. C

The problem-solving process consists of engaging, assessing, planning, intervening, evaluating, and terminating. Thus, planning is done after an assessment is complete (see Unit III—Chapter 11, *The Problem-Solving Model*).

25. A

Symbolization occurs when emotional feelings are associated with an object or, in this instance, the client's tattoo. The tattoo represents internal ideas, attitudes, and/or feelings of the client's mother. It evokes emotions that were present during her illness and represents her bravery (see Unit II—Chapter 7, *The Impact of Defense Mechanisms on Behavior*).

26. B

There is a strong relationship between research and policy in social work. Research findings are very useful to inform policy development and research agendas must be driven by issues and problems facing clients (A). Resources are scarce so ensuring that services are efficient and effective is critical and allocations of funds are made based upon evaluation outcomes (C). Researchers and policymakers do not speak the same professional language (D). Thus, report findings must be jargon-free and presented in a manner that a lay person can understand.

Policymakers often have to digest a lot of information. Research articles in academic journals are not easily understandable. Social workers should highlight research results in formats that are useful to those with decision-making authority and power, NOT give them the full reports (B) in which key findings may be difficult to identify (see Unit IV—Chapter 20, *The Policy Implications of Research Findings*).

27. D

Social workers should not engage in sexual activities or sexual contact with former clients because of the potential for harm to a client (D). If a social worker engages in conduct contrary to this prohibition or claims that an exception to this prohibition is warranted because of extraordinary circumstances, it is the social worker—not the client—who assumes the full burden of demonstrating that the former client has not been exploited, coerced, or manipulated, either intentionally or unintentionally.

Given the high relapse potential in substance abuse, the social worker in this case vignette should decline the invitation because the former client may need to use the residential facility again. Having a romantic relationship with the former client would preclude use of the residential facility in the future, resulting in fewer service options or harm to the client. In addition, there is a potential for unintentional exploitation, coercion, or manipulation given the nature of the services provided (see Unit V—Chapter 25, *Professional Boundary Issues*).

28. C

The primary benefit of peer supervision is the reciprocal learning through the sharing of experiences.

Peer supervision is based on the use of feedback to assist with self-directed learning and evaluation. Cost savings is not always associated with peer supervision, and is not an intended benefit. In order for peer supervision to be effective, it should occur regularly and be scheduled, rather than just happen "on the fly" (see Unit IV—Chapter 23, *The Models of Peer Supervision and Consultation*).

29. A

Maslow's hierarchy of needs can be divided into basic (or deficiency) needs (i.e., physiological, safety, social, and esteem) and growth needs (i.e., self-actualization). "Deficiency needs" arise due to deprivation, according to Maslow (see Unit I—Chapter 1, *Basic Human Needs*).

30. B

Social work interventions or treatments MUST be selected based upon the biopsychosocial–spiritual–cultural assessments of clients, which include the strengths that they possess and the identification of feasible and desired outcomes within larger service contexts (see Unit II—Chapter 8, *Criteria Used in Selecting Intervention/Treatment Modalities*).

31. A

This social worker is assessing need using secondary data, which is information that has already been collected for other purposes. Use of existing data is efficient since time and money associated with data collection are spared. However, the completeness of existing data, as well as its reliability, may be a concern. Thus, clients who could benefit from this group may not be identified (A) if they did not disclose that they had children or issues with childrearing on their intake applications—even if both are true. Data collection is only being done to assess the need for developing this service, and since clients are not actually being selected for the group, B is not a primary concern. Data to determine whether clients can benefit from an additional service can be collected within an agency and need is best assessed using objective or empirical data, so C and D are not reasons for alarm (see Unit IV—Chapter 15, *The Methods of Data Collection*).

32. B

Data analysis procedures begin with preparation that involves cleaning the data and checking it for accuracy (A). It is eventually coded for analysis and entered into a computer database given that data analysis is usually now done electronically (D). Social workers must balance the level of detail that is generated by data analysis to avoid its being so overwhelming as to increase the likelihood that major findings will be missed (C).

In most research, analyses include use of both descriptive AND inferential statistics, making B incorrect. Descriptive statistics provide information about the basic features of the data, such as simple summaries about the sample and the measures. However, inferential statistics are also important and are used to answer research questions or test models or hypotheses (see Unit IV—Chapter 15, *Data Analysis Procedures*).

33. A

The main tasks in families with young children include realigning the family system to make space for children, adopting and developing parenting roles, realigning relationships with families of origin to include parenting and grandparenting roles, and facilitating children to develop peer relationships. Adjusting to children taking a more central role in family maintenance is usually associated with later family life when the children reach adulthood (see Unit I—Chapter 2, *Family Life Cycle*).

34. D

Risk factors are associated with an increased likelihood that a client or community will be affected by, or become a perpetrator of, violence. Risk factors can occur at the individual, family, school, and community levels. Not everyone who is identified as being "at-risk" becomes involved in violence. Risk factors are negatively associated with protective factors (i.e., the more likely that risk factors are present, the less likely that there are existing protective factors) (see Unit I—Chapter 3, *The Dynamics of Domestic and Other Violence in Relationships*).

35. C

Paxil and Zoloft are both selective serotonin reuptake inhibitors (SSRIs) for the treatment of depression. Although the client may have other diagnoses, she is MOST likely diagnosed with Major Depressive Disorder, which would require the use of an antidepressant (see Unit II—Chapter 10, *Common Psychotropic and Non-Psychotropic Prescriptions and Over-the-Counter Medications and Their Side Effects*).

36. D

Social workers should not provide clinical services to individuals with whom they have had prior intimate relationships. Providing clinical services to a former girlfriend has the potential to be harmful to her and it may be difficult for the social worker and the former girlfriend to maintain appropriate professional boundaries (see Unit V—Chapter 25, *Professional Boundary Issues*).

37. C

The need for services to complement one another and not be duplicative is central to meeting client needs. Although several of the response choices may be correct, the development of service networks must directly help clients navigate the delivery system. Service networks ensure that duplication is reduced and integration is increased (C).

All of the other response choices focus on benefits for agencies or payers, which are not the MOST important function of service networks (see Unit IV—Chapter 18, *The Methods Used to Establish Service Networks or Community Resources*).

38. D

Social workers are allowed to defend themselves when sued by clients. Such a defense usually involves releasing information related to treatment.

However, social workers should limit the information released to that which is directly relevant to the allegations in the lawsuit (see Unit V—Chapter 26, *Legal and Ethical Issues Regarding Confidentiality, Including Electronic Information*).

39. B

Social workers should not terminate services to pursue social, financial, or sexual relationships with clients or when they believe that clients are making poor choices.

Social workers in fee-for-service settings may terminate services to clients who are not paying overdue balances if the financial contractual arrangements have been made clear, if clients do not pose an imminent danger to self or others, and if the clinical and other consequences of the current nonpayment have been addressed and discussed.

Social workers who are leaving employment settings can terminate with clients after informing them of appropriate options for the continuation of services and the benefits and risk of those options (see Unit III—Chapter 12, *The Techniques Used for Follow-Up*).

40. B

The *DSM-5* has eliminated the multiaxial diagnostic system. This change means that there is no longer an Axis V for indicating a client's Global Assessment of Functioning (GAF). In addition, the GAF Scale, which provided a numeric rating as an indicator of a client's well-being, has been eliminated. Instead, the World Health Organization Disability Assessment Schedule (WHODAS) is recommended as a tool to determine functioning and level of disability (see Unit II—Chapter 10, *Use of the Current* Diagnostic and Statistical Manual of Mental Disorders *of the American Psychiatric Association*).

41. C

Legal involvement was removed as a diagnostic criterion from the Substance-Related and Addictive Disorders category of the *DSM-5* (see Unit II—Chapter 10, *Use of the Current* Diagnostic and Statistical Manual of Mental Disorders *of the American Psychiatric Association*).

42. A

A mental status examination is a structured way of observing and describing a client's current state of mind, under the domains of appearance, attitude, behavior, mood and affect, speech, thought processes, thought content, perception, cognition, insight, and judgment. It is NOT a psychiatric evaluation aimed at diagnosing disorders. Many disorders or conditions cause delirium, such as alcohol or drug abuse or withdrawal and infections. Delirium involves a quick change between mental states (for example, from lethargy to agitation and back to lethargy). Symptoms that can be detected by a mental status examination include changes in alertness (usually more alert in the morning, less alert at night), awareness, orientation to time or place, memory, recall, and mood (personality changes) (see Unit II—Chapter 5, *The Components and Function of the Mental Status Examination* and Chapter 10, *The Symptoms of Neurologic and Organic Processes*).

43. B

In social work, triangulation indicates that multiple sources or methods are used to gather information and/or check results. A social worker may be more confident that he or she has the information needed or is accurate with conclusions drawn if different sources or methods lead to the same result. By using multiple sources or methods, a social worker can hope to overcome the weaknesses, intrinsic biases, and problems that can be associated with a single source or method (see Unit II—Chapter 6, *The Methods Used to Collect and Evaluate Collateral Information*).

44. C

Case presentations are also used in professional development and learning to provide input into options for treatment and to ensure services are being delivered effectively and efficiently. Although there is no universal format for a case presentation, it should contain demographic information, client and family history, and the presenting problem. In addition, a case presentation should contain the social worker's impressions and treatment recommendations. Thus, the summary described is unsatisfactory because it does not contain these elements (B) (see Unit IV—Chapter 19, *Elements of a Case Presentation*).

45. B

SOAP stands for Subjective, Objective, Assessment, and Plan. In the subjective and objective sections, a client's subjective and objective well-being are reported by the social worker. In the assessment section, a social worker pulls together these subjective and objective findings and consolidates them into a short assessment. A plan is then made based upon the assessment. The SOAP format does not outline cost and/or payment for services or insurance coverage (see Unit III—Chapter 12, *The Differential Use of Intervention/Treatement Techniques*).

46. D

Crisis intervention focuses on the here and now, is time-limited (most crises last from 4 to 6 weeks), is directive, and requires high levels of activity and involvement from social workers. Social workers' primary goal is to return clients to equilibrium and meet their immediate needs. Although the first response choice indicates that the support is short-term, it is incorrect because social workers focus on meeting basic needs, not "restoring clients' psychological capacities" (see Unit III—Chapter 11, *The Crisis Intervention/Treatment Approach*).

47. B

Equifinality refers to the concept that similar outcomes may stem from different experiences. Different early experiences in life (i.e., parental divorce, physical abuse, parental substance abuse) can lead to similar outcomes (i.e., diagnoses). In other words, there are many different experiences that can lead to the same problems, behaviors, and/or disorders (see Unit I—Chapter 1, *Systems Theory*).

48. C

The social worker has agreed to be an executrix, a woman legally named to carry out the provisions of a will. This is a conflict of interest or dual relationship and is unethical (C). Despite the social worker agreeing not to be compensated which often occurs when assuming this role, there is a risk that these responsibilities may interfere or conflict with those that are critical to social work services. For example, the social worker's duties as executrix may lead to discussions with the client that focus on financial matters, overshadowing the emotional feelings that the client may need to address as a result of his terminal illness diagnosis.

In addition, the social worker's education and training does not necessarily include the handling of legal and financial matters, leading to questions of competence as an executrix. Lastly, the social worker should not assume the legal authority to make decisions with regard to a client's personal or financial affairs, such as being his or her guardian or executrix, as these roles create a power differential between the two parties and can easily be conflicting, especially as related to matters of client self-determination (see Unit V—Chapter 25, *Dual Relationships*).

49. D

The receipt of an influenza immunization is the only response choice aimed at disease prevention. Participation in a support group and reducing strenuous activity are associated with managing or living with her COPD, which are tertiary prevention activities. Monitoring her medication is an activity aimed to slow the progression or long-term impacts of her conditions, including high blood pressure; thus medication monitoring is a secondary prevention activity (see Unit IV—Chapter 21, *Primary, Secondary, and Tertiary Prevention Strategies*).

50. C

Self-monitoring consists of clients systematically observing their own behavior. Most clients are not entirely aware of the extent to which they engage in various behaviors and/or antecedents or consequences of their actions. When clients are provided with the opportunity to observe their own behaviors carefully, dramatic changes often occur by the mere monitoring of the behaviors themselves (see Unit III—Chapter 12, *Client Self-Monitoring Techniques*).

51. D

Because the parents do not speak or understand English, the social worker should arrange for a qualified interpreter or translator. The use of the daughter to translate for her parents is not appropriate because the parents may be reluctant to identify the family's true needs to their daughter. In addition, the social worker will only hear what the parents say as per the daughter. Valuable information may be omitted or lost. The daughter also may not communicate what the social worker is saying in a manner that is appropriate or accurate (see Unit V—Chapter 26, *The Process of Obtaining Informed Consent*).

52. C

Expressed needs (C) are defined by the number of clients who have sought help. A major weakness of using expressed needs to justify program development is that it assumes that all those with needs seek help.

Social workers may want to use other methods for determining need to avoid this problem. Relative needs (A) are concerned with equity or comparing the needs of clients, with the goal of ranking them. Perceived needs (B) are defined by what clients think about their needs, with the standard set by each client. Absolute needs (D) are those which are needed for basic survival or well-being, such as food, shelter, clothing, and so on (see Unit IV—Chapter 18, *The Methods of Conducting a Needs Assessment*).

53. A

Tardive dyskinesia is a neurological disorder of involuntary movements that can be a side effect of long-term use of antipsychotic drugs. These medications may be used to treat Schizophrenia Spectrum and Other Psychotic Disorders. Symptoms include tongue protrusion, grimacing, lip smacking, or other involuntary movements of the head, face, neck, and tongue muscles (see Unit II—Chapter 10, *Common Psychotropic and Non-Psychotropic Prescriptions and Over-the-Counter Medications and Their Side Effects*).

54. D

Regardless of setting, a social worker who identifies that an ethical dilemma exists should determine an appropriate action in light of key social work values and principles as defined by the *Code of Ethics* (D). After implementation, the social worker should continue to monitor the situation and make further changes based upon these values and principles (see Unit V—Chapter 25, *Identification and Resolution of Ethical Dilemmas*).

55. B

Cognitive behavioral therapy aims to change patterns of thinking or behavior that are responsible for clients' difficulties. In this approach, the social worker assists the client to change attitudes and his or her behavior by focusing on the thoughts, images, beliefs, and attitudes that are held (cognitive processes) and replacing distorted thinking patterns with healthy ones (cognitive restructuring) (see Unit III—Chapter 11, *Psychotherapies*).

56. A

During middle adulthood, individuals establish careers, settle down within relationships, begin families, and develop a sense of being a part of the bigger picture. They give back to society through raising children, being productive at work, and becoming involved in community activities and organizations. By failing to achieve these objectives, individuals become stagnant and feel unproductive (see Unit I—Chapter 1, *The Psychosocial Model*).

57. D

Triangulation occurs when there is anxiety and tension between two individuals that may cause them not to communicate directly. In this situation, they communicate through a third person, leading to the formation of a triangle. Often the two people try to get the third to take each of their sides when disagreements arise (see Unit III—Chapter 12, *The Approaches to Family Therapy*).

58. C

Many of the problems reported by the couple appear to be caused by the alcohol use of the husband, including his unemployment, their financial problems, and her absence from the home. The social worker should FIRST determine the husband's willingness to address his drinking because many of the reported problems will not change if this behavior continues. Treating substance abuse and medical issues always comes first because they are often the etiological causes of negative impacts on psychosocial well-being (see Unit I—Chapter 1, *Addiction Theories*).

59. B

There are many influences on client behavior including individual, interpersonal, institutional, and community factors (A). In addition, human behavior can be explained through many theoretical perspectives, such as systems, conflict, rational choice, psychodynamic, developmental, social behavioral, and humanistic perspectives (C). Client behavior can also be explained using social constructivism which sees individuals as social beings who interact with each other and the physical world based on shared meanings (D).

Most importantly, social workers assess the interactions of clients with their environments and view all behavior using an ecological perspective, making B NOT true (see Unit I—Chapter 3, *Normal and Abnormal Behavior*).

60. D

The biopsychosocial–spiritual–cultural assessment provides critical information on the current/presenting issue or issues, including a client's past and present physical health and developmental milestones.

In order to be complete, the biological section should contain a client's medical history, developmental history, current medications, substance abuse history, and family history of medical illnesses. The information that was collected from the social worker in the case vignette is acceptable, but is not adequate or sufficient for a thorough assessment (see Unit II—Chapter 6, *The Components of a Biopsychosocial History*).

61. C

Legal practices refer to processes and policies to abide by laws dictated by government. Ethical practices refer to behavioral guidelines that result from personal morals and values, as well as standards of conduct that are set by social work professionals for those who are practicing within the field.

In this case vignette, the social worker is acting illegally, but ethically (C). The social worker is legally required to comply with the terms of the court order. By not providing the information, the social worker is breaking the law. However, by not placing the client and the client's family in danger, the social worker is fulfilling the primary mission of the profession: the enhancement of human well-being. Thus, the social worker is behaving ethically (see Unit V—Chapter 25, *Legal and Ethical Issues*).

62. C

Structural family therapy is based on the premise that there is an overall structure or organization that maintains family dysfunction. Restructuring is based on observing and manipulating interactions within therapeutic sessions. Enactments are suggested by social workers as ways to diagnose structure and provide openings for restructuring interventions (see Unit III—Chapter 12, *The Approaches to Family Therapy*).

63. D

Engagement is aimed at starting to build the therapeutic alliance. When a client is involuntary, he or she may be reluctant to trust the social worker and may think that the social worker does not understand his or her life circumstances. Thus, listening is the most effective action because it begins to build rapport. It shows the client that the social worker cares about what is being said and is nonjudgmental (see Unit III—Chapter 11, *The Methods Used in Working With the Unmotivated or Involuntary Client*).

64. D

Social workers in fee-for-service settings may terminate services to clients who are not paying overdue balances if the financial contractual arrangements have been made clear to clients, *if clients do not pose an imminent danger to self or others,* and if the clinical and other consequences of the current nonpayment have been addressed and discussed. In the case vignette, the client appears upset and states that he cannot "go on."

Such a statement may be an indication of suicide risk. The social worker must assess this risk and provide appropriate supports and referrals prior to termination (see Unit III—Chapter 12, *The Techniques Used for Follow-Up*).

65. D

The social worker should NOT begin the problem-solving process, including the intake or assessment, because she already has a prior relationship with the daughter in the school setting. The *Code of Ethics* states that social workers should take appropriate action to minimize any conflict of interest. An agreement for the social worker to be a consultant from the onset is also a conflict because the school social worker will then be serving her in different roles in each setting (see Unit IV—Chapter 25, *Dual Relationships*).

66. D

In *Jaffe v. Redmond* (1996), the U.S. Supreme Court ruled that the clients of clinical social workers have the right to privileged communication in federal courts. In various rulings, courts have identified numerous exceptions to clients' right of privileged communication. One of these exceptions is when a social worker's testimony about a client is required so that the social worker can defend himself or herself against a lawsuit filed by the client (D).

Disclosure of privileged information may also be permissible when a client threatens to commit suicide, has been abused or neglected, and/or may pose a threat to the public. Whether a social worker must disclose privileged information without a client's consent is often a matter of dispute and subject to relevant statutes, regulations, and judicial opinions (see Unit V—Chapter 26, *Legal and Ethical Issues Regarding Confidentiality, Including Electronic Information*).

67. B

Social workers who provide supervision are responsible for setting clear, appropriate, and culturally sensitive boundaries. They should not engage in any dual or multiple relationships with supervisees when there is a risk of exploitation of or potential harm to the supervisee.

However, in this case vignette, providing a written recommendation is an appropriate task for the social work supervisor as she would be aware of the supervisee's strengths and learning needs (B). It is critical that the recommendation be fair, accurate, and reflect only those areas of which the supervisor has direct knowledge. There is no inherent conflict of interest or dual relationship. She is instead promoting the professional development of the supervisee—an appropriate aim of a supervisor. The supervisor should not write the recommendation solely because it will benefit the agency, making D incorrect (see Unit V—Chapter 25, *Ethical Issues in Supervision and Management*).

68. D

Social workers should not engage in solicitation of testimonial endorsements (including solicitation of consent to use a client's prior statement as a testimonial endorsement) from current clients or from other people who, because of their particular circumstances, are vulnerable to undue influence (see Unit V—Chapter 28, *The Social Worker's Ethical Responsibility as a Professional*).

69. D

Self-image or how a client views himself or herself is critical to understand. Typically younger people describe themselves more in terms of personal traits, such as physical characteristics (D), whereas older people feel defined to a greater extent by their social roles (A). Emotional relationships (B) are critical during Erikson's early adulthood stage of intimacy versus isolation. Intellectual abilities (C) are described by Piaget as the formal operations stage, taking place age 11 through maturity which is marked by abstract thinking and assumption of adult roles. Thus, cognitive aptitudes are associated with positive self-image in adulthood (see Unit I—Chapter 3, *The Effects of Social Role on Self-Image*).

70. A

The client's actions are occurring during the first session. There is no indication that his outbursts are dangerous to himself or the social worker. Upon intake, clients are often upset and angry (even at themselves) for their current situations. The problem-solving process starts with engagement.

Because the case vignette is asking what the social worker should do FIRST, the answer should be directly related to engagement. Listening to the client as a way of building rapport will help facilitate change. The other answers will interfere with development of the therapeutic alliance and/or may come later in the process (see Unit III—Chapter 12, *Verbal and Nonverbal Communication Techniques*).

71. D

Releasing information is mandated under duty to warn and child abuse and neglect protections. A social worker should inform the client when seeking supervision and/or consultation and get the client's permission to release information. However, in instances in which disclosure is needed to prevent serious, foreseeable, and imminent harm to a client, the social worker can release only the minimum amount of information necessary to prevent such harm. The last response choice, using client information for a grant application, is unethical because it is not directly tied to client safety or duty to warn. Identifying client data should never be used in a grant application (see Unit V—Chapter 26, *Legal and Ethical Issues Regarding Confidentiality, Including Electronic Information*).

72. A

Risk factors can be categorized in a number of ways, but the most common distinctions in forensic risk assessments are between static and dynamic factors.

Static risk factors are historical factors that do not frequently fluctuate (i.e., genetic predisposition). Static risk factors include characteristics such as number of previous convictions, age, offense type, age at first conviction, and marital status. Many risk assessment tools are based entirely, or almost entirely, on static risk factors. A problem with such assessments is that it is virtually impossible for the offender to alter his or her risk assessment for the better.

Dynamic risk factors are those that can be changed by interventions, such as change in living situation, treatment of psychiatric symptoms, abstaining from drug and alcohol use, or access to weapons. Each client presents with a unique set of risk factors that require an individualized plan (see Unit II—Chapter 10, *The Characteristics of Perpetrators of Abuse and Neglect*).

73. A

The social worker is mandated to report this suspicion of child abuse. This question focuses on the FIRST action to be taken. According to the *Code of Ethics*, social workers should inform clients, to the extent possible, about the disclosure of confidential information and the potential consequences, when feasible, before the disclosure is made (A). This applies whether social workers disclose confidential information on the basis of a legal requirement or client consent.

In this case vignette, not telling the client about the need to report the suspected abuse prior to leaving the office will greatly affect the ongoing social worker–client trust. There also should be no delays due to any efforts to gather more information. The social worker should leave the interviewing of the youth to child protection agency staff who are trained in appropriate methods (see Unit V—Chapter 26, *Legal and Ethical Issues Regarding Mandatory Reporting of Abuse*).

74. B

According to the *Code of Ethics*, in instances when clients lack the capacity to provide informed consent, social workers should protect clients' interests by seeking permission from an appropriate third party (A), and informing clients consistent with the clients' level of understanding (C). In such instances, social workers should seek to ensure that the third party acts in a manner consistent with the clients' wishes and interests (D).

Clients' lack of capacity to provide informed consent may NOT require guardianship by others (B). In addition, there are many types of guardianship, including full and limited. Full guardianship means that another individual makes all legal, financial, and medical decisions whereas limited guardianship only allows another individual to make decisions in certain specified areas. (see Unit V—Chapter 26, *The Process of Obtaining Informed Consent*).

75. C

Social workers are charged with helping clients who have experienced discrimination by making policy and/or system changes. The social worker should not be seeking alternative methods to assist the couple to become parents because they have the right to adopt and the desire to do so. Although they may need support, developing coping skills or connecting them with others will not BEST assist the couple since these actions do not ultimately help them realize parenthood through adoption (see Unit IV—Chapter 20, *The Methods of Advocacy for Policies to Eliminate Discriminatory Practices*).

76. A

The mental development of older adults (age 65–79) and elders (age 80 and above) is characterized by being active learners and thinkers, but with declines in memory. In the oldest years, confusion may signal illness and/or medication problems. Older adults do continue to learn, but are not at their peak with regard to problem solving as a result of some declines associated with age (see Unit I—Chapter 1, *The Indicators of Normal Physical Growth and Development Throughout the Life Span*).

77. C

From age 6 to puberty, children begin to develop a sense of pride in their accomplishments. If they are encouraged and reinforced for their initiative, they begin to feel industrious and confident in their ability to achieve goals. If this initiative is not encouraged, it produces feelings of inferiority (see Unit I—Chapter 1, *The Psychosocial Model*).

78. B

The first step in ethical problem solving is to identify the ethical standards, as defined by the professional *Code of Ethics*, that may be compromised. The social worker should not rely on his supervisor or coworker to determine whether there is an ethical issue or dilemma. By referring directly to the *Code of Ethics*, the social worker can better weigh ethical issues in light of key social work values and principles, which are explicitly stated in this document (see Unit V—Chapter 25, *Identification and Resolution of Ethical Dilemmas*).

79. D

Evaluation methods can be classified as either qualitative or quantitative. In qualitative evaluations, data are collected through observations and/or interviews. Findings are generated via identification of themes in the language used and content contained in the communication observed or generated. The focus groups employed by the social worker are qualitative in nature.

Contrarily, quantitative evaluations are conducted by making numerical comparisons and statistical inferences. The social worker's comparison of the number of clients rehospitalized versus the number who were not is a quantitative approach. Since both qualitative and quantitative methods are being used, the social worker is using a mixed method approach to evaluation (see Unit IV—Chapter 15, *The Difference Between Quantitative and Qualitative Data*).

80. B

A role reversal is when two individuals switch roles. The 13-year-old girl has become the caregiver for her father, who is dependent due to his permanent injury. This is a role reversal because a parent would usually be meeting the physical and emotional needs of a child. The other response choices are all role issues, but do not contain a reversal in a parent–child relationship (see Unit I—Chapter 3, *The Effects of Social Role on Relationships*).

81. C

Protective factors are attributes that are associated with NOT engaging in dangerous behaviors. They are the opposite of risk factors. All of the options are associated with an increased likelihood of engaging in violence except the provision of clinical services for physical and behavioral care, which is a protective factor (see Unit II—Chapter 10, *The Indicators of Client Danger to Self and Others*).

82. C

Social workers should obtain clients' informed consent before audio or video recording of clients or permitting observation of services to clients by a third party. The consent forms should explicitly state that the sessions will be recorded and have information about who will listen to the recordings, how they will be stored, what will happen to the recordings after treatment has ended, and so forth. The risks and benefits associated with audio or video recordings should also be reviewed with clients as required for their informed consent. The permission of the client to make these recordings cannot be assumed or taken for granted as part of standard language about supervision on a consent form (see Unit V—Chapter 26, *The Process of Obtaining Informed Consent*).

83. D

Social workers should not terminate services to pursue a *social*, financial, or sexual relationship with a client (see Unit III—Chapter 12, *The Techniques Used for Follow-Up*).

84. B

The social worker was not aware of this potential conflict of interest at the start of treatment. Once it was discovered, steps such as minimizing contact and sitting across the room were taken to mitigate its existence. The client does not have to be referred to another social worker unless a change would be more comfortable for the client.

In addition, the social worker does not have to leave the church. However, the existence of this unanticipated conflict should be discussed so that the client is aware of its existence and strategies for minimizing its impact can be established (see Unit V—Chapter 25, *Dual Relationships*).

85. A

Shaping is used when it may be, or has been, difficult to achieve a goal or demonstrate a behavior. Shaping allows the goal or behavior to be achieved in steps, with each step positively reinforced. After a client achieves each successive step of the behavior or goal, a reward is received and the next step is presented until the desired end result is reached. If the client is having difficulty completing the steps, they should be broken down into smaller increments (see Unit III—Chapter 11, *Behavioral Approaches*).

86. D

Partialization is a good technique to assist clients in breaking down problems or goals into less overwhelming and more manageable components. However, it does not happen during engagement, but during planning and/or intervention. The remaining response choices do occur during engagement and are useful for helping alleviate the fears of resistant clients (see Unit III—Chapter 13, *The Process of Engagement in Social Work Practice*).

87. B

Because the receipt of the tickets by the social worker is clearly linked to the referrals, this is a form of "fee splitting," which is not allowed in social work practice. Social workers cannot receive incentives or remuneration for making referrals. The donation of the tickets to a local charity does not justify acceptance of these gifts. Although there is no additional cost to the colleague, the football tickets clearly have monetary value (see Unit V—Chapter 28, *The Social Worker's Ethical Responsibility to Colleagues*).

88. C

The evaluation is court-ordered and, therefore, the social worker does not need to get the consent of the client to perform services and/or release information to the court. However, it is essential that the social worker inform the client at the onset about what he has control over and what information will/will not be released. The client not wanting the social worker to release the information does not change the legal duty to do so (see Unit V—Chapter 26, *Legal and Ethical Issues Regarding Confidentiality, Including Electronic Information*).

89. C

Extinction is withholding a reinforcement that normally follows a behavior. Since the behavior is no longer reinforced, it will eventually cease. In this case vignette, the boy's reaction of crying is desired by the bullies, so removal of this response by walking away will hopefully reduce the incidents in the future (see Unit III—Chapter 11, *Behavioral Approaches*).

90. B

Youth who are not heterosexual and/or gender conforming face the same developmental tasks as their peers. However, they also face additional challenges that are different from their peers, such as the need to develop an identity with few role models. They may have a poor self-image; experience harassment, family rejection, stigma, social isolation; or engage in self-harm and/or risky behavior. They are often taunted and bullied, resulting in greater risk for mental and physical health complications compared with their peers (see Unit I—Chapter 4, *The Effects of Discrimination Based on Sexual Orientation, Gender and/or Gender Identification*).

91. C

The *Code of Ethics* indicates that consultation should follow all ethical standards, including avoiding conflicts of interest and maintaining boundaries. In the case vignette, the social worker's wife making changes to agency personnel policies that impact her husband is clearly a conflict of interest. Breaching this standard cannot be justified by the fact that the situation appears desperate and other resources are not evident. It remains a conflict of interest whether the wife charges for her services or not (see Unit V—Chapter 25, *Dual Relationships*).

92. B

Single-subject designs aim to determine if an intervention has the intended impact on a client. Data collected before the start of or during the withdrawal of services is a baseline (denoted by an "A") and is compared to that collected during service delivery (denoted by a "B"). Internal validity is the confidence that the social worker has that behavioral change is caused by an intervention. Thus, ABAB (A) is a design which is more effective in establishing internal validity than AB (C) because it provides two opportunities, rather than one, to observe changes in the target behavior once an intervention is introduced.

D is only a baseline measure with no intervention—denoted by a single "A"—so there is no ability to assess internal validity.

BAB (B) is the correct answer because it is the only design that begins with an intervention. Since the client in this case vignette is in crisis, it would be unethical to delay treatment to collect baseline data. The social worker must choose the design that begins with an intervention rather than a baseline assessment (see Unit IV—Chapter 15, *Social Work Research Designs*).

93. A

Termination is focused on reviewing accomplishments, anticipating how to address the problem if it arises in the future, and recognition of the loss to both the client and social worker that is connected to the ending of their relationship. Identifying *new* problems is NOT appropriate during termination (see Unit III—Chapter 11, *The Phases of Intervention/Treatment*).

94. C

Although the beliefs and behaviors of the family may be culturally based, there may be some adverse impacts to the children that threaten their well-being. It is not the responsibility of the social worker to determine the reasons for or impact of their actions. The social worker should get the child protection agency involved so they can investigate the situation further. There also may be some resources available to this family through the child protection agency (see Unit V—Chapter 26, *Ethical and Legal Issues Regarding Mandatory Reporting of Abuse*).

95. A

Hodgkin's disease is a type of lymphoma, a cancer of the lymphatic system. The first sign of Hodgkin's disease is often an enlarged lymph node. The disease can spread to nearby lymph nodes. Later, it may spread to the lungs, liver, or bone marrow. The exact cause is unknown (see Unit II—Chapter 6, *Basic Medical Terminology*).

96. B

Social workers should make clear distinctions between statements made and actions engaged in as private individuals as opposed to those as representatives of their employing agencies. In the case vignette, the social worker did not protest on agency time or identify himself in any way as an employee of the agency. He acted as a private individual and, therefore, his actions are ethical (see Unit V—Chapter 28, *The Social Worker's Ethical Responsibility to Broader Society*).

97. A

Congruence is the matching of awareness and experience with communication. It is essential that a client is able to express himself or herself and that this communication is reflective of his or her feelings. Congruence is essential for the vitality of a relationship and to facilitate true helping as part of the problem-solving process.

The client in the case vignette is saying that the relationship is "fine," but his physical symptoms clearly indicate that it is not. This is an example of a lack of congruence in his communication (see Unit III—Chapter 12, *The Concept of Congruence in Communication*).

98. A

Social workers should not disclose confidential information to third-party payers, including insurance companies, unless clients have authorized such disclosures. Only the first response choice includes reviewing the information requested with the client and getting his or her permission to submit (see Unit V—Chapter 26, *Legal and Ethical Issues Regarding Confidentiality, Including Electronic Information*).

99. C

Regression occurs when someone returns to an earlier state of being. In this instance, the daughter is using more infantile actions, such as "baby talk" and sucking her thumb. Because she did not do them immediately prior to the family's crisis, she may be relieving some of the anxiety of the situation through her dependency, which is further evidenced by clinging and wanting to be physically close to her mother (see Unit II—Chapter 7, *The Impact of Defense Mechanisms on Behavior*).

100. B

Case records are often an excellent source of information for evaluating the impacts of services. Because they are existing sources of data, there is no additional cost or time associated with their collection. However, there are a few limitations. If looking at records completed by multiple workers, there may be inconsistencies in recording styles or detail that may impact on evaluations. Also, information of interest may not be contained in the records and evaluations would need to be limited to information that is explicitly stated, which may not reflect all progress that has been made.

In addition, a client's own opinions and views on the process and outcomes of service delivery, which are also critical, may not be fully captured in the record (see Unit IV—Chapter 15, *The Methods of Data Collection*).

101. A

Permanency planning is an approach to child welfare that is based on the belief that children need permanence to thrive. Child protection services should focus on getting children into and maintaining permanent homes (see Unit II—Chapter 8, *Permanency Planning*).

102. A

When the ego is comfortable with feelings and/or behaviors, a client is said to be ego-syntonic. However, if a client is bothered by some of his or her feelings and/or behaviors, he or she would be ego-dystonic (ego alien) (see Unit I—Chapter 1, *Psychoanalytic Theory*).

103. B

Cluster B includes the personality disorders that are characterized by dramatic, emotional, and erratic behavior. It includes Borderline Personality Disorder, Narcissistic Personality Disorder, Histrionic Personality Disorder, and Antisocial Personality Disorder. Schizoid Personality Disorder and Paranoid Personality Disorder are in Cluster A (odd and eccentric behavior) and Obsessive-Compulsive Personality Disorder is in Cluster C (anxious and fearful behavior) (see Unit II—Chapter 10, *Use of the Current* Diagnostic and Statistical Manual of Mental Disorders *of the American Psychiatric Association*).

104. A

The *Code of Ethics* prohibits social workers who function as supervisors or educators from engaging in sexual activities or contact with supervisees, students, trainees, or other colleagues over who they exercise professional authority.

The social worker engaged in a dual relationship with her supervisee, which is unethical (see Unit V—Chapter 25, *Ethical Issues in Supervision and Management*).

105. D

Social workers often use collateral sources when collecting information to effectively treat clients. Prior provider information can be vital because it can relay what has been effective and ineffective in the past (D). Family members and friends may be collateral sources, providing important information about the length or severity of issues or problems; they can supplement information obtained directly from clients and provide contextual or background information that clients may not know.

It is essential that a social worker get informed consent from clients prior to reaching out to collateral sources (see Unit IV—Chapter 19, *The Use of Collaterals to Obtain Relevant Information*).

106. A

Agranulocytosis is a lowering of the white blood cell count that requires monitoring via bloodwork. A large number of drugs have been associated with agranulocytosis, including antiseizure, antibiotic, and antipsychotic medications such as Clozaril. All clients receiving Clozaril must get baseline bloodwork and be enrolled in the Clozaril National Registry, which records bloodwork results and adverse impacts from taking Clozaril (see Unit II—Chapter 10, *Common Psychotropic and*

Non-Psychotropic Prescriptions and Over-the-Counter Medications and Their Side Effects).

107. D

Negative punishment is when a desirable stimulus is removed following an undesirable behavior for the purpose of decreasing or eliminating the behavior. In the case vignette, the client takes away her daughter's cell phone (a desirable stimulus) with the desire to decrease her homework incompletion and tardiness (targeted behaviors) (see Unit III—Chapter 11, *Behavioral Approaches*).

108. A

According to the *Code of Ethics*, to obtain informed consent social workers must use clear and understandable language with clients to review service purpose and risks (B), limits due to third-party payers (C), and right of refusal or withdrawal (D).

Although it would be helpful for clients to receive information about the setting in which services are to be provided, reviewing the agency's mission (A) is not required. In addition, not all services are delivered in agency settings, but informed consent elements must be reviewed universally, even when services are rendered in private practices or government offices (see Unit V—Chapter 26, *The Process of Obtaining Informed Consent*).

109. A

A task-centered approach aims to quickly engage clients in the problem-solving process and to maximize their responsibility for treatment outcomes. The focus is on the "here and now." The problem is partialized into clearly delineated tasks to be addressed consecutively (*assessment leads to goals, which lead to tasks*). Termination, in this modality, begins almost immediately with the onset of treatment (see Unit III—Chapter 11, *Task Centered Practice*).

110. D

When social workers engage in group work, they should seek agreement among group members concerning preserving the confidentiality of information shared. However, social workers should inform members that they cannot guarantee that all group members will honor such agreements. Group members do not have the same legal obligations that social workers do to keep information private and protected. However, social workers engaged in group work should adhere to the same professional standards that govern their own conduct (see Unit V—Chapter 26, *Legal and Ethical Issues Regarding Confidentiality, Including Electronic Information*).

111. C

There are four main methods to assess reliability. The social worker is comparing the results of two tests that are believed to assess the same domain—client well-being. This method is used to establish parallel forms reliability (C).

Test–retest reliability (A) involves determining whether an assessment yields the same data in two separate administrations. Interrater or interobserver reliability (B) occurs when assessments of different raters or observers are found to be consistent. Internal consistency reliability (D) is confirmed when items within a single survey or test, thought to measure the same construct, yield consistent results (see Unit IV—Chapter 15, *The Methods Used to Assess Reliability and Validity in Social Work Research*).

112. A

Validation shows empathetic understanding of the client's problems. It lets the client know that she is not alone and others are experiencing the same feelings or difficulties. By realizing that her belief is one that is shared by those in similar situations, the client feels less isolated and gains strength by the realization that others have worked through the problem(s) that she is experiencing (see Unit III—Chapter 12, *The Use of Partializing, Supporting, Focusing, Clarifying, Confronting, Interpreting, and Reflecting*).

113. B

Social work interviews are always purposeful and involve verbal and nonverbal communication between social workers and clients through which ideas, attitudes, and feelings are exchanged. The aim is to gather important information used in the problem-solving process.

Social work interviews are designed to serve the interest of clients. Questions in a social work interview should be *tailored* to the specifics of a client, *not generic*, "one size fits all" inquiries.

The purpose of the social work interview can be informational, diagnostic, or therapeutic (see Unit II—Chapter 5, *The Principles and Techniques of Interviewing*).

114. A

Behavior change is best understood as a process with different stages of readiness. For most clients, behavior change occurs gradually over time, with a client progressing from being uninterested, unaware, or unwilling to make a change (precontemplation), to considering a change (contemplation), to deciding and preparing to make a change (preparation). This is followed by definitive action that attempts to maintain the new behavior over time (maintenance).

Contemplation is the first time that there is some movement toward change as a client, while ambivalent about changing, may weigh the benefits versus costs (i.e., time, expense, effort) of change. The client in the case vignette is willing to examine what his life would be like if change occurred; this is contemplation (see Unit II—Chapter 5, *The Methods Used to Assess Motivation and Resistance*).

115. D

Social workers should take appropriate steps to ensure that participants in research have access to appropriate supportive services (D).

The remaining response choices are NOT true for the following reasons. Social workers engaged in research must always obtain voluntary and written informed consent from participants, even when they are clients of their agencies. When research participants are clients, separate informed consent (A) is essential because of the risk of perceived or actual coercion to participate or the belief by clients that their participation is linked to service receipt. Social workers should never design or conduct research that does not use consent procedures—such as certain forms of naturalistic observation (B) and archival research—unless rigorous and responsible review of the research has found it to be justified by its prospective scientific, educational, or applied value and equally effective alternative procedures that do not involve waiver of consent are not feasible. Lastly, social workers must promote and facilitate research to contribute to the development of knowledge (C) (see Unit IV—Chapter 15, *Research Ethics*).

116. A

In social work, human behavior of clients is often explained using systems, conflict, rational choice, social constructionist, psychodynamic, developmental, social behavioral, and humanistic perspectives. Rational choice believes clients behave in a manner that tries to maximize rewards and minimize costs. A psychodynamic perspective is based on the view that unconscious, as well as conscious, mental activity serve as the motivating forces in human behavior. A developmental perspective sees human development as occurring in defined, age-related stages, which build upon one another and are distinct. However, the humanistic perspective is based on seeing each client as unique and responsible for choices made. Accordingly, clients have the capacity to change themselves because human behavior is driven by a desire for growth, personal meaning, and competence (see Unit I—Chapter 3, *Normal and Abnormal Behavior*).

117. D

Cultural competence involves working in conjunction with natural, informal support, and helping networks (i.e., neighborhoods, coworkers, churches, spiritual leaders, healers). The coworker is probably a member of the client's support network and can be useful in the problem-solving process. It is the client's decision of whether information can be shared (see Unit V—Chapter 26, *Legal and Ethical Issues Regarding Confidentiality, Including Electronic Information*).

118. C

Empowerment is a multidimensional social work process that helps clients gain control over their lives. It encourages clients to use their strengths and skills to make changes that they desire. Only C focuses on clients solving their own problems, a fundamental concept in empowerment (see Unit III—Chapter 13, *The Use of the Social Worker/Client Relationship as an Intervention/Treatment Tool*).

119. C

Social and political action is a social worker's ethical responsibility to broader society. Social workers should engage in social and political action that seeks to ensure that people have equal access to and expanded choice for needed resources (C). Social workers should promote conditions that encourage respect for cultural and social diversity.

Although empowering clients and educating them about the value of social and political action are important, the *Code of Ethics* does not mandate client behavior, but serves as a guide for social workers' actions—making D incorrect (see Unit V—Chapter 28, *The Social Worker's Ethical Responsibility to Broader Society*).

120. D

Ego strength is the ability of the ego to effectively deal with the demands of the id, the superego, and reality. It is a basis for resilience and helps maintain emotional stability by coping with internal and external stress.

Indicators of positive ego strength include clients:
- not getting overwhelmed by their moods
- using painful events to strengthen themselves
- taking responsibility for actions
- holding themselves accountable
- NOT blaming others
- accepting themselves with their limitations

(see Unit II—Chapter 9, *The Methods Used in Assessing Ego Strengths*).

121. C

Group development can be characterized by the sequential steps of forming (preaffiliation), storming (power and control), norming (intimacy), performing (differentiation), and adjourning (separation/termination) (see Unit I—Chapter 2, *Models of Group Development*).

122. D

The client has experienced discrimination. While the social worker must be concerned about the impacts of this discrimination, such as feelings of hopelessness and depression (C), he or she has an ethical mandate to assist the client to fight the housing discrimination (D) or the root cause of the problem.

Advocacy is essential to meeting the client's goal because she she is discouraged and thinking that change cannot occur but "would not like this treatment to happen to others." The social worker must work with the client to have her voice heard and educate her about tangible steps that can be taken to end such practices. A, B, and C may be included or addressed in treatment, but her goals have to "focus on" the discrimination because the feelings and alternative housing resulted from this core problem (see Unit IV—Chapter 19, *The Use of Advocacy Among Agencies and Disciplines*).

123. B

Referent power is derived from interpersonal relationships with others (B). It arises from charisma, as well as personal connections with key people who have decision-making authority and are influential.

Legitimate power (A) is also known as positional power. It comes from one's position within an organizational hierarchy. Expert power (C) arises from possessing knowledge or expertise in a particular area. Those with expert power perform critical tasks, are deemed indispensable, and are held in high regard. Reward power (D) results from the ability to influence the allocation of incentives, such as salary increments, positive appraisals, and/or promotions (see Unit IV—Chapter 19, *The Use of Informal and Formal Power Structures*).

124. D

Clients with Borderline Personality Disorder or its associated features are more likely to engage in transference. Transference-focused psychotherapy is, therefore, often used with clients who have Borderline Personality Disorder. Transference is unconscious, can be used therapeutically, and/or does not have to be sexual in nature (see Unit III—Chapter 13, *The Concept of Transference and Countertransference*).

125. C

Conversion is when mental conflict or disturbance is transferred into a physical symptom to relieve anxiety. The loss of movement in her arm may have resulted from the desire to strike her child (see Unit II—Chapter 7, *The Impact of Defense Mechanisms on Behavior*).

126. B

If the social worker has concerns about the consultant's recommendations and thinks they will be detrimental to clients, he or she cannot ethically implement them, but must make clear why such a decision is being made. It would be advisable for the social worker to speak to his or her supervisor, and even the agency director or the consultant if permitted and appropriate, to discuss the concerns. However, the social worker should not implement them because of the consultant's educational background and expertise or let the agency director decide. The social worker is also not responsible for hiring another consultant because the first one was contracted by the agency. In instances like the one described, the recommendations of consultants may not ultimately be implemented by the organization, may be modified based on the concerns, and/or may be studied further for their appropriateness (see Unit IV—Chapter 19, *The Approaches Used in Consultation*).

127. D

Statutory law is set by "statutes" or laws made by legislatures, locally or on the state or federal levels. Common law is made by judges. It is created by the courts deciding cases. When a court decides a case, it sets a "precedent" or binding example that other courts follow. When a large number of judges decide the same kind of case or question of law in the same way, the decision becomes "common law" (see Unit IV—Chapter 20, *Interpreting Legislation to Clients*).

128. A

None of the behaviors listed in the response choices are illegal when engaged in by social workers (unless they violate state statute or regulation related to the practice of social work). Adults can legally write recommendations, date other adults, borrow money, and/or have business relationships. However, dating, borrowing money, and/or having a dual (business) relationship with clients are prohibited by the *Code of Ethics*.

A social worker can certainly write a recommendation for a current (or even former) client, as long as the content is based on information collected as part of service delivery and the social worker is not making assertions or drawing conclusions beyond the scope of the therapeutic relationship (see Unit V—Chapter 25, *Dual Relationships*).

129. D

Social work roles in the problem-solving process include consultant, advocate, case manager, catalyst, broker, mediator, facilitator, instructor, mobilizer, resource allocator, and so forth.

Problems can arise when a client is not clear about a social worker's role. Initial clarification should be made during engagement and should be discussed during the therapeutic process if the role of a social worker changes. The social worker in this case vignette must address this situation immediately and should not ignore the comment. In addition, the social worker should not make this a therapeutic issue and question the client further about it because it may simply result from a lack of understanding on the client's part (see Unit III—Chapter 13, *The Methods Used to Clarify the Role of the Social Worker* and *The Social Worker's Role in the Change Process*).

130. C

DSM-5 does not include Caffeine Use Disorder, although research shows that as little as two to three cups of coffee can trigger a withdrawal effect marked by tiredness or sleepiness. There is sufficient evidence to support this as a condition, but it is not yet clear to what extent it is a clinically significant disorder. To encourage further research on the impact of this condition, Caffeine Use Disorder is included in Section III of the *DSM-5* (see Unit II—Chapter 10, *Use of the Current* Diagnostic and Statistical Manual of Mental Disorders *of the American Psychiatric Association*).

131. A

Connectedness between human beings can be understood within an *evolutionary* context. Children come into the world biologically preprogrammed to form attachments with others that will help them to survive. In addition, some theories suggest that attachment is a set of *learned behaviors*. Insecure attachment systems have been linked to psychiatric disorders and can result in clients reacting in a hostile and rejecting manner. Cultural influences impact on attachment. Thus, attachment and bonding must be viewed, keeping in mind a client's cultural background and traditions (see Unit I—Chapter 1, *The Concept of Attachment and Bonding*).

132. B

In the Asian culture, there is usually respect for elders and a hierarchical family structure with strictly prescribed roles and rules of behavior. The family and extended kinship network is often involved in treatment. The grandparents are traditionally viewed as the most knowledgeable and their opinions are held in high esteem (see Unit I—Chapter 4, *The Influence of Culture, Race, Religion/Spirituality and/or Ethnicity on Behaviors and Attitudes*).

133. A

Displacement is directing an impulse, wish, or feeling toward a less threatening object. The client is getting angry at his family instead of expressing this emotion with his boss (see Unit II—Chapter 7, *The Impact of Defense Mechanisms on Behavior*).

134. B

Social workers should protect the confidentiality of clients during legal proceedings to the extent permitted by law. When a court of law orders social workers to disclose confidential or privileged information without client consent, especially that which can be harmful, social workers should request that the court maintain the records "under seal." Filing "under seal" allows sensitive or confidential information to be filed with a court without becoming a matter of public record (B) (see Unit V— Chapter 26, *Legal and Ethical Issues Regarding Confidentiality, Including Electronic Information*).

135. C

Summarization seeks to bring together the important points of a discussion and to heighten awareness of progress made. It omits irrelevant information and organizes pertinent aspects of the interaction. It provides a sense of closure at the completion of a discussion. During summarization, social workers and clients strive to grasp the significance of what has been said, to formulate the meaning of the information, and to achieve new understandings.

In this case vignette, the social worker uses summarization at the end of a session to pull together the meaning of what has been said by each family member. This technique allows the family to better understand the common theme in session discussions and perhaps gain a new understanding about the behaviors of others (see Unit III—Chapter 12, *The Methods Used in Summarizing Communication*).

136. A

Entropy is associated with disorder in a system. Higher entropy means higher disorder and lower availability of the system's energy to do useful work. Although the concept of entropy originated in thermodynamics, it is applicable to communications, psychology, and sociology. The term is often used in systems theory (see Unit I—Chapter 1, *Systems Theory*).

137. B

Social workers should only seek the advice and counsel of colleagues who have demonstrated knowledge, expertise, and competence related to the subject of the consultation (B).

When seeking consultation, social workers need to get the permission of clients if any identifying information will be shared. Social workers should also only disclose information that is absolutely necessary when interacting with consultants. Lastly, social workers should follow all ethical standards, including avoiding conflicts of interest, when choosing consultants. Selecting family members or close friends as consultants would create dual relationships and violate professional boundaries (see Unit IV—Chapter 19, *The Approaches Used in Consultation*).

138. C

There are four different ways to assess reliability or consistency. Inter-rater reliability uses different independent raters/observers to see if there are consistent estimates of the behavior. Alternative or parallel forms uses two means of data collection constructed in the same way to see if they yield the same result. Test–retest reliability determines if assessments fluctuate from one time to another. Internal consistency looks at measurements within a test or assessment to see if they yield comparable results. Only interrater requires two or more independent staff to record the data (see Unit IV—Chapter 15, *The Methods Used to Assess Reliability and Validity in Social Work Research*).

139. C

External validity is concerned with the ability to generalize the results. In this case vignette, the director of the agency is worried about the effectiveness of the program with adults versus children (see Unit III—Chapter 14, *Utilization of Research Results in Practice*).

140. A

Despite the client's report that she will not act on her thoughts, she is at risk because she has these feelings. The case vignette does not describe the social worker taking any action. A safety assessment will determine the severity of the depression and whether she is at risk for a suicide attempt. It must be done FIRST before any other action is taken (see Unit I—Chapter 1, *Basic Human Needs*).

141. A

Folie à deux is very rare and describes when identical or similar psychiatric disorders affect two or more people, who usually have a close relationship. These disorders often involve delusions, especially those that are paranoid (see Unit II—Chapter 10, *The Symptoms of Mental and Emotional Illness*).

142. C

The "reasonable suspicion" of the social worker makes reporting to the child protection agency necessary. This report should not be delayed to monitor the situation and/or collect additional information. The social worker should tell the mother of her need to report and support the mother and child through the process. Having the mother present when the social worker contacts the child protection agency may alleviate the mother's fears about what is being disclosed and the social worker can help the mother to understand the next steps after such a report is made (see Unit V—Chapter 26, *Ethical and Legal Issues Regarding Mandatory Reporting of Abuse*).

143. C

Human development in social work uses a strengths-based approach to understanding how humans develop and grow throughout the life course. It does NOT pathologize or describe development in terms of problems that focus on deficit. Such an approach is often used in a medical model of medicine. Social work focuses on resiliency and adaptation (see Unit I—Chapter 1, *Theories of Human Growth and Development Through the Life Span*).

144. A

A subpoena is a request by the court for information. The social worker must respond. When receiving a subpoena, a social worker should claim privilege and not turn over records unless the court issues a subsequent court order to do so. A subpoena and a court order are not the same.

When a social worker gets a court order, he or she should try to limit its scope and/or ask that the records be sealed (see Unit V—Chapter 26, *Legal and Ethical Issues Regarding Confidentiality, Including Electronic Information*).

145. A

Erikson's first stage, which occurs in the first year of life, focuses on children learning the ability to trust others; they learn whether their needs can be met by others and that insecurities can develop if these attachments are not nurturing. Children then go through three states (autonomy versus shame/doubt, initiative versus guilt, and industry versus inferiority) that all focus on autonomy and exertion of independence. In adulthood, there is a need to begin to connect with others as part of intimacy versus isolation (see Unit I—Chapter 1, *The Psychosocial Model*).

146. D

Cultural competence involves working in conjunction with natural, informal support, as well as helping networks (i.e., neighborhoods, churches, spiritual leaders, healers). The social worker should help prepare the client for the meeting and provide other support as needed.

The social worker should not be evaluating the client's reasons for seeking guidance from her priest. In addition, the biopsychosocial–spiritual–cultural functioning of the client is the focus of treatment; the client should not feel that the social worker is not interested or able to address and consider her religious/spiritual concerns (see Unit I—Chapter 4, *The Influence of Culture, Race, Religion/Spirituality, and/or Ethnicity on Behaviors and Attitudes*).

147. B

Consent is the agreement of clients or their authorized representatives, who have legal authority to make decisions for them to participate in treatment.

Assent is a term used to express willingness to participate in treatment by clients who are too young to give consent or have been deemed by the courts as incapable of making legal decisions. Assent by itself is not sufficient. If assent is given, social workers must still obtain consent from clients' parents or guardians.

Court-mandated services do not require clients' consent, but clients should be advised at the onset what they have control over and what they do not in these situations. In some states, children can access limited services without parental consent, but the terms still have distinct meanings (see Unit V—Chapter 26, *The Process of Obtaining Informed Consent*).

148. A

When social workers involve consultants or others in the feedback process related to client care, clients should provide consent.

Social workers should ask for feedback in difficult circumstances—not just when circumstances appear neutral or positive. Sometimes the best learning can come from those who will be critical. Feedback is especially important at key decision points. Social workers must always be clear about why feedback is needed and what will be done with the information (see Unit III—Chapter 12, *The Methods Used to Obtain and Provide Feedback*).

149. B

Although all of the response choices reflect changes to the *DSM-5*, Disruptive Mood Dysregulation Disorder is listed under Depressive Disorders, not Neurodevelopmental Disorders. Recognition of this diagnosis is meant to address concerns about potential overdiagnosis and overtreatment of Bipolar Disorder in children. It can be used for children up to age 18 who exhibit persistent irritability and frequent episodes of extreme behavioral dyscontrol (see Unit II—Chapter 10, *Use of the Current Diagnostic and Statistical Manual of Mental Disorders of the American Psychiatric Association*).

150. A

Community organization and development are methods of intervention that focus on addressing social problems. Social workers assist communities in identifying problems, causes, and solutions aimed at improving the lives of community members. Basic tenets of these activities require full participation of community members in the change and development efforts.

In the case vignette, there are many broad reasons cited for the development of youth programs. In order to be most effective, the social worker should FIRST help community members prioritize the youth problems to be addressed; without a more defined focus, the program will not be successful. It would be impossible for a single youth program to positively address all the problems noted, so the social worker should initially work to narrow the goals of the program, thereby increasing its likelihood of success (see Unit IV—Chapter 18, *The Development of Programs and Services to Meet Community Needs*).

151. A

Social workers should seek the advice and counsel of colleagues whenever such consultation is in the best interests of clients, but should only do so from colleagues who have demonstrated knowledge, expertise, and competence related to the subject of the consultation.

Although willing, the colleague probably does not have expertise and competence related to the disorder because both social workers began working at the agency upon graduation and this disorder is not commonly treated in this agency setting. There is no conflict of interest in having a colleague in the same agency provide consultation if the colleague has the requisite knowledge and skills (see Unit IV—Chapter 23, *The Social Worker's Responsibility to Seek and Receive Appropriate Supervision*).

152. A

The woman is court-ordered to receive an evaluation and services from an agency. As this client is involuntary, the social worker should have told her at the initial meeting that information would be shared with the court and the scope of what was to be submitted. In this instance, the client does not have privilege (B) and a signed release is not needed (C). Trying to outreach to the client via other means of communication (D) is a good idea, but the social worker is required to submit the report, which is not mentioned in this response choice.

The protection of confidential information requires great care. Social workers should know the exceptions to confidentiality and how to handle practice records when working with court-ordered clients. In this case vignette, the social worker should send the court the report and information about the client not coming to appointments (A) (see Unit IV—Chapter 17, *The Management of Agency/Practice Records*).

153. B

Accreditation should not be used to justify higher salaries for agency workers (B), but instead to ensure that clients get the most effective services possible and resources are used appropriately and efficiently.

Accreditation provides accountability to the public (A) by having agency practices and outcomes reviewed (C) by an external entity which is objective. Accreditation reviews help social workers and other agency personnel learn more about best practices and how to critically think and analyze service delivery. Thus, accreditation aids in professional development of those involved (D) (see Unit IV—Chapter 16, *Accreditation and Program Reviews*).

154. A

The process and goals for completion of a child custody evaluation are vastly different than those used in marriage counseling. Making child custody recommendations would be inappropriate because both parties were not informed from the onset that discussions and information collected would be used for this purpose. In addition, both parties are current counseling clients. Child custody evaluation recommendations often are not favorable and/or acceptable to both parents. Providing such a recommendation may, therefore, not be in the best interest of or promote positive well-being for one or both of the current clients (see Unit V—Chapter 25, *Dual Relationships*).

155. C

Genetic counseling helps individuals understand the risk for an inherited disease or abnormal pregnancy outcome, discussing with men and women their chances of having children who are affected. When providing such counseling, social workers must have the experience and knowledge to help families understand birth defects and how inheritance works. They provide information that helps families make personal decisions about pregnancy and genetic testing.

All of the groups mentioned may be at risk and could benefit from genetic counseling EXCEPT new mothers suffering postpartum depression. Although there is evidence that depression may be due to both "nature and nurture," the best assistance for new mothers with a family history of postpartum depression is to be aware of the signs of depression and get assistance immediately if they recur. Genetic counseling will not help those who have already experienced such depression; these mothers will need to have heightened awareness of their vulnerability if they get pregnant in the future (see Unit I—Chapter 1, *Human Genetics*).

156. A

Summative evaluations examine the outcomes of programs. Since prisoner reentry programs attempt to ease the transition of those who are leaving jail or prison and provide support to avoid rearrest, reincarceration (A) is a good indicator of service effectiveness.

Program satisfaction (B) and length of services (D) are formative evaluation criteria because formative evaluations focus on the process of delivering services. Understanding clients' feelings and experiences is useful feedback that can help drive program improvements. It is also critical to assess whether clients stay in services or drop out.

Criminal history (C) is an extraneous variable that has to be controlled when assessing outcomes because it can be related to client success; however, it is not an outcome measure (see Unit IV—Chapter 16, *The Methods Used to Evaluate Agency Programs*).

157. C

Negative reinforcement is the removal of an aversive (negative) stimulus with the goal of increasing the targeted behavior. In the case vignette, the husband says that he will do more around the house (targeted behavior) if the wife stops (removes) the nagging (negative stimulus) (see Unit III—Chapter 11, *Behavioral Approaches*).

158. D

Most individuals who are transgender do not undergo sexual reassignment surgery. Gender identity is distinct from sexual orientation, and those who are transgender can be heterosexual, homosexual, bisexual, pansexual, polysexual, or asexual. A cross-dresser is someone who enjoys dressing in the opposite gender's clothing, but may not identify with that gender. Those who are transgender often experience stigma, bias, or discrimination due to myths and misconceptions (see Unit I—Chapter 4, *The Influence of Sexual Orientation, Gender, and/or Gender Identification on Behaviors and Attitudes*).

159. B

A delusion is a false or erroneous belief that usually involves a misinterpretation of perceptions or experiences. A delusion is a belief that is held despite evidence to the contrary. A hallucination involves the senses. An auditory hallucination—hearing something that is not said—is the most common type. In this case vignette, the client had a false, fixed belief despite a lack of supporting evidence, but there was no indication that it resulted from actually seeing or hearing anything that would support these beliefs (see Unit II—Chapter 10, *The Symptoms of Mental and Emotional Illness*).

160. D

The client and social worker are in the planning stage of the problem-solving process. Planning comes after engagement and assessment. The first two response choices are interventions. However, in order to determine their appropriateness, the social worker must clarify with the client the desired outcomes and what she means by "being more assertive." Clearly defining the problem and how it relates to positive and negative aspects of the client's life will assist in the formation of an appropriate intervention, treatment, or service plan (see Unit II—Chapter 8, *The Client's Role in the Intervention Process*).

161. B

Most practice situations are best handled with no self-disclosure by the social worker. In the case vignette, the social worker should not discuss her own marital breakup and remarriage. Instead, she should instill hope by providing the client with a feeling that she will be heard by the social worker and have the opportunity to address her feelings. The woman may benefit from meeting others who are going through similar experiences, but referring her at this point in the problem-solving process is not an appropriate method for instilling hope. The client's comments are indicative of those who are in this situation and do not alone indicate risk for self-harm (see Unit III—Chapter 12, *Verbal and Nonverbal Communication Techniques*).

162. A

The client's behavior is consistent with Bipolar Disorder. He was depressed upon admission and then appeared to be manic during the hospitalization. Only Lithium, out of those medications listed, is a mood stabilizer. Elavil is an antidepressant, Ativan is an antianxiety agent, and Haldol is an antipsychotic medication (see Unit II—Chapter 10, *Common Psychotropic and Non-Psychotropic Prescriptions and Over-the-Counter Medications and Their Side Effects*).

163. A

Persistent Depressive Disorder, formerly known as Dysthymic Disorder or Dysthymia, is a new diagnosis in the *DSM-5*. It requires that a depressed mood occur for most of the day, for more days than not, and for at least 2 years (at least 1 year for children and adolescents). It represents a consolidation of Chronic Major Depressive Disorder and Dysthymic Disorder (see Unit II—Chapter 10, *Use of the Current* Diagnostic and Statistical Manual of Mental Disorders *of the American Psychiatric Association*).

164. A

Sometimes missing appointments after achieving stated goals can be an indicator that the client is ready to terminate. The client may want to practice her new skills independently and does not think that she needs to continue to see the social worker. There is no indication that a new problem has emerged or the client is dissatisfied. Codependency occurs when a client does not want to end the therapeutic relationship despite having achieved goals. The client's behavior most likely means that she is ready to stop seeing the social worker (see Unit III—Chapter 11, *The Indicators of Client Readiness for Termination*).

165. A

Tertiary prevention focuses on managing complicated, long-term diseases, injuries, or illnesses. The goal is to prevent further deterioration and maximize quality of life because the disease is now established. Other types of prevention strategies are aimed at preventing the development of a disease and/or slowing its progression or minimizing its long-term impacts. Hospice is associated with care as a result of a life-limiting illness. The case vignette does not indicate that the cancer is terminal, so the management of the pain may be associated with treatment that is occurring (see Unit IV—Chapter 21, *Primary, Secondary, and Tertiary Prevention Strategies*).

166. D

The client file cannot be shared with the principal even if it will assist the client. Social workers should not be sharing information without consent unless necessary to prevent harm to self or others (see Unit V—Chapter 26, *Legal and Ethical Issues Regarding Confidentiality, Including Electronic Information*).

167. B

The standards that govern social work practice address the use of physical contact with clients. Setting clear, appropriate, and culturally sensitive boundaries that govern physical contact are essential for professional practice. Social workers should not engage in physical contact with clients when there is a possibility of psychological harm as a result of the contact (such as cradling or caressing clients).

Physical contact or other activities of a sexual nature with clients are clearly not allowed by social workers.

The *Code of Ethics* does not limit physical contact to only adult clients; however, social workers must clearly evaluate the appropriateness of having physical contact with children, especially because many of the youth served have experienced trauma (see Unit V—Chapter 25, *Professional Boundary Issues*).

168. B

An important clinical tool in the *DSM-5* is the revised diagnoses of "Other Specified" and "Unspecified" mental disorders. Replacing the "Not Otherwise Specified" categories, these diagnoses give social workers more flexibility. The first allows a social worker to specify the reason that the criteria for a specific disorder are not met, and the second allows a social worker the option to forgo specification (see Unit II—Chapter 10, *Use of the Current Diagnostic and Statistical Manual of Mental Disorders of the American Psychiatric Association*).

169. B

Social workers should protect the confidentiality of deceased clients consistent with the same standards that apply to those who are living. In this case vignette, the social worker should not disclose any information about the client. There is no reason to have the son put his questions in writing or to schedule a session to see him (see Unit V—Chapter 26, *Legal and Ethical Issues Regarding Confidentiality, Including Electronic Information*).

170. B

Person-first language names the person before a diagnosis, disability, or condition to avoid defining him or her by this trait. Its use began in the disability self-advocacy community but is now used universally. It is the belief that a person is not his or her disability and that by referring to those with varying physical and cognitive abilities as "the disabled," society is dehumanizing them. Thus, sentence structure should be used that names the person first and the condition second to avoid perceived and subconscious dehumanization when discussing people with diagnoses, disabilities, or conditions.

"Individuals with disabilities" (B) is the only response choice that lists individuals first and the presence of disabilities second (see Unit IV—Chapter 17, *Written Communication Skills*).

Index

validity
of research findings, 243
in social work research, assessing methods to, 249–250
variable costs, 301
VAWA of 1994. *See* Violence Against Women Act of 1994
verbal communication, 234
techniques, 227–228
violence
cycle of, 90–91
dynamics in helping relationship, 240
Violence Against Women Act (VAWA) of 1994, 281
vision/goals-based strategic planning, 302
visual learners, 30
voluntary clients, 315

Wechsler Intelligence Scale (WISC), 110
White American, behaviors and attitudes of, 93–94
WHODAS. *See* World Health Organization's Disability Assessment Schedule
WIA. *See* Workforce Investment Act

WIOA of 2014. *See* Workforce Innovation and Opportunity Act of 2014
WISC. *See* Wechsler Intelligence Scale
women, adult sexual behaviors in, 66, 67
work-centered sessions, 307
work environment, collegial and positive components, 299
Workforce Innovation and Opportunity Act of 2014 (WIOA), 282
Workforce Investment Act (WIA), 282
working environment, positive, 293
work relationships, dynamics of, 89
World Health Organization's Disability Assessment Schedule (WHODAS), 158
wrap-around services, coordinate services methods, 273
written communication skills, 259
written documentation, 259

young adult behavior and development, 60–61
young children (age 4–6), behavior and development, 58–59

zero-based budgeting, 301